# Political Paranoia

# Political Paranoia

## The Psychopolitics of Hatred

Robert S. Robins
Jerrold M. Post, M.D.

Yale University Press    New Haven and London

Published with assistance from the foundation established in memory of Philip Hamilton McMillan of the Class of 1894, Yale College.

Printed in the United States of America

Library of Congress Cataloging-in-Publication Data

Robins, Robert S.
Political paranoia : the psychopolitics of hatred /
Robert S. Robins, Jerrold M. Post.
p.   cm.
Includes bibliographical references and index.
ISBN 0-300-07027-6 (alk. paper)
1. Right and left (Political science)—Psychological
aspects.
2. Paranoia. I. Post, Jerrold M. II. Title.
JA74.5.R55   1997
302'.17—dc21     96-40336
CIP

ISBN 0-300-07027-6

A catalogue record for this book is available from the British Library.

The paper in this book meets the guidelines for permanence and durability of the Committee on Production Guidelines for Book Longevity of the Council on Library Resources.

10 9 8 7 6 5 4 3 2 1

To our grandchildren

Katherine Simone Robins
Emily Post Keller
Rachel Post Gramlich

May you grow up in a world
that knows less of hatred and more of
understanding and tolerance

# Contents

# Acknowledgments

We have been greatly helped by colleagues and students, family and friends, with whom we discoursed, often vigorously, about the book. All cannot be thanked, but we wish to express our gratitude especially to Fred Alford, Stephen Ambrose, Michael Barkun, Jason Berry, Roderick Camp, Brandon Clark, Lisa Cooper, David Chandler, Herman Freudenberger, Rajat Ganguly, Mark Gasiorowski, Lance Hill, F. Robert Hunter, Glen Jeansonne, Allen Johnson, Jr., Jeffrey Kaplan, Cheryle Koopman, Richard Latner, Roger Masters, Leo Ribuffo, Douglas Rose, Carol Rosenblum, Steven Rosenblum, Annelies J. Sheehan, Morris C. Sheehan, Kenneth Stern, Ray Taras, Robert Waite, and Robert Wood.

We are particularly indebted to Robert C. Tucker, professor emeritus at Princeton University, and Marvin Zonis of the University of Chicago for their longtime interest in this project and their helpful comments.

We are grateful to our wives, Carolyn Ashland Post and Marjorie McGann Robins, for their support and constructive criticism.

Special thanks to Gladys Topkis, senior editor at Yale University Press, for her vision, incisive intellect, patience, and sense of style. Thanks also to Jenya Weinreb and Brenda Kolb, whose careful editing and substantive corrections have helped in so many ways. Particular thanks to Keven Ruby, research assistant extraordinaire, whose thoughtful attention and perseverance were of indescribable importance in completing this project.

Robert Robins was a visiting scientist at the Tavistock Clinic and an honorary research fellow at the Wellcome Institute for the History of Science, both in London, as well as a participant in the New Orleans Psychoanalytic Applied Analysis Seminar. These institutions provided a stimulating intellectual environment during an important phase of work on this book.

Jerrold Post was a grantee of the Carnegie Corporation of New York, 1990–1993. The programmatic support for research in applied political psychology was of great assistance during the research phase of this book.

# Political Paranoia

# Introduction

[Pooh informs the boorish Eeyore that Eeyore's tail
is missing. With a long, sad sigh, Eeyore exclaims:]
"I believe you're right."
"Of course I'm right," said Pooh.
"That Accounts for a Good Deal," said Eeyore
gloomily. "It Explains Everything. No Wonder."
"You must have left it somewhere," said Winnie-
the-Pooh.
"Somebody must have taken it," said Eeyore.
"How Like Them," he added, after a long silence.
—A. A. Milne, *Winnie-the-Pooh*

paranoia, n.
mental disorder characterized by systematized
delusions and the projection of personal conflicts,
which are ascribed to the supposed hostility of others;
chronic functional psychosis of insidious
development, characterized by persistent, unalterable,
logically reasoned delusions, commonly of
persecution and grandeur
paranoid, n., a person afflicted with paranoia
a. characterized by oversuspicious, grandiose
delusions or delusions of persecution
—*Webster's New Universal Unabridged Dictionary*

Of the many letters of condolence that Eleanor Roosevelt
received upon her husband's death, the strangest came
from Joseph Stalin. After a few lines of sympathy, the
Soviet dictator implied that Franklin Delano Roosevelt
had been poisoned, and he went on to offer his assistance
in any investigation that Mrs. Roosevelt might conduct.

Apparently, etiquette in Stalin's Kremlin included suggesting the possibility of murder to a grieving widow and encouraging her to find the perpetrator.[1]

Aside from its grim humor, this story illustrates something important about the politics of what was then the world's largest country. First, it shows that that country was being ruled by a person who had a paranoid view of politics. From his perspective, even elderly men suffering from severe hypertension and morbid arteriosclerosis do not simply die from these diseases; they are poisoned. Second, his allusion to murder and the counsel of vengeance apparently reflected standard protocol in the Kremlin; an entire regime had adopted a paranoid worldview. Finally, Stalin assumed that the rest of the world—the United States in this case—shared this distorted view of reality. He projected his own and his society's psychopathology onto others.

But was this a projection of psychopathology, or was it a projection of the reality of life in the Kremlin? Recently released material from the Soviet archives reveals that when Lenin was lying stricken with a stroke, Stalin claimed that Lenin had asked for potassium cyanide to put him out of his misery (although he could not speak!). Stalin characterized giving the poison as a "humane mission" and promised to do the deed "without hesitation."[2] This anecdote suggests that Stalin wished to hasten Lenin's death and ensure his own total power, and it makes his comment to Mrs. Roosevelt more understandable.

The authors of this book—a psychiatrist who has devoted his career to the study of political psychology and a political scientist who has long been concerned with the role of psychopathology in political affairs—have become increasingly aware of the role of paranoid thinking in politics.[3] A paranoid worldview played a determinant role in the destructive policies of the most notorious mass murderers of this century, Adolf Hitler and Stalin. Ayatollah Ruholla Khomeini mobilized paranoid rage against the external enemy, the "Great Satan" of the United States, with extraordinary effectiveness in consolidating the Islamic fundamentalist revolution in Iran. The collective suicide and murders of the followers of the Reverend Jim Jones in the People's Temple in Guyana were driven by paranoid beliefs. And paranoid thinking has fueled the fires that have caused tens of thousands of ethnic murders in the Balkans, in India, and in Central Africa.

At its most extreme, this malign force exists on dramatic and bloody stages. But the paranoid dynamic is always present, even in stable, democratic, and humane societies; it is part of the human condition. This paranoid dynamic is conspicuous in such films as *JFK, Silkwood,* and *Missing,* which identify conspiracy as the "real" explanation for events. For much of the popular press, conspiratorial explanations are a basic stock in trade, whether applied to Marilyn Monroe's death or the attack on Pearl Harbor. The suicide of the U.S. president's chief counsel, Vincent Foster, on July 20, 1993, engendered a minor conspiracy cult. Nor is the phenomenon new. Other ages, such as the Tudor period in England, were held in its grip, and ancient traditions of persecutions are based on paranoid beliefs against Jews, Catholics, Gypsies, blacks, and a variety of "others."

Viewed simply as a personal disorder, the paranoid outlook is associated with a wide range of psychologies, from entirely normal to severely psychopathological. At its least malignant, it is an occasional human response to an ambiguous stimulus. Who among us, in reaction to a peremptory request to come immediately to the front office, has not wondered, "What did I do now?" Some persons, only mildly suspicious during most of their lives, become paranoid in old age. Others have a consistently paranoid outlook, never entirely losing touch with reality in the sense of developing psychotic delusions, but dominated by a paranoid orientation. These individuals, suffering from what is considered one of the most serious personality disorders, have paranoid personalities. The paranoid personality disorder is characterized by a pervasive distrust and suspiciousness of others such that their motives are interpreted as malevolent.[4] Individuals with the paranoid personality disorder

- suspect, without sufficient basis, that others are exploiting, harming, or deceiving them;
- are preoccupied with unjustified doubts about the loyalty, or trustworthiness, of friends or associates;
- are reluctant to confide in others because of unwarranted fear that the information will be used maliciously against them;

- read hidden demeaning or threatening meanings into benign remarks or events;
- persistently bear grudges—that is, are unforgiving of insults, injuries, or slights;
- perceive attacks on their character or reputation that are not apparent to others and are quick to react angrily, or to counterattack;
- have recurrent suspicions, without justification, regarding the fidelity of their spouse or sexual partner.

At its most malignant, the paranoid response is associated with serious mental illnesses, both functional and organic. Severe paranoid symptoms are associated with paranoid schizophrenia, manic-depressive disorders, the late stages of substance-abuse diseases, and organic psychoses.

The term *paranoia* was in use before the time of Hippocrates, signifying a mental disorder. The term was first used to refer to various persecutory and grandiose states by the German psychiatrist Karl Ludwig Kahlbaum in 1863, but it was the German psychiatrist Emil Kraepelin who specifically delineated the syndrome of paranoia, using the term to refer to a rare disorder in which a fixed delusional system developed insidiously, without hallucinations, and existed side by side with normal thinking. Another early psychiatric pioneer, Eugene Bleuler, in 1911 described paranoia as the "construction, from false premises, of a logically developed and in its various parts logically connected, unshakable delusional system without any demonstrable disturbance affecting any of the other mental functions and, therefore, also without any symptoms of 'deterioration' if one ignores the paranoiac's complete lack of insight into his own delusional system."[5] This disorder is characterized by a well-organized delusional system in otherwise clear consciousness, not associated with other psychiatric disorders. The paranoid is perfectly normal except for delusions of conspiracy and victimization. These are often well concealed, yet they may dominate the paranoid's every waking moment. Unless the area of walled-off delusional beliefs is addressed, those around the paranoid may be unaware of the severity of his distortions of reality.[6]

Of the four kinds of clinical paranoid states—persecutory, grandiose, jealous, and erotic—the persecutory is by far both the most frequent and the most significant. And the persecutory paranoid state and paranoid grandiosity lend themselves most readily to the world of politics. Paranoid grandiosity derives from an early phase of childhood development in which children think of themselves as having remarkable powers and abilities. In the face of frustration, the paranoid individual regresses to the imaginary position of an omnipotent individual whose powers cannot be diminished. Individuals who develop persecutory paranoia have a deep distrust of others and a strong tendency to deny their own hostility and project it onto others.[7]

Increasingly the term *paranoia* has been used to refer not only to this specific diagnostic entity but also more broadly to a personality trait and a personality style characterized by guardedness, suspiciousness, hypersensitivity, and isolation.[8] An important aspect of this style is a pattern of disowning uncomfortable personal feelings and attributing them to others, the psychological defense mechanism known as projection. With the understanding that the paranoid response springs from diverse sources and varies in consistency and intensity, throughout this book we will interchangeably use the terms *paranoid* and *paranoia* in this broader sense, to subsume both clinical paranoid illnesses and paranoid style and outlook.

Although the paranoid outlook affects many areas of human affairs, it is most evident in the adversarial world of politics, where it is a constant feature. Commenting on the mistrust that pervaded his relationship with his long-standing political rival, Israeli prime minister Yitzhak Rabin, Shimon Peres wryly observed: "Suspicion has its own charm. It makes you feel just and right. . . . Suspicion is a very pleasant commodity."[9] At its extreme, the paranoid style is more destructive than any other political style. Paranoids do not have adversaries or rivals or opponents; they have enemies, and enemies are not to be simply defeated and certainly not to be compromised with or won over. Enemies are to be destroyed. As Huey Long, onetime governor of Louisiana, would say to those who opposed him, "I'm not just going to beat you. I'm going to ruin you!"

What makes political paranoia so difficult to define and understand is that it begins as a distortion of an appropriate political response but then far overshoots the mark. Like fever in cases of disease, a certain amount of suspicion in politics is a necessary, even healthy, defense.

Lyndon Johnson, though not a paranoid leader, once noted that everyone in politics needs to be able to walk into a room full of people and sense who is for him and who is against. All politicians, whether in Moscow or the District of Columbia, must constantly look out for threats and must be especially sensitive to their opponents' efforts to organize secretly—conspire—against them. Politicians who lack this sensitivity will not last long. In some political systems they will not even live long. Lacking this sensitivity in the conspiracy-ridden Kremlin, for example, could be fatal.

When political leaders have actually experienced major betrayal or conspiracy, they will draw powerful lessons from these experiences and may overgeneralize. While there may be merit to the aphorism "Just because I'm paranoid doesn't mean they're not out to get me," it is also often true to state "Because they have been out to get me, I had better trust no one and assume I am surrounded by enemies." The scarred political leader learns to have a paranoid attitude in order to survive, retreating into isolation and becoming unable to develop trusting alliances.

This book proceeds in stages. We first describe the world as it is experienced by the paranoid, emphasizing suspiciousness as the sine qua non of the paranoid. Next we look at paranoid historical episodes, paranoid cultures, and conspiracy thinking, leading to an explanation of why the human species has such a powerful tendency toward paranoia. The analysis then moves to the crucial link between the individual and the collective. Finally, we consider leaders with a paranoid worldview.

The paranoid theme is a leitmotif in political life. Sometimes it is played loudly and rapidly by the brass section and sometimes slowly, in a delicate whisper, by the harp alone. At times it even seems to disappear completely. But it always returns. Paranoia, the quintessential political psychopathology, has had and will continue to have a profoundly destructive effect on human affairs, for it is deeply embedded within human nature.

# 1

## The Mind of the Paranoid

Our brain has developed a capacity to create for us
a world of our own making and imagination. Very
few of us live in the real world. We live in the world
of our perceptions, and those perceptions differ
dramatically according to our personal experiences.
We may perceive danger where there is none. If the
distortion is ever enough we may think we are living
among enemies even while surrounded by friends.
—Willard Gaylin, *The Rage Within*

The paranoid lives in a world of danger, as the center
of malevolent attention. The ever-present danger con-
centrates his senses. Believing that he is under unrelenting surveillance, his every move observed, he fears that
letting down his guard even for a minute may be fatal.
Like a submarine on patrol in hostile waters, its peri-
scope constantly scanning the horizon for the enemy, the
paranoid searches constantly for subtle clues of danger.

### The Seven Elements of Paranoia

Extreme suspiciousness is one of the principal components of the paranoid syndrome. The others are centrality, grandiosity, hostility, fear of loss of autonomy,
projection, and delusional thinking.

## Suspicion

Suspiciousness is the most evident presenting characteristic, the sine qua non, of the paranoid. To the paranoid, things are not what they seem to be. He does not permit himself to be distracted by apparently innocent facts but claims to see through them. He searches continually for hidden meaning, for clues to the enemies he knows are out there. Interpreting perceptions according to pre-existing ideas and pre-fixed conclusions, he employs "top-down" reasoning, avidly seizing upon the most minute clues that support his conspiratorial thesis.[1] He dismisses even the strongest disconfirming evidence as a sham designed to lull him into a false sense of complacency. But the paranoid is too smart to be thrown off; the apparently contradictory facts only prove how clever and sinister his opponents are. He *knows* the danger is there.

His quest is like that of a scientist, but with a crucial difference.[2] Seeking the truth, the scientist reasons both deductively and inductively and searches for an explanation of observations. The scientist tests his hypothesis, ready to disconfirm it if the evidence does not support it. The paranoid, in contrast, knows the "truth" already and searches for confirmation. His is a fixed conclusion in search of evidence. Thus the paranoid is not working to prove or disprove a hypothesis; he knows that if he works hard enough he will find the evidence to prove his suspicions. In his preoccupation with finding evidence, he selects only that "evidence" that confirms his conclusion of danger.

With keen attention to detail, the paranoid interprets away (often with great ingenuity) facts that do not fit in with his delusions and seeks clues and "real meanings" in every event and comment. The search is rigidly intentional.[3] In the paranoid's worldview, events do not simply occur; they are deliberately caused by someone. For the paranoid, coincidence does not exist. Everything happens by design. Finding that meaning behind apparently random events becomes an obsessive quest. If one searches hard enough, one will penetrate the surface obscurity and find the underlying truth. Seeing the same individual on the subway on two successive days, for example, confirms to the paranoid that he is under surveillance. If that individual nods to another, the existence of a network of observers is proven. The world of the paranoid admits no shades of gray; there is no room for uncertainty. There is an intolerance of ambiguity and a tendency to classify in either/or compartments: good/bad, friend/enemy. Much of the intense intellectual effort of the paranoid is in the service of resolving uncertainty.

Exercising reason without judgment, using facts without balance, the classic paranoid is thoroughly logical; it is his premises that are false. He is a great fact collector, but he collects only those facts that fit the logical system he has devised. In this sense, paranoia is the most intellectual of the mental disorders, the one most likely to be associated with complex political ideologies. Human beings are quintessentially reasoning animals, and the paranoid carries reasoning to a fault. The problem is not the reasoning process per se, but rather the fixed false premise of danger.[4]

The special psycho-logic of the paranoid has been called paleologic, referring to its primitive nature.[5] This psycho-logic is the logic of the child or of primitive people trying to make sense of the incomprehensible. It operates according to a principle first enunciated by Eilhard Von Domarus, who systematically studied the delusions of paranoid schizophrenics.[6] Whereas the normal person accepts identity only on the basis of identical subjects, the paleologician accepts identity based on identical predicates. That is, to the paleologician, two things that share any feature in common may be considered identical. When, to his mother's embarrassment, a little boy runs up to a strange man and shouts "Daddy," he is operating according to paleologic: "Daddy wears pants; this man wears pants; therefore this man is Daddy." A paranoid's delusion that she is the Virgin Mary follows the same skewed logic: "I am a virgin; Mary was a virgin; therefore I am the Virgin Mary." This associational logic underlies the significance the paranoid attaches to the simultaneous occurrence in time or space of two unrelated events.

Politics is rich in paleologic. If my grandfather was murdered by a Muslim fifty years ago, all Muslims are murderers and should be treated accordingly. If I have been cheated by a banker, all capitalists are thieves, and capitalism should be destroyed. To the paranoid, tragedies and misfortunes do not happen by accident.

## Centrality

The belief that the paranoid himself is the target of malevolent intent is prominent in paranoid thinking. For the paranoid, everything has meaning in reference to *him*. Actions and comments that have nothing to do with him are taken as being directed at him; he knows he is the object of great interest. The paranoid's world is populated by enemies, and he is the center of their attention. One of the most striking aspects of the paranoid, this centrality is defensive; it is preferable to be the center of a conspiracy than to be ignored.

The premise of centrality can lead to what Norman Cameron has called the paranoid pseudo-community, an "imaginary organization, composed of real and imagined persons, whom the patient represents as united for the purpose of carrying out some action against him."[7] As the paranoid's delusion crystallizes and the nature of the malignant community conspiring against him becomes apparent, it is not uncommon for the paranoid to say, "Everything became clear to me." And once the delusional "reality" snaps into place, it develops a force of its own. An innocent exchange of glances between strangers is taken as confirmation that the two are in league and part of the conspiracy. A scratch on a car door is proof that the car has been surreptitiously entered and bugged. This now well-organized community of conspiring enemies becomes the recipient of all the paranoid's aggressive projections.

## Grandiosity

Closely related to the paranoid's belief in his centrality is his arrogant grandiosity. The paranoid's certainty brooks no disagreement. He knows the truth and conveys a sense of contempt for those so foolish as to differ. The paranoid's arrogant posture regularly leads to disturbed interpersonal relationships.

## Hostility

The first characteristic to catch the attention of even the casual acquaintance of the paranoid is not so much his conspiratorial ideas or his arrogance as his generally hostile attitude toward the world. The paranoid is belligerent and irritable, humorless and extremely sensitive to slight, combative and quarrelsome, tightly wound and bristlingly defensive. And this defensive posture contains a poised readiness to attack. To be around a paranoid is to sense that one must walk on eggshells lest he be provoked and lash out.

The intensity of the paranoid's inner hostility is so great that he becomes caught up in an ever-growing need for love.[8] Because of his profound self-doubts, however, he is ready for rejection, and the search for love is bound to fail. The underlying insecurity and uncertainty may drive the paranoid coercively to extract proofs of love or loyalty. The paranoid's hostility, deep-seated suspiciousness and distrust, and the behaviors flowing from these feelings thus lead to his difficulties in sustaining close relationships. Because of the injustices he believes have been visited upon him in this dangerous world, the paranoid is chronically angry. He senses hostility all around him, believing he is surrounded by people out to get him. He acts antagonistically toward his perceived enemies and in a self-fulfilling prophecy provokes hostility, confirming that they are indeed out to get him.

Some paranoids flee rather than fight. They too are isolated and secretive, and no less suspicious than the fighting paranoids we have been describing.[9] Both are "injustice collectors," but while the combative paranoid is openly defiant, seeking vengeance for perceived mistreatment, the withdrawn paranoid secretly harbors his grievances.

## Fear of Loss of Autonomy

Like a coiled spring, the paranoid lives in a state of readiness. He is always prepared for an emergency, which he defines as an infringement upon his autonomy or free will; "don't tread on me" is his psychological motto. To give in to external pressure or authority is intolerable.[10] He is constantly wary of attempts by a superior force or by outside individuals to impose their will upon him, and he manifests an exaggerated independence.

It is ironic that the paranoid so often does put himself in danger, for he is driven by a desire to be perfectly safe, by a fear of the loss of control.[11] Consequently he spends his life imagining circumstances in which his safety would be compromised and then acting upon these fantasies. This demand for absolute safety is a perversion of healthy coping behavior, of adaptive prudence and caution. The paranoid fears weakness and despises soft or tender feelings. Underlying these fears may be the wish to be controlled, to passively yield to superior force. But this yearning is unacceptable to the paranoid, who erects strong psychological barricades against this dreaded (and desired) possibility.

A significant degree of political autonomy is indeed necessary to fulfill any leader's political goals and psychological needs.[12] But it is not possible to be perfectly autonomous any more than it is possible to be perfectly safe. An element of subordination and accommodation to the will of others and an acceptance of a degree of uncertainty are necessary accompaniments to living in society. Unable to tolerate this imperfection or to accept compromises, the paranoid finds himself in constant warfare with both real and imaginary adversaries seeking to control him and destroy his autonomy.

## Projection

If suspicion is the hallmark of paranoia, projection is its fundamental mechanism.[13] Projection, according to Sigmund Freud, is the result of a normal tendency to presume that internal states or changes are due to external causes. An example, which has implications for the world of politics, is the tendency of people who are small or frightened to attribute exaggerated size and power to their enemies.

Projection is an aberration of the relatively normal state of shame. Unable to tolerate a painful feeling, the person projects it onto his fellows and disowns it. The purpose of projection is to take unacceptable feelings and externalize them to the environment. It can be considered advantageous in that it transforms an intolerable internal threat into a more manageable external threat. But it is advantageous at the price of reality. Projection, a special type of reality impairment, represents an autistic view of the world. The paranoid person does not withdraw from the external world; rather, he attends extremely closely to it. He does not distort apparent reality; rather, the distortion is in the interpretation of reality. It is an interpretively biased cognition of reality. The paranoid projector is concerned not with the observable obvious but with the hidden motives of others that are behind the observable. The projection is a compromise with reality; the paranoid person "meets reality halfway."[14]

## Delusional Thinking

Delusions—false beliefs held in the presence of strong contradictory evidence—represent the fixed, crystallized extremity of projective thinking. The following vignette, from the case files of JMP, represents a delusion of reference: "A young man suffering from chronic paranoid schizophrenia had long-standing doubts about his masculinity, fearing he was a homosexual. When he traveled by bus, he became extremely uncomfortable, for he knew to a certainty that his fellow passengers were staring at him in disgust and saying under their breath, 'Queer.' " He had projected and disowned his self-reproach.

Of all paranoid delusions, those of persecution and grandiosity most readily lend themselves to the world of politics. These delusions and their associated feelings are paired in the paranoid, who has a sense of uniqueness.[15] He expects to be treated specially, but he himself tends to be manipulative and exploitative, while remaining largely unaware of his impact on others. When he is not treated specially, he reacts with hurt, anger, and at times vindictive rage.

> Rodney was a 54-year-old man who was sent to the hospital after attempting to drive his truck through the gates of the White House. Collateral social history revealed that he had been fired the previous day from his job as a dishwasher. In the psychiatric interview conducted to ascertain his dangerousness, he emanated a fiery righteous certitude as he explained that he was "king of the world." He had attempted to crash the White House gates in order to occupy his throne.
>
> When the examining psychiatrist [JMP] observed that someone was already occupying the throne, Rodney interjected, "You mean Mr. Johnson." When the psychiatrist observed, "Right, and he seems to be quite happy there," Rodney responded, "But he's only the President, and I'm the King." "And how," he was asked, "would you get him to relinquish the throne?" "I would persuade him" was the patient's response. "And if he would not be persuaded?" "If necessary," Rodney responded in a chillingly determined voice, "I would persuade him with force." With this it was decided to confine Rodney to the locked ward.

This patient defended against unbearable feelings of insignificance by developing a compensatory grandiose delusion. From the unbearable reality of being fired as a dishwasher he constructed the preferable reality of becoming king of the world.

Although distorted, the paranoid system is coherent, an integrated syndrome, each aspect supporting the others. The syndrome as a whole can be personally reparative ("I must be important because others conspire against me") and may even be politically helpful. The syndrome is also self-validating. Political failure confirms the paranoid's suspicions, and political success seems to confirm his grandiosity.[16] But with the exception of the blatantly delusional paranoid, this pathological posture is often masked. Typically, other aspects of the paranoid's personality are maintained: Stalin, for example, was known for his charm and affability.

## Defending Against Hostility and Insignificance

Many of the paranoid's surface manifestations are defenses against the opposite feelings.[17] This accounts for the paranoid's rigid insistence that he is the target of persecutors, despite overwhelming evidence to the contrary. The reason the paranoid cannot afford to question his fixed conclusion of danger is that it is psychologically essential to his emotional well-being. He cannot face the underlying shame of his insignificance; "proving" that he is the center of a conspiratorial plot reassures him. As the focus of this community of enemies, the paranoid has assumed great importance.[18]

Relying on the primitive psychological defenses of denial, distortion, and projection, the paranoid disavows feelings within himself. Hostility is a primary problem in paranoid conditions. Violently angry and afraid of their own aggression, paranoids defend against their rage by viewing themselves as the victims of persecutors.

The purpose of projection is to externalize to the environment unacceptable, usually aggressive feelings. Projection achieves an external substitute for an internal tension or threat, restoring stability to a threatened, rigid defensive system. Through projection, the paranoid externalizes the all-bad aggressive self and assigns these feelings to other individuals or groups. They in turn become external persecutors against whom he must defend himself. This is the reason the paranoid is suspicious of, or extremely sensitive to, other people.[19]

The paranoid appears both self-centered and arrogant, with little concern for the needs and feelings of others, but in fact he is extremely concerned with how others feel about him. The arrogance is a mask, concealing pervasive uncertainty and profound self-doubt. Because the paranoid feels inferior and despised, he is subject to envy and jealousy. Constantly surveilling his environment to see how he is regarded, he assumes the worst. This is the reason he is so sensitive to criticism. This defensive self-concern regularly leads to seriously disturbed interpersonal relationships.

The paranoid protects himself against unbearable reality by constructing an alternate reality. The newly constructed reality is a solace for the wounded ego. The paranoid's centrality is a defense against insignificance. The need to sustain a positive self-image explains why the paranoid clings so tenaciously to the idea that he is the object of a conspiracy. Even though one would expect the paranoid to be reassured to learn that there is no persecutory plot, in fact this would be devastating. It would deprive him of his sense of importance. It is better to be persecuted than to be ignored. If he feels inconsequential, the delusion of being the center of a conspiracy will make him feel important. If a person sees himself as a failure, attributing this failure to another's malicious actions restores his self-esteem, as illustrated by the following clinical vignette:

> Will, a 23-year-old pre-med student at a Washington, D.C., university, was admitted to the hospital in a state of psychotic decompensation, obsessed by the idea that the City Council was conspiring to keep his former girlfriend, Barbara, from seeing him. Apparently Barbara, a beautiful co-ed who was also a fashion model, had been in danger of flunking out of college. She had approached Will, told him how attractive she found him, and asked his help with her studies. By working with her night and day Will had helped Barbara pass her exams. In the process he had fallen deeply in love with her, a love she indicated she reciprocated.
>
> When the exam grades were posted, making it clear that Barbara would graduate, she immediately dropped Will. Unable to tolerate the reality that he had been cruelly used and manipulated by Barbara, who in truth did not care for him at all, he protected his self-esteem by developing the paranoid delusion

that Barbara did love him but that the City Council had conspired to keep them apart. The delusion had protected Will against two losses: the loss of Barbara, and, even more important in some ways, the humiliating shame of recognizing that he had been manipulated. In addition to denial, he had converted his inner sense of powerlessness and projected powerful control into the City Council. It wasn't the poor fool Will who was manipulated and rejected. They, the powerful City Council, were responsible. This delusion enabled Will to see himself not as an exploited and rejected dupe, but as the central object of an evil conspiracy, the romantic victim of a powerful force that prevented him from being united with his loved one. As he was helped to face the painful reality of Barbara's loss and her exploitation of him, his delusional thinking abated, to be replaced by a profound suicidal depression. The projected feelings had now been re-internalized and he was facing painful reality.

Paranoid ideas of persecution and grandeur are intended to overcome the sense of inferiority, unworthiness, and unlovability. Just as to be the center of a plot defends against insignificance, so too the paranoid's grandiosity is defensive, masking underlying insecurity. Better to be grand and of central importance than to be insignificant and inadequate. A person with exaggerated self-estimations and ambitions who is manifestly failing and is not considered important by others may well ascribe his lack of success to malevolent others. To varying degrees, paranoid ideation is always a compensation for feelings of inadequacy. The paranoid's feeling of worth is protected by the paranoid transfer of blame to other individuals.[20]

Paranoid grandiosity is a shield for a fragile ego. The paranoid person's jealousy, sensitivity to slight, and readiness to react to insult with anger all derive from the underlying insecurity beneath the arrogant facade. When that grandiose facade is pierced by reality, it results in unbearable shame, hurt, and rage.

The expectation of being treated specially—and the rage when that special treatment is not forthcoming—is a manifestation of narcissistic entitlement, for paranoia can be considered a primitive form of narcissistic pathology.[21] The narcissistic triad consists of (1) narcissistic entitlement, which inevitably leads to (2) disappointment and disillusionment at the frustration of insatiable narcissistic needs, which produces (3) narcissistic rage due to the rejection of the "entitlement."[22] This dynamic sequence is of central importance in understanding the close relations among grandiosity, feelings of persecution, and vindictive retaliatory rage in the paranoid. The reason for the magnitude of the rage is that the sense of entitlement has been breached, the grandiose self-image betrayed.[23] At the core of the paranoid's personality are feelings of depletion, inadequacy, shame, and vulnerability.

A psychodynamic formulation of Adolf Hitler's political psychology suggests that projection and paranoid transfer of blame were dominant mechanisms (see Chapter 11). In attempting to purify the German body politic by eliminating the contaminant of the Jews, Hitler was projecting the reviled hated parts of himself onto the Jews and then aggressively attacking them.[24] Hitler thus exemplifies the paranoid in politics.

## The Quintessential Political Disease

Paranoia, the most interpersonal of mental illnesses, is also the most political in the broad sense of centering on power relationships. Paranoids need their enemies, after all, and what richer source of enemies can be found than the world of politics?

The paranoid's underlying feelings of inadequacy, depletion, and vulnerability may translate into the sensation of powerlessness, an intolerable feeling that must be defended against. This can have political consequences, as was demonstrated by the case of Rodney, who tried to drive his truck through the White House gates. For the powerless, what could be a more potent symbol than the White House, the seat of power, the residence of the most powerful man on earth? The rash of attacks on the White House in 1994 were instances of the powerless striking out in frustration and in that brief instant gaining notice and significance. The man who crashed a plane on the White House portico after evading radar and penetrating the White House perimeter sought to die in a blaze of glory. And the failed dishwasher who would be king blamed the powerful establishment for his failures. He was prepared to attack the head of the establishment, the man he saw as responsible for his inability to succeed.

In addition to the fighting belligerent paranoid, the quiet, withdrawn paranoid has also been politically consequential. As a group, those who have murdered or attempted to murder U.S. presidents reflect paranoid psychopathology. Many of them led quiet, withdrawn lives prior to their history-changing acts. Brooding, distrustful loners, they manifested both grandiosity and bitterness. The gap between their majestic ambitions and their failed lives was extreme. In their acts of political violence they struck out at the powerful whom they blamed for their failures.[25]

The world of politics has powerful valence for individuals and groups with paranoid features. In the broader, nonpathological sense of the term, the paranoid response is not qualitatively different from other reactions often encountered in the range of human behavior. The paranoid response is a distortion of useful coping behavior. Paranoia is an exaggeration of the tried political style of alert suspicion, keen observation, and prudent preemption. Its power in politics also derives from its remarkable capacity to stimulate both intense aggressive behavior directed against delusional objects and vigorous and effective responses to genuine danger.

Paranoia, in other words, distorts conventional and useful responses to danger. Thus, political paranoia acquires its uniquely destructive force not only because of its pathological components of suspicion and delusion but, ironically, because it activates as well as distorts reparative psychological behavior and sound political practices. The paranoid response at first is capable of achieving considerable success. After it has wreaked its damage because of its excesses, it often self-destructs, but sometimes it does not. As the case of Joseph Stalin shows (see Chapter 10), the fearful insecurity of the paranoid in power can lead to a widening gyre of violence. The ruthless purging of enemies, both real and imagined, can appear to provide relative safety.

When the political actor is under stress, his characteristic reactions become magnified. Especially in the face of danger, the prudently suspicious politician can become frankly paranoid. Paranoia, then, is a caricature of ways of behaving and thinking that are indeed appropriate to dangerous situations. Suspiciousness is not itself dysfunctional. But *paranoid* suspiciousness is a malignant distortion of an otherwise adaptive response, a useful mode of behavior that has misfired, a dangerous—and often destructive—parody of prudent coping behavior.

The political paranoid has not fully departed the world of reality. Rather, he clings too single-mindedly to a part of it, exaggerating to a pathological degree. That part might be a fact: the reality of a minor conspiracy against him, the reality of some small and largely undeserved wrong. It might also be a distortion of some innocent event that could not unreasonably be interpreted as being hostilely directed. Becoming obsessed with these events, the paranoid exaggerates them, then builds an entire view of the world around the distorted images he has created.

Not only may the substance of his behavior be based on a piece of reality, but the form this behavior takes may also be a perversion of reality. The suspiciousness, the eagerness to strike at enemies before they strike at him, the tendency to relate events to his interests are themselves distortions and exaggerations of what in a not-too-different context and in a more proportional balance are effective patterns of defense. It has even been argued that paranoia is not a disease at all but simply a form of adaptation gone wrong.[26]

In the political sphere, blatantly delusional thinking is not the main concern. Such thinking is exceptional and evident to others. Far more dangerous is when the delusional thinking is borderline and consequently not easily recognized as the product of madness. For most political paranoids the delusion is likely to involve exaggeration and distortion of genuine events and rational beliefs rather than pure psychotic invention.

Leaders in power may fall victim to frank paranoid delusions. Some do great harm, like Rome's Nero, the Paraguayan dictator José Gaspar de Francia, Joseph Stalin, and Adolf Hitler. But like the delusional paranoids in the two previous vignettes, most leaders with paranoid psychoses, such as Britain's foreign secretary Lord Castlereagh and U.S. secretary of defense James Forrestal, do little harm. The psychopathologies of Castlereagh and Forrestal were so flagrant that these men were recognized as psychiatrically disturbed and their potentially harmful instructions were ignored. But it is the paranoid who is *not* recognized as psychiatrically disturbed (Hitler, Stalin, Jim Jones, David Koresh) who is most dangerous, for he can most readily attract followers and lead them on the path of political extremity.

The difference in potential political attractiveness between the paranoid recognized as mentally ill and the unrecognized paranoid was dramatically illustrated by two men encountered by one of the authors (JMP) on opposite corners of a Washington, D.C., intersection. Their messages were similar, but they elicited quite different responses.

On one corner was a bearded man in his mid-forties, wearing a sandwich board warning against governmental mind control. He was handing out fliers expanding on this warning:

> Are you being mind controlled by the subliminal radio? The government has developed a vast secret department involved in the study and advancement of mind control of individuals and groups by the silent radio.
>
> Tyranny always rules first. The radio is often being used to trick persons into every crime, sin, and stupid decision possible. The mind controllers are government, medical, lawyers, businessmen, psychiatrists, religious and educational. . . . All nations are using this subliminal radio in experiments of mind control on their citizens. . . .
>
> All are taught that a person who hears voices is automatically insane. As the advancement of the silent radio increases, more and more persons are hearing silent radio voices. It is common to place silent radio receivers in dental fillings, eye glass frames and earrings to insure communication. For group experiments, rooms and buildings are entirely wired. It is terrible that media covers this up as a national security issue.

Pedestrians studiously avoided this manifestly disturbed man. His delusional political tract contained two themes of paranoia: persecution and control, two ways of dealing with feelings of insignificance and helplessness. This man provides an example of a frequently encountered delusion, the "influencing machine" first described by Victor Tausk, a member of Freud's circle, in 1919.[27] Tausk observed that feelings of persecution begin with a sense of estrangement or alienation. The cause of this internal feeling is then projected externally upon a malevolent persecutory conspiracy that exercises control through the influencing

machine. (The nature of the machine has evolved in parallel with technological developments. Thus in the age of Freud, the machine sent electrical waves, later it sent radio waves and video signals, and now, in the
age of Star Wars, space-based laser rays are often invoked as the source
of control.) The man with the sandwich board, then, was denying his
responsibility for his inner feeling of helplessness and projecting it upon
a persecutory system.

On the opposite corner was an earnest young man handing out political tracts. The tracts described a widespread international conspiracy
that already had powerful influence over the unwitting citizens and threatened increasing control over all our destinies. The nature of this evil
conspiracy had been deciphered by Lyndon LaRouche, who, through his
newspaper, books, and political pamphlets, was attempting to warn the
world of the danger. He was also spreading the word through a legion of
followers, of which this earnest young man was one.

The danger from the conspiracy LaRouche warned of was extreme.
The language of his tract had striking resemblances to the pamphlets of
the man with the sandwich board on the opposite corner:

Stamp Out the Aquarian Conspiracy
Lyndon LaRouche

> The population of the United States of America is being
> brainwashed. This brainwashing is being done methodically,
> patiently by a large group of experts, the swarm of social psy-
> chologists deployed by their research institutes, employed in gov-
> ernment, business, labor and the media, and controlled by a
> powerful combination of business and financial leaders who run
> the high-technology areas of our economy, especially commu-
> nications, electronics and cybernetics . . . The social-psychiatrists
> and social-engineers . . . decided [in 1963–1965] to launch a
> massive, long-term brainwashing campaign in order to shift the
> underlying values and moral outlook of Americans away from
> rationalism, science and technology.
>
> The traditional values of this nation . . . are to be replaced by
> another set of values. This other set of values ranging from ho-
> mosexuality and oriental mysticism to ''cosmic consciousness''

and "religious fundamentalism" has been given the collective codename . . . "New Age" or "The Aquarian Conspiracy."

Every aspect of the mental and psychological life of the American people was profiled, recorded, and stored into computer memories. The institutions, personnel, and networks grew and penetrated deeply into every nook and cranny of federal, state, and local governments. . . .

Above this closely cooperating grouping of social psychologists, pollsters, and media manipulators, presides an elite of powerful patrons . . . Veteran intelligence officers refer to this awesome group . . . as the "Committee of Three Hundred." They prefer to be called "The Olympians." These are the real power in the land.[28]

The conspiratorial notions portrayed in LaRouche's material were no less bizarre than those of the influencing machine conveyed by the man with the sandwich board. Yet the warnings of the man with the sandwich board were discounted (he was dismissed as mentally disturbed), while Lyndon LaRouche was able to gain and sustain a substantial following. What was the difference between the two?

LaRouche, rhetorically persuasive and not obviously mentally ill, has the interpersonal and political skills to build an organization and appeal to a particular constituency (see Chapter 7). The key point is that he does not display a florid mental disturbance and accordingly is not recognized as psychiatrically disturbed by his potential followers. Indeed, LaRouche may be quite sane and only opportunistically exploiting a paranoid message. It is not possible to say whether LaRouche is a seriously disturbed paranoid or simply an exploiter of the theme. What does matter is that he has attracted a considerable following who see him not as an emotionally disturbed paranoid but as a visionary. Through his mastery of detail and ability to marshal selected "facts," LaRouche provides the evidence, the "proof," of the existence of the international elitist conspiracy whose goal is to control the destiny of the masses.

Often the political paranoid's beliefs in conspiracy and hostility originate in reality. Being a leader in any organization is always somewhat paranoiagenic. Subordinates and rivals may praise the leader to his face but plot against him behind his back. Leaders are rightly apt to be suspicious. As pressure mounts, the prudently alert leader may marginally overreact, going over the line into paranoia. Because his exaggerated fears have some basis, he may pull others along with him. As with hostility, there is a dynamic interaction between delusional suspicious thinking and the behavior of those surrounding the paranoid leader. The paranoid's behavior may in fact promote disaffection and conspiracies where there had been none. Fear of enemies can become a self-fulfilling prophecy.

By the same token, the grandiose self-concept and associated behavior can produce grandeur. Dreams of glory can be fulfilled. All the major political paranoids had grandiose self-images—Hitler, the admirer of Nietzsche, envisioned himself as superman; Stalin, as the leader of the greatest force in history; Ruholla Khomeini, as the savior of Islam.

There is accordingly a problem in determining whether leaders with grandiose self-concepts are out of touch with reality. Some indeed became significant historical figures. They did have major effects on the lives of their peoples. They were met with cheering throngs. People were willing to die for them. Scholars and journalists, presidents and generals, waited upon their words. For them, fantasy was actualized, dreams of glory fulfilled. Just as the paranoid discovers genuine plots, so too the grandiose paranoid will, if successful, find genuine admirers and genuine power.

Belief in an adversary, a rival, or an opponent is central to political life. But where rivals become enemies, we are entering the territory of paranoia. In the United States, Democrats and Republicans are (for the most part) not enemies. They are rivals, adversaries, or opponents. But Hitler and Stalin's rivals and opponents were their enemies.

This distinction between enemies and adversaries is critical in understanding the paranoid. The person or group who is the center of the paranoid fantasy is not a fully psychopathological object. Rivals for power are a necessary and inevitable feature of political life, but to the psychologically healthy political actor, their role is that of competitors. To the paranoid, they are pitiless foes who must be destroyed lest they destroy.

Was it delusional of Stalin to believe that other nations were plotting against the Soviet revolution? No. Many countries were doing precisely that—even fielding armies for the purpose. Was it delusional for Stalin to believe that subordinates and political rivals were plotting to destroy him? No. To be trusting, to be unsuspecting in the conspiracy-ridden Kremlin would have been naive, even fatal. But in his paranoid zeal to eliminate enemies, real and imagined, Stalin orchestrated purges that were to claim the lives of between 24 and 40 million citizens of the Soviet Union.

Stalin manifested all the cardinal characteristics of paranoia, with suspicion (amounting to an obsession with conspiracy) in the forefront. He acted out these beliefs in a hostile and disproportionate manner, creating ever more enemies in an escalating spiral of paranoid violence. But, like most political paranoids, Stalin was no fool. Robert Tucker, drawing on his studies of Stalin but informed by his examination of other militant leaders, has conceptualized a combative political personality pattern that is highly compatible with an effective paranoid appeal. He calls this pattern the "warfare personality."[29]

## The Warfare Personality and Richard Nixon

Leaders with the warfare personality induce societal paranoia for political aggrandizement through group manipulation. Such individuals thrive especially in totalitarian regimes but are found in democratic societies as well. Someone with the warfare personality exhibits the following qualities:

- He is the leader or strives to be the leader of a fighting bureaucracy—not a bureaucracy of a fighting organization but a bureaucracy that itself fights, like the Nazis or Bolsheviks.
- He has a great capacity for self-dramatization, which he achieves by pretending to be group-centered, at the service of the group, while in fact he is self-centered.
- His espoused delusions of enemies and conspiracies and his violent behavior approximate reality and conform to immediate political imperatives.

- He focuses his group's energies on defeating a demonic enemy. This focus gives the group coherence.

It is important to recognize that this pattern need not spring from psychopathological roots and does not necessarily reflect paranoid illness. One need not be paranoid to purvey a paranoid message. To be sure, to convey a paranoid message effectively is facilitated by a paranoid disposition, a capacity for conspiratorial thinking, but extremely paranoid messages can be conveyed by individuals who are not gravely paranoid but reap the political rewards that a paranoid appeal can bring. If their behavior does reflect a paranoid illness, it will eventually reveal itself when the leader pursues a policy that is irrelevant or contradictory to his political interests but consistent with his fantasies. Stalin, for example, revealed the paranoid dimension of his personality when he created the Great Purge (or Great Terror) of 1934–1939, a purge that was instituted after he had consolidated his rule and was no longer politically vulnerable. It was Stalin's desire to purge his own psychological demons that was being expressed.

Warfare personalities are not confined to totalitarian societies. An example in Western democratic society is Richard Nixon. Nixon, a complex character, displayed many of the features of the warfare personality, as his biographer Stephen Ambrose points out in *Nixon: The Education of a President*: "The inability to trust anyone is one of the principal personality traits of Nixon as an adult, a theme he returned to again and again in interviews, private conversations, and in his writings about himself. He insisted that 'in my job [he was then vice-president] you can't enjoy the luxury of intimate personal friendships. You can't confide absolutely in anyone.' "[30]

Richard Nixon was one of the most important figures in post–World War II America, and he also provoked the strongest hostility. A paranoid strain ran through Nixon's character and political style. Part of it was produced by his excessive response to the isolation that political leadership, especially executive electoral leadership, engenders. All leaders, whether in government, business, or any other large organization, know that many people cultivate confidences for personal gain and that these confidences are sometimes betrayed. In Nixon, who was temperamentally a loner, the paranoiagenic effect of leadership was compounded. He had political associates, but there was always a distance between him and them, and when the organizational bond was broken, so was the relationship. Bebe Rebozo and Robert Abplanalp were his only longtime friends, and they were nonpolitical listeners.[31] And Pat Nixon, unlike many other presidents' wives, was not her husband's confidante. Nixon was a solitary leader, and suspicion finds fertile soil in the garden of solitude.

There was more to Nixon's adversarial suspiciousness, however, than being lonely at the top. The intense hostility that existed between Richard Nixon and a substantial section of the American public developed out of decades of interaction. As a consequence of this interaction, Nixon's paranoid outlook and his obsessive hostile preoccupation with his adversaries were richly reciprocated: just because Nixon was a little paranoid didn't mean they weren't out to get him.

The wish to avoid conflict affects much social interaction. When individuals are challenged, they typically react by just meeting the level of provocation or even ignoring it to lessen the conflict. Some people, however, including those of a paranoid disposition, lack this basic social skill and thus create escalating social conflict.[32] The paranoid's readiness to meet hostility with hostility promotes greater hostility, although the individual will not be aware of his own role in producing tension. From his point of view, his feelings were produced by "them," when in fact the reverse is true. He is accurate in detecting hostility in the environment but oblivious to his own role in creating and compounding it. A genuine though minor conflict may exist, or the individual with a paranoid disposition may imagine a small inadvertent action to be a purposeful slight, causing him to commit a hostile act. Even where the provocation is genuine, the reaction is excessive. The opponent now also reacts, but, provoked, the politician with a paranoid orientation reacts at a higher level. An escalatory process becomes established. Eventually he sees himself as the victim, although he led in creating the hostile community. If the other person is similarly inclined, the process is that much more intense and the escalation that much more rapid. Whereas earlier the "victim" only imagined that he was the object of extraordinary hostility, now such

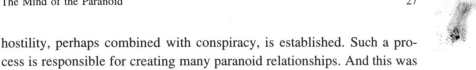

hostility, perhaps combined with conspiracy, is established. Such a pro-cess is responsible for creating many paranoid relationships. And this was the case with Nixon and his most extreme opponents.

Nixon's first campaign was against incumbent Democratic congress-man Jerry Voorhis, who was well entrenched, wealthy, and a liberal. As Nixon's political mentor, Murray Chotiner, argued, it was essential that the thirty-one-year-old candidate devalue the elder statesman. Unless the electorate were convinced that Voorhis should be replaced, they would not look at this upstart.

California's Twelfth Congressional District, with a population of 212,000, was influenced more by blue-collar workers and farm laborers than by any other group and "was listed as the Democrats' third most secure congressional stronghold in the entire country."[33] Voorhis, how-ever, was vulnerable. He was a poor, rambling speaker and had faced a succession of only mediocre opponents. Nor was he an active or partic-ularly effective legislator; he was known in Washington as a political saint, with cranky tendencies. He insisted, for example, on eliminating "Hon." before his name in the *Congressional Record* to save paper. Nixon made much of the fact that although Voorhis had introduced more than a hundred bills since 1942, the only one made into law transferred jurisdiction over rabbits from one federal department to another.

Most important, 1946 was a time for change. The Democrats had dominated American politics since 1930, and the first stirrings of the Cold War and the exhaustion of New Deal policies had turned America toward the right. Moreover, there was a feeling that the older generation of lead-ers should stand aside and that the generation who had won World War II should be given a chance to lead the country.

Nixon was a hardworking, effective campaigner, and he won the election by fourteen percentage points. Contrary to Nixon's later repu-tation (and subsequent revisionism), the "immediate press coverage of the election was favorable. *Time* [November 18, 1946] reported on how clean the fight for the 12th had been, praising Nixon for having 'politely avoided personal attacks on his opponent.' Even the displaced Voorhis recorded a pleasant handover meeting with Nixon and referred to the hope that they had parted as 'personal friends.' "[34] Nixon later said that he was happier on November 6, 1946, than at any other time in his political career.

At first glance this election does not seem to foreshadow Nixon's future career and reputation as an unscrupulous campaigner hated by liberals and the press. But on closer analysis, it does. Voorhis was generous in his post-election reference to Nixon as a personal friend. Nixon's campaign was dirty—he accused the mild and decent Voorhis of Communist sympathies. But the attack on Voorhis was not directly personal; it was guilt by association. The Democrats and the Democratic Party were anathematized, almost demonized. As Stephen Ambrose notes, Nixon was not a divider regionally, racially, or by class, but he was intensely partisan. Nixon was more motivated by ideas than most politicians, but he was not an ideologue. It was ambition, more than anything else, that drove him. The vehicle for his ambition was the Republican Party, and Nixon in his subsequent career had to deflate its better-established rival, the Democrats, as he did with Voorhis.

Alexis de Tocqueville noted even before the Civil War that American parties differed in their tendencies, not in their principles. Nixon contended the opposite: that Democrats were less loyal, less patriotic, less committed to a free society than Republicans. He charged that they were either unprincipled or had adopted sinister and corrupt principles. This charge, though not explicitly stated, was Nixon's "paranoid push," and it was one that committed Democrats sensed. They resented that Nixon was not playing the game straight. His sometime willingness, moreover, to stoop below the acceptable level of political rhetoric—accusing his liberal Senate opponent of 1950, Helen Gahagan Douglas, of being "pink right down to her underwear," for example, or later describing Democratic presidential nominee Adlai Stevenson as supported by "mobsters, gangsters, and remnants of the Old Capone gang"—confirmed the beyond-the-pale, almost slanderous nature of his political style.[35] Once his reputation was established, it became a political tool in the hands of his opponents and was invoked regardless of whether the reference was justified in any particular instance.

It made sense that a partisan politician would be resented by those he attacked. What was not evident in Nixon's first campaign was the mutual hostility that he and the bulk of the press, especially the elite media, would develop. The media came to have a "virtual chemical dislike of Nixon," especially after his prominence in the investigation of convicted perjurer and State Department official Alger Hiss.[36] In the Kennedy-Nixon presidential campaign of 1960, as William White describes it, "those forty or fifty national correspondents who had followed Kennedy since the beginning of his electoral exertions into the November days had become more than a press corps—they had become his friends and some of them his most devoted admirers. When the bus or the plane rolled or flew through the night, they sang songs of their own composition about Mr. Nixon and the Republicans in chorus with the Kennedy staff, and felt that they too were marching like soldiers of the Lord to the New Frontier."[37] To some extent this enthusiasm was pro-Kennedy (just as four and eight years earlier the press had showed a similar but more restrained ardor for Stevenson), but it was also anti-Nixon. Nixon realized this, and in his famous farewell address—"You won't have Nixon to kick around any more"—to the press after his defeat for the California governorship in 1962, he singled out the press for unfairness, depicting himself as victim.

As president, Nixon seemed obsessed by press criticism. He made lists of enemies among the press to be deprived of contact with him, and otherwise showed his hatred. The press disliked him as well and frequently gave him less than objective treatment. This personal conflict was compounded by the fact that Nixon became president in a time of great hostility toward all the major institutions of government and during the rise of adversarial journalism, both of which had helped bring down the Democrat Lyndon Johnson. Press hostility toward Nixon was so great that it leaped the Atlantic Ocean. One of the authors (RSR), who was living in England at the time of Nixon's resignation, recalls a news presenter on British television literally bouncing up and down on his chair in glee as he announced the event.

Nixon's political paranoia, then, was as complex as Nixon himself, a mixture of active and reactive prudence based on hard experience shading into provocative actions against imagined enemies that produced genuine enemies. It was a crucial factor in his rise to power and an essential ingredient in his ultimate fall from office.

## The Politics of Labeling the Paranoid

They called me mad, and I called them mad, and damn them,
they outvoted me.
—Nathaniel Lee, seventeenth-century playwright, on being
committed to Bedlam

Because exaggeratedly suspicious behavior can be useful as well as de-
structively irrational, what could be considered rational and prudent in
one setting might be irrational and disturbed in another. The political
dissident in Stalin's Soviet Union who was not always on guard, assuming surveillance, and suspicious would soon be imprisoned. Should he
win asylum in the West and continue to behave as if he were the object
of constant surveillance, trusting no one, he might well find himself diagnosed as suffering from a paranoid illness. It is adaptive to be suspicious in a conspiratorial environment. But the thoroughgoing paranoid is
not able to don his suspiciousness as a protective garment, discarding it
when it is no longer necessary. Always believing himself endangered, the
target of conspiracies, he sees no changes in the environment so never
changes his behavior.

The case of Major General P. G. Grigorenko of the Soviet army
vividly illustrates the contextual nature of what is paranoid.[38] General
Grigorenko became a dissident in 1961 at the height of his military career,
in the midst of the Cold War. He criticized the Soviet government for
what would now be called human rights violations and claimed that the
government was persecuting him. In 1964 he was incarcerated in a hospital for the criminally insane. Released a decade later, he was psychiatrically evaluated by Dr. Walter Reich of the U.S. National Institute of
Mental Health. The American evaluation determined that Grigorenko was
sane. The conclusions of the Soviet and American evaluations of the same
set of ideas and behavior patterns can be summarized as follows:

| Soviet | American |
| --- | --- |
| Obsessions | Perseverance |
| Delusions | Accurate beliefs |
| Psychotic recklessness | Committed devotion |

Soviet abuse of psychiatry for political purposes had been a major concern of the international psychiatric community since the early 1970s and eventually led to the expulsion of the All-Union Psychiatric Association of the Soviet Union from the World Psychiatric Association in 1979. The Soviet Union had developed a system of "special hospitals" for the criminally insane, staffed by psychiatrists who held senior rank in the GRU, the Soviet military intelligence service. The absence of due process and the lack of a concept of medical confidentiality facilitated the abuse of the psychiatric profession by the government.

Contributing to the abuse were vague and overly broad criteria for the diagnosis of so-called sluggish schizophrenia. The presence of "aberrant ideas" was viewed as representing the onset of serious paranoid mental illness. One of the aberrant ideas characteristic of sluggish schizophrenia was "delusions of societal reformation." Another serious symptom was "kverulanstvo," or querulousness. A factory supervisor could call the local KGB psychiatrist and indicate that a worker was falsely complaining about victimization. The diagnosis was related to position in the hierarchy: the worker could not call and complain that the supervisor was suffering from kverulanstvo.[39] The charge by a supervisor would result in a psychiatric evaluation, which in turn could lead to forced incarceration in one of the dreaded special hospitals. This process bypassed the legal system. After all, the government was providing "needed psychiatric care" to a "diagnosed mentally ill person."

In the hospital, painful "therapeutic" procedures were implemented to help extinguish the patient's "paranoid" ideas. The patient was pronounced cured when his "delusions of societal reformation" were no longer expressed and he acknowledged that they were symptoms of his mental illness. To ensure that he did not relapse after discharge from the hospital, the patient would be followed closely on an outpatient basis, with development of collateral information from the workplace and the social environment. Return of "paranoid delusions of societal reformation" would be seen as confirmation that the illness had reemerged, leading to rehospitalization and intensified "treatment."

In this case, a totalitarian system attempted to delegitimize a message of political dissent by diagnosing the messenger as a paranoid. Grigorenko did not suffer from a paranoid illness. The paranoid Soviet system *was* persecuting him. This emphasizes the cultural context in which the diagnosis is made. Is paranoia a diagnosis made by experts or a matter of majority consensus? Emily Dickinson answered this question poetically:

> Much Madness is divinest Sense—
> To a discerning Eye—
> Much Sense—the starkest Madness—
> 'Tis the Majority
> In this, as All, prevail—
> Assent—and you are sane—
> Demur—you're straightway dangerous—
> And handled with a Chain—[40]

Diagnosing the political paranoid is thus problematic within a paranoid culture because of the difficulties in discriminating paranoia from persecution.

## The Wilderness of Mirrors

One can consider counterintelligence offices within Western intelligence agencies as microclimates of paranoia within open democratic societies. The world of counterintelligence has aptly been characterized as a "wilderness of mirrors."[41] To be effective in rooting out espionage penetrations, one must suspect conspiracies. To fail to be professionally "paranoid" is to be ineffective. But the difference between being professionally suspicious and alert to conspiracies and being psychologically paranoid is considerable. The professional counterintelligence officer can shed his suspicions when he receives strong disconfirming evidence. The thoroughgoing paranoid, in contrast, may be so obsessed with his opponent that he "knows" that a particular individual is a penetration, a provocation, despite strong evidence to the contrary. The paleologic formulation is, "Opponents will try to penetrate us by saying they are defecting and giving us information. Therefore, any person who claims to have defected and offers us information is a penetration."

This is exactly what happened during the tenure of James Angleton, the founder of American counterintelligence.[42] Angleton was aided in his

rise in the Office of Strategic Services (OSS), the World War II predecessor to the Central Intelligence Agency, and in the CIA by his natural
suspiciousness, which served him well early in his career. But, unchar-
acteristically, he was deceived personally and professionally by the British Soviet spy Kim Philby. Angleton overcompensated for his error—in
which nearly the entire Anglo-American intelligence community had
shared—by creating a superficially complex but essentially simplistic policy of doubting everyone except a few close associates and an early KGB
defector, Anatoli Golitsyn.

Angleton was completely taken in by the dark conspiratorial plots
portrayed by Golitsyn, who persuaded Angleton that Chancellor Willy
Brandt of West Germany was a KGB agent and suggested that Prime
Minister Harold Wilson of Great Britain, Prime Minister Olof Palme of
Sweden, former ambassador to the Soviet Union and governor of New
York Averell Harriman, and even national security adviser and secretary
of state Henry Kissinger were under Soviet control. He then described a
Soviet "master plan" to deceive the West, an integral element of which
was the broad use of agents provocateurs. The "revelations" of Golitsyn
were on their face so extraordinary that they should have been treated
with the greatest suspicion, though investigated. But Golitsyn was providing the "proof" for which Angleton had been searching. Accordingly,
when another Soviet intelligence agent, Uri Nosenko, defected, providing
potentially valuable leads and information that would have completely
discredited Golitsyn's fabrications, Angleton (with the acquiescence of
high officials in the CIA and FBI) treated Nosenko as a Soviet plant and
had him placed under punitive house arrest for several years. The exaggerated suspicions that Golitsyn had supplied led Angleton to disbelieve
and discredit a genuine defector.

Angleton, convinced that Nosenko was a provocateur, saw his clues
as attempts to discredit the "genuine" Golitsyn. Moreover, if Nosenko
vouched for someone, that person was automatically suspect. Angleton's
world was indeed a wilderness of mirrors. Convinced by Golitsyn that
there was a mole within the CIA, Angleton zealously pursued dozens of
senior CIA officials, tarring their reputations and severely damaging their
careers. The community of espionage is one of deception and suspicion,
and once suspicion has stained anyone, especially a senior official, it is

difficult for him to prove his loyalty. Caution comes to dominate fairness, and the organization may determine that even though the charge has not been proven, it is imprudent to assign the suspect to a sensitive or responsible position.

Like so many paranoids who maintain the rest of their personality intact, Angleton was remarkably persuasive. His long service in the agency and his presence at its creation, his resolute belief in the existence of moles, and his occasional successes in discovering genuine penetrations made him a powerful and destructive force for decades, until his retirement.

Society is an uncertain judge of its paranoids. Some are identified as manifestly ill, and their paranoid ideas are seen as delusional products of deranged minds. The poet Ezra Pound, for example, was incarcerated in St. Elizabeth's hospital in Washington, D.C., in part because of his pro-Nazi and anti-Semitic propaganda. Others, like James Angleton, are in positions that require extreme suspiciousness of conspiracies, and so the boundary between professionally required suspiciousness and personal paranoia becomes blurred. And some paranoids, like Lyndon LaRouche, find success with a paranoid conspiratorial political message.

Some paranoids will focus with great precision on an individual or, much more likely, on some group that is malevolent in intent and must accordingly be destroyed. It is readily apparent how this suspiciousness lends itself to the political environment, becoming the basis of conspiracy theories. Especially in time of economic distress, to have a leader who with certainty can point the accusing finger at "them" as the basis of problems is extremely appealing.

Because paranoia is a distortion of a healthy response to the danger that exists in politics, and because threats appear and disappear, a perception of enemies may be accurate at one time and inaccurate at another. Some leaders, for reasons of their own internal paranoid psychology, are compelled to see themselves as surrounded by enemies, whatever is going on in the external political environment. Such severely clinically disturbed paranoids rarely are able to sustain effective political leadership. Most political paranoids are not at the extremity of clinical paranoia. The degree of paranoid traits they manifest depends on the psychological and political stress they experience and on the response to their message. Some may discount as an extremist the hate-mongering demagogue who inflames his followers against imaginary enemies, but those needing the false assurance of the paranoid's appeal view him as a savior, the only one making sense out of a hostile and senseless world. External validation of a paranoid message will then strengthen the belief of the paranoid messenger.

Societies fluctuate in their readiness to respond to these paranoid messengers, and some societies are more susceptible to their lure than others. To meet success in promulgating a paranoid message requires a political culture that is receptive to a paranoid message.

# 2

## Paranoid Culture and Conspiracy Thinking

The Invisible Enemy Should Not Exist [name of the
street connecting the northern entrance of Babylon to
the sanctuary of Marduk, Babylon's patron god, c. 600
B.C.]
—*The Ishtar Gate*

All governments are obscure and invisible.
—Sir Francis Bacon

Paranoia is not an obscure illness that affects only the
mad. It is present in all societies. Every society has its
paranoid groups and its paranoid individuals. For the
most part, these individuals and groups will be recognized as mad—sometimes ignored, sometimes mocked,
sometimes harassed.

A would-be leader conveying a paranoid message is
destined to be a prophet in the wilderness, preaching
only to a small band of true believers, unless the political
culture is receptive to his theme. In some cultures, there
are moments in history—times of stress when the existence of the society is believed to be threatened—when
paranoid messages are particularly attractive. And in
other cultures, paranoia is bred in the bone and conspir-

acy thinking is the stuff of everyday life. In either case, a distinctive paranoid style is evident.

## The Paranoid Style

Richard Hofstadter, in "The Paranoid Style in American Politics," was the first contemporary historian to treat societal paranoia in a systematic way. He did this by applying what was then known about paranoia to the history of social movements. He borrowed a clinical term but did not apply it clinically. Hofstadter used the term *paranoid* just as art historians use the terms *rococo* or *baroque,* as historians of national expansion use the word *imperialistic* or political scientists the word *authoritarian,* and as sociologists speak of *alienation.*

The paranoid style is readily recognized. Its users believe that a vast and subtle conspiracy exists to destroy their entire way of life. What is notable about the paranoid's view of history is not that he believes conspiracies exist and are important—after all, they do exist and may be important—but that he sees conspiracy as *the* motivating force in history and the essential organizing principle in all politics.

Characteristically, the conspiracy is described as already powerful and growing rapidly. Time is short. Absolute and irreversible victory of the conspiratorial group is near. The few people who recognize the danger must expose and fight the conspirators. The conflict cannot be compromised or mediated. It is a fight to the death. The conspirators are absolutely evil, and so, as the opponents of this evil power, members of the paranoid group see themselves as the force for good. Indeed, they acquire in their own eyes the role of the defenders of *all* that is good. The struggle is cast in Manichaean terms as between good and evil.

The paranoid style is distinctive and remarkably consistent over time. Hofstadter offers four examples from different eras. The first is from a sermon preached by the Reverend Jedidiah Morse at Charlestown, Massachusetts, in 1798:

Secret and systematic means have been adopted and pursued, with zeal and activity, by wicked and artful men, in foreign countries, to undermine the foundations of this Religion [Christianity], and to overthrow its Altars, and thus to deprive the world of its benign influence on society. . . . These impious conspirators and philosophists have completely effected their purposes in a large portion of Europe, and boast of their means of accomplishing their plans in all parts of Christendom.[1]

Religion and distant outsiders continued to figure prominently in paranoid rhetoric, as in this extract from the *Texas State Times* of September 15, 1855:

It is a notorious fact that the Monarchs of Europe and the Pope of Rome are at this very moment plotting our destruction. . . . We have the best reasons for believing that corruption has found its way into our Executive chamber, and that our Executive head is tainted with the infectious venom of Catholicism . . . The Pope has recently sent his ambassador of state to this country on a secret commission, the effect of which is an extraordinary boldness of the Catholic Church throughout the United States . . . These minions of the Pope . . . [are] propagating the adulterous union of Church and state; abusing with foul calumny all governments but Catholic; and spewing out the bitterest execrations of all Protestantism.[2]

The power of money also figures strongly in paranoid ideation. Like the power of religion, it forms a realistic core for paranoid fantasy. The anti-banking, anti–big business American Populist Party noted in its 1892 platform that a "vast conspiracy against mankind has been organized on two continents and is taking possession of the world." Three years later several of the leaders of this party signed the following manifesto:

As early as 1865–6 a conspiracy was entered into between the gold gamblers of Europe and America . . . For nearly thirty years these conspirators . . . have pursued with unrelenting zeal their one central purpose . . . Every device of treachery, every resource of statecraft, and every artifice known to the secret cabals of the international gold ring are being made use of to deal a blow to the property of the people and the financial and commercial independence of the country.[3]

Accusations of gross and immoral political ambition, manifesting it-self in political conspiracy, are also prominent in the paranoid political style. In June 1951, with the Korean War under way and the presidential campaign of 1952 beginning, Senator Joseph McCarthy entered the fol-lowing analysis of America's foreign policy problems into the *Congres-sional Record:*

> How can we account for our present situation unless we believe that men high in this government are concerting to deliver us to disaster? This must be the product of a great conspiracy, a con-spiracy on a scale so immense as to dwarf any previous such venture in the history of man . . . A conspiracy of infamy so black that, when it is finally exposed, its principals shall be forever deserving of the maledictions of all. What can be made of this unbroken series of decisions? . . . They cannot be attributed to incompetence . . . The laws of probability would dictate that part of . . . [the] decisions would serve this country's interest.[4]

What is notable about these quotations is not their substance. In each case there was probably some basis for concern. First, a wave of anti-religiosity struck Europe at the time of the French Revolution, and this wave consisted in its most extreme form of those who wished to destroy religion as a social force because of the earlier abuses committed in its name. Second, mid-nineteenth-century Europe still experienced political conflicts in which Catholic struggled against Protestant. The Populists, furthermore, were not completely wrong in believing that international bankers sometimes entered into conspiracies at the expense of others. And finally, McCarthy had some reason to be wary of organized treason in the American government. In each case, however, the tone and the scale of the reaction were so disproportionate to the situation that they were clearly being compounded by private psychological needs that found res-onance in a frightened population.[5]

The focus on conspiracy as a universal political explanation means that those displaying the paranoid style see history and politics as com-pletely rational and ultimately predictable, if only one has the key. In a world of uncertainty, the paranoid leader offers his followers certainty. The systematic world the paranoid creates in his fantasy is far more coherent than the real world. Nothing happens that is not deliberately caused.

Although the political paranoid's relation to society is adversarial, he is likely to see himself as society's victim, cast out by his fellows, and to see his struggle as a search for belonging, for community.[6] In this sense, the paranoid process begins when a person comes to fear and hate society and so withdraws from it. He then finds himself in a state of adversarial, atomistic, community-less nature, rather like that described by Thomas Hobbes in *Leviathan*. The various aspects of the paranoid syndrome, such as the fear that others are plotting against the paranoid person, can be seen as expressions of the alienated human condition. Paranoia from this point of view is simply man's situation when he cannot fulfill his social nature and feels forced to live outside society. *Political paranoia is a perverse attempt to reconnect with others, to regain community.*

Society provides many institutions to satisfy the desire for social interaction and emotional support: among these institutions are churches, clubs, and more informal groups such as monthly card parties and early-morning running groups. For some, however, who are stricken with paranoid fears and already feel themselves separated from normal society, such groups are emotionally unavailable.

The paranoid, being a social animal like other humans, will seek a group that complements his beliefs and offers him community. Some political paranoids will join (or form) such intense and violent organizations as social-revolutionary terrorist groups, like Italy's Red Brigade or Germany's Red Army Faction (see Chapter 4).

A perspective on the paranoia of our time can be gained by examining how paranoia existed in the past.

## The Past May Be a Paranoid Country

Cultural anthropologists and cross-cultural psychologists use an ahistorical approach. But the past can be seen as a foreign country, a different and exotic culture. This is another way to fix a definition of paranoia in cross-cultural terms. Rather than view history as a succession of events, which is how we have been taught to regard it, we can also consider it a "history of attitudes, behavior, and unconscious collective representation" held by successive generations—in other words, a history of mentalities.[7]

Mentalities are the beliefs and attitudes that nearly all people of a time share uncritically, without realizing it.[8] The study of mentalities is the intellectual history of nonintellectuals; in contrast to conventional intellectual history, it does not concern itself with the development of great ideas. Nor is it the same as (though it encompasses) the history of ideologies.[9] Ideologies are more systematic than mentalities and, though widely held, are not universally followed. An example of a contemporary mentality, at least in the richer countries of the world, is the practice of interpreting the physical world in a rational, positivistic manner.

The study of mentalities, moreover, differs from cultural and popular history in that the focus is not on events but on conceptualizations and psychology. Another way of describing the study of mentalities is to say that it is the history of worldviews.[10]

Early examples of this approach—although the method was not yet known as the study of mentalities—are Johan Huizinga's *Waning of the Middle Ages,* which describes the tenor of life and the unquestioned assumptions of the late medieval period, and Georges Lefebvre's *Great Fear of 1789,* which describes the panic that swept through France because of a greatly exaggerated fear of the return of the aristocracy.

One of the central themes of this book is that paranoia is a characteristic mentality of the late twentieth century. The paranoid worldview, largely unchallenged, frames and focuses how events are interpreted. We can gain a perspective on the paranoid mentality by looking at it as it appeared three hundred years ago, in Tudor England. As L. B. Smith shows, paranoia was pervasive among the Tudors.[11] It appeared in homely advice literature (for example, a self-help book of the period advises that one's immediate family perhaps can be trusted, but that it is best to avoid testing this possibility); in comments by the great, such as Henry VIII; and in the Earl of Essex's convoluted and betrayal-strewn political career, which the usually indulgent Queen Elizabeth I finally was compelled to end by having him beheaded.[12]

The Tudor's intellectual world, like that of the paranoid, was one of absolute reason, of pervasive interconnection "where nothing happened

by chance" and "everything was imbued with a moral meaning."[13] The
paranoid delusion of universal conspiracy was fueled by the importance
of individuals. It was taken for granted that events were decisively
brought about not through chance (by the weather, for example) or the
workings of impersonal influences (the wealth of a region) but through
the direct efforts of individuals, generally carried out in secret and hedged
with deception. The monarch both symbolized and manifested this per-
sonalized interpretation of politics.[14] The Tudor period not only experienced paranoia but also planted the seeds of future paranoia.

## A Paranoid Culture Needs a Paranoid Tradition

One of the distinctive qualities of the paranoid appeal is its reliance on
ideas, explanations, and arguments of causality. Indeed, a paranoid literary tradition has been used to stigmatize various groups, accusing them
of abominable practices and conspiratorial activity. As far back as antiq-
uity, this tradition posits the existence of a society within the larger society but hidden from it, and dedicated through the use of conspiracy to
destroying that larger society. The early Christian Church was so stigmatized until about the time of Constantine.

One type of paranoid tradition comes from the bottom up: it is the
lower social groups that are most exercised about conspiracy, and their
hostility is directed against the religious and secular aristocracy.[15] In the
Middle Ages, for example, distressed groups gathered around apostate
monks or friars and even laymen. Such non-establishment unorthodox
leaders claimed a holy mission to save the world from a secret and rapidly
growing evil force located in the ruling class. These movements "owed
both their dynamism and their destructiveness to a shared phantasy of a
markedly paranoid kind."[16] Like the populist movements associated with
Joseph McCarthy and Lyndon LaRouche, these were paranoid movements
from below—populist mass paranoia.

Paranoid beliefs can also draw on a tradition associated with a ruling
elite.[17] Such leaders as the thirteenth-century witch hunter Conrad of Mar-
burg and the nobles in sixteenth-century Italy who persecuted the heretical Fraticelli are examples of paranoia from above.

In the fourteenth century, Philip the Fair of France and his reluctant ally Pope Clement V, themselves members of the elite, combined these discrepant traditions by accusing the prestigious and powerful Knights Templar of carrying out secret rites parodying the Catholic faith, eating infants, and indulging in promiscuous sex with each other. The alleged secret rites not only separated the Templars from the larger society but, it was believed, bonded their members to one another.

Variations of this charge of sexual promiscuity and religious insult have been applied time and again to different groups as the fear of imagined conspiracies periodically grips society. This mass paranoia peaks with the persecution of the accused group and then falls back to a temporary quiescence, eventually to rise again.

Thus, paranoid beliefs in literate societies are not simply the product of childhood socialization, innate tendencies, and societal stress. Such beliefs also require and are shaped by specific traditions (for example, designated demonized groups) and specific narratives (such as tales of orgies parodying the Catholic faith). Systematic and society-wide persecution requires a paranoid mythology. Groups cannot be paranoidally persecuted without an established legitimating myth. The accusation is often essentially the same: secret groups exist that are bound together by hidden practices considered abominable by the rest of society, and these groups are conspiratorially dedicated to the destruction of the larger society.

## How the Paranoid Culture Selects Its Victims

The quintessential conspiratorial group united by abominations and dedicated to the destruction of the larger society is the witches' coven, presided over by Satan himself. The most famous events in the Americas concerning a paranoid panic associated with witches took place in Salem, Massachusetts, in 1692. What most attracts us to the Salem Panic is that it enables us to discern how the objects of paranoia are chosen.

The outline of what occurred in Salem is well documented. We have here compressed the narrative and broadened its scope to include the associated panic that went beyond Salem Village.

In early 1692, eleven-year-old Elizabeth Parris and her cousin Abigail

Williams were sometimes unable to speak or see, would violently open
and close their mouths, and fell into convulsive fits involving grotesque
distortions of the neck, arms, and back; choking; temporary amnesia; and
loss of hearing, sight, and touch. A church member advised the husband
of the Parrises' Carib slave, Tituba, that the girls could be cured by
serving a "witch cake," made with the girls' urine, to the family dog.
This was done, and the fits ceased.

The making and use of the urine cake were acts of witchcraft, and it
was these acts—coming from a parishioner—that first alarmed the ministers who were investigating the fits. Not only was a West Indian slave
using magic, but a church member had advocated it, albeit in an effort
to offset the girls' "possession." On March 1, 1692, Tituba testified that
"the Devil had come to her in the shape of a man—a tall man in black
with white hair . . . He had shown her a book [that had nine marks] and
two of them had been made by Good and Osburne [two elderly women
of poor reputation] . . . Sometimes the black man . . . had forced her to go
with them and afflict the children. She had gone 'upon a stick or pole
and Good and Osburne behind me. We ride taking hold of one another;
don't know how we go, for I saw no trees nor path but was presently
there.' "[18]

The fits spread to other girls (aged nine to twenty) who "cried out
upon" other witches. Many of those accused, like Tituba, confessed and
implicated others, some of whom also confessed. Many, perhaps most,
of the confessions had the ring of sincerity about them. It was a basic
tenet of Puritanism that God's people were always vulnerable, born as
they were in sin. Given this worldview, it is not surprising that the citizens
of Salem accepted Tituba's statements, and others like them, as factual.
In one confession, two unidentified women from Boston were referred to
as involved in satanic events.

Two types of witchcraft existed in the popular mind and in the law.
The first and oldest might today be called sorcery, or black magic, and
was called *maleficium* then. This involved the use of words or objects to
harm others. It was a body of knowledge and techniques that anyone
could learn and practice. Maleficium did not require the cooperation of
others, nor did it necessarily involve a compact with the devil. In many

ways maleficium blended into accepted Christian practice, so Christian authority was inconsistent in the severity of its punishment for this offense.

Another view, much more strongly held on the Continent than in England, described witchcraft as involving a compact with the devil and suggested that such compacts were part of a demonic plot to destroy the larger society. This was of course the greater danger. Individuals who made their neighbors' cattle die or created storms through casting spells were a problem and should be firmly punished, but they were essentially a nuisance, not a threat to society. But if individuals were compacting with Satan, following his leadership in developing secret organizations that included prominent and influential persons, then a crisis was at hand, requiring severe action. It was also expected that any form of witchcraft would be largely confined to marginal members of society, not typical church members.[19]

Tituba's accusation gave rise to two fears. First, the urine-cake episode demonstrated the involvement of regular church members in witchcraft. Second, Tituba's report of nine marks in the mysterious book and the two unidentified women from Boston fueled the fear of a broad conspiracy. Even more important, a former minister of Salem Village, George Burroughs, was soon "identified" as presiding at witches' sabbaths. He was brought back from Maine in early May, examined, tried, and hanged. Cotton Mather himself stated that Burroughs was the master conspirator. Over the next seventeen months more than fifty confessions took place. About a third of those accused confessed.[20]

People confessed because they had practiced witchcraft, because they had not practiced witchcraft but were persuaded that they had, and because they were coerced physically or psychologically. Many confessed because, although they were innocent, it had become evident that confession, the accusation of others, and a statement of repentance would safeguard them from further harm.[21] Many of those accused were urged by relatives to confess and even to implicate others to save themselves. It was this multiplicity of factors that created the large number of accusations (141 in all). Men as well as women were accused, as were six children, including the five-year-old Dorcas Good, whose mother was one of the first accused. Although a quarter of the accusations were against men, typically the men had some familial connection to an accused female.[22]

By May 14, 1692, a new governor, Sir William Phips, noting the growing list of confessions involving Satan, decided that prompt action had to be taken to "discourage the weak-willed from signing the devil's book."[23] It was not so much the fear of an outbreak of malicious magic that drove Governor Phips at this point as the fear of a broadening conspiracy presided over by the devil.

Phips appointed a Court of Oyer and Terminer to hear and decide cases. The court met on June 2, 1692, to hear the case of Bridget Bishop.[24] She was convicted and was executed on June 10, and other trials, based principally on depositions, proceeded rapidly. Another eighteen of those accused were hanged by September 22. The accusations were vigorously contested. Several witnesses acknowledged that they had been prompted to cry out certain names, and one of the afflicted girls admitted having made accusations "for sport." Many people shouted objections during the five hangings on August 19, especially in defense of George Burroughs and the generally respected John Proctor. But due process was carefully followed throughout, and charges were vigorously contested. People were not simply accused and dragged off to be hanged. Many accusations resulted in countersuits of defamation, and many of these countersuits succeeded.

The early confessions, especially the detailed and corroborative ones, frightened the judges into believing they faced a satanic attack. In a lengthy confession, for example, William Barker of Andover said that he had been a witch for three years and that heavy debts had led him to make a pact with the devil, who promised to pay off his obligations. He had not only signed a covenant and afflicted three women but had also attended a witches' meeting at Salem Village. He gave a detailed account of that event, claiming that George Burroughs was there and had blown a trumpet, and that almost immediately many witches appeared. He estimated that about one hundred of the three hundred who practiced in the neighborhood attended the meeting. The devil addressed the gathering, demanding to be worshiped and predicting the destruction of Salem and the surrounding area. This speech was followed by a ceremony involving wine and bread. At the end of his confession Barker apologized to the court and asked for their prayers.[25]

Such confessions confirmed the fear of many of Salem's inhabitants that the millennium, which would see the end of the devil's influence on earth, was approaching. If that were so, the devil would make a last effort to obtain recruits. Were not the pagan Indians in revolt? Were not the demonic Catholic powers encroaching on God's Massachusetts colony? The Puritans had reason to fear Indians, the French, and the subversive influence of Quakers. Nor were they unreasonable in being suspicious that London would somehow drain off their growing prosperity. This fear of loss of autonomy through invasion or oppression was keen. As Richard Godbeer notes in *The Devil's Dominion,* the "predisposition . . . to locate evil outside the self is the key to understanding what happened in 1692."[26] It is also the paranoid disposition. The girls and other members of the Salem community could have interpreted their convulsions as divine punishment for sinfulness or simply as inexplicable illness, but they looked to an external malevolent force.[27]

It is noteworthy that only members of the Puritan community were accused. Although Irish, Scots, Dutch, French, Catholics, Quakers, Baptists, Jews, and Indians all lived in the area, none of these seemingly likely candidates for witchcraft was accused. The panic was completely inwardly directed.[28]

As the number of the accused grew, the leaders of Salem began to doubt whether so many could be in league with the devil. Forty-three confessions (containing multiple accusations) were made between February and October.[29] Increasingly, "people of good conversation"—even Lady Phips, the governor's wife, and Captain John Alden of Boston, son of John Alden of the *Mayflower*—were accused.[30] Governor Phips suspended the trials and executions on September 22, calling for a reconsideration of the rules of evidence. The new rule, on the advice of Increase Mather, excluded spectral evidence (reports of seeing spirits, especially when others present could not see them). Cotton Mather began preaching that the witch frenzy was itself the devil's work, devised to divide Christians. Governor Phips dismissed the Court of Oyer and Terminer, and he began to have the prisoners released on bail. Although a superior court made three further convictions, no subsequent action was taken. In May 1693, the governor issued a general pardon to the surviving accused.

The 1692 Salem Panic had all the characteristics of a paranoid episode. There was a conspiratorial delusion (the devil and his confederates), significant hostility was mobilized (against the large number of "witches"), and the twin characteristics of centrality (the devil had chosen Salem for the beginning of his final pre-millennial campaign) and grandiosity (Salem would defeat the devil and save Christianity) were present. Projection and a fear of loss of autonomy were the principal psychological forces driving the creation and manifestation of these delusions. What distinguished this episode from the typical witch panic were the large number of hangings and the conflation of accusations of maleficium with accusations of conspiracy with the devil.

This paranoid episode shared many features with Stalin's purges and Pol Pot's terror, but unlike those broader events, the Salem Panic involved a specific group of victims (those accused), and later scholars can draw on a detailed record of why, when, and how they were accused. The choice of victims in Salem and elsewhere can be traced to three factors. Other historical contexts will offer a different emphasis from the Salem scenario but will involve the same factors.

*Victims are chosen within a complex and well-established tradition of belief.* The idea of witches, witchcraft, and the necessity for their discovery and destruction was not only part of the tradition of Christianity but preceded it. The Book of Exodus specifically ordered, "Thou shalt not suffer a witch to live" (22:18). The tools of the trade—certain potions, images with pins in them, and so on—were evidence that the owner was a practitioner. So too were physical signs, especially insensitivity to pain on certain areas of the body (such as the "witch's tit," from which the devil sucked blood). Certain events were also incriminating, such as the recovery of the afflicted upon being touched by the accused.

The idea of a heretical element beyond maleficium dates principally from the fifteenth century. Increasingly after the Reformation gained momentum, those who violated religious practices and expressed opposition to or doubts about Christianity were believed to be especially likely to be allied with the devil.

The tradition of belief can apply not only to what people do but also to whom they are. Some groups are embedded as paranoid objects within traditional beliefs or within ideologies. There was a tradition of xenophobia in Cambodia, on which the Khmer Rouge drew to select their Westernized victims. In his analysis of the *Protocols of the Elders of Zion* forgeries, Norman Cohn has demonstrated that modern anti-Semitism conforms to a tradition of suspicion and hostility to Jews stretching back to classical times.[31] Stalin's choice of marginally better-off peasants (the kulaks) for victimization depended in part on the place of these relatively rich peasants in Marxist-Leninist ideology. More important, a long tradition in Russia consists of explaining phenomena as due to conspiracy. For any paranoid movement, like any political movement, to succeed, it must draw upon a tradition. This tradition will guide it in choosing its special victims.

*Victims are chosen because they have assumed roles, acquired characteristics, or displayed behaviors that partially fit the profile the paranoid group describes.* People who practiced magic or healing were especially at risk of being accused of witchcraft. Tituba, for example, practiced magic by casting fortunes. Because witches shared the devil's evil nature, those who had a reputation—sometimes justified—for contentiousness or casualness toward religious matters were likely to find themselves accused. Pugnaciousness seemed to be a particularly important characteristic of those denounced. Not only were they belligerent toward others, but the accused had particularly quarrelsome family relations. Husbands not infrequently accused wives, and vice versa. Assaultive speech and theft were more common among the accused than among the general population, and this was especially the case with accused women. Accused females were more than twice as likely as other women to have a reputation for assaultive speech and thievery.[32]

Many of the accused were unpleasant people.[33] One Rachel Clinton deliberately poked her fellows with her elbows as they were seating themselves in the meeting house and referred to them as "hellhounds." John Godfrey of Andover had started 132 cases of litigation in the area.[34] Godfrey, a thoroughly obnoxious person, was tried several times and finally released with the verdict "suspiciously guilty of witchcraft, but not legally guilty, according to lawe and evidence . . . received."[35] But those accused who were brought to trial often had the virtues of their defects. Truculent and provocative, they also stood up for themselves. After all, they could have avoided all danger simply by confessing and accusing others.

We have suggested that some of those accused had in fact practiced witchcraft or quasi-witchcraft, especially healing arts.[36] The distinction between scientific doctoring and witch-doctoring was less clear then than it is now. Most important, those who actually practiced or claimed to practice witchcraft sometimes identified themselves. Abigail Hobbes, for example, boasted that she had "sold herself body and soul to the Old Boy."[37]

Although those who were accused tended to be of low status, a specially vulnerable group were those perpetual marginals, individuals who had risen to a higher status than their parents.[38] People like to take the newly risen down a peg, and a charge of witchcraft could do that.

Similar "marks" and behaviors appeared among victims in other times and places. Pol Pot's victims were often somewhat Western in outlook and education, and they often wore what were seen as tokens—watches, eyeglasses—of Westernization (see Chapter 10). Many of Stalin's victims were opposed to him, and some probably did conspire against him. The kulaks probably were less reliable supporters of the Communists than were those who replaced them. Many Jews in Germany were more prosperous than the average German and formed a community marginally separate from Gentile Germans.

Paranoia—especially political paranoia—is seldom a complete delusion. It is typically a distortion of a truth.

*Victims tend to be chosen from those whose death or humiliation can symbolically or materially enrich the accusers or from those who have angered the accusers.* Being on the wrong side of a factional quarrel can greatly increase one's chances of being accused of malevolent characteristics or behavior, including witchcraft. Salem Village had a population of about two hundred persons over the age of twenty-one.[39] Like most small communities, it had factional divisions. The principal division was between the supporters and opponents of Samuel Parris, the minister of an independent congregation in Salem Village, which had long sought autonomy from the larger, older, frequently interfering Salem Town.[40]

The division seems petty to contemporary observers, but to people at the time it was intense. Parris was one of the strongest advocates of the witch hunt, and it was his children who initiated it. As early as two years before the panic he described his opponents, both within Salem Village and in Salem Town, as having "a lamentable harmony [with] . . . devils, in their opposition of God's kingdom and interests."[41] It is not surprising that when the panic broke out, Parris found no witches among his supporters.

Another form of victimization was more subtle. The pattern of accusation was gender related. Both accusers and accused tended to be female, especially women who deviated from established female roles and expectations. In seventeenth-century Puritan communities, childbearing was considered a religious and a community obligation, perhaps the most important activity of any Christian woman. Women who were childless were under special obloquy. One in six of those accused in the Salem episode was childless, twice the average for the Salem area. Even those accused who had children tended to have fewer than the average.[42] Moreover, the accusations of witchcraft tended to be connected with matters concerning children, such as "children thought to have been made ill, or murdered, by witchcraft; mothers apparently bewitched while bearing or nursing children; witches alleged to suckle imps (in implicit parody of normal maternal function); witches observed to take a special (and suspicious) interest in other people's children; witches found to be predominantly of menopausal age and status."[43] Punishing the less fertile was a way of enhancing the status of the accusers (who were presumably fertile). That they were made to suffer for their condition probably led some to turn to witchcraft and other deviant behavior. Female witches were also much more likely to have charges of assaultive speech and theft levied against them than either the general population of women or male witches.[44] The connection of witchcraft to children also related to those accused: in Salem, children were especially afflicted and were leading accusers.

Self-interest, symbolic and material, is the principal factor determining the pattern of accusations. Whether the revolution is from above or below, paranoia's victims will often be those whose wealth can enrich the new rulers or whose humiliation can enhance the tormentors' self-regard. The European Jews of the 1930s and 1940s were vulnerable not only because they were considered outsiders and traditional objects of paranoid fears but also because many were propertied. The Asian merchants whose property was expropriated by Uganda's Idi Amin and the marginal landowners Stalin starved are two examples of paranoia's victims chosen at least in part on the basis of their wealth. Symbolic victimization has also been a powerful force. Pol Pot's illiterate peasants killed those Cambodians who wore glasses and wristwatches not to seize the glasses or watches but to assert their cultural dominance over the wearers.

The importance of symbolic politics in the paranoid dynamic is demonstrated by the fact that the defeated are not simply impoverished but humiliated. Enforced public apologies, the assignment of particularly demeaning tasks, and even public executions conducted in a degrading manner are designed to confirm the aggressor's position.

So it is that the most vulnerable in any society in any time are those who occupy a role traditionally associated with being a victim, who are outsiders or are different in some way, who confirm that role by some action or trait, and whose conviction can lead to the improvement of the accusers' situation. But we must add a caveat: chance plays a large role in the heat of any paranoid movement. Salem's Rebecca Nurse, though not free of imperfection, was a regular churchgoer and enjoyed a general reputation for goodwill and humility—but her Salem neighbors tried and hanged her. No one is safe when the paranoid beast is in the streets. And in some societies, conspiracy thinking is the stuff of everyday life.

## Where Paranoia Is the Norm

In her classic study of the Dobu of New Guinea, Ruth Benedict describes a society that believes in witchcraft and practices poisoning.[45] Suspicion is pervasive, misfortunes are always believed to be caused by malign human intent, and hostility is universal.

The Dobu live on bleak volcanic islands off the southern shore of eastern New Guinea. Unlike many of the islands in the region, their land offers little fishing and poor farming. Dobu society is even less inviting than the land. There are no legal institutions, and there is no trust. Disease is common, and all disease is believed to be due to the casting of spells.

Indeed, certain people "own" special spells for the creation of specific diseases. The most likely person to cast a spell is whoever is closest to you—your wife or child or hunting partner. Each husband and each wife cultivates his or her own yam patch, planted in yams descended from yams in each spouse's family. Even the yams are jealous: laughter is never permitted in hearing of the yam patch, as the yams would resent it or would think it some curse. Any type of wealth or pleasure is hidden, for the happiness implied would call up more than its owner's due share of curses. All this malice is hidden under a constant show of bland pleasantness. As Benedict observes, this deeply ingrained cultural pattern of deceptiveness engenders suspiciousness: "The Dobuan['s] . . . view of . . . virtue consists in selecting a victim upon whom he can vent the malignance he attributes alike to human society and to powers of nature . . . Suspicion and cruelty are his trusted weapons in the strife and he gives no mercy, and he asks none."[46] No wonder that Benedict comments, "Suspicion, in Dobu, runs to paranoid lengths."[47] In such a society it is indeed difficult, if not impossible, to apply norms of trust common in almost all other societies.

If paranoia is the norm for an entire society, can we call it paranoia? One way of evaluating whether a behavior is pathological is simply to accept the society's own evaluation of it: a behavior is mad if the society believes it to be so and sane if that pattern is locally accepted.[48] This in fact is the position of the pure cultural relativist, who would take issue with Benedict's suggestion of societal paranoia. To this purist, Dobu society is simply one form of human interaction, like any other. If such behavior is normal for Dobu society, we must accept it as such and not apply a pejorative, universalistic label like "paranoid."

The more common approach is that psychopathologies (paranoia, depression, mania, and so on) appear in all societies, but the circumstances in which they are defined as illness are culturally determined.[49] Thus the paranoid pattern would be seen as universal, but how often, under what circumstances, and to what degree it is defined as outside the mainstream would vary from society to society.

Throughout most of the world and throughout history, there have been near-universal behavioral and ideational patterns shared by all sane members of society.[50] Conversely, distortions or contradictions of these same patterns are also universal. Paranoia is one of those universal distortions or contradictions, manifesting itself in different forms in different societies to different degrees.[51]

Thus, the principal cross-cultural psychologists conclude that paranoia is almost always an exaggeration of existing patterns and not a qualitatively distinctive phenomenon.[52] Of the two forms that deviant behavior can take—opposing norms or exceeding them—paranoia almost always falls into the second category. That is, it is typically an exaggeration of what the society expects. And when the historical record is replete with conspiracies, it can be argued that these societies, not without reason, are consumed by suspicion of their enemies.[53]

In the Middle East, the cultural disposition toward paranoid thinking has been powerfully reinforced by a conspiracy-dominated historical record. The result is a region where suspicion of conspiracies is endemic and conspiracy thinking is regularly found in political discourse.

## Conspiracy Thinking in the Middle East

An American academic attending an international conference in Tunisia during the 1990 Persian Gulf crisis was startled when a Tunisian colleague congratulated him ''on the brilliance of your president.'' He went on to explain that ''it was brilliant, brilliant, for President Bush to create the appearance of a major conflict in order, once and for all, to guarantee America's oil supplies.'' According to this theory, President Bush and Saddam Hussein had together conspired to create the appearance of an impending war. They would then pull back from the brink and divide Middle Eastern oil between them. What startled the American professor was that he had always known his colleague to be a sensible man with no trace of emotional instability.

In the late 1980s, contrasting conspiratorial theories circulated when what appeared to be the sign of the cross appeared on the veils of Muslim girls of Upper Egypt, as reported in a Cairo newspaper: ''Some people said that Christians had sprayed a chemical on the veiled women's clothes and this material assumed the form of a small cross no larger than an ant; as soon as the clothing was moistened, the size of the cross would increase to about three centimeters. Some people offered another interpretation, which held that the cloth of the head covering had been im-

ported from Israel and that it was scientifically treated to form crosses
with the purpose of stirring up dissension between Muslims and Christians.''[54]

The most powerful value of conspiracy thinking is to remove responsibility from the person or group believing itself to be the victim of
the conspiracy. In the Middle East, conspiracy thinking typically is employed ''to explain that it is not the Arabs who are to blame for their
backwardness, but malevolent foreign factors.''[55]

To promote pan-Arabism, Egypt's president, Gamal Abdel Nasser,
invoked an imperialist plot against the Middle East, which he traced to
the Crusades. The imperialists employed the Crusades ''to degrade us
and acquire what was in our hands and under our feet . . . [and to] sow
the seeds of corruption and dissension among us, liquidate the foundations
of our nationality, and muzzle us to prevent our recalling the grandeur
of our past . . . and steal away our minds and this world of ours.''[56]

An ambassador from the United Arab Emirates to Great Britain propounded a more convoluted theory: although the British and the Jews
were both conspiring against the Muslims, the British were really manipulating the Jews. Israel ''is an invention of . . . the British,'' who created
Israel out of fear that the Jews ''would rule Britain.'' It was the British
who ''put the idea in [the Jews'] head of creating a homeland.''[57]

At a state dinner with Henry Kissinger, the late King Faisal of Saudi
Arabia argued somewhat the opposite. He suggested a Communist-Zionist
connection instead of a British-Zionist or the more commonly invoked
American-Zionist conspiracy. Israel, he argued, was created by the Jews
and Communists for the purpose of dividing the Arabs from the Americans.[58]

Decrying the moral decline in Muslim society, an Egyptian Islamic
leader, speaking on Cairo radio, offered the following ingenious explanation that related Darwinism to a Jewish plot to encourage immodesty
among Muslim women: ''Darwin's theory is another faded theory, . . . a
child of Jewish thought and should not be taught in our Islamic country.
America and Britain now prohibit its teaching because of its weakness.
And we try to study it! Why? As for Freud, he wanted to interpret Darwin's plot against our Islamic society, as indicated when he said, 'My
mind will not rest nor my eye close until I see humanity return to its

origin'—i.e. to its ancestor the ape. He meant that women should go out with their genitals uncovered like apes. The lewdness we see in our streets is merely an immediate translation of this proposition and this sinful plot."[59]

It should not be surprising that some entrepreneurial spiritualists have been able to profit from the Middle Eastern readiness to succumb to conspiracy thinking. "Jinn theory" concerns the characteristics of minor supernatural beings, like elves or sprites, a legacy from the Middle East's pre-Muslim polytheistic past. It is a traditional part of Middle Eastern folklore, and since the intifada (the Palestinian uprising in the occupied territories of Gaza and the West Bank) erupted on December 9, 1987, contending with jinns has become a growing business in Gaza. Sheikh Abu Khaled, an exorcist, said the number of possessed Muslims has more than tripled: "I suspect that Jewish magicians send jinns to us here in Gaza. In fact most of my patients are possessed with Jewish jinns."[60] Both Jewish and Christian jinns are reported to be black in color, but the Jewish ones are distinguished by the horns growing from their heads.

Conspiracy thinking is also prominent in the non-Arab Middle East. According to a *New York Times* article, a taxi driver in Teheran blamed American intelligence agents for the city's notorious traffic jams: "They get people to do unnecessary things and make the drivers frustrated and lose their temper." The CIA was also blamed for creating friction among itinerant vendors setting up shop in front of established businesses and so irritating the store owners.[61]

The readiness of the Iranian man in the street to believe conspiracy theories is adroitly manipulated through radio broadcasts by clerical leaders for political purposes. The Western media were accused in a January 19, 1990, broadcast of the *Voice and Vision of the Islamic Republic* (the official organ of the clerics) of "enacting [their] Satanic role" in a "sinister plot" against Azerbaijani Muslims.[62] Indeed, the Iranian constitution is the only constitution in the history of mankind that mentions conspiracy not once but twice. Its preamble refers to the Shah's White Revolution as an "American plot." Later in the document, the rights of non-Muslims are guaranteed *if* they "do not get involved . . . in conspiracies hatched against the Islamic Republic of Iran."[63]

Not only is there a readiness to believe that they are surrounded by enemies, but the power they attribute to these enemies suggests their underlying feelings of powerlessness. Indeed, a central psychological motivation for conspiratorial thinking is to serve as an antidote for the poisonous feeling of powerlessness. Just as the paranoid delusion is a solace for the psychologically disturbed individual, isolated and failing, so conspiracy thinking is a solace for the social group or society failing to achieve—a defense against humiliation. This is not to deny that there have been genuine conspiracies or that groups have been subject to persecution. It is the psychological propensity to believe in conspiracies and persecutory victimization with which we are concerned.

In some cases, a pattern of suspicion and hostility can become almost a national tradition, as in the case of Russia. In the Middle East, where conspiracy theories abound, it is striking that historical and political processes have produced on opposite sides of the cultural divide two national groups with similar persecutory mind-sets. Both the Palestinians and the Israelis feel cast out, virtually alone in the world. Each group feels like the victim, righteously justifying its aggression against the perceived enemy.

## Siege Mentality in Israel

When a nation has been victimized by conspiracy, its people become sensitized to conspiracy, and conspiratorial explanations of events are confirmed.[64] Correspondingly, when a nation has been the continuing object of enmity, its people may be sensitized to expect hostility in the external world. When a group comes to believe that the rest of the world has highly negative behavioral intentions toward them, they fall into a siege mentality.[65] The critical extrapolation is from detecting hostility from immediate (and genuinely hostile) out-groups to detecting hostility from the entire world. Subscribers to the siege mentality give voice to such beliefs as ''No one will help us in time of need'' and ''The world should be glad to get rid of us.''[66]

The siege mentality is widely shared by the Jewish population because of its long experience of persecution dating back to the Roman era. Persecution is a prominent theme in the Old Testament:

And he said unto Abraham, know of a surety that thy seed shall be a stranger in a land which is not theirs, and they will make them serve, and they will afflict them for four hundred years. (Genesis 15:13)

Lo, it [the Jews] is a people that shall dwell alone, and among the nations it shall not be reckoned. (Numbers 23:9)

Many are my persecutors and my assailants yet from thy testimonies did I not turn away. (Psalms 119:157)

The Holocaust, in which 6 million Jews perished as the world turned a blind eye, confirmed for many Jews the lessons of history that the Jews had to fight for their own survival, because the world was against them. In "Vital's Diary," the Holocaust poet Rachel Katznelson writes, "And so the nations of the world did not get involved, did not protest, . . . did not threaten the murderers . . . It was as if leaders of the world were afraid that the murderers would stop killing us."[67] Indeed, the siege mentality is the primary basis for today's Zionist ideology. According to this mentality, Jews are universally the victims of persecution, and safety can be found only in their own homeland.

References to the persecuted Israeli are regularly found in Israeli poetry, prose, and education. Analyses of Israeli history texts indicate they disproportionately emphasize the hatred of the world in characterizing the relations between Israel and other nations. The siege mentality is also reflected in Israeli media and comments by political leaders. The Israeli media, for example, frequently portray as fact the genocidal intentions of the world toward Israel: "The antisemitic movement in all its anti-zionist and anti-Israel revelations" proves that its perpetrators wish to complete the "final solution which Hitler initiated."[68] And Prime Minister Golda Meir, in response to a question from columnist Stewart Alsop, stated: "And you Mr. Alsop, you say that we have a Masada complex . . . It is true. We do have a Masada complex. We have a Pogrom complex. We have a Hitler complex."[69] In a 1988 speech, Prime Minister Yitzhak Shamir sardonically observed: "We have plenty of . . . 'friends' in the world who would like to see us dead, wounded, trampled, suppressed. And then it is possible to pity the wretched Jew, to commiserate with him."[70]

Political behavior flows from the siege mentality. If the world is seen as invariably hostile, the nation with a siege mentality will behave accordingly. Distrust and negative attitudes will be manifest in their relations with outsiders, and there will be pressures toward conformity and self-protection. These attitudes and behaviors can contribute to the perpetuation of a garrison state and can provide a major barrier to negotiations seeking to resolve conflict between, for example, Israel and its neighbors. Other national groups manifesting the siege mentality include the Albanians, Tokugawa Japanese, Iranians, the Afrikaners of apartheid South Africa, and post–World War II North Koreans.

## Conspiracy Thinking in Mexico

In 1980 a severe drought struck Mexico. For reasons that were never fully explained, the director of Mexico's National Meteorological Service charged that U.S. hurricane-tracking planes might be responsible.[71] For three weeks this accusation appeared on the front pages of Mexican newspapers, accompanied by articles with titles like "The Hurricane Hunters Are Protecting Florida's Tourism." One such article contained the detailed description of the history of hurricanes in Mexico. The researcher concluded that the only possible explanation for the drought was the "deliberate and effective program carried out by the United States."[72] Nor was this "reportage" simply a journalistic fancy. The Mexican government's foreign minister barred future National Oceanographic and Atmospheric Administration missions from Mexican airspace.

The historical legacy and the unequal power relationship support the propensity for paranoid thinking. There have been instances of American interferences, both covert and overt, in Mexican affairs, although for the most part Americans have ignored Mexico. Living so close to a country much larger, richer, and more powerful than their own, and one that tends to dominate others, Mexicans can be expected to manifest exaggerated fearfulness of the United States. Moreover, not only does America border Mexico, but many of its government agencies, such as the Departments of State, Agriculture, and Justice, and such specialized agencies as the Agency for International Development and the Drug Enforcement Agency, are active in that country. Their endeavors, though often uncoordinated and even more often poorly coordinated, do have a common thrust, which can give a conspiratorial cast to these activities.

Information, furthermore, is more restricted in Mexico than in the United States, and Mexico has a long history of self-censorship and government threats of censorship. Thus rumors are widespread in domestic politics because the truth is difficult to ascertain, and these rumors carry much more weight than they would in the United States. Because Mexicans accept conspiracy notions within their political culture, they are equally inclined toward such charges involving the United States.

The Mexican scholar Jorge G. Castañeda, in an essay in an appropriately titled book on U.S.-Mexican relations, *Limits to Friendship* (1988), offers an illustration of how lack of coordination on the part of Americans suggested a plot.[73] In May 1984 Mexican President Miguel de la Madrid made an official visit to Washington, D.C. Errors in protocol, garden-variety leaks to the press, and loosely coordinated policy proposals were seen by his supporters as designed to hurt their president at home. As Castañeda recounts, "Indeed, this was a textbook case of conspiracy theory fitting the available 'evidence' perfectly, *if* one had the slightest bent for such constructions. True, each event could be individually interpreted, and the ensuing multiple, isolated, and adequate explanations could be easily accepted . . . But if looked at from the other side, the view of the America monolith lumbering into conspiratorial action was not farfetched. There was a motive: Central American and Nicaraguan policy, and a general (conservative) ideological dissatisfaction in Washington with the way Mexico was being governed." Castañeda continues, giving a conspiratorial interpretation to each event: "Was this a realistic assumption [of conspiracy] or merely another instance of Mexican official paranoia and penchant for conspiracy theories? To a large extent, the 'factual' answer is less relevant than the conditions leading to the presumptions that there was a conspiracy afoot and that the United States was, once again, intervening in a deliberate fashion in Mexican affairs to further its own interests."[74]

As Castañeda notes, the same events can be interpreted conspiratorially or not, depending on the orientation of the interpreter. In this way, a conspiracy-thinking culture feeds on and validates itself.

## Suspiciousness in the Cultures of Vietnam, China, and Malaysia

All cultures have a paranoid dimension. For example, the Confucian cultures of China and Vietnam operate "as though decisive force was somehow beyond the total command of anyone," an assumption that has led to the doctrine of *wu-wei,* or non-effort, in which "stratagems, deception, and winning with minimum effort" are emphasized.[75]

In Vietnamese society deception is considered the very essence of politics, with the suspicion constant that no relationship is what it appears to be.[76] In the birthplace of Confucianism, the Chinese "normally suspect that others, who are almost by definition their 'enemies,' have stronger *quanxi* ties [personal connections], and hence they fear that the reality of *quanxi* in their culture is working against their own interests."[77] Even in the dominantly Islamic Asian culture of Malaya, power is believed to be invisible.[78] But Chinese, Vietnamese, and Malay cultures are not paranoid. Like all others, they have a paranoid component, one that never fully sleeps and can arise at any time.

## Anti-White Racist Populism:
## Conspiracy Thinking Among African-Americans

Although the paranoid tendency affects all groups, contemporary groups that have experienced a history of persecution are particularly apt to view the world in a paranoid manner. Just as adults who have been abused as children may themselves become abusers, groups that have suffered from the paranoid behavior of others are especially at risk of acquiring the "virus" from their tormentors.

Thus paranoid behavior is not only directed against, for example, blacks, Jews, and Muslims, but also is practiced by some of them. Because paranoid beliefs can restore a person's self-regard (assuring him that he bears no responsibility for his condition), the most paranoid members of a group are almost always most resistant to argument. They tend to view attempted persuasion as attack, disagreement as assault, advice as censure. Similarly, paranoid beliefs can restore the entire humiliated group's self-regard.

Anti-white and especially anti-Semitic rhetoric is prevalent in black America today. The claim of being victimized by a conspiracy offers great restitutive value. Why is the individual or the group in such difficulty? Because others—jealous and fearful of the genuine superiority of the suffering group—have conspired to keep them down. Such beliefs, although psychologically reassuring, even flattering, will divert the sufferer from dealing with genuine problems and will lead him to tilt at the imaginary windmills of conspiracy.

For the most part conspiratorial beliefs among late twentieth-century African-Americans appear in the particular rumors and urban legends of popular culture. The following beliefs were current in the mid-1990s:

- AIDS was developed by whites to murder blacks;
- AIDS was developed by whites, was tested in Africa on blacks, and escaped to the rest of the world;
- A conspiracy exists, directed by whites in the government, to put drugs into black communities to oppress blacks;
- The makers of a sports shoe popular among blacks are using the profits derived to maintain apartheid in South Africa;
- A popular sportswear company patronized by blacks is owned by the Ku Klux Klan, and the word *Troop* in the product name stands for "To Rule Over Oppressed People";
- A series of murders of black children in Atlanta, Georgia, for which a black man was convicted, was in fact perpetrated by the FBI for the purpose of performing tests on black genitalia;
- A prominent fast food chain puts a substance in its fried chicken and soft drinks to sterilize black men;
- Black patients in hospitals run a substantial chance of being experimented upon unless they have a black doctor.[79]

Some black studies programs foster a conspiratorial explanation of historiography. As Mary Lefkowitz, a professor of classics at Wellesley College, notes, "Egyptians, and other ancient peoples of Africa, [are depicted] as victims of a conspiracy: In [the view of certain black scholars], European historians have banded together to suppress the truth about the derivative and fraudulent nature of European civilization."[80]

When filmmaker John Singleton wanted to depict the attitude of the average poor urban black in his film *Boyz N the Hood* (Warner TriStar 1991), he has a character say to a crowd of blacks, "They [whites] want us to kill each other off. What they couldn't do in slavery, they are making us do to ourselves."[81] The theme song in *Do the Right Thing* (UIP/Forty Acres and a Mule Filmworks/Spike Lee 1989), a film about racial conflict centering on an Italian-owned pizza parlor in a black neighborhood, contains a chant advocating fighting an abstract power. Joseph Lowery, president of the Southern Christian Leadership Conference, commented that "African-Americans are pretty much convinced that there is a national assault on black life."[82] Lowery, a Christian minister, then gave his support to this belief: "The marketplace for drugs is very intentionally placed in the black community. Because wherever the marketplace is, that's where the war zone is, so they can kill each other."[83] According to this argument, heroin was introduced to black areas by whites to put down the black civil rights movement.

This impressionistic and anecdotal material is also supported by systematic public opinion surveys.[84] In 1990 the Southern Christian Leadership Conference commissioned a survey of 1,056 black church members throughout America. Among the questions they asked was whether the person polled believed that AIDS was a form of black genocide. Thirty-five percent said yes, and 30 percent said they did not know.[85] In a smaller but more focused poll (348 residents of southwestern New Jersey) conducted in April 1992, respondents were asked, without regard to their race, a series of questions regarding a variety of conspiracy theories. Topics included not only the question of AIDS as a government-created plot but also race-neutral questions involving flying saucers, George Bush's alleged involvement with arms to Iran, and Japanese conspiracies against the United States. Of those queried, 93 percent believed in at least one of the listed conspiracies.

The willingness to believe in the conspiracies, however, was not evenly distributed: "African-American respondents were more likely than white or Hispanic respondents to believe in the conspiracies which specifically affected their community. Sixty-two percent of the black respondents believed that it was definitely or probably true that the government deliberately put drugs in black communities. Sixty-eight percent believed that the F.B.I. had been involved in the killing of Martin Luther King. Thirty-one percent believed that the government deliberately put AIDS into the African-American communities."[86]

Although the margin of sampling error of such polls is 11 percent and although the survey was taken in a geographical area in which racial polarization might be higher than in the general population, the poll indicates that belief in white-directed conspiracies adversely affecting African-Americans is widespread among American blacks. Of the three groups sampled (black, Hispanic, white), African-Americans were substantially more likely to believe in conspiracies, whether directed at them (for example, the FBI assassination of Martin Luther King) or not (for example, flying saucers).

Assuming that the alleged conspiracies did not exist, how can we explain the prevalence of conspiracy beliefs among American blacks in the 1990s? Two factors suggest themselves. The first concerns the history of black people in America. As the English writer Jean Rhys (who recognized that she herself had a tendency toward oversuspiciousness) commented, "When people are paranoid you can bet your life they have something to be paranoid *about*."[87] The second cause is also related to blacks' history of oppression. Conspiratorial beliefs are common in the United States and tend to receive a sympathetic hearing beyond what the evidence suggests. It is not surprising, therefore, that such beliefs would figure prominently in any group's beliefs, including those of African-Americans. They supply a binding force for many in the black community, functioning as identifying myths do for any people. For this reason, and because there is often a reluctance in some white elite media circles to criticize black leaders publicly, paranoid statements concerning blacks are legitimated—or go unchallenged—to a degree that other such charges are not.

Patricia A. Turner, for example, author of *I Heard It Through the Grapevine: Rumor in African-American Culture* (1994), relates several of the paranoid rumors described in the previous paragraphs. In an interview in the *Chronicle of Higher Education* she acknowledged the falsity of such rumors but described them as a type of resistance to consumer culture.[88] A leading scholar, she did not condemn them or suggest their potential for destructiveness.

Mainstream media also suggest that a white conspiracy exists to oppress blacks, as the following quotation from the *New York Times* illustrates: "Since it's hard to imagine creating a world worse than Stateway

Gardens [a poor black neighborhood in Chicago], even if we tried, the mind takes a conspiratorial turn: maybe someone *did* try; perhaps this is what the power structure plotted.''[89]

Even when conspiratorial accusations are exhaustively researched under black leadership and no evidence is produced, the accusation lingers. In 1993 an investigation of charges of a widespread conspiracy behind the assassination of Martin Luther King, Jr., came to an end. After ''dozens of hearings, scores of witnesses and 487 trips by investigators to track leads in five countries,'' Congressman Walter Fauntroy, chair of the House Select Committee on Assassinations, said that, despite gathering no new evidence, he, like many Americans, black and white, remained suspicious.[90]

It is difficult to fight a fashionable idea. A belief in conspiracy as the motivating force in politics is very much the political fashion in the United States in the 1990s. That bizarre conspiracies have occurred provides a factual basis for remaining paranoid. Nevertheless, the toleration of the assumption of conspiracy through the collusion of silence or the false camaraderie of dishonest accord damages all.

## The Community of Nations as a Paranoid Community

Earlier we described how the paranoid, believing himself the object of the world's hostility, seeks to correct his situation by joining or forming a group, inevitably of a paranoid nature. We also noted that this belief is typically delusional. It is almost impossible for a person to find himself in a genuine state of nature where each person is turned against the others, where no community exists. Thomas Friedman, in *From Beirut to Jerusalem,* points out that when a society like Lebanon in the 1980s appears to have degenerated to a Hobbesian state, in fact just the opposite has occurred. Small, intimate, intense groups based on blood and religious belief grow stronger, people cling to them with greater intensity, and these groups give equally intense support to their members. Remarks Friedman: ''I don't know if Beirut is a perfect Hobbesian state of nature, but it is probably the closest thing to it that exists in the world today. If so, Hobbes was right about life in such a world being 'nasty, brutish, and short,' but he was quite wrong about it being 'poor' and 'solitary.' . . . When authority breaks down and a society collapses into a state of nature, men will do anything to avoid being poor or solitary."[91] Friedman elsewhere states, "When the larger, macro Beirut society and government splintered, people's first instinct was to draw together into micro-societies based on neighborhood, apartment house, religious, or family loyalties."[92]

But if the Hobbesian state of nature is seldom encountered in individual experience, it may be found in the experience among nations, in the international arena. The international system operates according to an inherent bad-faith model.[93] Each action taken, each undertaking entered into by independent states, will be carried out only so long as it is in the long-term interest of both parties. As soon as either decides that an agreement is no longer in its long-term interest, it will begin to move to break it, regardless of the promises made. With such an assumption, international relations are necessarily riven with suspicion, deception, and betrayal. Even the promises of the best and longest of allies are lies, and each party, in the dead of night if not in the usual course of business, realizes this.

Although the theory of the inherent bad-faith model was developed in connection with the foreign policy outlook of Eisenhower's secretary of state, John Foster Dulles,[94] it is not simply a limited historical phenomenon. The bad-faith model is more evident between adversaries than between allies, and it will be more prominent, or closer to the surface, in the foreign policies of some countries than in others, but it is always present. To varying degrees, this reality is nearly universally sensed but rarely acknowledged. To admit that all alliances and undertakings are in fact conditional upon their future effectiveness would weaken their present practical utility. Bad-faith assumptions are an unconsidered part of the mentality of contemporary international relations. The unthinking dominance of the bad-faith model is, moreover, not merely a description of what exists; it is also a self-fulfilling prophecy.

With the inherent bad-faith model in mind, consider the principal characteristics of paranoia: projective thinking, hostility, fear of loss of autonomy, suspicion, centrality, grandiosity, and delusional thinking. It would be remarkable if those responsible for the foreign policies of their nations did not acquire these characteristics. Each would think: "Of course, if I and my country are prepared to double-cross those with whom we have agreements, my 'allies' must be willing to do so as well. And this isn't just me and them. Every country is the same way, so I had better trust no one—although I will try to convince them that I trust them and that they can trust me. I had better look out for plots and conspiracies, and organize a few myself as well.''

The objective situation so blurs the line between paranoia and prudent reaction that we are led to characterize the normal condition of international relations as paranoid, or at least as significantly paranoiagenic.

Political paranoids join paranoid cultures, and if they do not find one that suits them, they may create one. Paranoid cultures also engender paranoid behavior. In this, as in other areas of social behavior, causation is reciprocal. Paranoia dozes but never sleeps.

# 3

## The Roots of Paranoia

In brief, I hold that from the very beginning of
human evolution, the conduct of every local group
was regulated by two codes of morality, distinguished
by Herbert Spencer as the "code of amity" and the
"code of enmity." There were thus exposed to
"natural selection" two opposing aspects of man's
mental nature. The code of amity favored the growth
and ripening of all those qualities of human nature
which find universal approval—friendliness, goodwill,
love, altruism, idealism, faith, hope, charity, humility,
and self-sacrifice—all the Christian virtues. Under the
code of enmity arose those qualities which are
condemned by all civilized minds—emulation, envy,
the competitive spirit, deceit, intrigue, hate, anger,
ferocity, and enmity. How the neural basis of such
qualities, both good and bad, came into existence
during the progressive development of the human
brain, we do not know, but it is clear that the
chances of survival of a struggling, evolving group
would be strengthened by both sets of qualities . . . It
will thus be seen that I look on the duality of a
human nature as an essential part of the machinery of
human evolution.
—Sir Arthur Keith, *Essays on Human Evolution*

Often suspecting of others comes of secretly condemning ourselves.
—Sir Philip Sidney

We has met the enemy, and he is us.
—Pogo (Walt Kelly)

What is it that makes us so susceptible to the siren song of the paranoid?
Why is it that large numbers of otherwise mentally healthy people will
follow a demonstrably paranoid person? When people begin to listen to,
believe, and then follow a Hitler, a Stalin, or a Jim Jones, what was an
individual aberration becomes transformed into a collective reaction. Left
unchecked, this can have catastrophic consequences.

That there is a universal readiness to follow the paranoid path—to be
suspicious of the outsider, to distrust, to fear the enemy—suggests that we
are wrestling with a deeply rooted human capacity. But what are the roots?
Is paranoia purely a social disorder, or is it fixed in our biological nature?
We can never specify the precise genesis of any human behavior. To ascertain whether a given train of conduct derives from natural selection would
require the manipulation of breeding and environment in ways that are in-
appropriate for *Homo sapiens*.[1] To say that a behavior is solely a product of
social conditioning and individual choice would be to deny much of what
we know about evolutionary biology and to reerect the barrier between
man and other species. But to attribute complex psychological reactions,
such as paranoia, solely to evolutionary psychology is to deny what is
uniquely human. Every complex human behavior is an interaction of evolutionary history and immediate human context. We cannot untangle the
threads, but we can see some of the brighter evolutionary strands.

A wide array of data indicates that fear of the enemy and distrust are
biologically rooted and have survival value, and a large body of observations from developmental psychology and psychoanalysis concern the
psychological roots of paranoia in childhood. We will first survey the
realm of evolutionary biology.

## Sociobiological Roots

The opposing tendencies of competition and cooperation coexist in the
animal kingdom. Struggling for space, food, and mates, nature's creatures

are at war with one another. Yet they will find it in their interest to cooperate, and often will do so, when

- they are closely related genetically;
- two or more unrelated individuals produce offspring together over a lifetime; or
- external threats can only (or best) be met by cooperation.[2]

Social collaboration produces such benefits as more effective food acquisition, better protection against predators, better care of young, and task specialization.[3] In general, the foundations of social collaboration are nepotism (the favorable treatment of kin); reciprocity (when interactions are mutually beneficial); and exploitation, although one-sided exploitation of one species by another tends to be short lived.[4]

The genetic basis of cooperation in social life is demonstrated by the fact that no conflict exists within certain groups of insects that reproduce asexually and so are genetically nearly identical.[5] In such cases, extraordinary cooperation occurs. Cooperation is also dramatic where identical or near-identical genetic interests are achieved by sexually reproducing species, such as large social insect colonies (for example, honeybees, ants, and termites), and by monogamous partners. When males and females of any species commit themselves to lifelong monogamy, their common interests and cooperation increase. In contrast, altruism diminishes with decreasing degrees of relatedness in humans and nonhuman species.[6]

But each social animal that reproduces sexually has a unique genetic complement. Would it not be in his interest to cheat, to take advantage of his fellows' altruism, in the interest of expanding the place that *his* genes will occupy in the future? Would it not be an evolutionary advantage to have such a capacity? At first blush, this seems obvious. We see this intuitively (being social animals), and the obvious has also been demonstrated formally from the perspective of game theory.[7]

The previous line of reasoning suggests an evolutionary purpose for behavior, a species-related goal for individuals. This view, characterized as the group selection fallacy, has been cogently challenged by Robert Trivers, who argues that "all traits must begin as rare in a species and can increase in frequency only if they increase the survival and reproductivity of those bearing the traits."[8] Referring back to the contest between the cheater and the altruist, the cheater's goal is not to expand the place that his genes will occupy in the future—it is to conquer and survive. Cheaters *do* prosper. This being the case, animals will lie, animals will cheat, and animals will deceive.[9] Michael Gazzaniga, a prominent brain researcher, in arguing for a selection-based evolutionary theory of human intelligence, notes: "Finally our ancestors' social interactions gave rise to other activities such as deceit. Establishing quid-pro-quo relationships and suggestion mechanisms for enforcing them have led some investigators to suggest that there was a sort of cognitive arms race during our evolution. Deceit in one caveman encourages reciprocal distrust in the caveman's neighbor, which promotes more distrust, and so on. While coming in out of the rain may not take much brain power, figuring out how to outsmart the sneak who lives in the next cave requires some intelligent functioning. Indeed one of the big events in human cognitive development occurs when we learn how to mask our true perceptions."[10]

In a contest between honest signalers and deceptive signalers, the deceivers should win. Although a conventional definition of a signal is "any sign, gesture, look, and so on, that serves to communicate information," signals are also sent which deceive and manipulate the receiver. A preferable, and more cynical, definition of a signal would be "a means by which one animal (the actor) exploits another animal's (the reactor's) muscle power." The counterpart of manipulation by the actor is mind reading by the reactor.

From this perspective, the evolution of animal signals can be seen as an interplay between manipulation and mind reading,[11] or, in the lexicon of this book, between deception and the ability to penetrate deception. Thus suspiciousness of the adversary's deceptive signals and reading the adversary's mind are adaptive. It is the ability to penetrate the manipulating adversary's deceptive signals that is the animal analogue to a suspicious attitude.

Natural selection will favor animals that become sensitive to subtle clues of danger.[12] Animals are "nature's psychologists."[13] The faculty of subjective consciousness and self-awareness is a product of evolution, a device to facilitate reading the minds of others. The animal that is an unwilling victim of mind reading may resort to disinformation; that is, he may feed the enemy deliberately misleading information. In other words, the victim of mind reading might exploit the fact that its mind is being read in order to manipulate the behavior of the mind reader. In effect, mind reading and manipulation are locked together in an "evolutionary arms race."[14]

To cooperate, to operate according to a "code of amity," requires honest communication. But with individuals whose interests are adverse, who are operating according to the "code of enmity," such as predators and prey, honesty in communication can be fatal. To survive in conflictual relationships requires deceptive communication signals. Moreover, there is a premium in such circumstances on detecting deception. Most communication signals lie between the extremes of total honesty and total deception.[15] Deception is imperative when there is no overlap of interests. The degree of honesty is correlated with the degree of relatedness and common interests, but the correlation is not perfect. In many negotiations it may be easier to reach agreement if a reaction is "faked." The leader, when frightened, for example, may pretend to be unafraid and thereby rouse his troops to victory. Moreover, it is a rare relationship that can tolerate total honesty. Brutal honesty between husband and wife is guaranteed to disrupt marital cooperation.

Cooperation requires honest communication signals; when the interests of the pair are adverse, deception is the path of choice. But the deceived soon learn to distrust, so that in order to gull the wary object of deception, one must give the appearance of honesty. The deceiver will get away with as much as the gullibility of his adversary will permit. The more able one is to penetrate deception, the greater the likelihood that the target of deception will survive. So there is an adaptive value to suspecting deception. To be naively trusting in a dangerous situation can have deadly consequences.

Where there is substantial overlap in interests, deception is destructive, and the core of truth is substantial. A series of categories of behavior are related to the evolutionary theory of social cooperation:[16]

- asociality (no need to cooperate)
- kinship or nepotism (shared genes by descent—not between mates but between offspring and parents, uncles and cousins, and so on)

- direct reciprocity (I scratch your back today, and you scratch mine tomorrow)
- indirect reciprocity (I help you when George is watching because otherwise George will say bad things about me)
- pure altruism or helping (I help unknown, unrelated others by contributing to collective goods from which others can benefit without contributing)

All these categories can occur at the same time or for the same individuals. Parent-offspring conflict, for example, arises from the tension between asociality and nepotism: the child wants more than the parent wants to give in part because the parent is also related to other kin (especially other offspring). In addition, the sexual division of labor in lion hunts favors the male, which has the less demanding—and less dangerous—task of going upwind and frightening wildebeest to move downwind, where the female's task is to isolate and kill a wildebeest out of the herd. Yet the males take the "lion's share" of the meat so that the females bear a greater cost, while the males enjoy preferential benefits, a "selfish interaction within the larger cooperative exchange."[17]

A wealth of ethological studies concerns animal aggression and cooperation and the roles trust and deception play in such interaction.[18] Both chimpanzees and vervet monkeys, for example, have been observed sending false signals of reconciliation only to become aggressive at the last moment. Vervet monkeys have also "used" each other as social tools to gain an advantage over their rivals.

Of particular relevance to the study of paranoia is evidence of the survival value of the detection of deception, the ability to penetrate false signals and detect danger. In a "cry wolf" experiment, a vervet monkey was duped into sending warning signals to the colony by an artificial silhouette of a predator, such as an eagle. The predator then did not materialize. When this happened repeatedly, the other vervets learned to discount the eagle warning signals from this particular monkey. But they did not develop a generalized skepticism concerning this monkey and would respond, for example, to its leopard warning signals.

A dialectic exists between deception and detection of deception. In effect, there is a "co-evolutionary struggle between deceiver and deceived.''[19] For as deception increases in frequency, it magnifies selection for detection. And as the ability to detect increases, it magnifies selection for deception.

Research on human children suggests that the capacity to deceive is both biologically rooted and age-specific. In a recent experiment, young children were told that two puppets would approach them and ask which of four stickers was their favorite. (It was known that each child had a favorite sticker.) They were also told that one of the two puppets was a friendly sort and, after learning which sticker a child wanted, would choose another sticker. The other puppet would most certainly grab the child's favorite. The three-year-olds were unable to deceive the mean puppet, whereas from age four, the children quickly learned to trick the mean puppet while remaining truthful to the nice one. Powerful selection pressure is at work in the species to develop such strategies.[20]

We are ''hard-wired'' to fear the enemy, to deceive, to penetrate deception—and to cooperate. The social behaviors associated with amity and enmity, including deception, are associated with specific neuroanatomical structures.[21] The human brain is composed of three main neural assemblies, reflecting an ancestral relationship to reptiles, early mammals, and late mammals. These three divisions form a ''triune brain'': a reptilian brain, a paleomammalian brain (the limbic system), and the neomammalian brain, composed of the neocortex and the thalamus. During evolutionary development, the more primitive structures have been not replaced but added to. Thus the higher forms of mammalian development and man contain the neomammalian brain in addition to the reptilian brain and the paleomammalian brain.

Many of the reactions that concern us—especially the almost visceral fear and defensive aggression toward strangers—are biologically rooted in the most primitive and reflexive aspects of the human brain, in the lowest neural organizations in the hierarchy: the reptilian brain and the paleomammalian brain. Different forms of thinking tend to have their origin in different parts of the brain. Higher-level thinking, for example, is associated with the newest and developmentally most differentiated part of the brain, the neocortex of the neomammalian brain. Whereas the forebrain is essential for directed activity, the more primitive elements of the brain are also essential for self-preservation and the preservation of the species. The neural basis of the brain is like a vehicle without a driver, acting viscerally, reflexively, without conscious direction.

Specific areas of the paleomammalian brain are associated with conflict and aggression behavior—fear, dominance, aggression, defenses, and calming.[22] Among the behaviors with relevance for our subject are the establishment and marking of territory, patrolling territory, ritualistic display in defense of territory, formalized fighting in defense of territory, triumphal display in successful defense or aggression, assumption of distinct postures in signaling surrender, and formation of social groups.[23]

Of particular interest to our examination of the biological precursors of paranoia is the reptilian behavior of deception. Deception, after all, protects against aggression and is essential for survival. But in order to survive, animals must also be able to penetrate deception, using the biological equivalent of suspiciousness and alertness to hidden danger. Deceptive mimicry is one way reptiles fool their prey and their enemies. And when certain parts of the reptilian brain are surgically altered or excised, these and other behaviors can be changed or removed from the behavioral repertoire.

The influence of neurochemical factors on behavior is also of considerable interest. By raising the serotonin levels in monkeys through such drugs as Prozac, the dominance hierarchy can be reversed.[24] In humans, clinical findings suggest that serotonin not only alleviates depression but also increases self-esteem, reduces fearfulness, and increases assertiveness.[25] And it is the primitive brain, the seat of the emotions, that contains high concentrations of serotonin and other neurotransmitters, all associated with emotional responses.

Thus there is abundant evidence of the biological roots and adaptive value of the two sides of man's nature: cooperation and conflict, amity and enmity. While there is value to cooperation among one's own kind, the biological universe is populated with predators and enemies. In this dangerous world, it is adaptive to be alert to danger and wary of strangers. But where is the boundary between adaptive suspicion in the service of detecting deception and pathological paranoia?

## Psychological Roots

We cling to that which is familiar and fear that which is not. The paranoid specializes in this innate human quality. His psychological life is dominated by fear and hatred of strangers. This fear of strangers can be traced back to the cradle.[26]

Pick up an infant for the first time, and he or she is likely to cry. Introduce your three-year-old to a stranger, and the child is likely to turn away, burying his head on your shoulder. This is a normal and healthy response—"stranger anxiety"[27]—beginning as early as eight months. The young child is a raw bundle of powerful feelings, of terrifying fears and uncontained aggression. It is the task of socialization to transform this raw bundle into an adult who can contain and alter these basic powerful emotions and drives, tolerate frustration, trust others, and function cooperatively in society. This, after all, is the basis of civilization.

Through the process of socialization in the family, the young child acquires mechanisms for coping with stress, both internal and external. These coping mechanisms, called ego defenses, are the basis of personality, the character armor.[28] The infant and young child characteristically use the primitive ego defenses: denial, distortion, and delusional projection.[29] Projection is the sine qua non of paranoia, but, as we have observed, it is widespread in everyday life.[30]

Observations of the behavior of infants and young children by the British psychoanalyst Melanie Klein became the foundations of an important body of psychoanalytic theory called object relations, which has become particularly influential in Great Britain and Latin America.[31] Klein's theory is especially helpful in explaining why some people will hate and fear others with little or no provocation.[32] The infant has only a fragmentary sense of self, with little understanding of where the outside world begins and where he or she ends. Both pleasurable feelings and painful and uncomfortable feelings are associated with the mother, who is the source of both nurturance and frustration. The child psychologically treats these two aspects of the mother as two different objects: the good mother, a warm and nurturing part, and the bad, frustrating mother. The child projects its aggressive impulses onto the bad mother, who is experienced as a hateful persecutor. Both the loving object and the persecuting object are introjected (psychologically internalized) and become part of the child's emerging self-concept. From our earliest days, each of us has a divided self.[33]

From the sequence described above, Klein posited the "paranoid-schizoid position" as a normal phase of childhood development—a position beyond which some individuals never mature and to which many individuals revert under psychosocial stress. The paranoid-schizoid position is a primitive psychological state characterized by a split between the idealized good loving object and the bad persecuting object. Psychoanalytic theorists consider the archetypal religious concepts of God and the devil as projected representations of these early fantasy objects. Roger Money-Kyrle, for example, conceives of God as a projection of the idealized object, which serves the function of protecting against the internal persecutor.[34]

The paranoid-schizoid position, characterized by the splitting process, relies centrally, according to Klein, on the mechanism of projective identification: "Identification by projection implies a combination of splitting off parts of the self and projecting them on to (or rather into) another person. . . . [Projective identification] underlies the feeling of identification with other people, because one has attributed qualities or attitudes of one's own to them."[35] The child's distress concerning the aggressive hatred within himself is relieved by splitting off and projecting the bad part—the *internal persecutor*—outward, onto other persons or objects, and retaining the good parts inside, idealizing them.[36] Thus the loving, nurturing part becomes the foundation of the idealized self-concept, while the negative destructive feelings are disowned and projected outward, onto strangers or groups.

Anna Freud has observed that internal aggressive destructive feelings are particularly threatening and that the function of projection is to break the connection between these dangerous impulses and the ego.[37] The child "finds it more manageable to cope with a monster of his own making than to carry within himself his own menace."[38] In order to preserve the child's sense of goodness, of well-being, "the sense of inner destructiveness and evil must be gotten rid of, must be escaped."[39] The solution is projection. In effect, the infant disowns the uncomfortable feelings within. "The human capacity for projection and displacement of its noxious psychic content is an ego mechanism operative since infancy''[40] and remains a potentiality throughout life. This capacity to project and displace, under internal or external stress, is at the heart of individual and collective paranoid reactions.[41]

The other side of hatred is love. As the aggression and hatred within are disowned and projected outward, they are associated with an intense need for love to counter the hatred. This is the reason the paranoid is so sensitive to loss of love or rejection.

In addition to aggressive and destructive impulses, painful feelings of reproach and shame are disowned. The young child is spared self-reproach by projecting it outward. The repression of self-reproach and its projection outward lead to the expectation of criticism from others and a distrust of others. In effect, this is a persecutory projection of critical parents, a projection of conscience.

The discovery that good and bad objects are different aspects of the same object is distressing for the child, who loves and hates the same object simultaneously. Unable to distinguish fantasy from perception, the young child has unconstrained hateful aggression toward the object that he at the same time loves. This discovery brings about what Klein calls the ''depressive position.'' The paranoid-schizoid position is at one end of the continuum of thinking styles conceptualized by Klein. When something goes wrong, the individual in this position seeks an outside reason or person to blame. He denies the negative feelings within and projects them onto outside objects. In contrast, individuals in the depressive position, at the other end of the continuum, react with guilt and self-reproach. These dispositions become ingrained features of the personality and remain throughout life. They are not stages of development but positions to which all return at different times.[42]

Some individuals remain fixated in the paranoid position. Placing primary reliance on the primitive ego defenses of denial, distortion, and delusional projection, these individuals are vulnerable to psychotic decompensation under stress.[43] Others remain locked in the depressive position—under attack by the internal persecutor, guilt-ridden, and vulnerable to depression.

In the process of becoming an adult, however, most individuals move beyond these early psychological stages, although they never completely leave them. They develop increasingly sophisticated ego defense mechanisms and more realistically appraise their environment and distinguish the internal from the external world. By developing these increasingly mature coping strategies, most individuals progress beyond the world of polarized idealized love and hateful persecutory evil, where the good object and the internal persecutory object are widely separated. Their own self-concept comes to contain all aspects, neither disowning uncomfortable feelings nor idealizing. They combine the split objects of the good mother and the bad mother into one object. In the felicitous phrase of Donald Winnicott, they integrate the disparate aspects into a "good enough mother."[44] As this is accomplished, they develop an integrated holistic sense of objects, for the most part no longer idealizing and demonizing.

But because of these movements back and forth during the process of developing an integrated self-concept, residues of the earlier positions always remain. Residues of the schizoid-paranoid position are associated with a tendency to exaggerate the "goodness" or the "badness" of those one meets. Residues of the depressive position lead to a sense of guilt whenever the individual is in conflict with his conscience. From this perspective, moral behavior can be considered behavior required by the fear of a sense of guilt. It contains both fear of punishment by the internal persecutor and fear of injuring or disappointing the internal benefactor.

The pain of being under attack by the internal persecutor cannot be overstated. One solution is suicide. "The hating introject calls out for the execution of the evil self. From life, a desert of loneliness and helplessness, . . . [man] turns to death in flight from internal persecutors."[45] The psychologist William James wrote of man as a "divided self." Within is a "battleground for what [is experienced as] two deadly hostile selves." This leads to "self-loathing; self despair; . . . an intolerable burden" for which "suicide naturally" [is the] course dictated by logical intellect."[46]

A solution for this "intolerable burden" is to disown the internal persecutor. This is what the paranoid does. He projects the internal persecutor onto an outside presence against which he must defend himself. It is rare that a paranoid commits suicide. More commonly he attacks his perceived enemy. If he does commit suicide, it is to escape his projected internal persecutor, his hidden executioner.[47]

For the most part, then, the paranoid successfully defends himself against devastating despair and emptiness. Paranoia is a defense against depression and loss. Recall the pre-medical student exploited by his girlfriend. His delusion that she still loved him but was being kept from him protected him against the humiliating recognition that she had never loved him but had exploited him and rejected him when she no longer needed him. When the paranoid defenses were broached, he fell into a suicidal depression.

The psychologically healthy individual has a flexible array of defense mechanisms to cope, for the most part successfully, with internal and external stress. But always, under the facade of civilization, of mature psychological organization, lurks the primitive psychological savage, prey to destructive feelings, fearing enemies, defensively aggressive. These feelings are contained by the character armor. That array of defenses provides psychological control.

An individual who does not have a healthy array of ego defenses and has specialized in the primitive defenses of denial, distortion, and delusional projection is vulnerable to paranoid decompensation when his control is threatened.[48] Being in control, not being subjected to another's will, and being autonomous are continuing issues for the vulnerable ego of the paranoid. Delusions of being under the control of powerful others, deriving from inner feelings of powerlessness, are common in paranoid psychosis. Recall the man with the sandwich board whose thoughts were being electronically controlled by the government.

The breakdown of the defensive armor leads to psychosis. The most terrifying experience is loss of control, the feeling of being overwhelmed by powerful emotions, the fear of annihilation, of unconstrained aggression. James Grotstein has likened this inner turbulence to black holes in the universe described by astronomers.[49] In the physical universe, the black hole (so called because it emits no light) has such extraordinary density and gravity that everything in its path is swallowed up and disappears into it. Grotstein, who characterizes the human being as "meaning-obsessed," has described the terror of the psychological black hole as the result of unknowable forces deriving from catastrophic disintegration of the self, the dissolution into a state of nothingness. The terror derives from the state of meaninglessness. So overwhelming is this dread of meaninglessness that there is an imperative to create meaning, to escape from the emptiness and despair of the inner void.[50] Making meaning to escape meaninglessness is central to paranoid dynamics.

The individual in an acute state of psychosis is experiencing psychological disintegration, a personal apocalypse.[51] Most psychiatric patients on the edge of psychosis experience apocalyptic fantasies and dreams of the end of the world. In Freud's classic analysis of the paranoid illness of the jurist Daniel Paul Schreber, Freud described Schreber as being "under the influence of visions which, in Schreber's own words, were 'partly of a terrifying character, but partly too of an indescribable grandeur.' "[52] Convinced of "the imminence of a great catastrophe," during the culmination of his illness Schreber came to believe that this catastrophe had occurred and that he was the only man left alive. Thus he projected his own personal experience of psychological disintegration onto the world.

Schreber's solution was to develop the belief that God had given him a mission to save the world from annihilation and to re-create an Eden.[53] The sequence for Schreber was death and rebirth, annihilation succeeded by a grand mission. Schreber's paranoid delusion was restitutive. He progressed from nothingness to grandeur, from meaninglessness to a special destiny, an exalted position superior even to God.

At its grandiose extremity, Schreber's delusion reveals the relation between paranoia and power and illustrates why paranoia lends itself so well to the world of politics. Schreber saw himself becoming, in effect, the last man on earth as all souls flowed into him, the savior of the world. Yet Schreber developed a conspiratorial delusion (closely linked to grandiosity) that dark forces were conspiring to prevent this ultimate power. The goal of the conspiracy was to render him an imbecile, robbing him of the brilliance of his gifts and keeping him from exercising ultimate leadership. In the full expression of his grandiose delusion, however, all enemies were vanquished and all mankind's power and vitality were embodied in him.

For an individual whose psychological world is disintegrating, the structure of constructed paranoid meaning is vastly preferable to psychological nothingness. The individual who returns from the edge of psychological disintegration experiences a purification, an ecstatic new world. In a state of euphoria, the patient has reconstituted himself through a grand scheme that centers on him. Recall the man who tried to break into the White House. Fired as a dishwasher, he recovered from his shattering loss of self-esteem by developing the grandiose delusion that he was the king of the world. He passed from total insignificance to magnificent grandeur. Once totally out of control, he was now in control of everything. The paranoid belief system is the structure that holds the paranoid together, his protection against psychological disintegration.

This sense-making belief system typically fuses grandeur with persecution. The enemies within, the powerful overwhelming forces, are psychologically transformed into the enemies without. It is a state of siege centered around the individual fighting off the (now) outside dangers, the corrupt, malevolent, destructive evil in the world.

This sense of being an innocent victim is associated with feelings of righteousness. A sequence can ensue that has violent potential. Under attack by the outside persecutor, the innocent victim feels aggrieved and increasingly angry. As the dynamic escalates, he can become consumed with righteous retaliatory rage. This in turn may lead him to attack his (feared and imagined) attackers in order to compel them to cease attacking him. The responsibility has been shifted in this enterprise. Instead of being guilt ridden over his own inner rage, the paranoid is now indignant over his enemies' unjust persecution of him and must defend himself against them. The aggression is required by them. It is defensive aggression. His aggression is, quite literally, self-defense. How much better to be all-powerful than to be powerless; how much better to be the center of a worldwide conspiracy than to be insignificant and ignored. Impaired in his ability to form relationships, the paranoid in his delusion finds himself the center of a vast network of relationships, the paranoid pseudocommunity.

This pseudocommunity is extremely valuable psychologically to the paranoid. It emphasizes his importance, as he is its center. But it also gives a focus to his fears and his strategy to counter their design. This is far preferable to chaos, to the earlier vague inchoate feelings of danger. It is because the paranoid delusion provides solace that it is so resistant to change. It is *not* reassuring to a paranoid to tell him that there are no enemies plotting to destroy him. In fact, such a comment will often provoke anger, for it threatens important psychological props. The paranoid holds tenaciously to his comforting, sense-making delusion that he is surrounded by enemies.

Just as the paranoid can find comfort in creating a pseudocommunity of enemies, he can also find comfort in belonging to a group united against common enemies. This transition from individual to group paranoia is critical to understanding how large movements and nations can become mobilized to attack the enemy, to go to war.

## From Individual to Group Paranoia

The group is the basic state of human existence,[54] and the psychological dynamics of group situations are especially apt to stimulate paranoid feelings. Most of us have served on committees where the rivalrous feelings were so intense as to interfere with the stated goals of the committee. The same is often true of interagency task forces established by the United States government. The Departments of State and Defense, for example, may be required to develop a joint estimate of the likelihood that Iran will initiate armed conflict in the Persian Gulf, but when the task force meets, it may appear that the major adversary is not Iran but the department across the Potomac. An army officer told one of the authors (RSR) that when he was promoted as an aide to a high-ranking officer he was asked, "Who is the enemy, major?" The naive major replied, "The Russians, sir." "No dummy," the general shot back, rising from his desk. "The Russians are our adversary. The navy is our enemy. Remember that!"

Working initially with psychiatric casualties in military hospitals during World War II, the British psychiatrist Wilfred Bion found similar self-defeating group processes in the healthiest of groups and organizations.[55] Drawing on the work of Melanie Klein, Bion was particularly struck by the manner in which the group setting facilitated projection. He observed that the group frequently behaves as if it were operating according to certain tacit, basic psychological assumptions that drive the group's behavior and interfere with its task.[56] Bion pointed out that, sometimes in a mild way and sometimes in a powerful way, these unconscious assumptions cause groups, organizations, and societies not only to behave in a paranoid manner but also to make them highly susceptible to the leadership, control, and manipulation of paranoid individuals.

Bion identified three distinct emotional states of groups, from which basic assumptions can be inferred.[57] He calls these group psychological states *basic assumption groups.*

In the *fight-flight group,* the members behave as if they have met to do battle against or escape from outside enemies. When it is in the fight mode, the group behaves like a frenzied mob out to destroy the identified enemy. In the flight mode, it is united in its flight from a common enemy. The leader of such a group is adroit at identifying suitable targets for aggression—that is, external enemies. The leader mobilizes group hatred and spurs the group either to attack or to flee, inspiring courage and sacrifice.[58] These actions are seen as necessary to preserve the group, and each member gains security from them. Preservation of the group in the face of the perceived enemy is key, and concern for the individual is secondary, to the point that individual needs and lives may be sacrificed in order to preserve the group.

In the *dependency group,* members behave as if the leader were all-wise and all-powerful. They are unable to function without the leader. They behave as if their primary goal were to gain security and protection from the leader, whom they treat as omnipotent and omniscient—an idealized God-like figure. Although this fantasy is unrealizable, by the manner in which they relate to the leader, the members act as if they could create a situation that would conform to their wishes. In the dependency group, the members behave as if they have no judgment or knowledge of their own, giving unlimited authority to the leader no matter how experienced and knowledgeable they in fact may be.

The *pairing group* operates as if it were to produce a messiah or introduce a millennium. The discussion is future oriented but vague. The hope is that what is produced will save the group from intense feelings in the present. Such political revolutions as the French and Russian Revolutions have this quality.

Drawing on the tradition of Bion, Earl Hopper posits that the fundamental psychological needs for the individual and for the group are for coherence, integration, and relatedness. The most dreaded state is dissolution or psychological disintegration—psychological apocalypse—the core feelings of what Hopper has called the incohesion basic assumption state. The *incohesion group* has a fear of annihilation. Undergoing fission and fragmentation, it may defensively seek a state of fusion in which boundaries are lost and confusion results. There is a hunger for merger to avoid incohesion and alienation.[59]

All the basic assumption groups—incohesion, fight-flight, dependency, and pairing—are relevant to political activity and to both individual and group paranoia.

Group paranoia, in Bion's view, is a manifestation of the leader's pathology and represents the victory of the psychopathic leader over other healthier forms of group development.[60] But this explanation underestimates the power of the group. There is a deep-seated human readiness to externalize inner frailties—a need for enemies. The role of the leader is crucial, but he is facilitating and giving form and meaning to a group sentiment. He stimulates the members' tendency to blame the outsider for their problems, legitimizes attacking their enemy, and provides a sense-making diagnosis; it is a diagnosis the group is eager to hear.

In this sense, the leader may be considered the creation of the group.[61] Especially under circumstances of group trauma, a group may be receptive only to a leader with paranoid tendencies and may psychologically recruit such a leader. One of the primary cohesive elements binding individuals into institutionalized human association is that of defense against psychotic (paranoid and depressive) anxiety.[62] Accordingly, groups will regularly display hostility, suspiciousness, and the other forms of maladaptive behavior that individuals display, but will often exceed individuals in the degree of these distortions of reality.[63] The social organization is the reservoir or holding mechanism for such primitive distortions, which if expressed individually would seem psychotic.

This is particularly true of terrorist groups. Behaving as if they were surrounded by enemies, the terrorists in fact create enemies. The terrorist group almost caricatures the fight-flight basic assumption. By virtue of their acts vis-à-vis society, the terrorists transform their psychological state into reality. Fleeing from the emptiness in their lives, they powerfully express the incohesion dynamic. The dependency dynamic is present in the group's uncritical acceptance of the leader's directives. And the pairing dynamic is the raison d'être of the terrorist group—its ideal is to create a utopia. If the corrupt, dehumanizing system of the present is destroyed, surely some utopia will emerge, whether socialist, anarchist, ethnic, or racial. Thus, for the terrorist group there is a fusion of the work task and the four basic assumption groups—incohesion, fight-flight, dependency, and pairing.[64]

All the basic assumptions come into play in large groups and mass movements and may even come to characterize entire societies, especially traumatized nations. Leaders then can mobilize the pain of the discontented. When these forces are mobilized in the service of creative accomplishment by such leaders as Mohandas Gandhi, Martin Luther King, and Franklin Delano Roosevelt, "they are not tempted to use the slime of frustrated souls as mortar in the building of a new world,"[65] as were Hitler and Stalin.

*Fight-Flight.* At the conclusion of the Vietnam War, the work task for the Cambodian nation was to restore internal cohesion. But under the leadership of the Khmer Rouge and Pol Pot, the path taken was pathological, with the country isolating itself not only physically from the world but also spiritually. The Cambodians acted as if they were being pursued by outsiders (see Chapter 10). On the national scale, this is a striking example of the fight-flight dynamic. Although flight was the principal behavior, fight was also present. Fifteen percent of Cambodia's population was murdered by the Khmer Rouge to "cleanse" the country of external influences. They acted as if the Westernized Cambodians—some of whom were Westernized only to the extent that they wore eyeglasses or had driver's licenses—were attacking the intensely nationalistic isolationist regime. The dependency dynamic was also present, manifested by the absolute power of the anonymous organization "angka," which vaguely stood for the Khmer Rouge, an organization that "kills but never explains." The Cambodians acted as if angka were a god. The pairing dynamic also was prominent: the elimination of non-Cambodian influences would institute a return to an idealized, pure Khmer culture. And finally, the Cambodians acted as if they were creating a millennium. While all the basic assumption states were present, Cambodia was dominated by paranoid flight.

The fight response as a principal mode of dealing with problems is all too familiar in history. Mussolini's Italy, for example, seeking national dignity, economic development, and international prestige, began a policy of direct aggression, starting with the Abyssinian campaign, and aggressive alliances to achieve these ends.

*Dependency.* The complete subordination of a population's will to a single person was characteristic of Mao Zedong's People's Republic of China and Kim Il Sung's North Korea. In describing the popular response to the charismatic leaders who fostered deifying cults of personality, we do not mean to imply that all who manifested slavish devotion to Kim Il Sung did so because dependency feelings were universally mobilized. In totalitarian states, fearful compliance can also produce this posture. In North Korea in the mid-1990s, the fight-flight dynamic was also powerfully mobilized.

*Pairing.* The belief that the group or nation exists to bring forth a salvationist leader or a millennium is characteristic of most revolutions in their early phases. In the first days of the Iranian revolution, Mao's initial decade, and Fidel Castro's early days, leaders proclaimed the imminent coming of a far better world.

*Incohesion.* This was the underlying feeling gripping all these nations and movements. It is to avoid the dreaded state of incohesion that nations, organizations, and groups succumb to the attractions of fight-flight, dependency, and pairing.

The fervor that grips a nation in a social or religious revolution sweeps up almost everyone, even those who will suffer under it and who had previously opposed its coming. Note that great revolutions contain all four of the basic assumption states. At a time of societal disintegration, millennial movements typically fight against others or flee from them, and these movements often have a leader who claims to protect his people, to be "the father of his country," and to offer a vision of a glorious future. Similar combinations occur in equally intense but historically less important organizations. The tragedy of Jim Jones's People's Temple and David Koresh's Branch Davidians, discussed in Chapter 8, were characterized by all four basic assumptions.

There is a comfort in belonging to an association of like-minded individuals on the side of the angels and together opposing the evil, conspiring other, whether that association is a union in conflict with management or a nation at war. This human tendency to adopt the paranoid position when enmeshed in social organizations, especially at times of stress, becomes intensified when a paranoid leader is at the helm of the organization and shapes it to reinforce his own paranoid disposition.

If the fear of enemies is biologically rooted, the identification of friends and enemies is socially conditioned. One of the important functions of socialization is to differentiate for the vulnerable child that which is safe from that which is dangerous. This becomes the basis for affiliation with the in-group and fear of the out-group, and ultimately is the foundation of ethnocentrism and nationalism.

# 4

## The Need for Enemies
### Nationalism, Terrorism, and Paranoid Mass Movements

How much blind night there is in the hearts of men!
—Ovid, *Metamorphoses*

There is a readiness in the human psyche to fear strangers and seek comfort in the familiar. The strangeness of some things and the comforting familiarity of others take on political significance as the child grows into adulthood. Political paranoia is not confined to individuals and groups who have not progressed beyond the paranoid position. No one is ever completely free from the paranoid dynamic. It is an innate human tendency, and under stress, otherwise psychologically healthy individuals, groups, and societies are susceptible to the paranoid appeal. As the paranoid capacity to project hatred is mobilized, "stranger anxiety" and fear of the other mount.

This fear of the stranger and projection of hatred upon the other are the psychological foundation of the concept of the enemy.[1] The crystallization of the shared comfort of the familiar is the psychological foundation of nationalism. Significant others—parents, teachers, peers—sponsor "suitable targets of externalization" for the developing child. They teach whom and what to fear.

Such externalized anxiety is produced not only by unknown persons but also by unfamiliar places, foods, and sounds. The group-specific externalizations they identify tie the children together.[2]

Vamik Volkan has drawn on both his psychoanalytic training and his own life history to illustrate this process, making the bridge from the family to the nation and the development of the sense of national identity.

> In Cyprus [Volkan's birthplace], although Greeks and Turks lived side by side for centuries until 1974, when the island was divided, they remained—and still remain—mutual antagonists. A Greek child learns from what his mother says and does that the neighborhood church is a good place; he unconsciously invests in it his unintegrated good aspects and feels comfortable there. The same mechanism, fueled by his mother's influence, makes him shun the Turkish mosque and minaret, in which he deposits the unintegrated bad aspects of himself and important others. He is more himself when playing near his church and distancing himself from the mosque. . . . Although the child would have his own unique individualized psychological makeup, he would be allied to other children in his group through the common suitable target of externalization . . . that affirms their ethnic, cultural, and national identity.[3]

As personal identity is consolidating, it incorporates elements of national identity. The sense of comfort and belonging spreads to the national flag. Those who oppose the nation or desecrate the flag may threaten the sense of self. This helps explain the rage engendered, for example, in the United States by flag burning. Especially under stress, we cling all the more tightly to those symbols of our national, racial, ethnic, or religious identity that have become incorporated as part of the self-concept. Thus, Volkan points out, Palestinians living in the Gaza Strip wear talismans—rings and other jewelry incorporating ethnic symbols: "Like songs often repeated among the Arabs, they are shared only within the in-group, providing a magical [psychological] network for maintaining group narcissism under adverse conditions as well as contributing to the self-esteem of individual Arabs. It is not enough for Palestinians in the Gaza Strip simply to be aware of their Arabic identity; they need to exhibit its symbols in order to maintain their self-esteem.''[4]

We are comforted by familiarity and by others like us. But to maintain the sense of group—and self—cohesion we must differentiate ourselves from strangers. Strangers, then, are necessary for our process of self-definition. To say "these things are specially good and are specially part of me" is to say "those other things are specially bad and not part of me but part of others." Because enemies are necessary for self-definition, it is necessary to have enemies in our midst.

This is the phenomenon of what we describe as the "familiar enemy." The Greeks and the Turks, as Volkan points out, have lived near each other for centuries. So have India's Sikhs and Hindus; Bosnia's Serbs, Croats, and Muslims; Northern Ireland's Catholics and Protestants; Israel's Arabs and Jews. To one another, these groups remain feared— but familiar—strangers. Maintaining boundaries is the foundation of an integrated psychological, social, and economic system that excludes strangers and ensures the continuity of the group. We project into strangers what we disown in ourselves. We end where they begin.[5]

Thus, marriages between familiar enemies are always prohibited; the ban is essential in order to maintain psychological boundaries. Although members of the various groups often carry on trade with one another, preference is given to members of one's own community. In the most intimate areas of trade—partnerships and loans—the patterns will seldom cross community boundaries. The major events of life—such rites of passages as baptism, confirmation, marriage, and burial—are laden with group symbols, and often other groups are excluded.

Holidays are special occasions for emphasizing group solidarity, and they sometimes do so by providing opportunities for antagonistic rituals at the boundary between groups. In India, for example, Muslims may slaughter a cow in front of a Hindu temple while a special ceremony is taking place within, and Hindus may make loud music and shout offensively in front of a mosque on holy days.

The situation is at its most extreme when major socioeconomic incongruity exists between adjoining groups. That is, hostility at the boundary is most intense when one group is rich and the other is poor, so that one ethnic group looks upon the other with contempt or bitter envy.

The more "different" the stranger in our midst, the more readily available he is as a target for externalization. An important aspect of the development of group identity is symbols of difference shared by the other—symbols on which to project hatred. But because it is representations of the self that are being projected, there must be a kinship recognized at an unconscious level. We are bound to those we hate. Nevertheless, there must be a recognizable difference, a distinct gap to facilitate the distinction between "us" and "them." A "good enough enemy"[6] is an object that is available to serve as a reservoir for all the negated aspects of the self. In this way, the enemy provides the valuable function of stabilizing the internal group by storing group projections. Just as the paranoid delusional system makes sense and provides cohesion for the individual ego under threat of fragmentation, so too does the enemy provide cohesion for the social group, especially the social group under stress (see Chapter 5). Ironically, those groups from which we most passionately distinguish ourselves are those to which we are most closely bound. The enemy who we are certain is a despicable "other" is littered with parts cast out from the self.[7]

Enemies, therefore, are to be cherished, cultivated, and preserved, for if we lose them our self-definition is endangered. But this identity-creating process—a psychological necessity—results in a world populated by groups with varying degrees of animosity, excessive self-regard, and fear of others. A mature, integrated person learns that "enemy" objects are at most adversaries or distasteful beings, not objects to be hated or destroyed. For some people, and for many when under stress, however, the bad objects become true enemies.

Creating bad others is a necessary part of acquiring a distinct identity in childhood, but insofar as a national identity becomes part of the personal identity, deep-seated feelings that transcend childhood become fixed within the social personality. Making friends and enemies, then, is central to man's social psychological nature.

Especially at times of stress, the self, and objects with which the self has identified (such as one's ethnic group or political party), are idealized; other objects (such as historical adversaries of one's ethnic group or political party) are viewed as dangerous persecutors and are demonized. The internalization of the good cultural symbols is expressed thus: "I must be good because my people's history—which is part of me—is good, our food is delicious, our religious buildings are impressive, our architecture is beautiful.'' The converse also occurs: ''All those others I see around me, especially those with whom my group has lived, are bad—their history is one of deception and violence, their food is inferior, their architecture is ugly,'' and so on. All badness is outside, all goodness inside.

Such racial or ethnic or religious identification has helped produce great poetry and music and has stimulated self-sacrifice in the interest of fellow group members. But group identification has also provided a fertile field from which wars and massacres have grown. Pride in one's heritage often manifests itself as destructive narcissism and political paranoia. It is a world of friends and enemies, good and evil, self and not-self.

For most people this splitting is a minor part of a wider healthy personality. The good enough mother, or the good enough self—the entirety, human and flawed, of the nurturing mother, of the self—is accepted. To reject the other is to disown the flawed aspects of ourselves: ''Christian anti-Semitism and Jewish anti-Christianism are defenses that prevent each from becoming more fully human. They are symptoms of our incompleteness and our struggle with the half we have rejected at such terrible cost. Only one who is whole can allow wholeness (indeed, otherness) in another . . . The fateful question for Jew and Christian alike is whether we shall persist in sustaining our venerable pseudo-identities by living parasitically off the projected and lived-out identities of others.''[8]

This innate tendency to idealize the in-group and demonize the out-group can never be eradicated. The germs of that more primitive psychology remain within the personality, ready to be activated at times of stress. Thus otherwise psychologically healthy individuals can be infected by paranoid thinking when the group with which they identify is attacked, when economic reversals occur, or even when epidemics of disease or forces of nature, such as earthquakes, afflict the group.

Recall that the image of the enemy that the paranoid creates is often a projection of his own feelings, a mirror image of himself. The paranoid sees his actions as reactions required by the enemy. If the enemy is seen as deceiving through writings, the paranoid will make use of the most detailed and elaborate pseudo-scholarship. Conspiracy will have to be fought with conspiracy, organization with organization. The paranoid motivations, fears, anxieties, and desires will be ascribed to phantom opponents. The relationship with the enemy is thus one beginning in fantasy and externalization, but if the adversary is drawn into responding, what began as fantasy is transformed into reality. These mechanisms contribute to the psychology of nations at war, with each nation externalizing its bad objects and aggressive impulses onto the enemy.[9] Each nation's own side is idealized, its aggression required by the persecutory enemy.

The search for group identity frequently leads to the development of the fight-flight paranoid dynamic. An institution set up to preserve a group's cultural traditions, for example, may turn paranoid. Such was the case with the German-American Bundists during the period just before World War II. Members of the Bund, an organization founded largely to develop German and American cultural ties, felt increasingly isolated and besieged by society. And the Bundists did become a source of Nazi influence in America. Were they agents of influence from the onset, as the surrounding society feared, or did the fear of the other become activated during this period of internal conflict, with intensification of nationalist feeling, promotion of a paranoid fight-flight dynamic, and a self-fulfilling prophecy?

## The Paradoxical Solace of Belonging to a Paranoid Group

As humans, we need our privacy and are uncomfortable with the touch of strangers. This is especially true of the paranoid, who is consumed by distrust. The paranoid tends to be a loner, averse to association. But paranoids find comfort in gathering together against the enemy. Arm in arm with former strangers, they are now part of a collective.

In such a collective, without watchful external authority, individuals may more easily yield to the wish to strike out, to give vent to frustrations. Individual responsibility is vitiated by collective action. An important role for the paranoid leader is providing a target for collective frustration and rage.

When the group swells, becoming a mass movement, its collective belief overwhelms individual resistance. Not only does the reality testing of its members become faulty, but normal inhibitions against the expression of individual hatefulness and aggression are diminished, for there is safety in numbers and anonymity. We melt together in the mob, become as one, and each member suspends individual judgment. All are equal within the group. It is as if the group had a mind of its own. The individual, swept along by its force, is unable to resist this powerful wave.[10] Elias Canetti likens the dynamics of the crowd to a flood or a fire gathering strength, destroying everything in its path. This is a force of primeval power.[11]

The absolute certainty with which the paranoid leader radiates his externalizing hatred is compelling to followers who have lost their moorings. That conviction of rectitude is essential to the maintenance of self-esteem and psychological integrity.[12] To admit error would be to acknowledge a personal defect and would be a blow to the paranoid's already fragile self-esteem. To breach the paranoid leader's certitude would unglue the connection between him and his followers. For it is his possession of the truth that permits the paranoid leader to take an assemblage of frustrated, angry individuals and, by the power of his rhetoric, inflame them, focusing their aggressive energy on the enemy without. Thus, disaggregated individuals become a powerful social movement.

The feeling of oneness with the crowd is powerful, but equally powerful is the feeling of distrust and persecution toward those who do not belong, the outsiders who are perceived to be intent on destroying the crowd. Those who do not subscribe to the belief system challenge the very foundations of the crowd. Insiders who question the unifying beliefs of the movement are an even greater threat. Skepticism is treason, and the insider who persists in questioning will find himself an outsider. The feelings of persecution, then, are directed against both the "attack" from without and the "conspiracy" within. Like a besieged city, the movement must strengthen its walls against the enemy without and search for enemies within.[13] True belief does not permit question and doubt.

The surge of excitement in becoming a member of the protesting crowd is well captured in the autobiographical memoirs of Egyptian revolutionary leader Gamal Abdel Nasser, who recalled seeing, as a teenager, protesters surging through the streets outside his home in Cairo. He joined in and was caught up in the throng. "I did not know what they were protesting," he said, "but I knew this was the life for me."[14]

Socially isolated individuals who are experiencing alienation are especially drawn to mass movements. Fleeing the dread of isolation, such individuals experience a "merger hunger." Surrendering to the leader, abandoning one's self to the movement, is paramount. Belonging to the mass movement is much more important than the movement's ethos. The cause is *not* the cause. The espoused cause of the movement is the rationale for joining, but the underlying need is to belong.

The frustrated, alienated individual who becomes a member of a mass movement now belongs, his self-concept has been expanded, and purposelessness has been replaced by a mission. Thus the individual subordinates his individuality to the mass movement. Striking out against authority, he yields to the authority of the movement and its leader. Ostensibly seeking freedom, in the words of Erich Fromm, he achieves an "escape from freedom."[15] Eric Hoffer quotes a young Nazi who, extolling his loyalty to Hitler, indicated he had joined the movement in order to be "free from freedom."[16]

The movement provides an escape from responsibility that permits individuals—now anonymous in the mass—to express their rage and frustration. That the Nazis on trial in Nuremberg disclaimed responsibility for their acts suggests (aside from its self-serving aspect) that they had joined the Nazi movement to escape individual responsibility and had yielded their individuality to the collective self of Hitler's followers.

Societies vary in their readiness to yield autonomy and submit to authority. In fiercely individualistic societies the authoritarian leader demanding total, selfless obedience will not flourish as easily. Other societies, however, have a history of passive subjugation to powerful authority. Russia is a notable example. Although Russians revolted against the tyranny of the czars, they readily succumbed to the authoritarian leadership of the Bolsheviks.

By providing the protective cover of the mass movement, the leader lets the members vent their frustration and aggression, unconstrained by conscience. "If the leader says it is the right thing to do, and others are doing it, it must be all right" is the members' rationale. Normally, the individual conscience represents the internalized standards and prohibitions of parents and other key figures. But in the mass movement, a group mind develops as the standards of the leader and the movement replace those of the individual. As the leader's adherents march together, build monuments together, and scapegoat enemies together, their united action strengthens their bonds.

The leader cannot exercise full authority over his group if his followers bear allegiance to others. Ties to the family are a threat to the power of the group. Closed religious cults therefore attempt to sever bonds between new recruits and their families and friends.[17] Jim Jones and David Koresh systematically attempted to break down the bonds between husband and wife, parents and children, to ensure that they received the total allegiance of their followers (see Chapter 5). In the early Soviet Union and during China's Cultural Revolution, youth were rewarded for betraying their families, for loyalty to family weakened the establishment of new Communist man. Jesus, too, recognized this revolutionary principle: "For I am come to set a man at variance against his father, and the daughter against her mother, and the daughter-in-law against her mother-in-law. And a man's foes shall be they of his own household. He that loveth father or mother more than me is not worthy of me: and he that loveth son or daughter more than me is not worthy of me" (Matthew 10: 35–37).

The contented individual in a rewarding society does not tear himself from family and the nation's institutions to follow a leader attacking the society. In even the healthiest society some alienated individuals will lose themselves in a paranoid group, but paranoid mass movements arise only in disintegrating societies. In these circumstances, ordinarily self-sufficient and psychologically healthy individuals overwhelmed by a society in chaos swell the ranks of the alienated and psychologically discontented.

But at the heart of the mass movement are many who are not at peace with themselves. Beneath the discontent with society is discontent with the flawed self. The paranoid leader sings to these discontented selves, "It is not you who are the problem. It is they. Join us against them. Strike out against them." And if there is any doubt, the thronging numbers already in the movement put the doubts to rest.

The leader who can identify an enemy for his distressed group is providing a sense-making function.[18] By attributing conspiratorial power to the other, he provides solace for his followers' inner sense of powerlessness, but at the cost of reality. In contrast to the group therapist who

helps his patients take responsibility for their lives and accurately deal
with reality, the paranoid leader, in shaping the group's fears of the enemy, serves as a malignant group therapist for them. It is as if the therapist
said to the paranoid-schizoid patient, "You really are being persecuted.
Let me help you by naming your persecutors and telling you who your
true friends are, friends who are also being attacked by these persecutors.
Together you and your true friends can fight the persecutors and praise
each other's righteousness, which will help you realize that the source of
aggression and evil is out there, in the real world. And you thought it
was all in your head!"[19]

Moreover, the group, in validating the leader's construction of reality,
magnifies the leader's influence, further weakening the individual's hold
on reality and easing his doubts by providing an "objective" external
focus for his anxiety. While an individual may be wary of the conspiracy
theory, his doubts are assuaged by the group's validation of the existence
of the enemy. The projection of self-reproach is a central dynamic of
paranoia, a dynamic that the skillful externalizing leader facilitates. Nothing pulls together a disparate group of followers more effectively than
hatred. One cannot facilitate the externalization of blame without a clear
enemy, and the gifted demagogue is adroit at enemy making. In his *Catechism of the Revolutionist*, Sergey Nechayev recognizes the utility of
the enemy for mobilizing hatred.[20] In identifying villainous categories to
be eliminated, he warns revolutionaries against eliminating the most villainous too early, for the hatred they provoke may be useful in inciting
popular rebellion.

Hitler's focused hatred on his enemies was by no means unbridled;
it also reflected thoughtful strategy. He considered that the genius of a
great leader was to mobilize hatred in his followers in such a way that
apparently disconnected adversaries "seem to belong to a single category." The unifying malevolent force in Hitler's paranoid worldview, of
course, was the Jew: "Behind England stands Israel and behind France
and behind the United States . . . It is impossible to exaggerate the formidable quality of the Jew as an enemy."[21] Asked early in the course of
the Nationalist Socialist Movement about destroying the Jews, Hitler,
echoing Nechayev, responded, "No . . . We should then have to invent
him. It is essential to have a tangible enemy, not merely an abstract one."

A member of a Japanese delegation studying Hitler's movement found it "magnificent." He added, "I wish we could have something like this in Japan, only we can't, because we haven't got any Jews."[22]

This is the mass-movement expression of the paranoid dynamic—relocating the wounded self's internal persecutor to the outside enemy who must be destroyed. The internal terrifier is boundless; the external enemy is finite.[23] As the threatened individual masters his fears and becomes the threatener, so the threatened group unites against and attacks the (perceived) outside enemy. It should be emphasized, however, that while the paranoid dynamic may be expressed in the mobilization of the mass movement, for the nation at war it is not paranoid to fear the enemy. The enemy is real, and the danger the enemy poses is real.

Thus the paranoid appeal, a fantasy at first, can come to be a reality. Just as individual paranoids create genuine enemies, so groups and even nations create theirs in war. When the paranoid group finds itself at war with the larger society, as do religious cults and terrorist organizations, or paranoid nations with other nations, the paranoid fears are realized. They *are* out there; it *is* true that it is *us versus them* and that they will destroy us unless we attack them and are successful. If the incentive to join a mass movement is collective feelings of fragmentation and isolation, going to war cements the alienated into a cohesive whole. For each party to the war, the aggression is defensive, justified, indeed required by the external enemy.

## Deception, Merger, and Sacrifice

To escape from the self and join in a transcendent movement requires self-deception. The leader facilitates that by casting the present in the bleakest of terms and promising a glorious future. He imbues the movements with a quasi-religious significance so that joining the movement and going to war become a holy cause. A religious fervor grips the participants and becomes the basis for sacrifice. It is the worthlessness of the present and the rewards of the future that so powerfully motivate the discontented souls who join the movement. The price of joining may be anonymity, becoming a nameless, selfless part of the mass. For many, this is not a cost but a benefit. The individual who is psychologically ripe for plucking by the paranoid leader is incomplete and yearns to merge.

But one does not lightly give up one's life, no matter how miserable the circumstances of everyday existence. How then can we explain the followers' characteristic willingness—indeed, avidity—to sacrifice for the cause? They have yielded their individuality to the collective good of which they are an organic part. So what serves the whole serves them, and if they serve the whole by their sacrifice, it is for their collective good.

The critical elements of the follower are a deprecation of the present and a blemished self with a readiness to hate, to imitate, to uncritically believe, and to attempt the impossible.[24] There is, then, a close relation between the willingness to sacrifice and a proneness to mass action. It is the role and genius of the leader to inspire the discontented to be ready to sacrifice for the common good. What more selfless act could there be than to give up one's life for the cause, the ultimate act of self-abnegation?

Ideology—be it religious or political—is important to the follower. But it is not the words that persuade, not the ideas that convince. They simply provide a rationale for the follower who yearns for a calling, for a group to join, a leader to follow, in order to flee from the self. The difference between the individual isolated and in despair and the individual in a collective, dedicated to a cause, is profound in terms of the willingness to take risks. Hoffer observes the perplexity of the British military administrating Palestine: "Since Hitler had managed to exterminate six million Jews without meeting serious resistance, it should not be too difficult to handle the 600,000 Jews in Palestine. Yet they found the Jews in Palestine . . . a formidable enemy: reckless, stubborn, and resourceful. The Jew in Europe faced his enemies alone, an isolated individual, a speck of life floating in an eternity of nothingness. In Palestine he felt himself not a human atom, but a member of an eternal race, with an immemorial past behind it and a breath-taking future ahead."[25]

The ignoble present becomes the springboard for a noble future, which for some groups means a return to the idealized past. This is not only the message of all fundamentalist religions but also an important appeal of the secular ideology of Nazism. The reason for your wretched state, the leaders explain, is your departure from the true faith, from tradition. Only by returning to those basic principles can you regain our glorious past and revitalize the followers of the true faith in the future.

## Protecting the True Believers from Doubt

Because belief in the true faith, be it Islam or Marxism, is obligatory to sustain membership in the movement, the true believer must suspend doubt and deny evidence that disconfirms his beliefs. Thus the true believer in a group setting has psychological qualities similar to the individual paranoid. Having already come to a conclusion, he searches for confirming evidence and denies disconfirming evidence. As suspiciousness is the sine qua non of the paranoid, so too is distrust of outsiders a central feature of the fanatic movement. Doubt and doubters threaten commitment to the cause, which requires uncritical loyalty to the movement and its leader. So it is that uniformity of thought is required within the group. For if doubts persist and grow, the unity of the movement is threatened. Doubt implies an ability to stand outside the group and take measure; the capacity to doubt dogma implies self-assurance. There is no room for questioning, self-assured individuals in fanatic movements, for doubt is the enemy of unquestioning commitment. If the group has strength, it is a rigid strength, which permits no question or challenge— thus the pervasive suspiciousness at the boundary between the group and the outside world. Doubt threatens the bonds of the individual to the collective. It is a cancer that must be eliminated, violently if necessary. Blind faith depends on insecurity, and the more self-doubt, the more powerful the passion of the true believer.

If there is no ambiguity in the mind of the true believer, neither must there be ambiguity in the doctrine to which he adheres. The certitude of the doctrine is central to its appeal. The body of ideas is an exoskeleton, holding the believer together—thus the rage when those ideas are attacked. When Salman Rushdie published his novel *The Satanic Verses,* he was, from the point of view of the fundamentalist Islamic clerics, assailing the organizing creed of the Islamic true believers by questioning important beliefs. As a consequence, a *fatwah* (religious judgment) was issued by Iran's Ayatollah Khomeini, condemning Rushdie to death. Free-

dom of expression, with the attendant possibility of stimulating doubt in
true believers, is poisonous to leadership attempting to transform society
ideologically.

Intellectual arguments are irrelevant. True belief is not a matter of
reason. Blaise Pascal observed, "It is the heart that is conscious of God,
not the reason," a principle invoked by Rudolf Hess when swearing in
the entire Nazi party in 1934. He exhorted the audience, "Do not seek
Hitler with your brains; all of you will find him with the strength of your
hearts."[26]

## Traumatized Groups and the Dynamics of Terrorism

However effective the leader, he cannot develop a passionate, unified
movement unless powerful dissatisfaction already exists. The moment
must be ripe; the feelings simmering. Of course, an important quality for
a leader is the capacity to "ripen" an issue.[27] When a foundation of
discontent is present, a traumatized group can powerfully exert "role
suction"—that is, the group can induce a leader to behave in a paranoid
or caretaking manner. The two postures, paranoia and caretaking, are not
in opposition, for one can take care of a group by protecting them against
the enemy. The swirling currents of paranoid fears, irrational dependency,
self-righteous aggression, and unrealistic expectations of a millennium
are manifest in extreme form in terrorist groups.

If one strips away the national contextual substance, the form of
terrorist rhetoric is strikingly uniform. It is "us versus them": "us," the
terrorists, fighting for what they claim is a righteous cause against
"them," the corrupt establishment. The terrorists claim that once this
corrupt establishment is destroyed, a better society will arise.[28]

Within the spectrum of terrorist groups, this dynamic was particularly
intense for social-revolutionary terrorists inspired by Marxist-Leninist
ideology, a phenomenon exemplified during the turbulent 1970s by such
groups as the Red Army Faction of the Federal Republic of Germany,
the Red Brigade of Italy, and the Weathermen of the United States. Although no single terrorist mindset exists, social-revolutionary terrorists in
these groups contained a high proportion of "angry paranoids," espe-

cially in the leadership. The terrorist group ethos is particularly attractive to individuals with paranoid personalities.[29]

In their minds, the terrorists are at war with the establishment, in what has been conceptualized as a "fantasy war" that becomes actualized.[30] The terrorists, seeing themselves in the vanguard of the revolution, have identified the establishment as the cause of society's problems. The terrorist group is idealized and society demonized. "They" (the establishment) are responsible for "our" problems, so it becomes a moral imperative to destroy "them." This is the upside-down psycho-logic of social-revolutionary terrorism. In the terrorists' view, the establishment is out to destroy the revolutionary group because of the danger it poses, and social justice cannot be achieved until the establishment is destroyed. Projection and grandiosity are closely linked in the terrorists' rhetoric and action. Paranoid flight (they are out to get us) and paranoid aggressiveness (we must destroy them) dominate.

It is not irrational for the group to believe that "society is out to get us." This self-fulfilling prophecy is characteristic of the paranoid dynamic. When the group mounts its anti-establishment attacks—killing judges, bombing government buildings—society will respond, and the fantasy war will be transformed into reality. This in turn consolidates the "us versus them" mentality and dissolves whatever incohesion there was within the group, magnifying its solidarity. As one of the Red Army Faction terrorists asserted, "The group was born under the pressure of pursuit, [and group solidarity was] compelled exclusively by the illegal situation, fashioned into a common destiny."[31] Another went so far as to claim that outside pressure was the "sole link holding the group together."[32]

Although there is no one terrorist mindset, many drawn to the path of terrorism have a paranoid disposition and find the externalizing rhetoric attractive. Under the dominating direction of an angry paranoid leader specializing in such rhetoric, the terrorist group can take on a paranoid coloration. It is, after all, a comfort to have an external target for one's frustrations. A comprehensive study of West German terrorists revealed that 25 percent had lost one or both parents by age fourteen, a significant percentage had been incarcerated for juvenile offenses, and a substantial number had experienced significant difficulties in school and the workplace.[33] If one is out of work, a loner, isolated from one's family, or an educational dropout, it is a comfort to be told, "It's not you. It's not your fault, not your responsibility, how badly things are going for you. It's them. The establishment. They are responsible for our troubles."

With this psycho-logic, it becomes morally permissible, indeed morally imperative, to destroy those seen as representing the establishment, for they are the source of society's (and the terrorist's) problems.[34] The terrorist leader, with his absolutist paranoid vision, has provided an external reason for their difficulty, has made sense of their empty, failed lives, with his siren song "It's Not Us, It's Them, for They Are Responsible for Our Problems."

## The Enemy as Legitimated Focus of Aggression

A consequence of threatened social identity is frustration and an unfocused readiness to strike out. In the Iranian revolution, for example, Ayatollah Khomeini adroitly focused the frustration and aggression of a population suffering from a fragmented, threatened identity by identifying the enemy first as the Shah of Iran and then as the "great Satan" of the United States.

But consolidating identity by focusing aggression against "them" has a deadly cost. One of the consequences of defining the in-group as "not them" is to deny a sense of responsibility for them. In other words, by defining ourselves in terms of who we are not, we separate ourselves psychologically from an empathic connection with the enemy. They are not us, and one can be merciful and compassionate to those like us, while being ruthless and aggressive toward others. The sense of responsibility and human concern are reserved for those like us. At its most extreme, this tendency leads to dehumanizing the enemy, to persuading followers that the enemy is subhuman, a different species. This is what Erik Erikson calls pseudospeciation.[35] Pseudospeciation helps explain the apparent paradox of the group whose ethos is compassionate and loving of mankind but which manages to inflict violence on other groups apparently without moral qualm. Their love is reserved for those within the boundary of their own pseudospecies. Those outside the boundary are "the other," a different species, to be exterminated like vermin.

That two peoples have lived alongside one another does not mean they are friends. They may remain strangers in all the things that truly matter. The fear that one group has for the other, moreover, may not be simply a consequence of the social or ceremonial distance we have been describing. Many of these peoples have been participating in cycles of genocidal violence for generations.

Even some hardened observers of Balkan politics believed that the antagonisms among Croats, Serbs, and Muslims had been permanently blunted by the decades of peaceful Communist rule. The revival of ferocious ethnic wars in the early 1990s demonstrated, however, that the historic wounds had not healed and the deep-seated antagonisms had not died but had merely been suppressed by the powerful leaders of the socialist state. In the wake of the fall of Communism, widespread economic and social dislocation ensued. The people were accustomed to blaming the Communist leadership for all their problems, but since the Communist enemy had disappeared, whom could the people blame? The need for enemies produced a bloody revival of ancient hatreds. The revival of age-old tensions in Eastern Europe in the wake of the dissolution of the Soviet empire is a special case of the destabilizing consequences of losing one's enemy.

## Searching for New Enemies, Reviving Old Hatreds

Two generations earlier, Lenin saw the inculcation of loyalty to the Soviet Union as a crucial task in institutionalizing the revolution. To develop an identity as "new Soviet man" required the suppression—indeed destruction—of other loyalties and identities, nationalistic and religious. Even family loyalties were seen as reactionary vestiges—a principle carried to its most dreadful extreme with the celebration of Pavel Morozov as a hero of the Soviet Union for denouncing his family.

This ruthless stamping out of national identity under the hypocritical motto of "national in form, socialist in content" extended to the socialist nations of Eastern Europe in the wake of World War II. In the pursuit of the new socialist man, for forty years expressions of nationalist identity were forbidden to the people of Central and Eastern Europe—the intensely nationalistic Poles, Hungarians, Bulgarians, Romanians, the

Czechs and Slovaks of Czechoslovakia, and the Serbs, Croats, and Bosnian Muslims of Yugoslavia.

In this exaggerated emphasis of one identity and the attempt to eliminate other identities by force, the essential quality of identity—difference—was attacked. Such attempted destruction of identity nearly always fails, and it did in Eastern Europe. In totalitarian regimes this leads to a duality of identity: the publicly espoused identity—new socialist man— and the private identity. The regime's intense pressure on private life led to an extensive erosion of private identity, which can occur in three ways:

- the *repression* of identity elements that have been deemed undesirable;
- the *transformation* of undesirable identity elements into "negative identity fragments" (the "self-criticism" in Communist China is an example of such enforced transformations); and
- the *marginalization* of private identity, "squeezing certain identity elements to the margins of awareness, thereby rendering them seemingly insignificant."[36]

But the Communist regime's attack on these private identity elements did not destroy them. Rather, the social basis of private identity was forced underground. Allusion became the "mother tongue of collective experience." Thus the social basis of private identity was weakened and forced underground, but not eliminated.[37]

Nevertheless, as expressions of national identity were forbidden, the associated expression of "us-them" tensions between ethnic groups was weakened as the locus of these tensions shifted. Now "they" were the Communist leaders. "They" were the deprivers of freedom, the cause of problems. And "they," the Communist leaders, were the target of hatred (albeit rarely expressed).

In the fall of 1989, that most remarkable season of freedom, with bewildering rapidity the Communist empire collapsed and one socialist government after another in Eastern Europe was displaced as the long-suppressed peoples rose up in democratic protest. It was an exultant moment. Free at last! But within a few years, that spirit was replaced by the revival of age-old hatreds in exaggerated form, as Serbs slaughtered Croats and Muslims, and Slovaks asserted their individual autonomy and

split from the Czech lands. Free expression, moreover, was given to hatred of minorities, which became an active ingredient in political campaigns. These events were not surprising, for after forty years of enforced
suppression of national identity, at last these intensely nationalistic people
were free to express in intensified form the core of their identity—difference, and with it expressions of hatred of the "other." As one mocking
poem put it,

> Free at last
> Free to choose
> To eat at McDonald's
> And hate the Jews.[38]

More than difference was expressed, for the intensity with which
hated groups were blamed for the troubles of the in-group was remarkable. A particularly painful example is found in Poland. Before World
War II, Poland was the center of world Judaism, with a population of
more than 3 million Jews. About 2.9 million perished in the Holocaust.
Today fewer than ten thousand of the estimated 38 million Poles are
Jewish, and the average age of those Jews is seventy. Approximately 30
percent of the population of Warsaw was Jewish when the Nazis invaded;
as a consequence of the Holocaust, only about three hundred or four
hundred Jews are now reported to live in Warsaw.

Poland not only has fewer Jews than in 1939; it also has fewer other
minorities. Hitler's murder of the Jews, the expulsion of the Germans
from East Prussia and Silesia, and the westward shift of the Ukrainian
border has made Poland perhaps the most ethnically and religiously ho-
mogeneous country in eastern Europe. Although Poland retains its historical memory of "enemy" minorities, it has almost none within its
borders. Absent the Communist leaders, absent traditional enemies, when
things went wrong in Poland—and initially they went very badly indeed—who could be blamed?

Reports of anti-Semitism surfaced almost immediately after 1989.
The new president of Poland, Lech Walesa, stated that anti-Semitic attitudes "would not be tolerated."[39] But monuments and cemeteries were
desecrated, with swastikas painted on gravestones.[40] On the monument
of the ghetto fighters who fought against the Nazis was inscribed, "The

only good Jew is a dead Jew.''[41] The largely nonexistent Jewish population was blamed for Poland's economic distress, with an invocation of the international Zionist conspiracy. A poll conducted in the early 1990s indicated that a quarter of the Polish population believed that although Jews constituted only a small part of the population, they nevertheless exercised too much influence. Only 3 percent of those interviewed found it acceptable to have Jewish neighbors.[42] The pollster Slawomir Nowotny, commenting on the intensity of the anti-Semitism in the face of the virtually absent Jewish population, characterized this phenomenon as ''platonic anti-Semitism.'' He explained that if love without sex is platonic love, then anti-Semitism without Jews is platonic anti-Semitism. Nowotny saw the power attributed to the Jews as a reflection of the powerlessness of the populace and their need for someone to blame.[43]

The leadership played an active role in fanning the flames of anti-Semitism. In August 1990, Walesa said that his earlier charge that a gang of Jews ''had gotten hold of the [country's] trough and is bent on destroying us'' applied not to ''the Jewish people as a whole'' but only to those ''who are looking out for themselves while not giving a damn about anyone else.''[44] In the 1990 election campaign, Walesa asserted he was ''clean,'' ''100 percent Pole,'' because he had no Jews among his ancestors.[45]

During the 1990 political campaign, Lech Walesa's main opponent was Tadeusz Mazowiecki, head of the Citizen's Movement–Democratic Action party (ROAD). At a press conference during the campaign, Mazowiecki was ''accused'' of being Jewish. Asked if he thought ROAD was a Jewish party, Walesa responded, ''Persons of Jewish origin should not conceal their identity. . . . When Jews hide their identity they provoke attitudes of anti-Semitism. Why are Jews not proud of the fact that they are Jewish? I am proud of the fact that I am Polish and, similarly, I would have been proud of my origin if I had been Jewish.''[46] (It should be noted that, for Walesa, Polish equals Polish Catholic and that to be Jewish was to be not Polish.)

In fact, Mazowiecki is not Jewish, although he did receive the support of the editor of *Gazeta Wyborcza,* Adam Michnik, who is Jewish. Not recognizing the anti-Semitism in their response, the Catholic Church ''defended'' Mazowiecki, asserting that they had gone back through two hundred years of church records and found "not a drop of Jewish blood" in Mazowiecki's family. In the campaign, most of the candidates stressed that Poland is a Christian nation.

In Romania, too, there is anti-Semitism without Jews. Before World War II, more than 1 million Jews were estimated to live in Romania. Today there are seventeen thousand, most of them elderly. More than four hundred thousand Romanian Jews were killed during World War II by Germans and Romanian security forces, and the climate under President Nicolae Ceausescu fostered a large emigration to Israel.

Romanian politics were distinctly anti-Communist in the interwar period. Most of the Communist Party's support came from the disaffected minorities, including Jews, Hungarians, and Bulgarians. Hostility toward the now-departed Communist leaders has been accompanied by denouncements of Jews and Hungarians as Communists. This "Communist equals Jew" rationalization for anti-Semitism was demonstrated in the manifesto of the National Defense League, made public during a violent demonstration in April 1990. The leaflet began with a declaration that the Communists had "sown only blood and woes" and that "blood calls for blood." It then went on to attack the National Salvation Front as having been "bought by the Bolsheviks and the international Jewish conspiracy." The manifesto declared that the Jews, under the direction of Chief Rabbi Moses Rosen, have a "secret mission . . . in your new communist government . . . of setting up a new form of communism and socialism for the benefit of the Jewry."[47]

Anti-Semitic articles have appeared in national newspapers, reviving the anti-Semitic organization known as the Legion of the Archangel Saint Michael, later renamed the Iron Guard.[48] In one message, reported to be from the anti-Communist Iron Guard Army, their goal was declared to be restoration of the "purity of the Rumanian soul, which has been poisoned." The pamphlet ended with the words, "Our time has finally come. Heil Hitler. We shall be victorious." There were swastikas in all four corners.[49] An article by a former submarine commander, Captain Nicolae Radu, claimed that Israel planned to turn Romania into a Jewish colony, that Jews were plotting with the International Monetary Fund to turn Romanians into "street sweepers," and that the Jews controlled the Romanian government and had brought Communism to Romania.[50]

In 1991 in Iasi, Romania, Elie Wiesel, the Nobel Prize–winning chronicler of the Holocaust, was taunted at a talk commemorating the deaths of eight thousand Jews at the hands of the Romanian army and police in 1941. Before the war, of the ninety thousand people living in Iasi, forty thousand were Jews. Today only nine hundred remain. A woman disrupted the meeting, shouting, "It's a lie. The Jews didn't die. We won't allow Rumanians to be insulted by foreigners in their own country."[51]

In April 1991, the Romanian chamber of deputies rose in a minute of silence in tribute to the memory of Ion Antonescu, the dictator executed as a war criminal who allied Romania with Germany and ordered the deportation and killing of thousands of Jews. During the spring and fall of 1991, similar tribute was paid to another architect of the Holocaust, Father Josef Tiso, a Catholic priest who was president of Slovakia during the one period of its functioning as an autonomous nation (1939–1945). Under Tiso's leadership, Slovakia was allied with Germany. Tiso arranged to pay the Germans five hundred crowns for each Jewish man, woman, and child deported to the death camps. He was later convicted of war crimes and executed. A cross was consecrated and erected on the grave of Josef Tiso in March 1991 on the occasion of the fifty-second anniversary of the Slovak Republic by a new, intensely nationalist political force, the Slovak National Unity, which had declared as its central goal the establishment of an independent Slovak state. "It was not the first time in history when power humiliated the law and justice and an innocent man had to die," the eulogist said. During the rally, the eulogy was interrupted by cries of "Glory to Tiso," "Enough of [President Václav] Havel," and "Long Live Slovakia."[52]

When Chaim Herzog, the president of Israel, visited Czechoslovakia, the Slovak fascist party erected a plaque on Tiso's birthplace. President Havel, wishing to avoid further fueling a controversy, did not make a statement decrying this act. On a prior visit to Bratislava, Havel had been attacked by a crowd who called him King of the Jews. The resurgence of Slovakian nationalism was coupled with an intense resurgence of the feelings associated with the brief period of national independence—fascism and anti-Semitism.

Reflecting on the suppression of identity, Peter Hunčík, a psychiatrist who served as special assistant to President Havel in the Czech and Slovak Federal Republic, observed that more than identity was suppressed. He wrote of the "deformation of personality" after forty years of socialism, observing that the socialist masters systematically extinguished initiative and, in emphasizing the primacy of state authority, created a climate that socialized a passive, dependent people who expected the state to take care of them. With a marked atrophy of individual responsibility, the populace blamed the omnipresent authority for society's shortcomings. With the disappearance of that authority, the populace floundered. The long-sought freedom was frightening, as it required individual identity and responsibility. The resentful, dependent populace had to find a target to blame.[53]

The readiness to externalize blame is another social-psychological consequence of forty years of Communist rule, for one of the legacies of Communism was societal paranoia.[54] The massive security organizations throughout the Communist bloc led to pervasive fear and distrust and an erosion of communality. The inability to trust friends and even family had led to deep scars and an atrophy of mutuality and sharing.

What happens when that all-powerful authority disappears, when the caretaking enemy is gone? As Communist governments were overthrown, leaving social and economic chaos in their wake, it was at last safe to express the long pent-up anger at the Communist leaders. For many, "Communist equals Jew" was an equation in the collective psychology.[55] Anger and blame went to the departing enemy. But new enemies must be found as well, and so old enmities were revived. A Czech journalist asserted, "The politics of Slovakia is looking for an enemy—everybody who is different."[56]

In the Czech lands of Bohemia and Moravia some anti-Semitism exists, but the most intense feelings are directed at Gypsies. Indeed, it has been suggested that the resentment of the large Gypsy population has defused feelings that otherwise might have targeted Jews. The Gypsies have been the object of brutal attacks by young toughs, but the attitudes of ethnocentric resentment are maintained by Czech intelligentsia as well. A Czech diplomat, shaking his head in disgust, stated: "They are responsible for most of the crime. They are lazy, and shiftless, and don't hold regular jobs. And they have all of these children. It makes me angry that there are these special welfare programs for them, when the money should be going to the hard working people of this country."[57] (These feelings also bear a remarkable similarity to the anti-black stereotypes exploited by David Duke in economically distressed Louisiana.)

Similar feelings were voiced in Hungary. When the main opposition party in Hungary called attention to the plight of the Gypsies, it was characterized as the party of the Gypsies and the Jews in leading newspapers and demonstrably lost votes at the polls because of its stand.

The intensity of nationalistic passions and associated violence has several roots. After decades of suppression under socialist rule, these expressions of nationalism represent an exaggerated search for identity, which at heart depends upon difference. At the same time, the forty years of socialist rule did indeed lead to "a deformation of personality," including societal paranoia, the atrophy of personal responsibility and initiative, and an expectation of being cared for, however badly, by the autocratic leadership. With the disappearance of that leadership, the populace floundered. The long-sought freedom was frightening, as it emphasized qualities long suppressed: individual identity and responsibility.

The revival of hostility among existing groups with a history of conflict is not surprising. Nor, given the long-standing history of anti-Semitism in these nations, would it be surprising to see the revival of anti-Semitism in post-Communist Eastern Europe, *if there were Jews there*. The fact that anti-Semitism has been revived so powerfully in the virtual absence of Jews demonstrates the power of the paranoid dynamic and the associated need for enemies. When the real enemy disappears, the need for enemies becomes intensified; in the absence of real enemies, substitutes will be created.

When the powerful disappear, someone must be found to blame for the chaos left behind. The accustomed externalization of authority lends itself in this climate to blaming outside enemies—Slovakians blaming the arrogant leadership in Prague or Poles blaming the nonexistent Jewish population.[58] The political and economic instability in Eastern and Central Europe in the wake of the loss of the Communist enemy is ripe territory for the paranoid dynamic. Here as elsewhere, demagogues have provided meaning for distressed populations by identifying new enemies and reviving old enmities.

# 5

## From the Individual to the Collective Apocalypse

The individual whose world is falling apart is experiencing his own psychological apocalypse. From this state of ultimate powerlessness and meaninglessness, some create a world of meaning in their mind, a new world in which they have power and significance. Through this vision they have found personal redemption.

Groups, too, can experience overwhelming stress and undergo collective apocalyptic thinking—an event that creates a psychological predisposition for group paranoia. Collective apocalyptic thinking is associated with two major historical circumstances: the oppressive occupation of one people by another, with the apocalyptic vision bringing hope to the oppressed; and periods of social decay, with the apocalyptic vision as an antidote to immoral and irreligious behavior.[1] Each set of circumstances can produce a compensatory vision—hope out of despair. Just as the paranoid delusion is sense-making and restitutive for the individual on the verge of psychological disintegration, so collective apocalyptic vision and ultimate redemption are sense-making and restitutive for social groups facing disintegration.

Whereas apocalyptic thinking can provide false re-

lief at times of social disintegration, apocalyptic thinking itself can produce social disintegration. For the most part, members of apocalyptic
movements, infused with renewed hope, await the day of redemption.
Members of such movements are often spurred to action by charismatic
leaders in order to correct the grievous flaws in society. When these
powerful forces are mobilized, profound social disorder can result.[2]

The relation between the twin delusions of apocalypticism and mil-
lennarianism is an intimate one. The apocalyptic refers to what will happen at the end of history: typically such disasters as war, famine, and
flood. This time of struggle and misery ushers in the millennium, a period
of perfect and perpetual peace in which all is resolved. The apocalyptic
period demands struggle and may require—in the service of the millennium to come—acts that would otherwise be forbidden. Mass murders
and lifelong imprisonments, for example, were perpetrated by Bolsheviks, midwifing, they believed, the dawning of a Communist millennium,
and similar acts were perpetrated by Nazis in their attempts to create a
Thousand-Year Reich (see Chapters 10 and 11). During times like these,
distressed populations may also turn to a charismatic religious leader.
Some people, on the verge of psychological collapse, find comfort and
meaning in a highly structured religious belief system. When one is on
the edge of meaninglessness, immense relief and a sense of purpose can
come from the belief that God loves one.

At times of social and political distress, a troubled individual, struggling to make meaning of his own life, may enlist followers to fulfill his
redemptive vision and create an apocalyptic or millennarian social system. If such an individual is a paranoid with a messianic delusion, possesses leadership abilities, and can identify himself with a vulnerable
population, the ingredients are present for a charismatic apocalyptic religious cult. His delusion is sense-making not only for him but also for
other wounded individuals whose world is falling apart. He is a collective
diagnostician. Initially alone against the paranoid pseudocommunity, now
the paranoid with religious delusions has followers. Moreover, his followers confirm the truth of his inspired religious convictions. For the
followers, such an inspired leader has provided a diagnosis of the ills
afflicting the world and has given them a special role to play. He has
made sense for them of the surrounding chaos. Their impression of the

outside danger has been confirmed, but they are no longer alone in facing the enemy. Rather, they are united with their fellow true believers under the banner of a gifted leader. In this closed cult, he and his followers are in a shuttered system, in which each reinforces the beliefs of the others. This was the case with Jim Jones, who committed suicide with more than nine hundred of his followers at the People's Temple in Guyana in 1978.

## The Jonestown Mass Suicide

On November 18, 1978, a group of 912 persons willingly ingested a cyanide-laced soft drink at the direction of their leader, Jim Jones. These voluntary victims had already fled to the jungles of the Caribbean nation of Guyana on the northeast coast of South America. They were told by Jones, who joined them in death, that their suicides and their children's deaths were the only escape from imminent persecution by the outside world. These people were not insane people. Most of the surviving members showed no signs of psychopathology, according to H. R. S. Sukhdeo, chief of psychiatry at the New Jersey Medical School, who worked with them on their return to the United States.[3]

What was the basis of the powerful grasp Jones held over his followers—so powerful that he could lead individuals who were not seriously psychologically disturbed to their deaths? What caused them willingly to yield control over their lives to their leader? What was the nature of the social system they created in the jungles of Guyana?

The political personality of Jim Jones had three major elements: narcissism, the ability to work well within a conventional political environment, and a paranoid leadership style. Jones could not have had a better start on the road to becoming a charismatic narcissistic leader. His mother recounts that she married for one reason: to produce a savior.[4] She always believed that young Jim was that savior.

In contrast to the powerful presence of his mother, his father was a weak and passive figure who returned from World War I crippled by mustard gas, so that Jim's mother was obliged to support the family. In one of his evening lectures to his flock, Jones delivered a self-pitying diatribe describing the loneliness of his early years and the anger that consumed him. Note how Jones's theme, tone, and language are used to connect with the experience and feelings of his largely rejected and poor followers: "I was ready to kill by the end of the third grade. I mean, I was so fucking aggressive and hostile. I was ready to kill. Nobody gave me any love, any understanding. In those Indiana days, a parent was supposed to go with a child to school functions . . . There was some kind of school performance, and everybody's fucking parent was there but mine. I'm standing there alone. Alone, I was always alone!"[5]

It is not surprising that Jones sought another father figure, the successful and flamboyant black minister Father Divine.[6] When Father Divine died in 1965, Jones indicated that Father Divine—"like Jesus Christ and Lenin—had entered my soul."[7] Thus young Jim emerged from his early years wounded but sharing his mother's messianic aspirations.

Despite his fundamentalist upbringing, as a young man Jones had turned against religion. It was only in 1952—when, by chance, the newly married twenty-one-year-old looked at a Methodist church bulletin board and read that Methodists "stood for the rights of racial groups"—that he was drawn back into religion.[8] Within months Jones had entered the ministry as a student pastor at the Somerset Methodist Church in Indianapolis. Although his congregation was poor white, Jones began to spend more and more time at nearby black churches. He invited blacks to his home and, to the distress of many of his parishioners, to his services.

Jones became increasingly drawn to Pentecostalism. Its emotional style and the charismatic role of its preachers suited him better than Methodism. Soon he was preaching at Pentecostal meetings and, unusual for a Methodist, was performing "miracles" of healing. By 1956 he had developed his own social creed, which combined the self-discipline of Methodism, the emotional and charismatic appeal of Pentecostalism, and a strong practice of racial integration.

Jones sought out the disadvantaged, the needy, the marginally psychotic, the confused, and the rejected. These vulnerable individuals tended to have poor interpersonal attachments, and so they easily bonded to the magnetic Jones and the quasi-religious institutions he created around himself. They were poor people, many of them former drug addicts, and almost always with few personal ties. Some had suffered at society's hands—from racial discrimination or from being born poor. All had suffered within society, sometimes simply from bad luck, or a bad marriage, or a personality that made it difficult for them to cope. They found in Jones a promise of strength and redemption. For Jones, the trip from the abyss of loneliness and abandonment to the center of a group of loving, adoring followers was profoundly rewarding.

Adequate though not extravagant funding for Jones's largely unexceptional uplift projects came from liberal politicians and institutions. Before long, he had acquired a reputation as an effective Christian activist clergyman and received the various minor honors and offices associated with that status. In 1960 he began his public career as head of the Indianapolis Human Rights Commission. Years later he was appointed to the more powerful position of chair of the San Francisco Housing Authority. An interfaith organization, Religion in American Life, included him in its list of America's One Hundred Most Outstanding Clergymen, the *Los Angeles Herald* named him Humanitarian of the Year, and he even received the Martin Luther King, Jr., Humanitarian Award.[9] Clearly, Jim Jones was an effective local political activist operating largely within the mainstream of liberal politics. He raised money, acquired prestige, and generated a following.

During this period, however, Jones was becoming more and more consumed with private fears and fantasies. He was extraordinarily suspicious of his co-workers, and fearing betrayal and danger, he hired bodyguards. Jones also became obsessed with nuclear war. In 1960 or 1961 he had a vision of a nuclear explosion. In January 1962 he read an article in *Esquire* magazine listing the safest places to be in a nuclear war.[10] He temporarily moved to Brazil and often panicked when the topic of nuclear war was raised. At times he would cry when he heard an airplane. These psychological problems were complicated by his increasing addiction to drugs.

Private neurosis, political skills, a distressed and receptive audience, and a geographical "home" all came together. Jones announced that he would form a self-help and therapeutic community that would settle in some place distant from the threat of nuclear war. His flock would escape the destruction of this war, and in the post-nuclear-war period the "ideals of the People's Temple would replace corrupt, racist, oppressive societies that were doomed to destroy themselves."[11] (By this time Marxist rhetoric was becoming increasingly prominent in his explanations.) The government of the Caribbean nation of Guyana agreed to permit him and his group to settle in an isolated area of the country.

With about a hundred followers, Jones established a community in the Guyanan jungle. Marital and other family bonds were discouraged, and sexual promiscuity was encouraged. He particularly humiliated his male parishioners by the flagrant seduction of their wives and humiliated many of the women by the requirement—both unstated and stated—that they make themselves sexually available to him. As in all would-be totalitarian systems, family unity was a threat, and by forced humiliation and degradation Jones secured his control. Jones obtained detailed information on the members by an internal espionage system. While followers were at services, for example, members of the inner circle would break into their houses, read their mail, go through their garbage, and examine their medicine cabinets.[12] Most important, communication with the outside world was strictly controlled. To a large degree it was prohibited. Jones spoke frequently of the danger to the community from armed mercenaries. It is not clear whether he believed that this danger existed or only said so to intimidate his followers.

In this closed society,[13] isolated from the outside world, Jones held forth each night with an idiosyncratic religious service in which his own grandeur was exalted while his followers were humiliated.[14] His "sermons," more like tirades, were recorded and portray the thrall in which he held his followers: "You are stupid piss-ants and reptiles, who are lower than the primates, you make whoopee if you want, but your whoopee makes me sicky . . . Peace, peace . . . You make your whoopee, while I do something that's far more significant, because I know exactly what's going to take place. I've made some big plans, honey . . . You fuckers, I like to look at you now, because you don't know how clever I am. I made plans for your treason long ago, because I knew I couldn't trust nothing, only Communism, and the principle that is in me—that is me!"[15] In these nightly sermons, Jones often referred to the threats represented by armed mercenaries and CIA "fascists." This had the effect of intimidating his followers and drawing them closer to him. They probably also reflected Jones's paranoid siege mentality.

The political problems the jungle state confronted were, however, real. Like the leaders of other fighting millennarian cults before him, Jones faced diminishing conversions, resentment against the suffocation of individuality, and the danger of increasing penetration by outside ideas. Other leaders might have tried to reverse this erosion by aggression against the outside, by trying to provoke the world and so find converts in new battles. But Jones had already determined that the outside world would not fall to his appeal.[16] During this period, Jones's drug use intensified, including barbiturates and amphetamines.[17] Jones's doctor had diagnosed him as suffering from coccidioidomycosis (a fungal infection), and it may be that he had acquired coccidioidal meningitis, which would have led to confused and irrational behavior.[18] Whatever the reason, Jones became increasingly psychotic.

A few members managed to escape, so word of the practices at Jonestown spread. It may be that some of the accusations were exaggerated by the former members or became exaggerated when repeated by others. The families of some of the members of the Jonestown community expressed fears that individuals there were being held prisoner. A U.S. congressman, Leo Ryan of San Francisco, decided to make a visit. He was not hostile but was seen by some of the community's members as being so. When Ryan and six disaffected cult members prepared to leave Guyana, they were wounded in the airport by Jones loyalists.

The self-fulfilling dynamic of paranoia was now under way—a genuine community of antagonists had been created out of the paranoid's own fantasies. Now there would be a massive and hostile investigation. Before Ryan's murder, Jones had staged several "loyalty exercises," in which members, including children, were brought together and told that because they were in danger of attack they were to commit suicide by swallowing a poisoned soft drink. Soon after Congressman Ryan's assassination, the community was assembled for one of these tests. This time there was cyanide in the drink. Nearly all the community—912 members, including Jones—died. Some of them may have been coerced, but most apparently willingly "passed the test."

The relationship between Jones and his followers was a complex one.[19] What particularly interests us is how Jones was able to manipulate the fears of others (which sprang from their inability to function in society) and to persuade them to follow him, follow his degrading directives, and even follow his example into death. Jones accomplished this gruesome feat by employing a variety of techniques within an environment in which he had total control:

> *Control of property and income.* On joining the People's Temple, Jones's followers had to turn over their social security checks and personal property to Jones, who then fully supported them. Thus there was an enforced dependency.
>
> *Weakening of family ties.* Jones systematically weakened ties between husbands and wives. He encouraged extramarital affairs. All followers were to call him Dad. He was to be the most important love object.
>
> A *sociopolitical caste system.* In Jonestown there was a power pyramid with Jones at the top, then a "planning commission" and guards, then the common people. All power was in the hands of unconditionally loyal followers.
>
> *Control of mobility.* Not only was it geographically difficult to leave Jonestown, but Jones made trying to leave equivalent to treason and subject to severe punishment.
>
> *Control of verbal expression.* Overt criticism was harshly punished, and a network of spies and informers reported expression of dissent to Jones.
>
> *Cognitive control.* No information from the outside was allowed. There was constant indoctrination, the equivalent of brainwashing.
>
> *Emotional control.* Meetings at Jonestown were frightening experiences reflecting the power of mass emotional contagion. The intensity of these meetings was enhanced by the public punishment of dissenters. Members of the audience were encouraged to boo and hiss the victims, and to identify with the aggressor. These events of public humiliation (much like the "vomit hatred" sessions of the Chinese Cultural Revolution) were instances of group regression that led to an acceptance of Jones's delusional system. Jones's techniques of political control were

an expression of both his paranoid personality and his grandiosity.[20]

Part of the reason that otherwise sensible people will follow a paranoid leader is that the leader is able to relate his personal obsessional paranoid objects to those of his followers. A leader who has a pathological fear of external control may find weak and vulnerable followers who have in fact suffered at the hands of others and who share a similar deep-rooted psychological fear. Such was the case with Jim Jones. Jonestown was remarkable because it combined so many aspects of paranoid dynamics. At its base, however, it depended on an obsessive and pathological fear of strangers. Ultimately, Jones led 912 followers to commit mass suicide rather than yield to the threatening world that surrounded them.

The fusion of paranoid dynamics and passive but militant withdrawal from the world was also characteristic of David Koresh, the messianic leader of the Branch Davidian religious cult. The siege and storming of the Branch Davidian compound, Ranch Apocalypse, by the Federal Bureau of Investigation on April 19, 1993, led to the death of seventy-five Branch Davidians, including David Koresh and twenty-five children, confirming Koresh's apocalyptic prophecies. A government investigation determined that some of the victims had been shot through the head and the fire that ravaged the corpses had been lit by the Branch Davidians.

## David Koresh: The Messiah of Ranch Apocalypse

David Koresh's early years were marked by instability and abuse.[21] A ninth-grade dropout, Koresh began life as Vernon Howell, the son of Bonnie Clark, a high school dropout who gave birth to him when she was an unmarried fourteen-year-old. Shortly after the birth, Bonnie married a hard-driving "macho man," recently released from prison, who was physically abusive both to her and to her son. After eighteen months, Bonnie left her husband and sought help from her mother, who took her grandson into her Houston home and shortly had two more children of her own. Vernon and his two younger uncles were essentially raised as siblings; Vernon called his grandmother Momma.

Bonnie eventually divorced her abusive husband, remarried, and reclaimed Vernon. She took him from her mother's home in Houston to live with her and her husband in Dallas. Vernon's new stepfather was a strict physical disciplinarian. The adult Vernon recalled, "When I got a bad report card . . . [I got my] tail whomped." He later spoke of the physical abuse he endured, showing burn scars that he said were the result of being forced to kneel on a heat register.

School was difficult for Vernon, and he was soon diagnosed as suffering from dyslexia, a severe learning disability. Held back to complete first grade twice, he was put in a special class for learning-disabled children in the third grade. At age fourteen, he was again sent to live with his grandmother, where he made a small shed in the backyard into a private retreat. There he taught himself to play the guitar, and his ambitions to become a rock star took form.

His grandparents were practicing Seventh-Day Adventists, and these years were steeped in religious study and strict adherence to biblical prohibitions against smoking, drinking, and fornication. School continued to be difficult for Vernon, but he became fascinated both with Bible study and with radio preachers during these years.

Howell dropped out of public school and briefly attended a church-run academy, reportedly leaving after a dispute with a teacher. Difficulties with his grandparents led him to be returned to his mother. He had serious problems with her and her husband, however, and was once more returned to his grandparents.

Thus Koresh's formative years were marked by rejection by parents, grandparents, and school authorities. In addition to this general instability, Vernon suffered the lack of any secure model of male authority. Neither father, stepfather, grandfather, nor teachers accepted him. Howell's underlying self-concept must have been deeply wounded.

At age eighteen, Vernon was doing construction work while honing his skills on the electric guitar. A local businessman, the proprietor of the Lone Star Music and Sound Company, described him as an odd mix of religious zealot and would-be rock star: "He was a frustrated musician who wanted to be a rock star, gave up on that dream, and then wanted to be Jesus Christ." Demonstrating even then the charismatic appeal that would later become so striking, he was idolized by young teenagers. He formed a band and wrote his own lyrics, many of which had a satanic flavor, such as "Mad Man from Waco":

There's a mad man living in Waco
Pray to the Prince of Hell
Please, please, please won't you listen?
It's not what it appears to be
We didn't want to hurt anybody
Just set our people free.[22]

Howell was very active sexually. After a teenage girl he was seeing became pregnant and her father refused to let Howell marry her, he began attending a Seventh-Day Adventist church. Seeking atonement for the guilt he felt over his preoccupying sexual thoughts, he prayed a great deal and lost considerable weight.

Howell's intense involvement in the church marked a major turning point. Coming from a background characterized by instability and lack of meaning, he found stability and meaning in the church. It provided the home he had never had, and his evident seriousness attracted attention. From a life marked by failure, he now began to find success. He absorbed the strict prohibitions of the Adventists and soon became an outspoken and moralistic judge of the behavior of others. He was especially critical of sexual matters, for example, telling a father that his daughter was dressed immodestly.

This strict, highly structured adherence to religion was beginning to play a positive and central organizing role for Howell. Then, however, he was exposed to a fire-and-brimstone evangelist, Jim Gilley. Gilley, conducting Revelation Seminars, prophesied an imminent Armageddon, using a video construction of the Apocalypse as foretold in the Book of Revelation, which depicted earthquakes, plagues, and religious persecutions.[23]

Howell attended the seminars each night and was mesmerized. He told his sister that what was missing for the next great prophet was the Seventh Seal. (In the Book of Revelation, a scroll held by God predicting the calamities that will precede the Apocalypse is bound by seven seals. The Seventh Seal could be opened only by a new prophet.) Howell told his "sister," his younger aunt Sharon, that he was quite possibly the person who could unlock the secret of the Seventh Seal. He came to believe that he was destined to be ''a new prophet and a new light'' in the Seventh-Day Adventist Church.[24]

Howell had shifted his own apocalyptic drama to the universal stage. Howell, in a development reminiscent of Daniel Paul Schreber's transition from the edge of psychological annihilation to the role of divinity, became a messenger of God; from being without a psychological center, he became intensely centered on God and his own mission.

Howell, however, was unable to persuade the church leadership of his divine role. His hectoring dogmatism had already offended many, and his prophetic pretensions were the final straw. He was ''disfellowshipped'' from the Tyler, Texas, congregation in April 1983.

Howell, rejected by this relatively conventional congregation, now found his way to the Branch Davidians. This group was an offshoot of Adventism and had been formed sixty years earlier by Victor Houteff. Houteff called his new church the Davidian branch of Seventh-Day Adventists. Thus the doctrine of the Branch Davidians has as a central element a prophet in their midst, a doctrine suited perfectly to the now divinely inspired Howell.

Houteff had attracted a large following with his prophetic preaching. They gave up their property to join him at his communal farm, which he called Mount Carmel, in Waco, Texas. After Houteff's death, his widow led the group. She predicted that the Kingdom of God would arrive on Easter of 1959. Davidian Adventists across the country sold their possessions and came to Waco to await the end of the world. When Easter came and went, disillusioned followers eventually straggled away. This event, which came to be known as the Great Disappointment, almost led to the dissolution of what had been a thriving movement. Only fifty true believers kept the faith. This group suffered further disorganization until a member named Ben Roden declared himself the leader of a new assembly, which he designated the Branch Davidians.

Roden's widow, Lois, assumed the leadership upon her husband's death. She, however, was a heterodox among heterodoxes; she offended many members by declaring that the Holy Spirit was feminine. Between her feminist doctrines and her advancing age (sixty-seven), she was unable to exercise clear leadership. Thus, the arrival of the twenty-three-year-old Howell seemed divinely inspired. Howell endeared himself to Lois Roden literally—they became lovers and even tried to have a child together.[25]

Howell began to attend Branch Davidian revival meetings, where he aggressively preached, annoying the anti-Lois meeting organizers, who had police ask him to leave. In these fervent sermons, he strongly emphasized religious freedom, the right to bear arms, and the right to be free of government interference.

In November 1987, a bizarre incident consolidated Howell's leadership of the Branch Davidians. Lois Roden's son George, an emotionally unstable man, hoped to succeed his mother as leader of the Branch Davidian cult. Lois, however, designated Howell as her successor. When she died in 1986, a succession struggle ensued. The resentful George Roden announced a test of religious authenticity to determine who was divinely inspired and hence the rightful heir to the leadership throne. He disinterred the corpse of a former cult member, an eighty-five-year-old woman, and declared that whoever could bring her corpse back to life should be the new cult leader.

Howell called the local prosecutor, charging that Roden should be arrested for corpse abuse. With seven armed supporters, he infiltrated the religion's home base, the Mount Carmel compound, to photograph the corpse. Roden met them with a semiautomatic rifle, and a shoot-out ensued in which Roden was slightly wounded. Howell was tried for attempted murder. At the trial, he demonstrated such mastery that the occasion became a turning point in his leadership. When no witnesses would stand in response to the judge's request that they do so, Howell, with almost saintly calm, reportedly told them, "It's all right. You've done nothing wrong. Stand." They did. Howell's confederates were acquitted, and his charges led to a hung jury.[26]

After the trial, the sheriff's truck was observed being loaded with weapons, which previously had been seized from the compound and now were to be returned to the Branch Davidians. This moment of singular symbolic triumph ensured Howell's leadership. A former cult member recalls the collective interpretation of that dramatic moment: "You don't have to stretch your imagination to appreciate how his followers must have interpreted that. He had won the verdict, the weapons and the compound. In his mind, and in those of his people, he must have felt that he was guided by the hand of God.''[27]

From uncertainty to total command, from dyslexic difficulties with written words to total mastery of the Word—this was the road Howell had traveled. Howell, now twenty-eight, took command of the Waco section of the Branch Davidians. He systematically transformed the grounds into an armed compound, acquired a large arsenal, and began to train his followers in military tactics to prepare them for the coming Apocalypse. In 1990 Howell legally changed his name to David Koresh (*Koresh* is Hebrew for Cyrus, the Persian king who allowed the Jews to return to Palestine).

Koresh's divine role was by now established in his own mind, and he conveyed this powerfully to his followers. His oratory was of almost hypnotic quality, according to former followers, and he was highly successful in proselytizing for the Branch Davidians. He traveled widely in pursuit of recruits and was especially successful in Australia, Israel, Great Britain, and Jamaica. His message was especially appealing to individuals who had lost their moorings, who were searching for meaning, whose personal worlds were crumbling. David Koresh, on the verge of individual apocalypse, had translated his own psychological state into a unique religious doctrine.

To others like himself, whose world had been shattered, he offered a shared vision: ''These feelings you have, which you thought reflected personal weakness, reflect a transcendent reality. So you are not alone. And I who am divinely inspired possess knowledge of that awful reality, and I have the keys to paradise.'' No longer alone, the weak and dispossessed found a message of ultimate hope and redemption in the prophetic words of Koresh, and they followed him to Mount Carmel.

According to his vision, he was the seventh and final angel, destined to be the agent of God who brings about the end of the world. He preached that the triggering event would occur in Texas at the Mount Carmel compound in Waco, and he urged his followers to prepare themselves for this final battle of the forces of good against the forces of evil. As a consequence of this battle, in which the world would be consumed and purified in flames to receive Christ, the messiah, David Koresh, would return as Christ, and those who believed in him would find paradise in the New Jerusalem.

Koresh had originally preached that the end would come when he moved to Israel and began converting the Jews. The conversion, he claimed, would cause worldwide upheaval, would start a war, and would cause American armed forces to invade the Holy Land. That would signal the beginning of Armageddon. Then he would be transformed into a warrior angel who would cleanse the earth in preparation for the New Jerusalem.[28] He did move to Israel in the late 1980s, but when his prediction was not fulfilled, he returned to the compound at Mount Carmel and began prophesying that the end would come not in Israel but in Texas. The American army would attack the group, precipitating a fiery confrontation and the end of the world.

Using a unique interpretation of Scripture to justify his leadership actions, Koresh systematically developed a closed and controlled social system that required total devotion to his divine personage and enshrined himself as "the chosen one," while totally subordinating the followers to his whims. Prolonged Bible study sessions—as long as fifteen hours—were hypnotic in their effect upon his followers. By 1987, Koresh was living in what detectives described as a harem of young girls, some as young as twelve. They believed he was Jesus Christ, and he had persuaded them of their duty to serve him sexually, indicating that it was his divine right "to plant his seed" in order to "fill the house of David."[29] Later he was to order the men in the group to practice celibacy and require that they offer up their wives and daughters to him. Parents gladly sent to him their daughters and husbands, their wives, honored that they had been chosen. A dozen women proudly proclaimed that they belonged to Koresh. The young teenagers and pre-teens he chose wore Star of David pendants as signs they belonged to David Koresh. It is estimated he fathered as many as seventeen children, most of whom perished with him. He justified this sexual entitlement on the basis of the Forty-fifth Psalm, in which it is written that the king is anointed with the "oil of gladness." Koresh interpreted the "oil of gladness" as vaginal secretions and that it was his penis that was to be anointed.

Guilt-ridden over his sexual drives as an adolescent, the divinely inspired Koresh had reinterpreted Scripture not only to justify but to sanctify his sexual proclivities. In this he followed the practice established by the Mormon leader Joseph Smith, who indulged his sexual appetites and those of his close colleagues, enshrining polygamy as religiously sanctified. The manner in which Koresh became the sexual hub of the Branch Davidian compound is also reminiscent of Jim Jones's requirement that husbands watch as he had sex with their wives, and that wives watch as he had relations with their husbands. As in all would-be totalitarian systems, family unity was a threat, and by this forced humiliation and degradation, Koresh, like Jones, ensured his control.

It is striking that Koresh was able to persuade his followers to embrace this sexually licentious lifestyle as required by a reformulated morality, and a very harsh morality at that. What were the psychological dynamics underlying the willingness of his followers to degrade themselves?

First, a great principle is often invoked to violate long-standing morality. A person's commitment to the ideal is proved by his willingness to do things that he would otherwise despise. Jones's followers accepted his claim that he was divinely inspired, that his words were God's, and they could therefore see themselves as fulfilling a divine mandate, not degrading themselves. Koresh indicated that God had told him to build a new House of David by having many wives and spreading his seed, as King David had done.

Second, individuals often rationalize their desires, excusing what they want to do by their alleged dedication to some principle. At least some of Koresh's followers were rationalizing their desires, excusing their promiscuous actions as proofs of their dedication to God's word.

Finally, like many narcissistic leaders, Koresh made an exception of himself and wrapped this exception in theological justification.

As he gathered his flock to him, Koresh preached constantly about the approaching end of the world and the need to protect themselves against the coming attack.[30] And so it was when the Bureau of Alcohol, Tobacco, and Firearms attacked the compound, it seemed to be the fulfillment of Koresh's prophecy. During the fifty-one-day siege that followed, the FBI and the Bureau of Alcohol, Tobacco, and Firearms profoundly misread the nature of the social system within the compound and the nature of Koresh's personality. They defined the circumstance as a hostage-and-barricade situation, and hostage-rescue doctrine indicates a two-track strategy: negotiating while increasing pressure. They applied pressure through what they termed "psychological operations," an array of tactics including continuous high-intensity sound bombardment. They misdiagnosed Koresh as a psychopath, a con man.

Koresh's followers, however, were by no means hostages; they were committed followers of the charismatic leader of a closed apocalyptic religious cult. In addition to being manipulative and sociopathic, Koresh was paranoid, grandiose, and delusional, moving in and out of reality—traits consistent with the psychiatric diagnosis of a "borderline disorder." Individuals with this diagnosis can function quite normally but when under pressure can slip into psychosis. When such an individual is hanging from the edge of the cliff of sanity, you do not subject his hands to merciless pounding with a high-frequency drill. That was the equivalent of the FBI's unremitting pressure on David Koresh and his followers. Moreover, the government and media's focus on Koresh, the failed rock star who longed for prominence, must have rewarded his grandiose narcissism. He was the center of America's attention.

This pressure pushed Koresh over the edge, into the grandiose paranoid world he had constructed with his true believers. He entered a psychotic realm in which he was the biblical Cyrus who delivered the message of the Seven Seals of Revelation. Consumed with the apocalyptic prophecy, Koresh believed and communicated to his followers that there would be a fiery confrontation between the forces of good and the forces of the devil and that death in the struggle would bring entry into paradise.

While a core of true believers supported Koresh during the standoff, many had doubts about his leadership, and a number of them defected. But if individuals had any doubt about the "truth" Koresh was conveying to them, the spectacle of armor-plated vehicles and the experience of sound bombardment during the FBI's campaign of psychological warfare were not designed to magnify those doubts. To the contrary, they seemed to confirm Koresh's apocalyptic visions: in prophesying the final battle, Koresh quoted from the Book of Revelation, which speaks of dragons and the sound of trumpets. When the armor-plated vehicles began to punch holes in the compound and pump in tear gas, one did not have to be a paranoid psychotic to disbelieve the government's message, trans-

mitted via bullhorns, that this was *not* an attack. For the Branch Davidians, the nature of the government's actions confirmed their belief that
this was the prophesied final battle. Along with Koresh, seventy-five died
in the fire that consumed Ranch Apocalypse. Like many paranoid movements, this messianic paranoid leader and his followers interacted with
the surrounding environment in a tragically self-fulfilling prophecy, producing the very reactions they both feared and anticipated.

The People's Temple and the Branch Davidians came to violent ends,
but in fact both groups were passive millennarians, withdrawing in despair from the world. As the outside world approached, Jones led his
followers in a collective suicide; Koresh prepared his for the final battle.
The irony of the apocalyptic and millennarian appeal of the charismatic
leader is that he can fulfill only one promise—not the millennium but the
apocalypse.

But not all followers of new religions are passive, withdrawing in
despair from the secular world. The Aum Supreme Truth, led by the guru
Shoko Asahara, sought to precipitate the apocalypse. The poison gas attack in the Tokyo subway on March 20, 1995, which killed 12 people
and injured 5,500, was the beginning of what was to be a widespread
campaign whose goal was to precipitate World War III.

## Shoko Asahara and Aum Supreme Truth

Before the 1995 nerve gas attack, Asahara had long predicted a world
war in which the United States would take over Japan. In a 1988 speech
entitled "Prediction and Salvation," Asahara foretold a nuclear war near
the turn of the twenty-first century, a war that could be avoided only by
following Asahara's teachings as spread through branches in different
countries.[31] The source of his knowledge was, he claimed, "my astral
vision, intuitive wisdom, and my knowledge inferred through Jnana
Yoga."[32]

In 1994 Asahara made the delusional claim that U.S. jets were delivering gas attacks on his followers, a projection of his own paranoid
psychology. Asahara became increasingly preoccupied not with surviving
the coming war but with starting it. Twelve days before the Tokyo subway attack, the Aum leadership sent its members a written "last warn-

ing'' stating that they faced death by biological weapons and set up an emergency meeting at the cult's Aoyama training grounds.[33]

Somewhat contradictorily, Asahara had in another place assured his followers that even nuclear war would not be a problem for his true believers because an emancipated person may be born into this world again with a new physical body. He emphasized, however, the need to protect the world so that a place exists for reincarnation.[34]

The gas attack was to be the opening move of an elaborate plan to start World War III. On May 5, 1995, bags of chemicals were found burning in Tokyo's Shinjuku station. Police said that, had the chemicals been properly ignited, they could have killed twenty thousand people. The major action was scheduled for November, when the cult's plan called for attacks on government buildings, the Diet, and the Imperial Palace.[35] Raids on the Aum complex in the aftermath of the gas attack revealed the magnitude of the planned destruction. There were weapon stockpiles, "truckloads of chemicals that could be used to make, detect and treat Sarin," a Russian helicopter, and millions of dollars in cash and gold.[36] The cult had constructed a series of munitions factories, and microbiologists recruited by Asahara were attempting to develop biological weapons, including the Ebola virus. Behind a false wall at Aum headquarters, a seven-hundred-thousand-dollar research laboratory was discovered, capable of producing enough of the poison gas sarin to kill 6–8 million people a month. The entrance to the laboratory was concealed behind a giant relief of Siva, the Hindu god of creation and destruction venerated by Aum. One of the plans detailed in documents called for releasing sarin over Tokyo from 512-foot-long remote-controlled helicopters. Also included in the laboratory was an industry-scale microwave oven reportedly to be used to reduce the bodies of victims to dust.[37]

The goal of Asahara's plan was defeat of the Japanese Self-Defense Forces (Japan's military) and Asahara's takeover of the country. In his 1988 speeches Asahara had warned of the growing police power. He predicted a crushing defeat of Japan's Liberal Democratic Party in the next general elections, followed by a focus by the mass media on three worldly pleasures: appetite, sexual desire, and sports. This would result in disorder followed by increased police power, so that the "Japanese people may be controlled to have uniform thoughts."[38]

In protecting against the feared police control, Asahara had systematically penetrated the Self-Defense Forces: the names of more than twenty serving and former members of the Self-Defense Forces were found on Aum's membership lists. Police investigators concluded that the SDF members were part of a special commando unit trained in the use of tanks, helicopters, and chemical weapons, including sarin. The investigation revealed that a "shadow cabinet" had been formed by Asahara to rule after the coup, with its members as ministers.[39] Although the shadow government has been described as being modeled after the Japanese government, with such ministries as Finance, Education, and Construction, some of the ministries and their designated leaders resembled more a nation at war or a paramilitary command and appeared to be Aum's power and enforcement arm. The Health and Welfare Ministry, headed by a genetic engineer, was apparently responsible for germ warfare research. The Science and Technology Ministry, headed by an astrophysicist, contained the chemical arms unit, which was apparently responsible for the development of chemical weapons.[40] The head of the Chemical Squad acknowledged that he oversaw the manufacture of sarin nerve gas. Clandestine Activities, which was headed by the number-two leader of Aum, procured and manufactured weapons and procured military hardware. The Action Squad, an important organization within that unit, was Aum's enforcement arm and was allegedly behind the abductions and killings of defecting sect members and opponents of the sect. Its director, Kiyohide Nakada, was formerly a member of the Yakuza (the Japanese mob).[41] This squad was believed to have engineered the March 30, 1995, assassination attempt on the head of the National Police Agency, who was responsible for coordinating the raid on Aum facilities and the arrest of Asahara.

To the astonishment of Japanese society, a high percentage of Aum's members came to the cult from prestigious universities, with advanced degrees in such scientific specialties as physics, chemistry, microbiology, and nuclear engineering. It is not uncommon for scientists, especially those among the first generation of their families to receive a higher education, to be attracted to extremist politico-religious movements. The cult also numbered members of Japan's ruling establishment in its ranks.

"Venerated Master" Shoko Asahara had founded the Aum Shinriko movement in 1987. According to the cult's mythic history, Asahara started the cult after reaching the state of nirvana in the Himalayas. He claimed to possess six mystic powers that he had acquired in Tibet after long, punishing training. One of his powers supposedly enabled him to levitate, to transform himself into any form, and to move objects and change their forms without touching them. Asahara's supernatural abilities were often advertised in Aum's promotional material, and one animated film showed a handsome and lean Asahara—a glorified image of the leader, who is homely and stout—going through walls and serenely flying over cities.[42]

The cult was presented as a means of obtaining self-enlightenment through a combination of Tibetan Buddhism and Hinduism.[43] At its peak, the cult was estimated to have ten thousand members in Japan and thirty thousand in Russia, and smaller clusters in other nations.[44]

Striking similarities exist between the life courses of Asahara and David Koresh. In both cases, backgrounds characterized by psychological and economic poverty underlay their compensatory grandiosity. Asahara, whose followers greeted the Venerated Master by kissing his big toe, came from extremely humble beginnings.[45] He was born on March 2, 1955, the fourth son of an impoverished tatami maker. Named Chizuo Matsumoto, the future venerated seer developed glaucoma as an infant, which left him without sight in one eye and with only a third of normal sight in the other. As a consequence, he could not follow his father's trade and at age six was sent as a full-time boarder to a state-supported school for the blind. He never again lived with his family.

In the land of the blind, the one-eyed man is king, and as a partially sighted student in the all-blind school, the young Chizuo quickly became a leader—a tyrannical leader at that. When he escorted fellow students to the snack shop, he insisted they pay for him. As a young boy he had fantasies about ruling a kingdom of intelligent robots—fantasies of unlimited power which sprang from his inner sense of powerlessness. He told a number of his fellow students that he hoped to enter politics and wanted to be prime minister. Traditionally, severely visually impaired children were trained as acupuncturists or masseurs, but in 1973, at age eighteen, Matsumoto enrolled in a cram course to enter prestigious Tokyo

University, aspiring to a political career. When he was not admitted to the university, it must have been a crushing rebuff.

From dreams of glory he retreated, taking up acupuncture and opening a shop selling traditional Chinese medicines in an area on the outskirts of Tokyo peopled by fortune-tellers, mystics, acupuncturists, and peddlers of herbal medicine. At this time he changed his appearance—and his name. Now bearded, with long, flowing hair, he adopted the name *Shoko,* a homonym for the word meaning "an offering of incense," and *Asahara,* a rather high-toned name in contrast to the plebeian Matsumoto.

He spent the next nine years in this realm of charlatans. During this period he started a yoga school and became increasingly preoccupied with mysticism. In 1982, Asahara lost his herbalist license after being jailed and fined for selling fake medicines—his first brush with the law. At about that time he married a partner in his religious enterprises. Tomoko Asahara later became a senior official of Aum. With the collapse of his herbal medicine business, Asahara and his wife started their first cult, the Heavenly Blessing Association. This failed, and in 1984 Asahara made a pilgrimage to Tibet, where, according to his account, he found enlightenment. He then returned and founded a small yoga and meditation group, which consisted of a half-dozen followers meeting in a rented room. He also started a small publishing house. He then established the Aum Divine Wizard Association. Drawing on his idiosyncratic interpretation of Buddhist principles, he decided that a mastery of these principles would permit him to defy gravity and fly, techniques that he has continued to try to teach his practitioners. Pictures of him levitating are prominently featured in Aum's brochures. In 1985 a Japanese occult magazine, *Twilight Zone,* featured a picture of Asahara meditating in the lotus position while apparently floating in midair. Although this picture gave his image a major boost in occult circles, the Aum Divine Wizard Association failed.

In 1987, he founded his third sect, which he initially called the New Society of Aum. Its name was subsequently changed to the current Aum Shinriko (Aum Supreme Truth). There is some controversy over the meaning of the word *Aum.* While some identify it as the Sanskrit word for an element of doctrine, others indicate that it is the sacred sound that Buddhist monks pronounce in seeking the blissful state of satori. Asahara claims in his book *The Ultimate Power* that he is the "only person in

Japan who has achieved the ultimate stage of satori.''[46] In 1989 the Tokyo metropolitan government recognized Aum Shinriko as a religious corporation, giving it tax-exempt status.

Asahara's personality was compelling, his marketing of his new religion impressive. He targeted youth who were alienated from Japan's materialistic culture, appealing to intelligent and educated young men and women seeking greater meaning in their lives. His new religious cult thrived and amassed great wealth, for Asahara persuaded members that, in order for them to become monks or nuns and achieve enlightenment, they had to turn over to him all their possessions. By the time Aum's protected religious status was reversed, setting in motion seizure of its assets, Aum's holdings were between $300 million and $1 billion, including substantial real estate holdings, computer shops, noodle stores, a publishing company, a travel agency, and even a dating service.[47]

As in other closed religious cults, once a new recruit succumbed to the initial embrace of the cult, he or she found it extremely difficult to leave. Those who tried were told they would burn in a Buddhist hell. ''Rescuing'' backsliders was the euphemism for kidnapping, and some who were forcibly returned were killed.

New recruits wore helmets that were fitted with an electronic apparatus and rented for as much as ten thousand dollars per month, depending on the recruit's ability to pay. The helmets were said to align the members' brain waves with Asahara's. Members also drank water from a special ''miracle pond'' filled with ''water from the bath used by Asahara.'' New initiates were also given such drugs as LSD, morphine, and certain stimulants to influence their thought patterns.[48] At the time of the raid on 130 Aum buildings (located from the northern island of Hokkaido to Okinawa in the south), eighty children between the ages of three and fourteen were found in a children's annex. Fifty-three of them, sick and malnourished, were removed. One explained that she could not go outside because the air was full of poison gas. Many of the children were wearing headgear specially wired with electrodes implanted in their scalps.[49]

The regimen was harsh, the devotion required for the Venerated Master total. One former member described the requirement of watching Asahara's sermons on video and chanting continuously. For a ''love donation'' of about one thousand dollars, a member would receive thirty-

six trillion units of DNA—human genetic material—from Asahara. Another member, a woman, recalled being locked inside a small, windowless
room, receiving only one meal a day, and enduring a regimen of sleep
deprivation. Guards sometimes beat members with rods, and members'
training was punishing, with dinner at 2:30 A.M., bedtime at 3 A.M., wake-
up call at 6 A.M., followed by cleaning and more immersion in the truths
of Asahara. When this member was able, after three months, to negotiate
the release of herself and her daughter, the cult would not return the
property she had given Aum on her entrance. The children in the compound received no schooling other than immersion in the writings of
Asahara. Another former cult member reported visiting Aum in 1990. He
had no intent of staying, but once he and his family entered the building,
they were locked up. Although he escaped, his wife and children stayed
behind. When he managed to rescue three of his children, the cult kidnapped them and regained their custody.[50]

Extremity of belief does not permit doubt, and one way of eliminating
doubt is to eliminate doubters, a responsibility entrusted to the Action
Squad. A lawyer who was representing families trying to get their children back from the cult became a priority target for the Covert Action
Group. Six followers, acting on Asahara's orders, broke into the attorney's apartment at three in the morning in November 1989 and killed
him, his wife, and their child by injecting them with drugs, hitting them
with a hammer, and strangling them. Their bodies were found in the
mountains of central Japan in September 1995.[51] A case in February 1995
concerned an elderly woman who had donated a hundred thousand dollars
to Aum, but when Aum insisted she also give Asahara a parcel of land,
she broke from the cult and went into hiding. Aum kidnapped her brother
to try to force him to reveal her whereabouts. They injected him with
Pentothal, and he died during interrogation. They then reduced his body
to powder in the cult's microwave oven and scattered the ashes.

In 1989, after disputes with locals in southwestern Japan, Aum purchased land near the village of Kamikuishiki, below sacred Mount Fuji.
The facilities were extraordinary for what was portrayed as a new religion. Asahara, an admirer of Hitler, ordered the construction of a sophisticated, computer-controlled chemical factory designed to produce
cyanide gas, mustard gas, and sarin, a nerve gas that had been developed

by the Nazis shortly before World War II. (When a strong odor emanated from a cult facility, a representative of the cult asserted that the group was the victim of U.S. and Japanese military, who were spraying poison gas on them.) Aum was also exploring the area of biological warfare: some 160 barrels of peptone, material used to grow bacteria, were discovered in the facility along with large quantities of the bacteria that causes botulism.

Encouraged by the adulation of his followers, Asahara decided to launch a campaign for the 1990 general election with his own party, Truth. The party had no program, no issues. The campaign consisted of dewy-eyed, white-robed followers chanting, "Sho-ko, Sho-ko, As-a-ha-ra." The most prominent campaign spokesman was a debonair young man, Fumihiro Joyu, who charmed television viewers, especially women, and claimed that Asahara had given him the strength to stop masturbating.

Asahara was badly rebuffed at the polls. Before the electoral failure he believed that first Japan and then the entire world would acclaim him as the new Buddha and the savior of mankind. He reacted to the defeat by taking a thousand of his followers to an isolated island in the Okinawa region, a rehearsal for the retreat when American bombers would one day launch a nuclear attack on mainland Japan (this paranoid flight was similar to those of Jim Jones and David Koresh). The media pursued Asahara, asking if he and his followers planned to commit mass suicide. Asahara called off the retreat.

Now that Asahara's grandiose aspirations were dashed, he was consumed with even greater retaliatory rage. The patient Buddhism that had figured so prominently in his appeal was replaced by a more exigent rhetoric. In the wake of his political failure, he increasingly identified with Jesus Christ, publishing in 1992 a manifesto entitled *Declaring Myself the Christ*. In this book, Asahara proclaims himself to be not only the fully enlightened master but also the Lamb of God, sent to take away the sins of the world. His rejection by the voters is taken to confirm his special mission. He quotes Matthew 24:9: "Then shall they deliver you to be afflicted and shall kill you: and ye shall be hated of all nations for my name's sake." Now the apocalyptic prophecies of Revelation, so crucial to the theology of Koresh, are incorporated into the vision of Asahara. (He also draws upon Nostradamus' predictions of war breaking out in

July 1999.)[52] Asahara's image in Russian-language pamphlets is that of a "stripped, beaten Christ wearing a crown of thorns and hanging from a cross—and also bearing a striking resemblance to the prophet-monk Rasputin."[53]

Aum had opened its first office in Russia in 1991. In 1992, Asahara visited Russia again, seeking out the Nobel Prize–winning physicist Nikolay Basov, apparently trying to extract from him knowledge to incorporate into an advanced weapons system of mass destruction. Later that year Asahara opened in Ishikawa Prefecture a weapons factory devoted to making Soviet-designed AK-47 assault rifles. Aum also purchased a forty-eight-thousand-acre sheep ranch in Australia and took out mining licenses (there are extensive uranium holdings in Australia). Such mining would have been technically difficult, but it was as if Asahara were exploring every avenue for acquiring the means of mass destruction, nuclear and otherwise. Aum apparently did test sarin on livestock at their Australia ranch: carcasses of twenty-four sheep revealed traces of sarin, as did soil samples.

Aum's scientists busily explored other avenues. Asahara became fascinated with Nikola Tesla, the Croatian-born electrical engineer who invented alternating current in the first half of the twentieth century. In the Tesla museum in Belgrade, Yugoslavia, are details of some of his science fiction concepts, such as a death ray that could destroy ten thousand airplanes at a time and shock waves that could split the earth in two. Asahara's lieutenants visited the museum and studied Tesla's documents, apparently with a view to creating a major earthquake in Japan. A team of Aum microbiologists traveled to Zaire in 1992, ostensibly to help curb an outbreak of Ebola virus, but according to U.S. Senate testimony, their mission was to collect a strain for germ warfare. An Aum scientist had even acquired the formula for synthesizing the deadly venom of the green-mamba snake.

As the Lamb of God, Asahara explained that his failing health was due to his giving his strength to his disciples. He spoke of serious illnesses, including cancer of the liver, and indicated that he did not have long to live. Asahara regularly predicted a world war in 1997, caused by a shadowy conspiracy variously identified with the Japanese government, the United States, Jews, Freemasons, and rival Japanese religions. The likeliest source was the United States, identified as the Beast from the Book of Revelation. Asahara's association of this apocalyptic prophecy with his own failing health suggests a projection of his own personal apocalypse upon the world.

In the revised preface to the 1992 edition of *Beyond Life and Death* (first published in 1986), Asahara compares the four years that had passed since the first edition to "a ship caught in a storm." But the storm, he asserts, was a joy for him, for "if not for this harsh and cruel 'Aum-bashing,' we should never have had the new growth and development." Asahara also declared, "We all die," and he urged people to attend an Aum program on "death and rebirth . . . Modern Japan has been unjustly deprived of the concept of life after death." He offered to teach about both. Apparently the 1995 gas attack was an object lesson.[54] Just before police broke into the Kamikuishiki complex, a taped message called upon Aum members to carry out his plan for salvation and to "meet death without regrets."

In his latest book, *The Land of the Rising Sun Is Headed Towards a Bitter Fate,* Asahara predicted a U.S. nuclear attack on Japan between 1996 and 1998. In particular, many of his predictions were of a U.S.-led gas attack on Aum headquarters, which accordingly was prepared with stores of atropine, an antidote for nerve gas. Asahara stressed that Aum members would survive. The most likely explanation for the holdings Aum purchased in Australia was to serve as a retreat in which to wait out the nuclear holocaust. Then Asahara's followers were to repopulate the world, with a society dedicated to the principles of Aum Supreme Truth rising out of the ashes.

The Aum Supreme Truth represents a transition between passive mil-lennarians, who withdraw in despair to await the millennium (as exem-plified by the People's Temple and the Branch Davidians), and religious warriors, who are not in a state of despair but fight against the unbelievers for their version of God's kingdom. The paranoia of Shoko Asahara and his followers led to defensive aggression. Believing they were going to be attacked, they attacked first.[55]

These three leaders—Jones, Koresh, and Asahara—all displayed the clas-sic paranoid traits of delusional suspicion, centrality, grandiosity, hostility, fear of loss of autonomy, and projection. In each instance the leader was able to dominate his followers psychologically, not only manipulating them into sharing his delusions but causing them to act upon these delusions. These examples are evidence that a politicized paranoia embedded within an activist organization invariably leads to violence.

This dynamic is not confined to extremist new religions. It also appears at the outer edges of mainstream religions, where it is most powerful when it calls on the pious to commit the ultimate paradox—killing in the name of God.

# 6

## Killing in the Name of God

[God directs Joshua to destroy the city of Jericho:]

Look [God said to Joshua], I have delivered
Jericho and her king unto your hands. . . .

Under the ban [not to plunder, the Hebrews]
destroyed everything in the city; they put everyone to
the sword, men and women, young and old, and also
cattle, sheep, and asses. . . .

Thus the Lord was with Joshua, and his fame
spread through the country.
—Joshua 6:2–27

Slay the idolaters wheresoever you find them, and take
them captive or besiege them, and lie in wait for them
at every likely place.
—The Qur'an 9:5

The deaths and losses which shall accrue from this
[resistance] are your fault, and not that of their
Highnesses [of Aragon and Castile], or ours, nor these
cavaliers who come with us.
—The *Requerimiento,* read, in Latin or Spanish, to
native peoples of the Americas by the Spanish
conquistadores, promising death or enslavement to
those who did not accept Christianity and Spanish
rule

The individual who is psychologically overwhelmed may withdraw from the painful world into the self, into a bleak depression, or into a mental world of his own construction. Similarly, the humiliated or ostracized social group may withdraw from the larger society. David Koresh led his group into the asylum of the Branch Davidian compound, leaving the corrupt world behind; Jim Jones led his group into the People's Temple in the jungles of Guyana. If one is beset by terrifying forces, what a comfort it is to belong to a group that offers an answer, whose leader has made sense of the overwhelming difficulties and whose members collectively understand and assign meaning to the bewildering events.

Some groups withdraw passively, waiting for the apocalypse and the subsequent redemption. Others strive to combat the immoral forces in the world, to demonstrate their piety to the world. These spiritual belligerents individually and collectively confront society aggressively in terms of their religious doctrine.[1] Living in a subjective, polarized reality, an us-versus-them world, they display a paranoid attitude and have a Manichaean view of the world.

Sometimes the paranoid aggression hides under a seemingly passive exterior. The Dead Sea sect, a fundamentalist ascetic group that lived in the Judean desert around A.D. 70, saw themselves as the Sons of Light in opposition to the Sons of Darkness.[2] They were quite peaceful on the surface, but their worldview was not pacifism but rather suppressed and delayed aggression. Their conduct was specified by *The Community Rule,* which required them to refrain from retaliation, adopt a humble demeanor, and forgive their adversaries. This posture belied zealous destructiveness toward those who did not share their beliefs, for *The Community Rule* prescribed restraint only "until [God's] day of judgment," when the killing in the name of God would occur. "On the Day of Revenge" the members' "wrath shall not turn from the men of falsehood" but shall smash them "until judgment is done."[3]

Religious belligerents are not confined to closed religious cults but are also found within the ranks of the mainstream religions. The dichotomization of the universe depicted in Scripture is fertile soil for the "spiritual belligerent"—justification for his aggression. A sharp division of the moral universe between good and evil is one of the principal attributes of the three largest monotheistic religions that originated in the Middle East: Judaism, Christianity, and Islam. This division between good and evil has given these religions their characteristic vitality, a quality that many see lacking in the more accepting great religions of Hinduism and Buddhism. This "edge" is made even keener by the other defining characteristic of the People of the Book: their insistence that there is only one God—a jealous, watchful, personal God who permits no compromise with his will. This is a world of light and darkness, in constant warfare with evil, its members having an unambiguous responsibility to fight on God's side.

Ardent practitioners of these faiths, committed to the literal word of God, are able to find ample justification in their texts for militant defense of their beliefs. One need consider only the bloody and violent imagery of Christianity, "the central symbol [of which] is an execution device—a cross—from which, at least in the Roman tradition, the body still hangs." For further evidence of militancy and bloodshed, consider the Christian hymns "Onward, Christian Soldiers," "The Old Rugged Cross," "Washed in the Blood of the Lamb," and "There Is a Fountain Flowing with Blood."[4]

The great religions emergent from the Old Testament are, like ourselves, divided between the life instinct and the death instinct, between love and hatred. The holy texts inspire with words of love and justice and have given rise to some of the greatest achievements of the human spirit. They have also, however, inspired believers to violent aggression in the service of their faith.

It is not difficult to find examples from history to demonstrate this point. The quotation from Joshua at the beginning of this chapter illustrates the destructive ferocity of the ancient Hebrews. Massacres by Christians in all the Crusades show that killing in the name of Christ was practiced by Christians. Islamic tradition also extols the honor of those who participate in a war to defend Islam in danger.

## The Psychology of Religious Violence

Killing in the name of God runs like a scarlet thread through the major events of the final decades of the twentieth century. When Islamic fun-

damentalist terrorists were found guilty of the 1993 bombing of the World
Trade Center towers—the most destructive terrorist act in the United
States inspired by an overseas issue and directed by non-Americans—the
defendants shouted in unison, *"Allah akbar"* (God is great). When Dr.
Baruch Goldstein obtained an automatic weapon and opened fire on Muslim worshipers at the Tomb of the Patriarchs in Hebron in 1994, killing
thirty of them, he believed he was on a divine mission and was hailed as
a saint by hard-line Israeli settlers, as was Yigal Amir, the twenty-five-
year-old religious extremist responsible for the assassination of Israeli
Prime Minister Yitzhak Rabin. Michael Griffin, the pro-life activist convicted in the 1993 murder of Dr. David Gunn, the attending physician at
a Pensacola, Florida, women's clinic, also believed that he was acting in
support of his faith. So did Rachelle Shannon, who attempted to murder
Dr. George Tiller in his Wichita, Kansas, abortion clinic later in 1993.
Shannon and Griffin both pleaded not guilty because they could justify
trying to kill people they perceived as murderers.

In all these cases, the perpetrators of the violence were striking out
at threats to their belief systems. Their actions were defensive aggression
against the enemy without. Strong religious beliefs may serve as a protection against psychological stress, especially for the fanatic believer,
whose sense of self rests upon the integrity of his belief system.[5] Accordingly, those perceived as threatening that belief system, by words or
deeds, pose a fundamental threat to the psychological integrity of the
fanatic believer. For the passionate believer, it is not the beliefs that
generate the passion. To the contrary, the rigid beliefs provide a sense-
making container for powerful feelings. Because attacks upon those beliefs threaten the believer's control and risk his being overwhelmed by
the feelings, such attacks provoke a passionate, often violent response.

Faith—which requires the rejection of all earthly evidence contrary
to belief—is at the center of this psychological system. Girded by faith,
the spiritual belligerent is impervious to reason. Faith in its passive form
requires rejecting or ignoring conflicting evidence. Faith in its active form
requires defeating or destroying the proponents of conflicting evidence.
Destruction of the challenger will not produce guilt; it will bring psychological comfort. Pascal observed, "Men never do evil so openly and
contentedly as when they do it from religious conviction."[6]

The community must punish the heretic who threatens the belief system. This is particularly true in a transformational mass religious movement for which faith is the motivating force (see Chapter 4). Thus, when the Iranian religious leader Ayatollah Khomeini issued the *fatwah* calling for the death of writer Salman Rushdie for defiling Islam in his novel *The Satanic Verses,* Khomeini was defending the true faith. When the Bangladesh feminist Taslima Nasrin wrote in the 1990s that traditional interpretations of the Qur'an have been used to inhibit the emancipation of women, she was forced into hiding by angry Muslims who demanded her death for blaspheming the Qur'an.[7]

It is the boundary between the religious community and outsiders that permits guilt-free violation of the fundamental religious prohibition against killing. The literal translation of the biblical injunction is not "Thou shalt not kill" but "Thou shalt not murder."[8] A group with a sacred belief system that is under siege may justify killing the threatening other. In such circumstances, killing is not murder but a religious sacrament, for it is in defense of the beliefs that hold the group together. These intensely held ideologies have many sources, but one feature they share is a willingness to use violence against outsiders who challenge their beliefs.

Man's capacity to project intolerable internal feelings on an external object—the defining characteristic of paranoid reactions—is an ego defense mechanism operative since infancy. This defense mechanism, which comes to the fore under stress, channels aggression to the external target. This is the basis for prejudice, for scapegoating, and, in its most catastrophic expression, for genocide.

The destructive charismatic leader exploits this mechanism by identifying a symbolically suitable target for the group's aggression. He claims to possess a salvationist truth for a distressed people. When that "truth" is conveyed by an authoritarian religious leader, such as Khomeini, all doubt is relieved for his fanatic followers. It provides justification to attack and even to kill. By channeling righteous rage against opponents of the faith, the destructive charismatic leader exploits, manipulates, and encourages the paranoid dynamic in his followers and thereby maintains the equilibrium of the group.

The paranoid follower attacks his own disowned feelings that he has projected on the enemy. Because the feelings must be disowned to restore psychological harmony, the follower can have no empathy for or psychological contact with the target. The zeal of the torturer, the alacrity of the killer, represents his eagerness to destroy the devalued and disowned part of the self. The other is not a victim or a sacrifice but the "deserving culprit."[9] After the murder of Dr. Gunn and his staff at the abortion clinic, representatives of the pro-life movement were striking in their lack of empathy for the victims. And 57 percent of the Palestinian population approved of Islamic Jihad's suicide bombing in Israel, in which twenty Israelis were killed and sixty injured. Palestinian crowds cheered "the death of 20 monkeys, the injuries of 60 pigs."[10]

It may be a paranoid leader who points the accusing finger at this "deserving culprit," who facilitates channeling of this self-righteous rage against the enemy of the faith. For true believers, the leader's identification of the enemy is sufficient. To an established paranoid group, however, a legitimating leader is unnecessary. This is the case, for example, with many violent anti-abortion Christian groups and violent civilian militias. The member becomes as one with the group, and the leader's and the group's moral code becomes that of the member, with no room or need for individual moral judgment. This pattern is particularly strong when the group believes itself to be under threat.

Religious language regularly addresses the tension between tranquil order and grave disorder, promising that through the path of faith, order will triumph as disorder is contained.[11] Accordingly, violence, the accompaniment of disorder, is often integral to religious discourse.

In both Judaism and Christianity, some believe literally in the Scripture, be it the Old Testament or the New Testament. And all Muslims believe in the literal sacredness of the Qur'an. Within each fundamentalist belief, there are two sentiments: the quietist and the activist. The majority are quietist, awaiting the arrival of the messiah. The activists, by contrast, believe that they can hasten the arrival of the messiah by acts of piety. This "duty" to force the end is a major justification of religious fundamentalist terrorism. God's will must be realized now, and so unbelievers are a threat that must be eliminated, either by forced capitulation or by destruction. Islam in particular has been closely intertwined with violence since its very beginnings.

## Killing in the Name of Allah

Fight these specimens of faithlessness . . . Will you not fight
those who broke their pledge and plotted to banish the Apostle,
and were the first to attack you? Are you afraid of them? If
you are believers you should fear God more. Fight them so
that God may punish them at your hands.
—The Qur'an 9:12–14

I would like to warn the governments of the Islamic countries
not to repeat their past mistakes but extend the hand of
brotherhood to each other. With humility toward God and
relying on the power of Islam, they should cut the cruel hands
of the oppressors and world-devouring plunderers, especially
the United States, from the region.
—Ayatollah Khomeini, radio broadcast, June 5, 1983

Islam has produced some of the finest manifestations of the human spirit
in art, literature, and philosophy.[12] Strict monotheism, a commitment to
the integration of religion in every aspect of life, and clear and universalistic rules on how to worship God form the essence of its appeal.
Yet Islam is a human organization, subject to the same infections as any
other—infections often borne on the winds of history. The paranoid
theme is neither specific to nor characteristic of Islam, but it does appear
there. There is a great irony here, for Islam practices the nonparanoid
qualities of mercy and forgiveness and owes much of its success to the
exercise of patient tolerance. Indeed, the first words of the Qur'an emphasize mercy and forgiveness: "Bismillah al-rahman, al-rahim" ["In
the name of Allah the most benevolent, ever merciful"].

But no institution is safe from the paranoid bacillus. Islam has a
strong tradition of violence as well as tolerance. It should not be surprising, therefore, that paranoia has drawn nourishment from that religion's
misfortunes and those of the region of its birth.

Islam was born a fighting religion. Since 610, when God first spoke
to Muhammad, the call to arms in the name of God has powerfully roused
Muslims. In the first century of the religion's existence, the Kharijites, a
group of violent dissidents committed to violent jihad (holy war), fought

against the enemies of their sect and assassinated the fourth caliph, Imam Ali.[13] They believed they had a holy mission to fight against the followers of Satan, a duty that permitted—indeed required—violence.[14] Many today would consider the Kharijites Islam's first terrorists.

Islam governs all aspects of life—political, social, and cultural. Every facet of life is prescribed by the *shari'a,* or Islamic law, including the circumstances under which Muslims should go to war. As exemplified by the verse that introduces this section, many verses of the Qur'an advocate violence against unbelievers and apostates. Many Muslims believe that jihad is an obligation of every Muslim. The Qur'an dictates that Muslims should go to war only in the name of God.[15] At the final judgment, the warrior who has given his life for the faith will, according to the Qur'an,

> Spend eternity in gardens of tranquility. . . .
> Youths of never-ending bloom will pass round to them decanters,
> beakers full of sparkling wine.
> Unheady, uninebriating.
> And suck fruits as they fancy.
> Bird meats that they relish.
> And companions with big beautiful eyes
> Like pearls within their shells. . . .
> We have formed them in a distinctive fashion,
> And made them virginal.[16]

Such delights await all pious Muslim warriors.

The first thousand years of Islam were centuries of conquest and expansion—and of magnificent cultural achievements. Thus military dominance and the glories of Islam are intertwined in the history of Islam and in the collective consciousness of Muslims. Near the turn of the seventeenth century, Akbar, the great Muslim Mughal ruler of northern India, wrote or commissioned a history of the world centering on his own people, the Indo-Persians, and his religion, Islam. The place he gave to the Christian peoples of Europe was especially small. He dismissed them as hopeless barbarians, the high points of whose civilization—their medicine and philosophy, for example—were imperfectly derived from the Islamic peoples. Akbar did note that the Christians had made an unsuc-

cessful effort to break out of their backwater into the richer lands of the
Muslims (that is how he described the Crusades), but of course they were
thrown back.

Akbar had good reason to write as he did, for until his own time the
Islamic world had overshadowed the West. As Akbar was writing, however, English, French, Portuguese, and Dutch soldiers and merchants were
establishing themselves in modest trading stations in several parts of the
subcontinent. Within a few decades they would be a power. Within a
century they would be the dominant power. Within two centuries a European people, the British, would rule all the Grand Mughal had claimed
and far more besides.

By the end of World War I, Europeans ruled over almost every Muslim in the world. From Morocco to Indonesia, from the steppes of central
Asia to the Hausa lands of Nigeria, the rulers were European—and Christian. The few apparent exceptions—Persia, almost all the Arabian peninsula, and Afghanistan—were regions of comparatively little economic
or military value, and even in these areas Europeans seldom were prevented from working their will. The last Muslim empire, that of the Ot-
tomans, collapsed at the end of World War I. As the Muslim peoples
were being dominated militarily and politically, their culture, too, was
being overwhelmed by Western influence. Economically, the Muslims
were suppliers to the Western capitalist machine. The European imperial
powers carried on a conscious policy of mercantilism, in which cotton
from Egypt, spices from Indonesia, and, increasingly, oil from the Persian
Gulf were sent to Europe, processed, and reexported at great profit.

Although Muslim culture was not destroyed, it was under siege.
Western languages, forms of social organization, and aesthetic and philosophical ideas prevailed. By the third quarter of the twentieth century,
the cumulative effect of these pressures, probably better called "modern"
than "Western," was the progressive weakening of Islamic society. Elements of cooperation among the Western powers at times suggested a
conspiratorial pattern. And at times Western rulers did conspire to extend
their power in the Middle East. There was hostility toward Islam on the
part of Western nations, which were often arrogant and assumptive in
their dealings with the Islamic world. Feelings of suspicion and powerlessness toward the imperialist West were a natural reaction, especially

since many of the Muslim societies had a predisposition toward conspiratorial thinking; adding the West to the list of plotters was not a difficult leap.

Society sets sharp limits on the expression of anger, and religion often serves as a socially sanctioned umbrella under which it may be expressed. This was especially the case with conservative Muslims, because their religion compelled the fusing of the religious and the secular. Several Islamic revivals took place, the most recent of which was associated with the loss of East Jerusalem, the third holiest city in Islam, to Israel in 1967. For many devout Muslims, the humiliating defeat, in only six days, of the armies of Jordan, Syria, and Egypt at the hands of the Jews was God's punishment for the corruption of Islam and its abandonment of the tenets of the Qur'an. Only by returning to first principles, the fundamental teachings of Islam, could the honor and glories of Islam be restored.

The principles of all fundamentalist Muslims, both those who seek to pursue these goals peacefully and those who take a more violent path, are the following:

- Islam is a total and comprehensive way of life, not merely a religion. There are no separate realms, like politics, law, and society— there is Islam.
- The failure of Muslim societies is due to their departure from the straight path of Islam and their following a Western path, with its secular, materialistic ideologies and values.
- The renewal of society requires a return to Islam, an Islamic religio-political and social reformation or revolution, that draws its inspiration from the Qur'an and from the first great Islamic movement, led by the prophet Muhammad.
- To restore God's rule and inaugurate a true Islamic social order, Western-inspired civil codes must be replaced by Islamic law, the only acceptable blueprint for Muslim society.
- Although the Westernization of society is condemned, modernization as such is not. Science and technology are accepted, but they are to be subordinated to Islamic beliefs and values in order to guard against the Westernization and secularization of Muslim society.

- The process of Islamization or, more accurately, re-Islamization requires organizations of dedicated and trained Muslims, who, by their example and activities, call on others to be more observant and who are willing to struggle (jihad) against corruption and social injustice.[17]

In the golden era of the past toward which the revivalists look, the glories of Islam were associated with militance and aggression. It is to be expected, then, that some who seek the Islamic revival believe that their religion and political reality require violent revolution—that the extremity of the situation requires an extreme solution. Claiming to be the victims of aggression, these radical Islamists believe that the Crusader mentality still exists in the West (which includes the non-Muslim successor states of the Soviet Union and Israel). International Zionism, they believe, has allied itself with this Western force.

Creating an Islamic state based on God's command is, for these radical Muslims, not an option but an imperative. Only Islamic governments are legitimate, and only governments that are based on Islamic law, the shari'a, are Islamic. In their view, both governments and individuals who fail to follow the shari'a strictly are guilty of unbelief and are the equivalent of atheists even if they call themselves Islamic. Their unbelief demands holy war. The official clergy and state-supported mosques are not immune from this stricture. If clergy are not strict adherents, they are considered to have been co-opted or corrupted, and they too must be destroyed. Indeed, these modernizing moderate regimes that call themselves Islamic are the first to be attacked by the radical Islamists, even before the West, precisely because their apostasy is so threatening to the true faith. Because jihad is a religious duty, all true believers are obliged to combat such governments and their supporters. Like the Kharijites in early Islam, these radicals demand total commitment and obedience. One is either a true believer or an infidel, saved or damned, a friend or an enemy of God.

According to radical Muslims, the long-standing practice of giving special latitude to "people of the book" (dhimmi, or scriptuaries; that is, Christians and Jews) is to be put aside. These people have lost their ancient protection because of their connections with Western (Christian) colonialism and Zionism. They are seen as partners in a Judeo-Christian conspiracy against Islam and the Muslim world. Thus, all non-Muslim minorities are often subjected to persecution.

An important source of inspiration to militant Islam is Muslim Brotherhood leader Sayid Qutb, who declared, before he was executed by the Nasser regime in 1965, that there was a "war to be waged in the name of Islam."[18] This refrain was echoed by the Islamic scholar Ayatollah Fazlallah Mahallati, who wrote that a Muslim who saw Islam insulted and did nothing would "end up in the seventh layer of Hell," but if he harmed or killed the offender his place would be "assured in heaven." An Islamic state consists of such believers, who remain at war with the world until the world accepts Islam.[19] Muhammad Navab Safavi, another Muslim fundamentalist, emphasizes that whatever serves Islam is justified—lying in the name of God, stealing in the name of God, killing in the name of God. Safavi commended killing in God's name, writing that such killing "is tantamount to saying a prayer when those who are harmful [to the faith] need to be put out of the way."[20]

Radical Islamists hearken to the original teachings of Muhammad, who affirmed that those who wage war in God's service are engaged in a religious-political act and will be divinely assisted. The struggle is to convert, to subjugate, or to eliminate the unbeliever. The Qur'an gives stronger voice to justifying violence in defense of the faith than do either the Old or the New Testament. Radical Islamists cite the Qur'an in support of their beliefs:

> And slay them wherever ye catch them, and turn them out from where they have turned you out; . . . Such is the reward of those who suppress the faith. (2:190–193)

> Fight and slay the pagans wherever ye find them . . . But if they repent and establish regular prayers . . . then open the way for them, for Allah is oft-forgiving. (9:5)

For those committed to this interpretation of Islam, conducting this struggle is not a choice. Muslims are divinely commanded to "strive and fight in the cause of Allah with their goods and their persons." Fighting is also a test set by God to let the Muslims demonstrate their piety, and those who die in the holy cause are assured a favored place in heaven.[21]

## Ayatollah Khomeini and Radical Shi'ite Islam

Whereas the Islamic revival was given impetus by the Arabs' humiliating defeat in the Six-Day War against Israel in 1967, the revival burst upon the world in the aftermath of the Shah of Iran's overthrow in 1979. The Shah's nemesis was the Shi'ite cleric Ayatollah Ruholla Khomeini. When the United States granted asylum to the Shah, who was gravely ill with cancer, militant followers of Khomeini seized the U.S. embassy in Teheran and held fifty-two American hostages for 444 days. Iran was to become the world's first modern Islamic state and the base for Khomeini's vision of an Islamic state extending throughout the Persian Gulf and the world.

Khomeini had developed a coherent ideological framework drawing on themes in the historical experience of Shi'ite Islam that justified violence and anti-state actions in the pursuit of the Islamic Revolution.[22] According to Shi'ite doctrine, the meek are the righteous, and the strong are evil. Therefore, Khomeini argued, the strongest nations—the superpowers—are the most evil, the most illegitimate, and "responsible for all the world's corruption."[23]

Khomeini not only justified striking out at the enemies of the true faith but made it obligatory to do so. His ideology was appealing on a highly personal level. In effect, he instructed Muslims that their personal trauma would be resolved through violent action for which they would be rewarded; they could resolve their personal existential crises by pursuit of political-military action against "illegitimate" regimes. Even though ruled by Islamic leaders, moderate modernizing Islamic regimes were a threat to Khomeini's expansive vision and became the target of his systematic strategy to destabilize them. They were viewed as corrupt and inauthentic Islamic regimes which had sold out to the West.

For Khomeini, there was either good or evil—true believers or the followers of Satan. Corruption, in Khomeini's absolutist view, could not be reformed; it had to be destroyed. He regularly employed the metaphor of the clean spring and the stagnant pond: however much sweet water the spring pours into the pond, the pond will remain stagnant. To preserve the purity of the water, the pond must be drained. Of the war against Iraq, he once said: "Why don't you recite the sura of killing? Why should you always recite the Sura of Mercy? Don't forget that killing is also a form of mercy."[24] Khomeini and his clerical followers regularly found justification for their actions in the Qur'anic suras calling for the shedding of blood. These suras were a common feature of Khomeini's prayer services and long continued to be cited in the prayer services of Shi'ite fundamentalist clerics in Iran and Lebanon. In the cemetery outside Teheran where the regime buried many of the dead from the Iran-Iraq war, they constructed a huge fountain, but instead of circulating water, the fountain was said to circulate blood—a potent symbol of the Khomeini era.

## Hezbollah

With the support of Iran, in 1982 a group of Lebanese Shi'ite Muslims formed a revolutionary party dedicated to establishing an Islamic state in Lebanon. They called themselves Hezbollah [the party of God], after the Qur'anic injunction "And verily the party of God is sure to triumph." Hezbollah leaders Ayatollah Sayyid Muhammad Husayn Fadlallah and Husayn al-Musawi provided the "moral logic" requiring kidnapping, assassination, and other terrorist acts.[25] According to them, the extraordinary circumstances of Islam's extreme degradation justified extraordinary means. The value of martyrdom was extolled in Fadlallah's speeches and writings. He regularly observed in his sermons that "there is evil in everything good and something good in every evil."

Hezbollah and other Iranian-backed Islamic extremists based in Lebanon were responsible for taking hostage thirty-seven American and other Westerners in 1982. The last American was freed in 1991. Hostage taking violates the Qur'an, which emphasizes hospitality toward strangers, but Fadlallah's clerical followers justified the extraordinary measure, asserting, "Just as freedom is demanded for a handful of Europeans, it is also demanded for the millions of Muslims."[26]

Iranian-backed radical Shi'ite Muslims were also responsible for the 1983 suicide bombing of the U.S. Marine barracks in Beirut, in which a lone Shi'ite driving a truck loaded with explosives crashed into the barracks and killed 241 marines. This ushered in a wave of suicide bombings by Shi'ite Muslims, which lasted from the spring of 1983 to the summer of 1985. Fadlallah offered a remarkable justification for suicide, which is strictly prohibited by the Qur'an. Ingeniously arguing that it was really a matter of timing, Fadlallah asserted that killing oneself as a means of killing an enemy "differs little from that of a soldier who fights and knows that in the end he will be killed."[27]

The calls to destructive action by Khomeini and Fadlallah are part of Shi'ite doctrine. Shi'ites have long been considered the more violent, intense and populist, and the less compromising, of the two major divisions in Islam. It is important, however, to emphasize the complex and infinitely variegated texture of Islam; the justifications of violence in the Qur'an cited by Khomeini and Fadlallah were selected from this rich tapestry and used by them to justify their goals. These goals and justifications were appealing to their followers but were by no means universally approved by Muslims. A similar call to violence can be found in the rhetoric of the majority Islamic group, the Sunni.

## Sunni Doctrine and Killing in the Name of God

Abd Al-Salam Faraj, leader of Al-Jihad, the Sunni Islamic group responsible for the 1981 assassination of President Anwar Sadat of Egypt, justified Sadat's murder as the fulfillment of a sacred obligation.[28] He claimed that the religious obligation to struggle when Islam is in danger was a "neglected duty"—the title of his book. The devout Muslim, according to his interpretation, cannot rest until the shari'a governs all human conduct, and this goal may require killing unbelievers, as prescribed by the Qur'an.

But how did Faraj justify killing Sadat, who, after all, was a devout, practicing Muslim? The problem was that Sadat was a moderate and modernizing Muslim willing to secularize parts of Egyptian society and was thus the enemy of practitioners of the true faith. Secularism offers latitude from many of the restraints that Islam requires: restrictions on sexual behavior, on relations between the sexes, on what one eats, even on the rhythm of one's day. Students of Islamic society suggest that the price that modernizing Muslims pay for this freedom and social permissiveness is loss of community and loss of personal serenity. Sadat, by being complacent about secular influences and not applying the shari'a, did not protect his people from these corrupting influences. In fact, he appeared to support these un-Islamic practices. So he deserved to die. Moreover, Sadat's signing of the Camp David treaties with Israel demonstrated his treason. His willingness to recognize and deal with "the Zionist entity" represented the final betrayal.

Sunni Islamic terrorism has entered the United States as well. On February 26, 1993, followers of Sheik Omar Abdel-Rahman, a radical Sunni Muslim cleric, detonated a car bomb in the parking garage beneath the World Trade Center in New York, killing six people, injuring more than a thousand others, and causing more than $500 million in damages. In his prayer services Abdel-Rahman regularly cited the Qur'an as justification for acts of violence. And at their sentencing the four convicted terrorists called on God to legitimate what they had done.

In the opening statement at the trial of Abdel-Rahman and the other accused terrorists on January 30, 1995, the prosecution depicted the Trade Center bombing as an act of war. Prosecutor Robert Khuzami portrayed the terrorists as soldiers in a war against the United States, with Abdel-Rahman as their general.[29] A follower of Abdel-Rahman testified in May 1995 that Abdel-Rahman had ordered him to assassinate Egyptian President Hosni Mubarak on his planned visit to New York in 1993. These events demonstrated that the paranoid dynamic was powerful outside the Shi'ite community and can be manifested in a non-Islamic society.

## Hamas

The genius of Khomeini was in conceptualizing a radical ideology based on a particularistic interpretation of the Qur'an, justifying violence in pursuit of the Islamic state. Hamas, the Islamic Resistance Movement, justified the unity of radical Islam with Palestinian nationalism and absolved violence on the basis of an absolutist and paranoid worldview.

Established during the *intifada* (a civil revolt by Palestinians against Israeli occupation, which began in December 1987), Hamas traces its origins to the Muslim Brotherhood in Palestine, founded in 1928.[30] The Brotherhood sought to revitalize Islam and to establish an Islamic state with no distinction between religion and the state. Its members considered Palestine a permanently and exclusively Muslim land, so designated by

God. In their view, it is the duty of Muslims to liberate the entirety of the Holy Land from non-Muslim authority: "Israel will be established and will stay established until Islam nullifies it as it nullified what was before it," stated the martyred Imam Hasan al-Banna, founder and "Supreme Guide" of the Muslim Brotherhood.[31] Sheik Hasan al-Banna also stated, "It is the nature of Islam to dominate, not to be dominated, to impose its law on all nations and to extend its power to the entire planet."[32]

When the intifada erupted in 1987, Sheikh Ahmad Yasin convened a group of Muslim Brotherhood leaders. They decided to establish a nominally separate organization to participate in the intifada. This would provide deniability should the revolt fail but would permit them to claim credit if it succeeded. They called the organization Hamas, which means "zeal," "force," and "bravery" in Arabic. The term is also an acronym for Harakat al-Muqawama al-Islamiyya (the Islamic Resistance Movement).

Paranoid rhetoric pervades the Hamas charter, which identifies Islam with Palestinian nationalism and the destruction of Israel.[33] Article 13 emphasizes the Brotherhood's belief that "giving up any part of the homeland is like giving up part of the religious faith itself." The conspiratorial foundation of this "religious cause" is spelled out in Article 22:

> The enemy planned long ago and perfected their plan so that they can achieve what they want to achieve . . . They worked on gathering huge and effective amounts of wealth to achieve their goal. With wealth they controlled the international mass media-news services, newspapers, printing presses, broadcast stations and more . . . With money they ignited revolutions in all parts of the world to realize their benefits and reap the fruits of them. They are behind the French Revolution, the Communist Revolution, and most of the revolutions here and there . . . With wealth they formed secret organizations throughout the world to destroy societies and promote the Zionist cause; those organizations include the freemasons, the Rotary and Lions clubs, and others . . .

With wealth they controlled imperialistic nations and pushed them to occupy many nations to exhaust their natural resources and spread mischief in them.

    . . . They are behind the First World War in which they destroyed the Islamic Caliph and gained material profit, monopolized raw wealth, and got the Balfour Declaration [which laid the groundwork for the creation of Israel]. They created the League of Nations so they could control the world through that organization. They are behind the Second World War . . . and set down the foundations to establish their nation by forming the United Nations and Security Council instead of the League of Nations in order to rule the world through that organization.

    There is not a war that goes on here or there in which their fingers are not playing behind it.

Article 32 cites as the authoritative source for this international Jewish conspiracy the anti-Semitic counterfeit text *Protocols of the Learned Elders of Zion:* "Today it's Palestine and tomorrow it will be another country, and then another. The Zionist plan has no bounds and after Palestine they wish to expand from the Nile River to the Euphrates. When they totally occupy it they will look towards another, and such is their plan in the 'Protocols of the Learned Elders of Zion.' "

Just as Khomeini saw modernizing Arab leaders as a threat to his cherished Islamic republic, so too the extremist Hamas organization views the more moderate Palestine Liberation Organization and the peace process as a threat to their mission to free the Holy Land from non-Muslim rule.[34]

Thus, the use of violence in the defense and expansion of Islam is not only accepted but embraced by a significant section of the Muslim political community. There are many reasons for this readiness to use violence, and a paranoid worldview is one of them.

### Killing in the Name of Jehovah

Like the radical Muslims who are impelled to violent acts in defense of their faith, some messianic Zionist settlers have become militant warriors in defense of the Promised Land and their faith. Some Orthodox Jews have reacted to the permissive modern age as a profound threat and have withdrawn into tightly knit communities, whether in or out of Israel, rejecting all of the modern world, including the state of Israel. Others see Israel as the promised kingdom of God, *Eretz Yisrael*.

Avraham Yitzhak Hacohen Kook was the chief rabbi of Palestine in 1948, at the time of the British mandate. Whereas many Orthodox Jews had turned away from secular political Zionism and rejected the concept of the Jewish state, Kook conceived of a union of the divine idea and nationalist sentiment, and his followers were to become spiritual belligerents in the pursuit of the kingdom of Israel.

## Gush Emunim Radicals

The 1967 Six-Day War was a singular moment in the history of Israel.[35] The dramatic victory reunified Jerusalem, enabling Israel to reclaim the Old City and the West Wall of the ancient Temple (among the most sacred sites in Judaism), biblical Judea and Samaria (the West Bank of the Jordan River), the Golan Heights, and the Sinai Peninsula. The largely nonreligious Zionist nationalists experienced a resurgence of pride and religious Jewish identity. With the regained land encompassing Judea and Samaria, the boundaries of Israel were now essentially those of biblical Israel. So astonishing was the victory that to many religious Jews it seemed like a miracle.

Rabbi Kook's son and successor, Rabbi Zvi Yehuda Kook, saw God's hand in the triumph of Israel in the 1967 war. The regaining of Eretz Yisrael signaled the imminent arrival of the Messiah. Three weeks before the war, Rabbi Kook had delivered a sermon entitled "They Divided Up My Land," in which he prophetically stated: "They divided up my land. Yes—this is true. Where is our Hebron? Do we let it be forgotten? And where are our Shechem [Nablus] and our Jericho? [Both cities were then under Jordanian rule.] Where are they? Can we ever forsake them? All of Transjordan—it is ours. Every single inch, every square foot, . . . belong to the Land of Israel. Do we have the right to give up even one millimeter?"[36] The Israeli victory three weeks later, which brought the land once again into Israeli hands, endowed this sermon with mystical force for the followers of Rabbi Kook. Believing that the secular Israeli army was the unwitting instrument of God's will, Rabbi Kook and his followers declared 1967 Year One of the Era of Redemption.

Six years later, however, in October 1973, the Yom Kippur War shattered the illusion of Jewish invulnerability. Israel was not defeated, though at one stage the country was on the precipice of defeat. The ruling Labor government was pressured both from within Israel and from the United States to relinquish occupied territory in order to defuse the explosive situation and achieve peace with Arab neighbors. In the view of Rabbi Kook and his followers, this situation threatened to undo God's will. In February 1974, they founded Gush Emunim (Movement of the Faithful), dedicated to fulfilling the biblical prophecy of the Promised Land, committed to not yielding "one millimeter" of the land that in their view belonged to the Jews by virtue of the covenant between God and his chosen people. To ensure this unity, Gush began to establish settlements in the occupied territories, trying to establish "facts on the ground" to guarantee that none of the God-given land would be relinquished as part of any peace negotiations. Their intent was to annex the occupied territories.

A precursor of Gush's settlement strategy was a particularly provocative act in 1967 in Hebron. Rabbi Moshe Levinger and a small group of followers occupied a hotel in this Palestinian West Bank city to claim it for Israel. Hebron had historical significance for Israel, and in 1970 ardent Zionists, following Levinger's example, founded the settlement of Kiryat Arba near Hebron.

The Labor government resisted the establishment of these settlements. But the situation changed when Menachem Begin's conservative and religiously oriented Likud party won the 1977 election. Gush found active support in the prime minister, a strongly religious Zionist with a deep sense of history, who supported a strategy of settlements throughout the occupied territories, congruent with Gush's goal of re-Judaization from above.

The Likud government's 1977 land-for-peace negotiations with Egypt were, however, taken as a betrayal by Gush. In their view the negotiations threatened a delay in the arrival of the Messiah, an arrival that had been foreshadowed by the regaining of the Promised Land in the 1967 war.

The Camp David accords and the 1979 peace treaty, which entailed the return of the Sinai, confirmed the betrayal.

In 1980 radicals within Gush reacted to Palestinian attacks on the settlements by initiating a campaign of counterterror. In May 1980, a group of Gush Emunim settlers were gunned down while leaving a synagogue in Hebron. The government deported three Arab leaders to Lebanon. Considering the government's response feeble, the Gush radicals booby-trapped the cars of three West Bank Palestinian mayors, seriously wounding them. The Israeli government did not press an investigation, and no punishment occurred. Violence flared again in 1983 after a yeshiva student was killed in Hebron; the radicals again retaliated, killing three Palestinians at the Islamic university in the same city. After Israeli buses were attacked in 1984, the Gush radicals were about to plant bombs on five Arab buses when Israeli security arrested the conspirators.

With the arrest and subsequent interrogation, a plan of alarming dimensions was revealed. The Gush underground intended to dynamite one of the holiest sites of Islam—the Dome of the Rock in Jerusalem—which sits atop the Temple Mount, the holiest Jewish site. (It is the location of the First and Second Temples and will be, it is believed, the site of the Third Temple when the Messiah arrives.)

Within Gush, a group of ardent messianic Jews had formed the Gush Emunim underground. They reasoned that the intensely religious Zionist Menachem Begin could not have voluntarily yielded part of Eretz Yisrael in the Camp David concessions. Therefore this was an act of God, reproaching the Jewish people. But for what? The offense, they concluded, must be the continuing presence of the "abomination," the Dome of the Rock, on the Temple Mount. Accordingly, the removal of this blemish was required to ensure the Messiah's arrival on earth.[37] The object of the destruction of the al-Aksah Mosque and the Dome of the Rock, the third holiest shrine in Islam, was to transform the secular state of Israel into the kingdom of Israel, which "will be no more an ordinary state."[38]

If carried out, the bombing of this Islamic holy site surely would have precipitated the most extreme Arab reaction, perhaps a major war. The Gush Emunim welcomed this possibility. The leaders of the Gush underground estimated that the destruction of the Dome of the Rock "would arouse hundreds of millions of Muslims to a jihad sweeping all mankind into an ultimate confrontation . . . Israel's victorious emergence from this longed for trial by fire would then pave the way for the coming of the Messiah.''[39] War or no war, the goal of this plan was to demonstrate their faith, to prepare for the rebuilding of the Temple by ''cleansing'' the Temple Mount of the ''abomination'' and to force the end.

When the population of Israel did not launch large protests against the 1979 evacuation of the Sinai, the organizers of the Temple Mount plot came to believe that their violent plan would not receive support within Israel. Rabbi Kook, rather more politically astute than his ardent followers, refused to sanction the act, and the plan was shelved. Although it was not enacted, the Temple Mount plot represents the extreme of Jewish justification of violence against their Arab enemies in the name of God.

## The Massacre at the Tomb of the Patriarchs

On February 25, 1994, when Dr. Baruch Goldstein walked into the mosque atop the Tomb of the Patriarchs in Hebron and fired his automatic weapon into the worshiping Muslims, killing or wounding at least 130 of them, the act was decried by Israeli Prime Minister Yitzhak Rabin as that of a mentally unstable man. The evening before, Goldstein, a physician, had tended to the wounds of friends injured in the Muslim uprising on the Israel-occupied territories on the West Bank, and he had become increasingly distressed. His act was the culmination of feelings that had been building over time—feelings at one with those of five hundred of his fellow settlers in the radical Jewish settlement of Kiryat Arba, who celebrated the massacre and hailed him as a hero.

Also on the night before the massacre, Goldstein had read to his two young daughters from the Book of Esther, which tells the story of the Jewish festival of Purim, to be celebrated the next day. According to a neighbor and friend, Goldstein had seen several of his neighbors die at the hands of terrorists and believed that militant aggression was the only course open to the settlers. Purim, the friend explained, ''is a holiday to kill the people who are trying to kill the Jews.''[40]

Purim celebrates the deliverance of the Jews in ancient Persia from a planned massacre at the hands of Haman, minister to King Ahasuerus. In what may be considered the first political use of anti-Semitism, Haman, shamed by the Jew Mordecai's refusal to bow before him, had persuaded King Ahasuerus to kill the Jews of the kingdom. With the intervention of Queen Esther, the niece of Mordecai, Haman's plan was reversed: he himself was hanged on the gallows erected for Mordecai, and the Jews killed their would-be persecutors. For most Jews Purim is a joyous celebration of deliverance. But for some it is a celebration of violence, commemorating an uprising of the Jews against their enemies, a day of righteous wrath when "the Jews smote all their enemies with the stroke of the sword and with slaughter and destruction, and did what they would unto them that hated them" (Esther 9:1).

It was on Purim that Baruch Goldstein gunned down the Arabs praying at the Tomb of the Patriarchs. Goldstein had given voice to his beliefs in an extended interview in the spring of 1988:

> I don't think Israel needs the help of America or any other country. We need the help of God . . . Anybody who acts to support the Jewish people in the end will be rewarded; anybody who acts against the Jewish people in the end will be punished. That's a promise God gave Abraham, and that's a promise that exists today: "I will bless those who bless you and curse those who curse you."
>
> The media is trying to portray [the Arab-Israeli conflict] as a problem only of Judea and Samaria, and is playing down what is happening inside the '67 borders. People say you can't live with the Arabs, and you can't keep so many soldiers here permanently, so the solution is coexistence. I say the land belongs to us, and the Arabs don't belong to us, so the land we should keep. The Arabs we should let go. . . .
>
> They are a people who want to spill blood. If they had the opportunity, they would make a holocaust in Israel.
>
> We have to act as Jews, and this means fulfilling the Commandments, which includes holding on to the land of Israel. Then God will protect us. If not, then we get punished. It sounds very simple, but that's the way it is. [God] continually recreates the world, and whoever fulfills his commandments he will reward, and whoever doesn't he will punish.

When the Jewish people is seen as weak, then the God of Israel is seen as weak. When the Nazis were able to trample the Jews and step on the Jews with their boots, then their obvious question was: So where is your God? Jewish weakness is seen by the world as a symbol of God's weakness, and that's why I say it's a desecration of God's name.

I'm not looking to punish the Arabs. I'm looking to rid ourselves of this danger, and any way that's possible, I think it should be done . . . I'm not saying we should be bad to others, but if someone is trying to hurt a Jew, I think he should be hit hard.

The Arabs are the Nazis of [today]. The same thing Hitler wanted to do in Germany they want to do here in Israel and any talk about territories is just covering up the main purpose. . . .

Will the world accept us driving them out? Eventually we're going to have to drive them out, or we'll be driven out. Either one or the other.[41]

These are the words of a committed Zionist, not one suffering from a mental disorder, but assuredly one under siege. The years between the 1988 interview and the massacre, when the violence perpetrated by Palestinian intifada activists against Jewish settlers became only more intense, would have done nothing to diminish the vehemence of his views.

The February 1994 massacre was greeted with enthusiasm by many Jewish settlers on the West Bank, although they realized that what Goldstein had done would endanger them and produce reprisals. But they applauded the massacre and honored the "martyred" Goldstein because he had acted out their collective fantasy, an expression of ideologically grounded defensive aggression.

## Meir Kahane

Goldstein was a devoted follower of the Jewish-American activist Rabbi Meir Kahane, whose book *Never Again!* is an exposition of the "fighting Jew," grounded in the Old Testament and Talmudic commentary. Kahane started with the unexceptional Talmudic statement "If one comes to slay you—slay him first."[42] This principle is simply one of self-defense. A second principle of Kahane also seems unexceptional: "Ahavat Yisroel" (love of Israel).[43] Kahane cites the Old Testament verse "Thou shalt not stand idly by your brother's blood" (Leviticus 19:16) and the Talmudic commentary that states that if a person "sees someone pursuing his comrade with the purpose of killing him, he is free to save a life through killing the pursuer."[44]

There is nothing paranoid about these quotations from Leviticus and the Talmud. They provide a moral sanction for defending a relative or friend under attack. What is dangerous is interpreting such obligations in a paranoid manner. If a person believes that the world consists of enemies desiring to kill one's group, then these religious injunctions provide moral license to kill almost any outsider.

Kahane and his followers drew on many other commentaries, such as Maimonides' exhortation to wage "obligatory war" against Jewish enemies,[45] the duty of Jews to lay down their own lives for another Jew,[46] and the obligation of Jews to be skilled in war.

## The Assassination of Prime Minister Yitzhak Rabin

In Kings of Israel Square in Tel Aviv, at a peace rally attended by more than a hundred thousand people on November 4, 1995, Israeli Prime Minister Yitzhak Rabin, winner of the 1994 Nobel Peace Prize, was assassinated. The assassin was not a Palestinian terrorist but a twenty-seven-year-old Orthodox Jew who was a law student at Bar-Ilan University and a member of Israel's extremist religious right. At his arrest, the assassin, Yigal Amir, told the police: "I acted alone on God's orders. I have no regret."[47] Shortly after the arrest, Avishai Raviv, leader of Eyal, the outlawed right-wing group founded by Kahane and to which Amir belonged, indicated in a television interview that his group "admires the lad [Amir] for his sincerity, for standing behind his words . . . This man Rabin is responsible for the murder of hundreds of Jews."[48] He was referring to the ideology of the extreme right, which held that the government's agreement to cede control of parts of the West Bank was a surrender of the Jews' biblical heritage and posed a mortal threat to Jews by creating a haven for Palestinian terrorists. Subsequently Raviv and other members of Eyal were arrested, and officials indicated their belief that the assassination was the result of a conspiracy.

As the peace process advanced, the stridency of the rhetoric in Israel's extreme religious right had increased to incendiary proportions. The land-for-peace terms of the Oslo agreement meant relinquishing Israeli control over the West Bank of the Jordan River, called Judea and Samaria by the religious right. The militant Orthodox opponents of the Rabin government believed that the land had been given to the Jewish people by God, and for the secular government to give away the Promised Land was a violation of God's command. Extremists had branded Rabin a traitor and murderer, and effigies of Rabin in a Nazi uniform were prominent at right-wing rallies. This inflammatory rhetoric was not confined to the extreme right. Opposition Likud Party chairman Binyamin Netanyahu had invoked the threat of a Palestinian state on Israel's border in a speech shortly before the assassination: "You, Mr. Prime Minister, are going to go down in history as the Prime Minister who established an army of terrorists."[49]

At his interrogation, Amir stated that he killed the prime minister to prevent the handing over of land to the Palestinians and that he had followed Jewish religious law in doing so. He called Rabin a "pursuer," quoting the Talmudic commentary so frequently cited by Kahane: a person is free, indeed obligated, to kill an assailant who poses a mortal threat, "to save a life through killing the pursuer." "According to Jewish law," Amir asserted at his hearing, "the minute a Jew betrays his people and country to the enemy, he must be killed . . . I've been studying Talmud all my life, and I have all the data."[50] Commenting on the interrogation, Police Minister Moshe Shahal indicated that the assassin was influenced by militant rabbis who had regularly indicated that Rabin's policies posed a mortal danger to Israel and the Jewish people. Amir's motives drew on halakic (Jewish religious law) rulings made by the rabbis that the "pursuer's decree has effect on Rabin."[51] Students at Bar-Ilan University recalled a Talmudic colloquy of several days' duration among Amir and his yeshiva classmates several months earlier in which Amir had drawn on the twelfth-century Law of Kings. Amir claimed that Rabin qualified for a *din rodef,* the "judgment of the pursuer," entitling a righteous man to kill him, because Rabin was poised to spill the blood of other Jews by giving up control of the West Bank.

At a meeting of religious nationalist leaders after the assassination,

Rabbi Yoel Ben Nun, a prominent West Bank rabbi, revealed that certain rabbis had invoked the "law of the pursuer" against Rabin and Shimon Peres, the former foreign minister who had negotiated the Oslo accords and who assumed the prime ministership after Rabin's assassination. He indicated, "There are those among us who still say that Rabin deserved death because of the injunction [in Jewish law] regarding someone who wants to kill you."[52]

Amir had devoted his life to the study of the Old Testament and the Talmud. He was a true believer whose extreme religious ideology was central to his self-concept. The abandonment of Judea and Samaria by the secular Rabin government was a threat to his psychological integrity and that of other ardent Jews of the extreme right. He struck out, finding justification for his act in the religious writings he had studied throughout his life.

Statements from the Old Testament and the Talmud, pillars of moral force, have been drawn upon to provide a religious rationale for striking out against the enemies of one's faith. Some Jews, then, like some Muslims, have invoked their holy literature to justify killing in the name of God. And Christians have done the same.

## Killing in the Name of Jesus

We're in a battle between good and evil.
—John Burt, fundamentalist Christian minister and regional
director of the anti-abortion organization Rescue America

Although initially heralded as a religion of love, Christianity soon became a religion of violence as well. In western and southern Europe Christianity spread largely through conversion of kings and other rulers, but in eastern Europe military-religious orders like the Teutonic Knights presented a harsher face and forced conversions. The spirit of the Teutonic Knights was present at Charles Martel's victory over the invading Muslims near Poitiers in 732, which, although defensive, was followed by seven centuries of aggression in the Iberian Peninsula.

Most Christian violence was directed against other Christians, even when the followers of Jesus set out to free the Holy Sepulchre from Islam.

The ill-disciplined mobs that made up the People's Crusade so provoked their fellow Christians in Hungary that the Hungarians destroyed them. (The People's Crusade, however, succeeded better against the Jews of the Rhineland, the least unfortunate of whom were dispersed eastward.) One People's Crusade reached Constantinople, pillaging and murdering to such an extent that Emperor Alexius Comnenus arranged for the Crusaders to be massacred by the Muslim Seljuks.

The disordered People's Crusade was followed by the first organized effort to reconquer the Holy Land. Beginning in 1097, the First Crusade also directed much of its venom against fellow Christians, although the Crusaders were far from averse to slaying Muslims as well. Fueled by idealism, as so many murderous enterprises are, another six Crusades followed, ending only in 1250 with the capture and ransoming of Louis IX of France.

Most of the religious killing, however, took place not on Crusades but close to home. In the early thirteenth century many Albigenses in the south of France adopted the ancient doctrine of the Persian Mani, who stated that all existence was a struggle between light and dark, perfect good and absolute evil. The Albigenses believed themselves to be good Christians, and they did lead lives of exemplary virtue, but their criticism of the pope and their doctrine that Jesus had been a rebel against the harsh God of the Old Testament, not Jehovah's mild and dutiful son, provoked massacres against them so widespread as to amount to genocide.

The thirteenth century also saw the beginning of the Spanish Inquisition. Its evil reputation has been exaggerated. Much of what occurred simply lived up to its name—inquisitions, inquiries—without violence. Yet this body, which operated well into the nineteenth century, had as its object the imposition of orthodox thinking and often used torture to that end. Some thirty thousand Jews died for their faith during the Inquisition. In a particularly bloody pogrom which swept through Spain in 1391, the cry of "Convert to the Holy Faith or die" presented the Jews with only two alternatives (although sometimes expulsion was permitted). Religion was as much a matter of political loyalty as confessional unity. Here we see how a stressful situation (the Christians were in a life-and-death battle with the Muslims) and a legitimate political demand (that there be political unity behind one's own lines) can feed a paranoid dynamic. Those who do not believe exactly as we do are a threat to our political unity and our belief system, and they must either be coerced into capitulation or be destroyed. By the mid-fifteenth century, the *conversos* (Jewish converts) of Spain had become the enemy as well, and race and religion had become fused. In a foreshadowing of the Holocaust, laws of racial purity were passed, and high-ranking conversos were expelled from their positions because of "impure blood."[53]

The apogee of Christians killing Christians in the name of Christianity was reached in 1618 in the Thirty Years' War in the Germanic lands. The Protestant Reformation's elimination of a common Christian society led to an entire generation of looting, pillaging, and murder. It exceeded the misery accompanying the barbarian invasions at the end of the Roman Empire.

Although killing in the name of Jesus continued after the war ended in 1648, nationalism and imperialism then became the great sources of violence in the Christian lands. These became the new religions of Europe—that is, those things for which people were willing not only to kill but also to die.

But if the Christianity of the modern West is a far different institution from its seventeenth-century ancestors, and a less bloody one, it can still sometimes behave like them. While Christianity, especially in its milder versions—Episcopalianism, Presbyterianism, and Methodism—is not often seen as having a paranoid dimension and indeed appears particularly resistant to this psychopathic virus, here too the paranoid organism can find a susceptible host and spread the paranoid infection.

C. S. Lewis was one of the most prominent popular writers of Christian doctrine in the mid-twentieth century. A modest and moderate man, he gave short (and uncontroversial) talks about Christianity on BBC radio during World War II. He later wrote the amusing *Screwtape Letters,* in which a minor demon argues (unsuccessfully) against Christianity. Lewis' own faith was Church of England, which appears in somewhat altered form in the United States as Episcopalianism. It is an establishmentarian and temperate doctrine.

Yet Lewis, in *Mere Christianity,* an expanded revision of his BBC lectures, describes an aspect of Christianity—one he believed in—that was paranoid:

> One of the things that surprised me when I first read the New Testament seriously was that it talked so much about a Dark Power in the universe—a mighty evil spirit who was held to be the Power behind death and disease, and sin. The difference is that Christianity thinks this Dark Power was created by God, and was good when he was created by God, and went wrong. Christianity [believes] that this universe is at war. But it does not think this is a war between independent powers. It thinks it is a civil war, a rebellion, and that we are living in a part of the universe occupied by the rebel. Enemy-occupied territory—that is what this world is . . . When you go to church you are really listening in to the secret wireless from our friends . . . Christians, then, believe that an evil power has made himself for the present Prince of the World.[54]

Lewis further notes that the devil works in many disguises, especially those of rationalists, seemingly well meaning and kindly persons who mock and denigrate religion. Not only are we in enemy-occupied territory, but we cannot know whom to trust.

This paranoid theme appeared with great power in several American politico-religious movements beginning in the mid-1970s. Seeking to re-Christianize America, they provided important support to the election campaign of Ronald Reagan. Jerry Falwell's Moral Majority was particularly prominent at that time. In his Action Program, he indicated that there are "five major problems that have political consequences, political implications, that moral Americans should be ready to face: abortion, homosexuality, pornography, humanism, the fractured family." Among these issues, Falwell gave the issue of abortion highest priority.[55]

Since the 1973 *Roe v. Wade* Supreme Court decision, which largely legalized abortion on demand, abortion has been the political issue that has galvanized fundamentalist Christians in the United States. Until that time, abortions were illegal in almost every American jurisdiction, and this prohibition had general religious support. The massive changes in the direction of personal choice in the Western world in the 1960s resulted in the abandonment of many restrictions—especially regarding sexual practices—and also in a decline in the status of many institutions, especially religious ones. Fundamentalist Protestants suffered more from this decline in status than any other group. The abortion issue struck a strong emotional chord in this group, and they could receive support on this issue from their erstwhile antagonist, the Catholic Church. In addition, many non-fundamentalists and non-Catholics felt uneasy about legalizing abortion.

The four topics that politicians most fear to discuss—because they are so emotive—are sex, violence, the treatment of children, and religion. The abortion issue draws on all four topics.[56] It is ironic that the issue over which some religious extremists have committed murder has been the preservation of life.

The question of when a fetus can be granted status as a full human being has been central to the debate over abortion rights. Members of the pro-life anti-abortion movement believe that human life begins at conception, so there is no moral difference between killing a fetus and killing an infant. By this reasoning, abortionists are not only murderers but also child murderers, and mass murderers in most cases. Women who have an abortion are killing their own children. Some, especially liberal Catholics, argue against abortion for the same reason that they oppose war or capital punishment—that only God may take life.

The concept of abortion as murder has led the extremists of the movement to liken the legalization of abortion to genocide, to a "resurrection of the spirit of Nazism." Holocaust rhetoric is prominent among anti-abortion activists. A position paper of the Fundamentalist Bible Tabernacle states: "The response of Bible-believing Christians has been almost the same as it was in Hitler's Germany. Those who claim to believe their Bibles have responded to the abortion holocaust in America by doing little if anything."[57]

Following the logic of their beliefs, anti-abortionists have murdered abortionists. David Gunn, medical director of the Women's Medical Services Clinic in Pensacola, Florida, was assassinated by abortion activist Michael Griffin in March 1993. Griffin, a member of Rescue America (an extremist anti-abortion organization), told police that he had acted for God.[58]

Soon after three Christmas Day fire bombings of abortion clinics in Pensacola in 1984, two young Christian fundamentalist defendants, James Simmons and Matthew Goldsby, said that God had instructed them to bomb the clinics. The young perpetrators called the bombs a "birthday gift for Jesus."[59] They had planted their first bomb in a clinic in June 1984, escaping undetected. In their view, this escape was a sign from God that what they had done was right, and the event encouraged them to plan the Christmas bombings.[60]

This level of violence had been building for more than a decade. The beginning of the movement, in 1973, was characterized by relatively mild protest: stink bombs were thrown, clinic locks were cemented, clinic entrances were blockaded, and so on. From 1982 to 1992 the following acts were committed by the anti-abortion movement in the United States:

- 32 bombings,
- 54 incidents of arson,
- 76 cases of assault and battery,
- 129 death threats, and
- 296 acts of vandalism against abortion providers.

Between 1987 and 1993 thirty-three thousand arrests were made in the United States in connection with the anti-abortion movement.

Although few of the official pro-life organizations openly condone violence, one group that has actively advocated it is the Army of God, which has published a handbook detailing ways to commit terrorism without being captured while causing the largest impact.[61] Another such group is Defensive Action, a "small group of about 30 pastors and church leaders from across the country who have signed a declaration proclaiming the Godly justice of taking all action necessary to protect unborn life." Paul Hill, leader of Defensive Action, stated, "The police use force to protect abortionists. Abortion is murder, and murderers deserve to be executed." Hill (a former minister who had been excommunicated from his Presbyterian church) insisted that "executing abortion providers was a moral imperative."[62]

Protestant fundamentalists seldom draw on pre-Reformation doctrine to support killing abortionists. But David C. Trosch of Mobile, Alabama, a Roman Catholic priest, has defended killing abortion doctors as "justifiable homicide,'' citing the writings of St. Augustine and St. Thomas Aquinas: ''There is full human life, by Christian common belief, in the womb following conception. They are persons worthy of defense, like any born person, and they must be defended by any means necessary to protect them, including the death of the assailants, which in this case would be the abortionists and their direct accomplices.''[63]

Roman Catholic archbishop Oscar H. Lipscomb criticized Trosch in a letter of pastoral instruction, citing the biblical commandment against killing and stressing that citizens must not usurp the role of civil authorities. Trosch dismissed the archbishop's arguments, stating that God's law supersedes civil law. He wrote to the Vatican, warning of ''coming catastrophes'' that would wipe out a fifth of the world's population. He wrote to members of Congress, warning of a possible civil war with ''massive killings'' of abortion doctors. Asked if he would not feel guilty if his sermons and speeches incited someone to murder an abortion doctor, Trosch responded, ''Defending innocent human life is not murder. You're comparing the lives of morally guilty persons against the lives of manifestly innocent persons. That's like trying to compare the lives of the Jews in the incinerators in Nazi Germany or Poland or wherever with the lives of the Gestapo.'' He also made an analogy to the French Resistance in World War II: ''When they killed their enemy soldiers, did anybody ever admonish them? In fact, they were considered heroes.''[64]

In the view of these religious warriors, the women's movement, feminism, abortion rights, and the decline of religious influence are all connected. There is a distinctly paranoid flavor in imputing a dark organizing force to these social movements. They are all part of the trend toward personal choice or permissiveness, originating in large part in the 1960s, which fundamentalist Christians abhor. To echo C. S. Lewis, the most extreme and violent of the abortion activists see themselves living in ''enemy-occupied territory'' dominated by a dark power that ''has made himself for the present Prince of the World.''

A perspective on the violent Protestant anti-abortion movement can be gained by looking at the Roman Catholic Church's position on anti-abortion violence. The church's opposition to abortion is as uncompromising as that of the Protestant fundamentalists, and it uses the same arguments. But Catholics, who are encouraged to demonstrate peacefully

against clinics, are forbidden to use violence. The church also notes that
God permits killing only in the most extreme cases, and it does not consider abortion such a case. Thus, the church balances values and considers
alternatives.

It is the overvaluation of a single idea that is the hallmark of the
paranoid mindset. Paranoid characters are dominated by one concept.
That idea may have merit, but the paranoid grossly and obsessively exaggerates its importance, subordinating every other value to it and willing
to commit any act to fulfill it. The complete dominance of this idea means
that paranoid fanatics live within a closed ideational system, a sealed
castle of invincible ignorance immune to competing considerations.[65] It
is this commitment to logic without sense that leads some fundamentalist
Protestants to use violence, including murder, to "preserve life."

One can have strong religiously based opposition to abortion without
taking life in pursuit of that cause, just as one can be committed to Zionism or Palestinian nationalism without taking innocent life. Yet in all
three of these cases, those who take life in pursuit of their causes claim
religious justification.

But Judaism, Christianity, and Islam are not the only religions that
advocate killing in the name of God. Consider Sikhism, a religion that
developed largely outside these traditions.

## The Religion of Warriors and Saints

Sikhism was established in the early sixteenth century in the Punjab, a
region that now is divided between India and Pakistan.[66] The Sikhs today
number about 18 million—2 percent of India's population. Aside from
their strategic prominence in the Punjab, India's granary, they enjoy
prominence owing to their importance in such security-oriented occupa-
tions as the military and the police. Sikhs constitute about 12 percent of
the military's enlisted men and 20 percent of India's officer corps. Male
Sikhs are known for their proud bearing and virile aspect. They generally
wear turbans (their religion forbids the cutting of hair), which adds to
their height, and they carry weapons because of their religion's requirement that male Sikhs always be armed. Sikhs who are police officers,
guards, or soldiers may also carry the weapons associated with their pro-

fessions. The Sikh community is relatively well off, with an average income about twice India's national average.

Sikhism, although it grew out of Hinduism, is a distinct religion—it rejects the holiness of the Hindu Vedas, any suggestion of idolatry, and the entire caste system, including the special authority of Brahmins. Its origin in Hinduism is manifested by its retention of the concept of karma (the continuity of personal responsibility through rebirth). Its separate status is frequently not recognized by Hindus, who often consider Sikhism a branch of Hinduism. This belief and the sometimes condescending attitude associated with it have fueled anger and insecurity among many Sikhs.

Part of the impetus for Sikhism's development was Islamic pressure in the sixteenth and seventeenth centuries. In this period the Sikhs—then properly considered a Hindu sect—became the protectors of the Punjabi Hindus against Islamic aggression. They gradually came to be the rulers of the Punjab, defeating the Muslims and the fierce invading Hindu Marathas from the south and succumbing only to the British, with whom they eventually allied themselves.

So it was that Sikhism developed from a sect into a religion, and the Sikhs developed from a people into a nation. Like Islam—historically its great opponent—Sikhism continues to be influenced by its warrior origins while maintaining a strong ethical system. Calling themselves the *khalsa* (the pure or elect), Sikhs frequently take the name *Singh* (lion) as an indication of their bravery. Two of the religion's symbols—a short sword that every Sikh is to carry at all times, and brief undertrousers that are always to be worn—mark each Sikh man as a warrior ready for battle. Among the khalsa, there is an even fiercer faction, the *akali*—the religion's shock troops pledged to accept death for their faith. Violence is a central theme in Sikhism's traditional recounting of its history.

With the partitioning of the British Indian empire in 1947, the new Muslim nation of Pakistan expelled the Sikhs from the western Punjab. They concentrated themselves in the eastern Punjab, under Indian rule. Peace, hard work, and the agricultural benefits of the Green Revolution permitted the Sikhs to prosper. Ironically, the economic prosperity and generally higher educational levels of the Sikhs attracted immigrants from the rest of India, and the previously strongly Sikh eastern Punjab gained many Hindus. The dilution of Sikhism was compounded by the increased secularization of some low-status and low-income Sikhs.

In this period, a conflict developed concerning language: Punjabi Muslims more and more often spoke Urdu; non-Punjabi Hindus, Hindi; and Sikhs and Punjabi Hindus, Punjabi. The languages are closely related, and all those in the region could and often did speak Punjabi, but the Sikhs claimed Punjabi as their special language. The Sikhs also called for the script of their holy works, Gurumakhi, to be made the official script. In seeking a Punjabi-speaking, Gurumakhi-writing state, the traditionalist Sikhs were in effect seeking a Sikh state. Competition, moreover, was not only for linguistic dominance but also for converts. The uncertain status of the Sikhs gave rise to conflict not only with non-Sikhs but also with those Sikhs who were less orthodox, more sympathetic toward Hindus.[67] The establishment of the states of Punjab and Haryana in 1966 temporarily satisfied Sikh demands, but many Sikhs rebelled again in the 1980s and 1990s.

By mid-1984 the Punjab had become a land of civil war, with radical Sikhs fighting other Sikhs and the Indian government. It was widely believed that the radical Sikhs were receiving covert aid from their traditional enemies, Pakistani Muslims, who disliked the government of India even more than they disliked the Sikhs. The Muslims hoped to fragment India by supporting the radical Sikhs, who believed that the practice of their religion required a separate country, Khalistan. Thus, we again see the dynamic where a group identifies its political status with its religious mission and asserts the divine right to kill others in the furtherance of that mission.[68]

The militant charismatic Sikh leader, Jarmail Singh Bhindranwale (who, like David Koresh, died with scores of his followers at the hands of a besieging government), proclaimed the Sikhs' separate identity as a religious community with national characteristics. In his fiery sermons Bhindranwale demonized opponents of Sikhism and exhorted his followers to kill those who insulted their faith: ''Unless you are prepared to die, sacrificing your own life, you cannot be a free people. . . . If you start thinking in terms of sacrifice to your community, you will be on the right path and you will readily sacrifice yourself. The Sikh faith is to pray to God, take one's vows before the Guru Granth Sahib [Scriptures] and then act careless of consequences to self . . . Seek justice against those who have dishonored our sisters, drunk the blood of innocent persons, and insulted Satguru Granth Sahib.''[69] This provocative rhetoric led to internecine killing in the Punjab, the Sikh shrine known as the Golden Temple being used as a base for terrorism, the storming of that temple (at the cost of many lives), the assassination of Prime Minister Indira Gandhi, anti-Sikh riots, and continuing bloodshed.

The ideology of the radical Sikh follows a familiar pattern:

1. *The cosmic struggle is played out in history.* In order to commit violence, the devout must believe that the cosmic struggle can be realized in human terms. The struggle between good and evil as depicted in the great Hindu epics has continued in historical time. The contemporary adversary is identified with the legendary demonized foe.

2. *Believers identify personally with the struggle.* Under the guidance of their spiritual leaders, the devout feel personally responsible for the moral decadence in the world. A battle between good and evil is taking place within the soul, but by joining forces with others, the true believer can externalize the battlefield.

3. *The cosmic struggle continues in the present.* Despite the appearance of calm and tranquillity, under the surface the battle between the forces of good and evil still rages.

4. *The struggle is at a point of crisis.* Apocalyptic rhetoric is used to promote a sense of urgency to join in the momentous battle.

5. *Acts of violence have a cosmic meaning.* To act in the service of one's faith is to demonstrate great valor and piety. Not to so act is a sin. In exhorting Sikhs to defend their faith, Bhindranwale said, "There is no greater sin for a Sikh than keeping weapons and not using them to protect his faith."[70]

As of late 1996 the militant Sikhs have been suppressed. As in other religious struggles, the violence and the provocation were not only on one side. The religious Sikhs were at times abused, deceived, and persecuted. It is commonly believed in the Punjab, for example, that Indian security forces involved in suppressing the revolt were given substantial bounties for the corpses of Sikh militants. The Sikhs will not forget, and killing in the name of God is not a habit easily broken. Thus, such killing is not limited to one religion or even to one group of religions, such as those with ties to the Old Testament.

Each of these instances of killing in the name of God reflects a paranoid social system with a powerful governing idea. The perpetrators felt besieged by an aggressive world of unbelievers. Their belief systems, central to their psychological integrity, were under attack. If the outside world does literally attack, as dramatically exemplified by the Branch Davidian siege and the attack on the Golden Temple of the Sikhs, their beliefs are further strengthened.

Aggression is required to defend against the world of unbelief. This defensive aggression is intended to protect the true believers from victimization. Their feelings of persecution are not wholly delusional: for example, Palestinians have died at the hands of Israeli soldiers, Israelis have been killed by Palestinian terrorists, and Hamas has called for the destruction of Israel.

When a population is overwhelmed by the world around it and sinks into despair, the path may be one of withdrawal. But when the situation is desperate and the population has not succumbed to despair, the path may be militant fundamentalism.[71] The religious fanatic in a crumbling world needs to attack the threats to his structure of meaning. The corruption and immorality of the modernizing world may threaten the pillars of the belief system, so that world must be attacked to defend the faith. Righteous rage, channeled perhaps by a destructive charismatic, confirmed perhaps by a widely and intensely held belief of the members of a group, thus maintains and restores the psychological equilibrium of the group and of the individual.[72]

This dynamic is represented broadly in the realm of politics. The ideology may be Marxism or Serbian nationalism rather than Islam, Judaism, or Christianity. Fanatic belief, religious or secular, is regularly at the heart of political extremism. In order for a group to become a mass movement, in order for a nation to be led into war, inchoate feelings of discontent and frustration are insufficient. The paranoid leader, to channel these powerful but unfocused feelings, requires a body of ideas.

# 7

## Paranoia's Theorists

A new disease? I know not, new or old,
But it may well be call'd poor mortals' plague;
For, like a pestilence, it doth infect
The houses of the brain . . .
Till not a thought, or motion, in the mind,
Be free from the black poison of suspect.
—Ben Jonson, *Every Man in His Humor*

Mass movements can rise and spread without belief in
a God, but never without belief in a devil.
—Eric Hoffer, *The True Believer*

Welding an inchoate, discontented mass into a coherent
mass movement requires a powerful central idea. Political activists cannot succeed without a sense-making intellectual framework to organize and inspire their
followers. The theoretician, the man of ideas, creates this
intellectual framework. The activist, the man of deeds,
brings it to the public. Both roles are necessary. Marx,
the theoretician, required Lenin, the man of action, to
give flesh to his doctrine. Lenin needed the theoretical
framework Marx provided to mobilize the discontented.

The paranoid theorist offers "facts" and "reasons"
demonstrating the existence of and purpose behind the
conspiracy. The activist creates an organization and

179

broadcasts the argument, at times assisted, often unwittingly, by the entertainer, who profits from the popularity and appeal of the message through the media.

These roles overlap in the field of politics. The theorist tailors his ideas to the demands of the political market; the organizing activist often develops his own theoretical variations concerning the conspiratorial enemy; the profiteer as entertainer may not only add a theoretical comma or two but become part of the paranoid agitation. Not infrequently, a person shifts roles. Hitler, for example, was a theorist when writing *Mein Kampf,* an agitator activist as an early member of the National Socialist German Workers' Party, and a dramatist when he presided over the Nuremberg rallies.

Men of words and ideas are critical, especially at the beginning of this process. At the heart of the paranoid delusion is, after all, an argument, supported by "facts." Without an argument that will persuade otherwise normal and reasonable people, the political paranoid is just an impotent crank.

For the paranoid theorist to succeed, he needs more than his paranoid conspiracy theory. He needs a fighting ideology. Unlike philosophers, ideologues seek not truth but rather a change in society. One of their first tasks, accordingly, is to magnify discontent with the present, for it is discontent that is the engine for change. The theorist provides an explanation for that discontent and a pathway to a desirable future.

The ideologue interprets facts and employs reason to support what he already believes, not to challenge it. Dispassionate interpretation would obstruct his reformation of the world. The ideologue believes he has a truth that others have slighted in the service of their self-interest or to which they have inexplicably remained oblivious. But the ideologue sees this truth. Indeed, he sees little else. Contradictory facts and arguments become invisible or, if they do appear, are brushed aside. Reason and fact appear only in the service of the ideologue's program. Arguments and evidence that support the program are searched out; others are ignored or denied. The ideologue has a fixed conclusion in search of confirming evidence; his personality has a paranoid core.

Many twentieth-century ideologies have produced militant variants: Marxism (arguing that a radical change in economic relations is necessary to reform society), fascism (arguing that a radical change in favor of order and solidarity based on tradition or race combined with an emotional appeal is necessary to reform society), feminism (arguing that a radical change in the relation between the sexes is necessary to reform society), Zionism (arguing that the establishment of a homeland for the Jews is necessary for the full expression of Jewish culture and the security of the Jewish people), Gandhism (arguing that a rejection of violence is necessary for a reformation of politics), and the varieties of religious extremism (each one arguing that the reform of society requires strict adherence to the tenets of its religion). Not all of these ideologies, however, have had a major paranoid component, and not all their proponents are fanatics.

Ideologies are seldom without merit. There is generally some, and often a great deal of, truth in their doctrines. Fighting ideologies are not so much incorrect as simplistic or reductionist. It is their simplicity and clarity that make them so appealing and so suitable as an organizing framework for action.

Ideologies, like paranoia, offer direction, understanding, and moral authority. Fighting ideologues, like paranoids, are deaf to contradicting arguments and intolerant of neutrals; they scorn conflicting facts and view opponents as enemies. Paranoia and fighting ideologies are not the same, but they are natural allies. When the paranoid presents his text, it will be a revision of the ideologue's draft.

The paranoid theorist must take a delusion ("They are out to get us," when in fact no one is) and make many people believe it. Although paranoids lack judgment, they have great facility in argument and immense energy in seeking out supporting evidence. Only rarely, if at all, will the theorist use lies. Self-deluding fantasies will be prominent. Most common, however, are genuine facts, selected and interpreted within the paranoid argument.

The effective paranoid theorist creates and then offers a credible formulation, a sense-making interpretation of reality. Drawing on heightened suspiciousness, this interpretation may be just over the edge of reality, or it may reflect psychotic distortions of reality and lie deep within the land of lunacy. But in either case, it will draw upon "facts" and be presented dogmatically with irrefutable "logic." The delusion's location will be difficult for many to identify because it will be obscured in the shifting shadows of corrupt reason and selective evidence.

The paranoid delusion first appears as the servant of a fighting ideology. Eventually, as with Stalinism and German fascism, the servant becomes the master. Neo-Nazism, for example, has an ideological foundation supporting its racist and anti-Semitic beliefs: the Christian Identity Movement.

## The Christian Identity Movement

When such racist groups as the Aryan Nation and the Ku Klux Klan can provide a religious as well as a racist rationale for their program, it enhances their moral footing and broadens their appeal.[1] The people attracted to these groups are white and typically come from a background in which religion, especially fundamentalist Protestantism, is important. Christian Identity is a pseudo-Christian belief system that combines traditional elements of fundamentalist Protestantism with a paranoid explanation and a paranoid set of policies. This combination has so distorted its traditional Protestant elements as to make its relation to Protestantism almost unrecognizable, converting a religion of love into one of hatred. But its appeal rests in large part on its religious authority, and a lineal connection exists between it and Christian doctrine.

Christian Identity churches claim that the Bible teaches the racial superiority of Aryans (defined as those of Nordic and Alpine racial background, principally the inhabitants of the Scandinavian and Germanic countries and the British Isles, although for the most part any Gentile white person is included). Its members denounce Jews and blacks, claiming that they are on the spiritual level of animals. Identity Christians also claim that Aryans are God's chosen people and that Jesus was not a Jew. Jews are depicted as the literal offspring of the devil. According to Jarah Crawford, proponent of the Christian Identity Bible, Jews are a "half-breed, race-mixed, polluted people not of God . . . They are not God's creation. [They are] the children of Satan, the serpent seed line."[2] Other proponents of Christian Identity, apocalyptic in their rhetoric, call on their fellows to fight in "these final days." Among their beliefs are the following:

- Aryans are descendants of the lost tribes of Israel and are the true chosen people. They have a special calling and are on earth to do God's work.
- Jews are not descendants of the biblical Israelites but are the offspring of Satan, descended from Satan's seduction of Eve in the Garden of Eden.
- The apocalypse is approaching. The final battle will be between the Aryans, the forces of good, and the Jews, the forces of evil. It is the God-given task of the Aryans to warn of the dangers represented by the Jews and the blacks and to destroy them.[3]

Christian Identity traces its origins to a late-nineteenth- and early-twentieth-century movement known as Anglo-Israelism, a doctrine that, peaking in the 1920s in Great Britain, had the support of many members of the British establishment. It is today much reduced in size and marginal in influence, with modest headquarters in Putney, South London.

In his *Lectures on Our Israelite Origin* (1876), John Wilson argues that the lost tribes had migrated to northern Europe. He distinguishes between the southern kingdom of Judah, in which the Jews originated, and the northern kingdom of Israel, which gave rise to the northern Europeans. It is for the northern kingdom and their descendants in particular that the bulk of God's blessings were intended. They are the chosen among the chosen people, considered far more important instruments of God's purposes and destined for greater blessings than the Hebrews of the southern kingdom. The southern Jews' status has been further diminished by intermarriage with inferior peoples, the "worst of the Gentiles."

Wilson finds "evidence" of the northern kingdom of Israel "not only among Germans and their Anglo-Saxon offspring" but also in France, Italy, Switzerland, and Scandinavia. He particularly links Britain and Germany, citing their common Teutonic origins. Thus it is the Danes, Scots, Germans, and others from northern Europe who are the "real" Jews, having retained an almost pure genetic connection with their biblical ancestors. Most important of these groups are the ancient Hebrews' descendants in the British Isles, who accomplished God's will in creating a worldwide empire for him.

Today Anglo-Israelism, which began to decline after World War I, is only a curious remnant of empire, a peculiar doctrine with insignificant support. It is not a force for anti-Semitism in Britain. Only when it crossed the Atlantic did it become a source of late-twentieth-century anti-Semitism.

Two other mid-nineteenth-century writers deserve mention, for their treatises provide both the terminology and the justification for the superiority of the white race. In 1864, Dominick M'Causland published *Adam and the Adamites,* which postulates the existence of several ancient civilizations before Adam. He called the descendants of Adam "the Adamic race," a term embraced by Christian Identity. Alexander Winchell, a Methodist minister and scientist, finds repugnant the notion that he and black people share a common ancestor. He postulates two streams of humanity: the black race of "pre-Adamites," who preceded Adam, and descendants of Adam, who "represented a decided and even a sudden step in organic improvement, . . . a noble and superior specimen."[4] This conceptualization has led Identity Christians to designate blacks as the "mud-people."[5]

Although Jews are demoted from their role as chosen people and blacks are deemed inferior, they are nevertheless human, according to Anglo-Israelite doctrine. To be sure, Anglo-Israelism was increasingly anti-Semitic, especially after about 1945, but it did not demonize the Jews. It was only when Anglo-Israelism became the foundation for Christian Identity that Jews and blacks were considered spawn of the devil.

Anglo-Israelism reached the United States in the latter half of the 1800s. In 1890 Charles Totten, a teacher of military science at Yale University, founded a periodical called *Our Race: Its Origin and Destiny.* According to Totten, the British are descendants of the ten tribes, but the Germans are descendants of the Israelites' hated enemy, the Assyrians. In Maine in 1893, a Christian evangelist, Frank Sandford, founded a millenarian movement known as the Kingdom to propagate Totten's views; according to Sandford, Totten's ideas were "to Bible study what Galileo was to astronomy."[6]

Sandford's students at the Shiloh Bible School spread the word in their evangelical ministries. A particularly influential follower of Sandford, Charles Parham, founded his own Bible college in Topeka, Kansas, where in 1901 the hysteric display of speaking in tongues was emphasized, contributing to the founding of the Pentecostal movement. Major revival meetings occurred on the West Coast under Parham's leadership. By 1936 slightly more than 11 percent of all Pentecostals lived on the West Coast, forming an important part of the demographic basis for the rise of Christian Identity in the 1930s and 1940s.

An important early figure in integrating this idiosyncratic theology with the psychopolitics of hatred was Reuben Sawyer. In the 1920s, Sawyer, who had helped to organize the British-Israel World Federation (an offshoot of Anglo-Israelism), lectured widely to promote the acceptance and growth of the Ku Klux Klan. The doctrine of the Second Klan (the first being the one that had defeated Reconstruction in the South) of the 1920s emphasized Americanism and morality while reviling ''foreign influences'' and spoke of the need for a ''cleansed and purified Americanism.''[7]

Among these malign foreign influences, according to Sawyer, were ''inauthentic Jews,'' or ''counterfeit Israelites,'' who were descended from the racially polluted southern tribes. Like many others who believed in the northern European diaspora of the ancient Israelites, Sawyer commonly used the term *Israelite* to refer to the ''true'' Jews (from whom he and his followers were descended) and *Jew* to refer to ''inauthentic'' Jews, the contemporary practitioners of the Jewish religion. Eventually, Sawyer and his followers came to believe that anyone practicing Judaism was an inauthentic Jew and that only he and his followers were genuine Israelites, the chosen of God, although they no longer called themselves Jews and typically practiced Christianity.

The real danger, according to Sawyer, came from the Jews who were persecuting the Gentile Israelites. He accused the inauthentic Jews of forming a ''government within our government,'' plotting the destruction of Christendom. They were either ''bolshevists, undermining the government, or Shylocks in finance or commerce gaining control and command of Christians.''[8] It was the mission of the Ku Klux Klan to destroy them.

It was not until the 1960s, however, that the theory of the Satanic origin of the Jews became fully developed and began to circulate broadly in Christian Identity circles. This theory is the ideological foundation of the political agenda of Christian Identity:

- God distinguished between two types of beings according to their paternity. Some, called Adamites, were descended from Adam and were human. Others, called pre-Adamites, were created separately, long before Adam, and were less than human.
- The serpent in Genesis's story of the Fall was not a reptile but an intelligent humanoid creature associated with the devil, if not the devil himself.
- Original sin consisted of Eve's sexual relationship with this serpent.
- Because of this liaison, the world contains two "seedlines." One (Adam's) consists of the descendants of Adam and Eve. The other (the serpent's) consists of the descendants of Eve and the serpent or devil.
- Cain, the product of Eve's liaison with the serpent, was a historical figure associated with evil in general and the devil in particular, and he passed his propensity for evil to his descendants.[9]

Thus, the Identity Christians trace a line of Jewish descent from the serpent or devil who literally seduced and impregnated Eve in the Garden of Eden. In some versions, the issue of this union, Cain, was the first Jew. His line passed through the Edomites and the south Russian Khazars to contemporary Jews. Christian Identity thus combines the delusions of a worldwide Jewish conspiracy with that of a cosmic satanic conspiracy.[10] This dehumanization of the Jews justifies acts of violence against them; such acts can be freely committed without violating biblical injunctions. Proponents of Christian Identity speak of a "final solution" in which the Jewish people, the seed of Satan, are obliterated in a religious war.

It is important to distinguish Christian Identity from Christian fundamentalism. Fundamentalist Christianity accepts as Jews those who are called and call themselves Jews, and sees a special role for them: their conversion will precede the second coming of Jesus. Christian Identity, in contrast, sees no role for Jews in any divine plan because they are creatures of the devil.

Given the paranoid nature of this theology, it is not surprising that its members have developed an aggressive political agenda. A key goal is to biblicize American law. Although initially the Identity Christians seek to bring American law into conformity with laws spelled out in the

Bible as they interpret it, their ultimate goal is to replace human law with divine law as they describe it.

The doctrine of Identity Christianity appears to be so bizarre as to be easily dismissed. But all religious doctrines are bizarre to those who do not believe in them. Identity Christianity locates its origins in a major religion and offers a pseudohistorical rationalization; it thus contains the sense-making appeal that the destructive paranoid movement requires. Indeed, Identity Christianity became the religious ideological foundation of such hate groups as the neo-Nazis (see Chapter 8) and of David Duke, a major political figure in the United States in the late 1980s and early 1990s (see Chapter 9).

Whereas Christian Identity has grafted a paranoid anti-Jewish and anti-black stem onto the tree of Christianity, Elijah Muhammad of the Nation of Islam has grafted a paranoid anti-white stem to the tree of Islam.

## Elijah Muhammad of the Nation of Islam

Religion, race, and material competition are the great engines of human emotion. In the twentieth century, ideologies of race, sometimes tied to religion and economic advantage, have been the principal source of paranoid thought. The writings of theorists of racial paranoia are romantic and emotional. Their arguments are myths, presented as literal to the gullible, symbolic to the elect. The theoreticians are often charismatic figures telling evocative stories, not gray scholars working in quiet libraries.

Black racism as a major theme in American culture is a recent phenomenon. In the mid-twentieth century, the dominant black movement, led by Martin Luther King, Jr., was hostile to racism in all its forms. Because the most prominent racist doctrines were anti-black, racism was too tainted to be adapted for black use. Given the importance of religion in the social organization of black life, an anti-white racism could succeed only if it had a religious dimension. But none of the established religions were receptive. Also, oppositional black leaders were often left wing—liberal or socialist—and the politics of the American left tended to be anti-racist. Eventually, however, a racist religion did arise. Believers received its unusual arguments as new light illuminating what they had always sensed but never understood.

Metaphorically, paranoia is an infectious disease. The objects of the paranoid message are as likely to be infected as to be resistant. When infected—that is, when the victims react to a paranoid attack by mounting one of their own—they are no less paranoid, no less dangerous, and are likely to be no less destructive than those who initiated the process.

Black people have been a particular object of paranoid hatred. It is not surprising, therefore, that paranoid thought, organization, and pro- grams have found a place within black politics. Blacks in the United States have been the object of paranoia far more than its instrument, more reactive than initiating. We note this fact not to excuse but rather to understand the context in which black racism developed and still operates.

The origin of what was to be a religion of paranoid hatred was a doctrine propounded by a peddler of silks and raincoats in Chicago in the 1920s and 1930s. This prophet was known variously as Wallace D. Fard, W. Fard Muhammed, F. Muhammed Ali, Wali Farrad, and often simply Mr. Fard.[11] Fard's race is not clear. He apparently was quite fair skinned and often identified himself as an Arab. According to Bruce Perry, Fard claimed to be white at San Quentin, where he served time for selling heroin.[12] Fard also claimed to come from Mecca and to be the son of a black man and a white Armenian woman whom he said was the devil.

Peter Goldman quotes Fard as having claimed, "My name is Mahdi [prophet]; I am God. I come to guide you."[13] He said that he had come to aid the blacks, the original people. Among his disciples was Robert Poole, later known as Elijah Muhammad, to whom he communicated his secrets: God was black and created black people trillions of years before he created Adam, the first white man. Blacks designated by God created all of the universe.

This story of universal creation and the history of the black race is presented in a mythic style, although it is clearly intended to be taken literally, at least by some. The all-black universe was a happy one, but an evil, dissident black scientist, Yacub, created whites, breeding them over centuries from black recessive genes. These whites lacked not only color but moral character. God decided that these whites should rule over blacks for six thousand years. This period would end in the twentieth century, at which time the whites would be destroyed and the former black paradise would then return. Thus the Fard myth provided for a creation, a Golden Age, a Fall, an oppression, a promised imminent redemption, and finally a millennium. The beliefs may seem bizarre, but they are no more so than the beliefs of Jews, Christians, and Hindus. Had the Fard myth gained enough of a following, it would be as respected as are the major world religions.

Fard, according to Elijah Muhammad, was the incarnation of God. Elijah Muhammad not only had been in his presence and received his truth but continued to be in communication with him. Thus, Fard's word was God's word. All black people were divine, although God was preeminent among them. This doctrine was presented in two holy works: *The Secret Ritual of the Nation of Islam,* which was never to be written down but was to be taught and memorized anew by each generation; and *Teaching for the Lost Found Nation of Islam in a Mathematical Way,* which was written but was highly obscure and needed to be interpreted by special persons within the church. Thus, the doctrine of the church, like so many paranoid dogmas, is highly esoteric. The credo appears to be "Those against us operate in secret, so we must keep our secrets as well."

The heart of the doctrine is racist and is explicitly acknowledged to be so. In a television documentary "The Hate That Hate Produced," aired on July 10, 1959, the following exchange took place:

MR. LOUIS LOMAX: Now if I have understood your teachings correctly, you teach that all of the members of Islam are god, and that one among you is supreme, and that one is Allah. Now have I understood you correctly?

MR. ELIJAH MUHAMMAD: That's right.

MR. LOMAX: Now, you have on the other hand said that the devil is the white man—that the white man is a doomed race.

MR. MUHAMMAD: Yes.[14]

About a month earlier, in the June 16, 1959, issue of the black-published *Pittsburgh Courier,* Elijah Muhammad was quoted: "The human beast—the serpent, the dragon, the devil, and Satan—all mean one and the same; the people or race known as the white or Caucasian race, sometimes called the European race. Since by nature they were created liars and murderers, they are the enemies of truth and righteousness and the enemies of those who seek truth."[15]

From the point of view of paranoid psychodynamics the myth was very effective. Black is good, white is evil. Black is human, white is less than human. Blacks will come to rule all, whites will be destroyed. This self-idealization was a reaction to, or an overcompensation for, the depressed position blacks occupied in American society. This racist message and others like it have come to form an important part of black political culture.

## The Paranoid Culture of the John Birch Society

Stopping the Communists, and destroying their conspiracy, or at least breaking its grip on our government and shattering its power within the United States, not only must occupy the front spot and most important spot in all of our thinking. It is the driving danger which should determine our thinking about almost everything else, and most of our actions too, for the foreseeable future. For unless we can win that battle, the war for a better world will again be carried on through long and feudal Dark Ages, after we have been killed, our children have been enslaved, and all that we value has been destroyed.
—Robert Welch, *The Blue Book of the John Birch Society*

American society in the late 1940s and 1950s was preoccupied by the dangers of Communism. This was a well-founded fear. And like most well-founded political fears, it produced its paranoid variant, the belief that American society was secretly controlled by Communists.

Political paranoia comes in different strengths and sizes. In what we call soft paranoid movements, supporters are seldom activists but are satisfied with simple participation. Such groups do not set off explosions, hijack planes, or imprison their own members. They function principally to provide a political home for those with political paranoid ideation. Members may be regarded as politically obnoxious or disagreeably strange, but they rarely threaten the destruction of their society. A typical soft paranoid organization was the John Birch Society. It was founded by Robert Welch, a retired candy magnate, in 1958, during the height of the Cold War. It was the culmination of Welch's years of certainty that a Communist conspiracy threatened the existence of the United States.

Welch's life and career led him to see the world in absolutist and apocalyptic terms.[16] His family was intensely religious (several of his ancestors were fundamentalist Baptist ministers) and admitted no shades of gray: there was good and there was evil—those on the side of God and those in the camp of Satan. Welch carried this approach into his later fanatical devotion to the cause of anti-Communism. "He who does not see things absolutely our way is against us" is the absolutist creed of the political paranoid.

Welch dates his concern with the dangers of Communism to his 1938 reading of Eugene Lyons' *Assignment in Utopia,* a memoir of the journalist's time in the Soviet Union.[17] Lyons described Stalin's government as brutal, repressive, anti-democratic, and expansionist. Welch's response to this factual description was not irrational in and of itself, but, as so often with paranoid personalities, it was disproportionate. He became obsessed with the Communist threat, exaggerated its degree, and came to interpret all politics in terms of this delusional exaggeration.

Welch used his business base to become politically active in support of conservative Republican candidates. He was embittered when the 1952 Republican national convention bypassed the conservative Robert Taft for the more moderate Dwight D. Eisenhower, and Welch later accused Eisenhower of being a Communist sympathizer. Welch became an unwavering supporter of Joseph McCarthy and remained so years after McCarthy had been discredited. In a gesture of continuing symbolic support, in 1989 the headquarters of the John Birch Society was moved to Appleton, Wisconsin, McCarthy's hometown.

In 1952, Welch was already demonizing the Soviet Union: "Soviet leaders are, without exception, murderers, liars, thieves, and ruthlessly cruel tyrants . . . These men are not human beings; they are predatory beasts . . . Communist infiltration into our government, and the recruiting and planting of Communist traitors in spots of vital control in every important branch of our economic, political and cultural life has already gone far beyond the wildest guess of the average American citizen.''[18]

Welch later added a theme that we have noted in other paranoid writings: the belief in the existence of a secret group within society, dedicated to the destruction of the larger society. These traitors, who ''are recruited from the richest families, [are] the most highly educated intellectuals, and the most skillful politicians,'' whom the naive would think would be the last to plot society's degradation, are in fact the center of the conspiracy, a ''gigantic conspiracy to enslave mankind.''[19]

In 1958, Welch called a meeting of eleven friends who shared his beliefs. The transcript of the meeting was privately published by Welch in 1961 as *The Blue Book of the John Birch Society*.[20] It was to become the Bible of the organization he founded to combat the Communist conspiracy.[21] The members of this group were to become the founders of the society, which was named after Captain John Birch, an army intelligence officer killed by Chinese Communists just after the end of World War II. Captain Birch was thus memorialized by the Birchers as the first casualty of the Cold War. Welch warned the founding meeting that they had ''only a few more years'' before the United States would fall under Communist domination and be ''ruled by police-state methods from the Kremlin.''[22] Among the functions of the governing council of the John Birch Society, Welch ominously noted, was to select a new leader in the event that Welch was murdered by Communists.[23]

Welch, a prolific writer, wrote several books and many shorter pieces over the succeeding years about ''the conspiracy.'' At the height of his movement's popularity, some sixty-seven thousand persons subscribed to the society's newsletter.

Welch stepped down as leader in 1983. Among his successors was Congressman Larry McDonald of Georgia, who perished when the Soviets shot down the Korean airliner KAL-007 in September 1987. Many members of the society believe that McDonald and other passengers on the plane may still be alive—held as prisoners.[24] Despite the dissolution of the Soviet Union in 1991, at that time the society's newsletter had about twenty-one thousand subscribers. Among the ''enemies'' of the Society who are suspected of aiding the Communist cause are supporters of the civil rights movement, the United Nations, and the sponsors of Earth

Day. In September 1991, the society warned of the planned "complete socialist takeover of the greater Los Angeles area."[25]

A core of reality underlay the central ideology of the John Birch Society. A reading of Lenin and Stalin provided ample support for belief in the aggressively expansionist aims of the Soviet Union during the height of the Cold War. The Soviet Union's attempts to penetrate Western governments through espionage were well documented. But the paranoid ideology of the John Birch Society expanded dramatically from this rational foundation. The ideology identifies an international Communist conspiracy as the cause of nearly all of America's problems, foreign and domestic.[26]

Although its rhetoric was uncompromising, there was something curiously cautious and pedestrian about the society. For example, it sought to fight this demonic, deep, and widespread Communist conspiracy through conventional electoral politics. One of its most prominent campaigns was an effort to impeach the moderate Republican Supreme Court justice Earl Warren. The members never advocated illegality, much less violence. Given the magnitude of the conspiratorial organization they described, which had allegedly infiltrated and even controlled large parts of American government and society, it is puzzling that they believed this conspiracy could be defeated by the efforts of retired merchants and obscure academics working through conventional channels.

The climate within the organization differed strikingly from the pervasive hostility and suspiciousness of others that characterize fighting paranoid groups.[27] Most members joined and stayed in the organization not to engage in combat and defend the nation but to experience its social life—the meetings, the circulation of petitions, and so on. The Communist enemy provided a focus for group solidarity. The society's paranoid ideology became the rationalization for joining a group of like-minded individuals and ameliorating one's feelings of isolation and alienation. In the more intensely paranoid groups, as one former terrorist ruefully acknowledged, "our only common destiny was fleeing from danger."[28] Indeed, it sometimes appeared that the Birchers' only common destiny was fleeing from boredom.

In America in the 1950s, the reality of the Cold War at its height made paranoid thinking attractive, a sentiment crystallized in Robert

Welch's belief system. It was not an evident military threat, however, that inspired our next example. It was an obsession with a fantasy built of distorted reason.

## Lyndon LaRouche: The Extremity of Reason

LaRouche was a man with a coherent program, subtle tactics, and . . . a long range plan of how to get from here to there. He was a serious ideologue.
—Dennis King, *Lyndon LaRouche and the New American Facism*

Recall that the image of the enemy that the paranoid creates is often a projection of his own feelings.[29] The paranoid sees his own actions as reactions required by the enemy. If the enemy is seen as deceiving through writings, the paranoid will make use of the most detailed and elaborate pseudoscholarship. Conspiracy must be fought with conspiracy, organization with organization. The paranoid's motivations, fears, anxieties, and desires are ascribed to his opponents, some real, some phantom. The relationship with the enemy is thus one beginning in fantasy and externalization, but then, if the adversary is drawn into responding, what began as fantasy can be transformed into reality.

We have found no person who has developed a more complex, or more ingenious, paranoid theory than Lyndon Hermyle LaRouche, Jr. LaRouche was born in 1922 in Rochester, New Hampshire, to Quaker parents. His parents were truly "fighting Quakers," although the object of their battles was not a bellicose or oppressive government but other Quakers. They were constantly accusing their co-religionists of leftist sympathies and misappropriation of funds.

The young Lyndon was forced to swear never to fight, in school or out, and he suffered greatly at the hands of bullies. Though not a studious child, he had a strong desire to read and was called Big Head by his classmates. At the outbreak of World War II, LaRouche, aged nineteen, volunteered as a noncombatant and served in the China-Burma-India theater. Somewhere along the way, perhaps during a brief period at Northeastern University, LaRouche acquired an allegiance to Marxism. On leave in Calcutta, he offered the Indian Communist leader P. C. Joshi his services to organize GIs. Rebuffed by this mainstream Communist, LaRouche decided to become a Trotskyite.

After the war, LaRouche returned to Boston and soon became an organizer at the General Electric plant in Lynn, Massachusetts. By 1954 he had abandoned organizing activity and was hiring himself out as a management consultant on labor problems. He did well, earning as much as a thousand dollars a week. One of his management principles, which foreshadowed his later paranoid politics, was, "If management tells you to stay out of any area, that is where you should go." Another foreshadowing of his later political ideology was an interest in the new field of computer technology.

By 1963, LaRouche had become a successful businessman but had maintained his association with the Trotskyist movement. As political radicalism and disorder grew in the 1960s, LaRouche, now in his early forties, became increasingly involved. His efforts on behalf of the Trotskyist Socialist Workers Party were unsuccessful, however. By 1974 LaRouche had abandoned Marxism and developed his own view of history, on which he built his political empire. His movement prospered into the 1980s, but in 1988 he was sentenced to fifteen years in a federal penitentiary for fraud and tax evasion. He was released on parole on January 26, 1994.

LaRouche proposed a view of history and society built on the belief in an ancient conspiracy, which purportedly grew out of a philosophical disagreement about the nature of truth. According to LaRouche, all history can be understood as a conflict between Platonists and Aristotelians. The Platonists believe in pure truth and hence, in worldly terms, in standards. The Aristotelians, in contrast, believe that truth is uncertain and relative and thus are opponents of standards. To LaRouche, if people do not believe in at least the possibility of certainty, there can be no progress, and humanity will slip into self-destructive hedonism. LaRouche argues that Aristotelians, aiming to distract people from the truth and to retain their own power and wealth, have entered into a conspiracy to fool the public with spurious doctrines (such as moral relativism), pseudomedicine (such as psychotherapy), drugs (heroin, marijuana, and so on), and degraded entertainment (pornography, acid rock).

The Platonists, according to LaRouche, are creators and builders, in favor of truth, standards, technology, and man's conquest of nature. Their members purportedly include Jesus, Johann Sebastian Bach, William Shakespeare, Gottfried Leibniz, and Franklin Delano Roosevelt. Aristotelians attempt to frustrate this desire for human control over the environment. Among this group, LaRouche lists Adam Smith (who described capitalism in order to encourage hedonism), Jeremy Bentham (who developed the hedonistic doctrine of utilitarianism), and the entire English empirical tradition associated with Thomas Hobbes, John Locke, George Berkeley, and David Hume.

This novel way of classifying all the political leaders, scientists, and artists who have ever lived creates strange alliances. Those believed by others to be adversaries (indeed, those who believe themselves to be adversaries) are seen as allies. And those generally believed to be allies are considered adversaries. The American Civil Liberties Union is part of the malign Aristotelian conspiracy, for example, but so are the FBI, the CIA, and their masters, the British Intelligence Services, MI5 and MI6. The Socialist International and the free-market-advocating Heritage Society are both Aristotelians under the skin; the Anti-Defamation League is part of the conspiracy, but so too is the John Birch Society. In fact, according to LaRouche, all these organizations are controlled by the same dark Aristotelian forces. Their apparent differences are just a smoke screen.

The conspiracy goes well beyond politics. Werner Heisenberg's development of the uncertainty principle, for example, which states that in the realm of very small units of matter movement cannot be predicted, was an effort to undermine belief in standards, virtue, and truth. Heisenberg and his followers, then, are part of the Aristotelian conspiracy. Jazz, rock and roll, and dissonance as an integral part of much twentieth-century music can be traced to the unsuccessful battle of the (Platonist) sixteenth-century musician Gioseffo Zarlino to maintain the tempered order of the keyboard in face of the disruptive efforts of (the Aristotelian) Claudio Monteverdi.

LaRouche or his followers offer an explanation for each of these examples. Some of the explanations are rather complex:

Because LaRouche includes Zionists and Jewish bankers such as the Rothschilds and Warburgs as agents of the British plot, the Anti-Defamation League has accused him of being an anti-Semite—even though a number of his closest followers are Jewish. An article LaRouche wrote in 1978 mentions the *Protocols of the Elders of Zion,* but he gives the legend one of his typically bizarre twists. "The fallacy of the *Protocols of Zion* is that it misattributes the alleged conspiracy to Jews generally," LaRouche wrote, rather than to a few select Jewish conspirators. Actually, he explained, Oxford University invented Zionism and "Israel is ruled from London as a zombie-nation."

LaRouche's position on the Holocaust is even more confusing. As an agent of Britain, Hitler killed 1.5 million—but not 6 million—Jews, LaRouche wrote. But now the British supposedly exaggerate the Holocaust, using it as a psywar technique to brainwash Jews into becoming Zionists. Zionism is part of the Dark Ages plot, LaRouche wrote, because the British, by signing the Balfour Declaration, helped establish Israel. LaRouche claims that neo-Nazis working with networks of Freemasons are responsible for Palestinian terrorism and that both Nazis and Zionists are British controlled. To him, the Middle East crisis is a British operation to destabilize the region, furthering the oligarchs' attempts to take over the world.[30]

What these Aristotelian forces are attempting to disrupt is progress, which, LaRouche argues, occurs as new technologies create new social relations. He draws an explicit correspondence between modern technology and the doctrine of neo-Platonism, which greatly influenced Christian thought in the Middle Ages and also influenced such early modern scientists and mathematicians as Johannes Kepler and Gottfried Leibniz. The neo-Platonic ascending spheres, leading to God in the early versions, are given an economic and social character by LaRouche. These spheres are technological or economic stages through which mankind rises toward perfection.

What is the nature of this perfection according to LaRouche? In accordance with his Platonism, it is elitist and authoritarian. But LaRouche adds a major non-Platonist twist. Human life, he says, is the greatest good. Therefore, the world must be made as efficient as possible to accommodate the largest number of people. Nuclear energy is necessary for this end. (Of course, the Aristotelian environmentalists, who are spiritual and intellectual descendants of the sun-worshipping devotees of Isis, oppose it.) The gradual elimination of Aristotelian influences combined with technology will eventually bring about the millennium. Millions of human beings, uncorrupted by Aristotelian influences, will then be able to enjoy Shakespeare undistracted by Ken Kesey, to relish Beethoven undisturbed by the Grateful Dead.

LaRouche has been called "a kind of Allan Bloom gone mad," supported by followers who, "like crazed graduate students, . . . crank out dissertations on who is in and who is out of the conspiracy."[31] La-Rouche's argument certainly shows no lack of "theory" or "facts." His organization has had vigorous leadership and, at least at times, has been well funded. To those who are not attracted to his theory, it appears to be simply screwy. To the susceptible, however, its novelty is seductive. Yet despite the theory's conceptual inventiveness, its elaborate system of supporting "evidence," and its organization's strong funding and consistent leadership, it has had little success.

The reason is that the doctrine does not ally itself with the great engines of human conflict: race, economic exploitation, and religion. La-Rouchism's followers must abandon at least most of their previous racial, economic, and religious commitments and even prejudices. Anti-Semites and racists of all hues would have to renounce Hitler; anti-leftists would have to give up their faith in capitalism and even turn against bankers; those who hate religion would have to accept *both* Muhammad and Jesus as great leaders; and those of a literal bent in religion would have to forsake sympathy for fundamentalism of any sort. Although LaRouche appears regularly on public access television channels and sought the Democratic nomination for the presidency in 1996, LaRouchism has declined greatly in influence and is now marginal to American politics—ironically, because of its being too paranoid.[32] It is pure cultural paranoia. All it emphasizes is conspiracy. Not only does LaRouchism not associate itself with the great breeders of paranoid fears—race, religion, and material desire—it denies them. Ideas alone are too thin a diet for a paranoid movement.

The paranoid theories we have looked at are based on racism, religion, and the distortion of logic. Each of them appeals both to emotion and to reason—that is, to base emotion and to deformed reason. The effectiveness of these doctrines, however, depends as much on their presentation in the marketplace of ideas as on their substance.

# 8

## Paranoia's Agitators and Activists

We believe that there are literal children of Satan in the world today. These children are the descendants of Cain, who was a result of Eve's original sin, her physical seduction by Satan . . . There is a battle and a natural enmity between the children of Satan and the children of the Most High God. . . . We believe that there is a battle being fought this day between the children of darkness (today known as Jews) and the children of light (God), the Aryan race, the true Israel of the Bible.
—Creedal Statement of the Aryan Nation and the Church of Jesus Christ, Christian

The paranoid leader needs a framework of ideas to focus the frustrated rage of his followers. The two paranoid religion-based theories we have discussed—Christian Identity and the Nation of Islam—have become important rationales for extremism and violence for some radical activists within these movements.

## The Paranoid Radical Right and Defensive Aggression

Right-wing extremism is not an organized movement with clear identifying characteristics.[1] Rather, it should be viewed as a pastiche, a mosaic, containing groups and organizations with both common themes and differences. There are many right-wing leaders, of somewhat different ideological hues. White supremacism and neo-Nazism are major but not uniform themes, as are "survivalism" and anti-government sentiments, united under a common banner of patriotism and religion. Not all right-wing organizations rely on religious theory, but Christian Identity does provide a theological justification for many right-wing extremist groups. In particular, it draws together religious fundamentalism and racism, providing a religious rationale (that Jews control America with the intent of destroying the white race) both for a "race war that would deliver our people and achieve total victory for the Aryan race" and for groups opposing the exercise of governmental control and power.[2]

Recall that the tenets of Christian Identity provide a rich basis for paranoid political activists of the radical right to support an extreme political agenda:

- Anglo-Saxons are the true descendants of the Israelites of the Old Testament with whom God made His covenant, and they are his chosen people. They are the last true defenders of the faith and the United States is the true State of Israel, the last bastion against evil.
- God's laws are absolute and the only ones that people are obligated to follow. Because His laws have been disregarded, the United States is on the brink of disaster and Armageddon is imminent. Loyalty is not owed to institutions that violate these laws. America's laws especially are invalid because the United States government is controlled by Jews, "a Zionist Occupied Government" (ZOG). The news media and economic institutions are also directed by Jews.
- Three types of people exist. Whites (God's chosen) are of a higher order than either Jews (the "Seed of Satan") or blacks (the "mud people"). Since members of the last group have no souls, they are subhuman and represent "false starts" before God perfected whites. They also are manipulated by Jews against the Aryans.

- Because Jews are the children of the devil, they are responsible for all the evil that has occurred throughout history and are the spiritual and moral enemies of white Christians. Armageddon will be a military confrontation between God's chosen (the Aryan race) and the forces of Satan (Jews, blacks, and other minority groups).
- For white Christians, there are no practical distinctions among race, religion, and nationality.[3]

Christian Identity tells its members that they must endure the apocalypse on earth and help prepare for it through paramilitary and survival training.[4] In the Aryan Nation's compound at Hayden Lake, Idaho, white supremacist groups gather each July to receive indoctrination in Identity Christian principles and paramilitary training. The Aryan Nation's religious organization is named the Church of Jesus Christ, Christian (as opposed to Jesus Christ, Jew). Robert Butler is the founder and leader of both the Aryan Nation and the Church of Jesus Christ, Christian.

The Aryan Nation's magazine *Calling Our Nation* has accused Jews of committing human sacrifice. In other publications and members' speeches, the organization elaborates on the satanic Jewish conspiracy, which, in the words of George Stout, leader of the Aryan Nation in Texas, exerts control over the "world's political system through the Babylon system of banking, finances, and economics."[5]

Robert Mathews, a leading lieutenant of Butler, split off from the Aryan Nation in 1983 and formed his own group, the Order, a violent, tax-protesting, neo-pagan, neo-Nazi cult that also called itself the Brotherhood of Silence. It sought to build a white American bastion. In 1979 Mathews recruited Gary Yarborough into the Aryan Nation from an Arizona prison, where he belonged to a white racist group called the Aryan Brotherhood. Yarborough became Butler's bodyguard and Mathews' principal lieutenant. The major preoccupation of the Order was the danger of the "genocide of the white race" at the hands of the "devil's children," the Jews. They saw Cain's murder of Abel as the prototype for the Jewish genocide of the white race and were obsessed by the powerful Jewish conspiracy that they believed controlled the United States through its domination of the media and banks. The Order's obsession with the

Zionist Occupied Government was not only defensive aggression but was fueled by projection—a desire to destroy the Jews.

Members of the Order swore an oath of violence in pursuing Aryan victory over the Jew. They claimed "no fear of death, no fear of foe," in doing "whatever is necessary to deliver our people from the Jew." Members of the Order, "true Aryan men," face the "enemies of our faith and our race," invoke the "blood covenant," and declare they are in a "state of war," which they will continue to wage until they "have driven the enemy into the sea."[6] To finance a guerrilla campaign that it hoped would lead to an uprising by the white population against the Zionist-controlled government, the Order embarked upon a campaign of bank robberies and counterfeiting. The most dramatic crimes committed by the Order in pursuit of its revolutionary goals were the July 1984 robbery of a Brinks armored car (which netted $3.8 million), the burning of a synagogue in Boise, Idaho, and the 1984 murder of Alan Berg, a Jew and a radio talk show host based in Denver.[7]

After the murder of Berg, the FBI traced Yarborough and confronted him on October 18, 1984, near his home in Sandpoint, Idaho. Yarborough fired at the FBI agents and fled. When police searched his house, they found an array of terrorist and racist tracts, including a list of "enemies of the Aryan people"—prominent California jurists, journalists, and entertainment figures. They also found explosives and weapons, including the Berg murder weapon. The FBI finally captured Yarborough in November 1984, but Mathews escaped. In a siege at Whidbey Island in Puget Sound (which has now achieved mythic status in the right wing), Mathews refused to surrender to the hundred officials surrounding his house. When a helicopter dropped a flare, the house went up in flames, and Mathews died in the fire. Liberty Net, the neo-Nazi computer network, accorded Mathews heroic stature for his role in the movement and for his death.[8] After his death, Liberty Net carried Mathews' last message: "By the time my son had arrived, I realized that white America . . . was headed for oblivion unless white men rose and turned the tide. The more I came to love my son, the more I realized that unless things changed radically, by the time he was my age he would be a stranger in his own land, a blond-haired, blue-eyed Aryan in a country populated mainly by

Mexicans, mulattos, blacks and Asians. His future was growing darker by the day."[9]

These neo-Nazi groups, the Aryan Nation and the Order, were intensely anti-Semitic and racist, but they also feared the federal government, which they saw as dominated by Jews. The balance of these themes is different in the Posse Comitatus and the militias, where the federal government is regarded as the greatest enemy and where anti-Semitism and racism, although present, have a lower profile.

The forerunner to the militia movement, the Posse Comitatus (now defunct), was fiercely opposed to government. It asserted that no public official above the level of sheriff is legitimate.[10] The extremist group began as the Citizen's Law-Enforcement Committee, an organization formed in 1969 in Portland, Oregon, to protest taxes and challenge the authority of the federal government over the local government. William Potter Gale then founded a branch in Glendale, California, calling it the U.S. Christian Posse Association. The national Posse Comitatus was formally organized in Michigan in 1972.

Over the next ten years, chapters were formed in nearly every state, focusing on tax protest, providing legal assistance to tax evaders, and advocating local constitutional authority. They sought to avoid taxes by establishing tax-exempt Christian Identity churches. In their view, the county level was the legitimate seat of government, hence the name *Posse Comitatus* (literally "power of the county"). Posse members believed that all legal rights derive from the U.S. Constitution and its first ten amendments, the Magna Carta, the Bible, the Articles of Confederation, and common law, and they were violently opposed to state and federal laws that they considered unconstitutional. They refused to pay state and federal taxes and declared the Internal Revenue Service and income tax "Communist and unconstitutional." The "Jew-run" federal government, in the view of the Posse, had usurped its powers. Posse doctrine advocated firearms and survival training in preparation for Armageddon, the approaching nuclear holocaust that is the goal of the "Communist-Jew run government."[11]

The Posse Comitatus, perhaps reflecting the group's antipathy to central authority, had no leader or central governance. Rather, the various Posses constituted a leaderless national organization of loosely affiliated chapters, which were often known by other names.[12] The average Posse member tended to be religious, a tax protestor, a loner, and self-employed. Most hated blacks and Jews. Members had to be white and Christian and were required to state that they were patriotic, of good character (in Posse terms), and interested in the preservation of law and order as that was understood by Posse members.[13] The legitimacy of killing federal officials was regularly cited in Posse documents. "Killing in the defense of freedom," members were advised, "is not murder any more than a soldier killing in war."[14]

The mail-order catalogues of right-wing extremist groups not only provide an insight into what they believe but also demonstrate the common thrust of the movement. The catalogues of the Christian Patriots, a group identified with the Posse Comitatus, and of the National Vanguard, a West Virginia neo-Nazi group, for example, include many of the same books. A best-seller is *The Turner Diaries,* written by William Pierce under the pseudonym Andrew McDonald.[15] Pierce served as an assistant to George Lincoln Rockwell, chief of the American Nazi Party, in the late 1960s, sold "Negro control equipment" from his home, and was a mentor of Robert Mathews, the founder of the Order. Pierce is a physicist who left academia in the 1960s to crusade against Jews and blacks. He would like "to see North America become a white continent" and asserts that "there is no way a society based on Aryan values can evolve peacefully from a society which has succumbed to Jewish spiritual corruption." First published in 1980, the novel is regularly cited by white supremacist groups and anti-gun-control militias.[16]

The plot of the *Turner Diaries* is a paranoid triumphalist fantasy. It describes America eighteen months after all private ownership of guns has been outlawed by the Cohen Act. The central character, the Aryan hero Earl Turner, recounts his role in overthrowing the U.S. government in the 1990s in the Great Revolution. Turner is a member of a clandestine group, the Organization, whose goal is to restore white control of the United States by killing nonwhites and Jews. In the final section of the book, millions of American Jews, blacks, Latinos, and "race traitors" are killed on the "Day of the Rope." California is liberated by the explosion of a nuclear bomb and the hanging from lampposts of thousands of blacks and Jews, as well as "White women who were married to or living with Blacks, with Jews, or with other non-white males.'' The book describes the mass hanging of thousands of these women at the triumph of the white nation, each woman necklaced with a placard proclaiming "I defiled my race."[17] The book, which attracted a wide following in right-wing circles, by 1996 sold more than two hundred thousand copies.

Other offerings by the Christian Patriots include such Holocaust denial literature as Arthur Butz's *Hoax of the Twentieth Century* and Richard Harwood's *Did Six Million Die?* along with Henry Ford's *International Jew* and Carleton Putnam's *Race and Reason.* This literature has a familiar paranoid flavor. The books identify a threat to the existence of Christian white society, mostly from Jews and blacks. Jews are portrayed as a malevolent force controlling nearly every aspect of life and growing ever more powerful. Blacks, an inferior species, threaten to destroy white society by racial mixing that produces "mongrelization." Again we see the posture of defensive aggression, "provoked" by the powerful conspiracy that threatens to engulf the victim. It is necessary to defend against the dangers posed by Jews and blacks. Often added to this list of corrupters are homosexuals and foreigners. Note the attribution of power and danger to "them"; "they" must be destroyed before "they" destroy us.

Tim Bishop, the security chief of the Aryan Nation, has expressed his organization's solidarity with the anti-abortion movement: "The Lord says abortion is a sin. Worse, abortion kills millions of white babies every year. We fight abortions all the time . . . Abortion is one of our battle fronts." He cited Operation Rescue and Rescue America for their good work: "They're pure white, pure Aryans. They do good work for the Bible and for God, . . . good Aryan work." But this is less a matter of religious principle than of support for the war against the blacks and the Jews: "I would gladly help any black woman to get an abortion. The less of them the better. Hell, we'd raise money for that. I'm just against abortion for the pure white race. For blacks and other mongrelized kind abortion is a good idea . . . It's part of our Holy War for the pure Aryan race." Jews, too, should be aborted to purify the Aryan race. Moreover, the Jews promote abortions. "The Jews are really behind abortion . . . the first to yell for it. Yeah, Jew York."[18]

We see that the radical right—a broad aggregation of organizations tied together by common delusional fears and not central leaderships—displays the paranoid theme of belief in external control (by Jews and the federal government), and their defensive aggressive reaction is manifested in a desire to overthrow the government of the United States, destroy those that they call non-Aryans, and restore an "ideal" America. One part of this movement, however, deserves special attention because it draws on *healthy* American themes. Political paranoia is at its most dangerous when it combines the propagation of delusions with the perversion of virtues.

## The Militia Movement

The bomb that destroyed the federal building in Oklahoma City on April 19, 1995, not only claimed 168 lives, it also shattered the widespread illusion that the United States was immune to domestic terrorism.[19] The devastating explosion was apparently perpetrated by American citizens who were consumed with rage against the federal government. A troubling mindset within the American political landscape was thus brought forcibly to Americans' attention—the mindset of the paranoid radical right, especially the militia movement.

The ideas that identify organizations and the social processes that unite them can be far more paranoid than their members. The militias demonstrate how such unexceptional personal beliefs as an allegiance to the right to bear arms and a distrust of government can be carried to paranoid lengths under the stimulation of a paranoid organization. The constitutional right to bear arms is upheld by the courts and adhered to by mainstream political groups. And a distrust of government, especially the central government, is America's oldest political tradition and one strongly espoused by individuals across the political spectrum.

For many of the most active militia members, the advocacy of these established liberties reaches paranoid dimensions. The three themes militias share, then, are a strong belief in the right to bear firearms, intense distrust and fear of the federal government, and collective paranoid beliefs. Statements made by John Trochmann, co-founder of the Militia of Montana, capture these three themes. Trochmann claims to have been the victim of death threats intended to deter him from uncovering a plot by "one-world" government authorities intent on disarming average citizens, violating their constitutional rights, and destroying America's sovereignty.[20] In Trochmann's view, an armed citizenry is the most important defense against this usurpation.[21] Trochmann and others in the militia movement cite the 1992 incident in which federal agents killed the wife and child of white supremacist Randy Weaver in a confrontation at Ruby Ridge, Idaho, as proof of the federal government's resolve to disarm its citizens. They also regularly cite the attack by the Bureau of Alcohol, Tobacco, and Firearms on the Branch Davidian compound in Waco, Texas, in order to disarm David Koresh and his followers, and the subsequent siege by the FBI, which ended in a fiery tragedy. The Ruby Ridge attack and the siege in Waco have assumed almost mythic significance for the militias.

The federal government, according to the conspiracy theories shared by many of the militias, seeks to control the lives of citizens and will crush resisters by any means possible, including sending in United Nations troops.[22] Fiercely independent and resenting control of any kind, they fear that the federal government will destroy American democracy. These self-styled patriots believe that well-armed grassroots paramilitary organizations offer the only protection against the tyranny to come or, in the minds of many, the tyranny already present. The intensive paramilitary training of the militias is to defend against the secret elites that plan an apocalyptic takeover of the United States, under the auspices of the United Nations or the North Atlantic Treaty Organization (NATO).

One of the suspects in the Oklahoma City bombing, Timothy McVeigh, was deeply influenced by *The Turner Diaries,* which he bought in quantity and sold below cost at gun shows. In the novel, one of the first and most dramatic acts of the Organization is to blow up the FBI building in Washington with a fertilizer bomb—the same explosive used to destroy the federal building in Oklahoma City. In Montana, three weeks before the Oklahoma City bombing, a militia official threatened several government officials, warning, "There cannot be a cleansing without the shedding of blood."[23]

The basic thrust of this classic conspiracy theory is that world history has been orchestrated for hundreds of years by a small, self-serving group. They were behind the French Revolution, the European revolutions of

1848, the Communist revolution of 1917, and the Great Depression. These "globalists" have a secret agenda to develop a socialist one-world government under the United Nations and to subordinate the United States to this New World Order. In fact, televangelist Pat Robertson's *New World Order* propounds just such a theory, which has received wide acceptance in the militia movement: "A single thread runs from the [Bush] White House to the State Department to the Council on Foreign Relations to the Trilateral Commission to secret societies to extreme New Agers."[24] Robertson warns that "our constitutional right to bear and keep arms would be one of the first casualties" when the New World Order is in place. Depicting the government as the potential enemy, he exhorts: "The task of good men now will be to fight with all their strength." Although Robertson has disavowed racism and anti-Semitism, his book has anti-Semitic echoes. He traces the conspiracy to the Illuminati (a secret organization that claimed special religious knowledge) and Free-masons of the eighteenth century, organizations that he said were funded by the Jewish Rothschilds, whose lodge in Frankfurt was the center of a conspiracy for world revolution. Robertson suggests that the Gulf War may have been a plot to persuade Americans to accept United Nations rule. He also charges that the attempt of disaffected Soviet intelligence and military officers to overturn Mikhail Gorbachev and restore Communism was designed to fail in order to accelerate the consolidation of the New World Order.[25]

According to some militia conspiracists, the bar codes on federal highway signs are secret codes for the United Nations army when it moves in to take over the country. They also speak of surveillance conducted via black helicopters and satellites. The surveillance is maintained through signals sent to the orbiting satellites from microchips implanted in militants' buttocks during their military service.[26] McVeigh spoke with conviction of the biochip in his left buttock.

What shall we make of individuals who read secret meanings into bar codes on highways signs, imagine surveillance helicopters hovering overhead, and believe they have microchips implanted in them? If an individual were to report such ideas in a clinician's office, he would be diagnosed promptly as suffering a severe paranoid disorder. But groups adhere to these beliefs, which they claim are "common knowledge."

Such beliefs—held by otherwise sane and sensible persons—are more a reflection of group dynamics than of individual psychopathology. The members hear their leaders repeat these "facts" and are exposed to common messages in both print and electronic media. Like the rest of us, they obtain their reality checks by comparing their beliefs with those of their associates. Wanting to belong, they do not question the group's beliefs. Once a paranoid belief system is established in a group, it is nearly impossible to dislodge.

The militias' fantasies about and fear of technology do not mean that they do not use it for their own purposes. Militia members, for example, have exchanged advice, "intelligence," and political views through such Internet bulletin boards as the Paul Revere Net, the American Patriot Fax Network, and the Motherboard of Freedom. Gaining full access to such networks requires commitment. One had a welcoming message that stated, "We are a network of doers, not whiners or fakers," and then asked newcomers whether they were willing to provide safehouses, training areas, and supplies to "patriots." An item that ran on the alt.conspiracy Usenet group was headlined "Clinton Orders Okla. Bombing?"[27] The Aryan Nation's Liberty Net was a national neo-Nazi computer network that, among other things, provided a list of Anti-Defamation League offices and a list of enemies, those who "have betrayed their race [and will] suffer the extreme penalty."[28] As of this writing, the network has been replaced by a home page on the World Wide Web.

A leading conspiracy propagandist, Mark Koernke of the Michigan Militia, broadcast "The Intelligence Report" every Thursday evening since August 1994 on World Wide Christian Radio. Koernke stated on the air that the government would enforce the New World Order with a national police force made up of National Guard units and foreign troops, including Nepalese Gurkhas and Los Angeles street gangs. He issued warnings that the "Mark of the Beast" in Revelation 13, the Antichrist's means of control, would take the form of implanted microchips.[29] Koernke's radio show sign-off was "Death to the New World Order! We shall prevail!" One of his commercial videotapes, which are widely circulated in the militia movement, showed the back of a cereal box listing "America's regions," with their chief industries and natural resources. These maps are propaganda, Koernke said, for a New World Order partition of America. At one time he had warned that detention centers were being constructed in Oklahoma City and other places, and that U.N. and NATO military vehicles were already being deployed within U.S. borders. Koernke characterized U.S. Attorney General Janet Reno as "the butcher of Waco" and suggested that the federal government might have been behind the Oklahoma bombing of the federal building.[30] This idea gained wide currency in the militia movement, one theory being that the blast was to justify the government's declaring martial law in order to seize the weapons of civilians. Another charge, voiced by the founder of the Oregon Militia, was that a "rogue agency" had carried out the terrorist act in order to destroy documents related to the Waco confrontation so there would not be a renewed inquiry into the case: "If they would blow up one of their own buildings, who knows what they could do to militias?" The network canceled Koernke's radio show immediately after the Oklahoma City bombing, but he continues to broadcast it via satellite.[31]

The head of the Michigan Militia, Norman Olson, sent out a news release that suggested that the Japanese government planted the Oklahoma City bomb. Japan allegedly committed this act in retaliation for a Tokyo nerve gas attack orchestrated by the CIA to punish Japan for lowering the value of the dollar against the yen. This charge went beyond the permissive boundaries of the Michigan Militia, and Olson was dismissed.[32]

Although only a minority of the militias are explicitly racist, forty-five militias in twenty-two states have links to white supremacist groups.[33] Ties between the militias and the Christian Identity movement are variable; some of the militias are closely connected, whereas others have no apparent relationship.

Some of the militias are more extreme in their actions than others. In testimony before Congress on June 15, 1995, in connection with the Oklahoma City bombing, five leaders of the militias described themselves as ordinary people who loved the Constitution, feared government abuse, and owned guns only to protect themselves. They stated that the government was using "weather-control techniques so the new world order could starve millions of Americans," that the government had caused as many as eighty-five midwestern tornadoes in order to disorient heartland America, and that there were actually two bombs that destroyed the

Oklahoma City federal building, which were accidentally detonated by the government itself. The head of the Michigan Militia accused the lawmakers of being part of the "corrupt, oppressive tyranny in government" and identified the CIA as the "grandest conspirator behind all this government."[34]

The power and malign design attributed to the U.S. government are central components of this mindset. The militias are preparing to defend themselves against this all-powerful government, which seeks to deprive the citizens of the right to bear arms and other rights. This identification of the outside enemy as the holder of power, with the concomitant feeling of powerlessness, are central features of the psychology of political paranoia.[35] As aggression is projected, so too are the associated feelings of strength and knowledge, so that a feeling of relative weakness and powerlessness on the part of the projector is the result. Recall the message of the man with the sandwich board, warning of the dangers of mind control by the U.S. government. His message was one not only of persecution and conspiracy but also of powerlessness, of being controlled by outside forces. External threats are substituted for internal threats and weakness. The process of projecting the unbearable affect outward contributes to and reinforces the perception of persecution. These powerful feelings, observed in microcosm in terrorist groups, are at the heart of many destructive mass movements and may come to characterize entire nations. Through the polarization of the environment into "good" and "bad" imagery, political leaders possess the power to externalize internal dangers and make the act of defending against and destroying the projected "monsters" a common good for the society, thus legitimating defensive aggression.[36] For the extremists of the radical right, the federal government has been identified as the enemy, with the tragedy in Oklahoma City as the dreadful consequence.

The militia movement is fed not only by the vicious delusions we have just described but also by the distortion of several virtues. Three American traditions influence the militias: rural romanticism, radical individualism, and American exceptionalism.

American rural romanticism and radical individualism, which originated with Thomas Jefferson and Andrew Jackson, and perhaps with the Rousseauesque idealism that influenced these two great presidents, also appear in extreme though seldom violent forms on the left—in, for example, the rural commune and hippie movements of the 1960s and among some of the extreme ecologists today. The belief in a conspiracy directed by those identified with cities—Jews and bankers, for example—draws on the Jeffersonian idea that the countryside is the source of virtue and productivity while the cities are corrupting and parasitic.

Radical individualism is as deeply American as rural romanticism. The American Revolution is portrayed as individual riflemen fighting overtrained Britons, and the even more powerful myth of the frontier idealizes the individual, his family, and his neighbors in their quest to conquer the wilderness without the aid of government. In today's capitalist society and fiercely adversarial political and judicial systems, radical individualism remains a powerful force.

Just as rural romanticism and radical individualism have been distorted by many militia members to paranoid lengths, so too has the idea of American exceptionalism. The belief that America is unlike any other society and that it has a salvationist message—that it is the last best hope of mankind—has been perverted by many in the militia movement into a paranoid xenophobia. Closely complementary to this belief is the idea that the wily foreigners are in the end always defeated by the straightforward, honest Americans, once they have been aroused to the danger.

An instructive manifestation of the psychological dynamics of the movement is found in the films that militia members are most attracted to—the Rambo series, released between 1982 and 1988.[37] These films, which some dismiss as nothing more than comic strip fantasies, idealize the traditional virtues of honesty, loyalty to one's friends, bravery, and self-reliance. To do right, to save his friends, and to vanquish Communism, Rambo must fight the "suits"—the effete, cunning, and sneering Ivy League types in the CIA and State Department. This class conflict (Rambo is clearly working class) is expressed in American, not European, terms: honest small-town patriotism versus Europeanized Washingtonians. This is the same conflict the marginalized militia members believe they are engaged in.

Watching the Rambo movies, the susceptible audience understands why America lost the war in Vietnam. It was not because the American soldiers were ineffective or the war lacked merit; it was because the high-level officers and Washington bureaucrats betrayed the common soldier and sabotaged America's ideals. The lesson of Vietnam that the American audience draws from these films, a lesson it had already sensed, is that their values, their America, can triumph only after they have defeated Washington and New York.

More than revanchism, however, underlies the militia movement. Like the violent anti-abortion movement (see Chapter 5), the militia movement is in part a reaction against feminism: man as protector and man as warrior are the defining archaic myths and archetypes. But the militia members are not merely overgrown kids playing soldier in the woods. The movement is fueled by alienation, race, power, and historical memory, cast in the name of honor.

But why now? Why did the militia movement, which was only fragmentary in the 1980s, gain such momentum in the early 1990s? Why did the paranoid fantasy novel *The Turner Diaries,* published in 1980, become so popular in the United States in the late 1980s and 1990s?

To some extent the militia movement is the extreme manifestation of the mainstream suspicion of government that had grown so strong not only in America but throughout the world in this period. We have noted other factors as well. But there is another, and less obvious, influence. Just as the end of the Cold War was destabilizing for Eastern Europe and led to the revival of old enmities, so too has the United States lost its enemy. The advent of domestic terrorism and the rise of the militia movement reflect aggression turned inward. For some, the Communist enemy abroad has been replaced by the federal government at home.

## Racist Black Activism

We hated our head, we hated the shape of our nose—we wanted one of those long, *dog*-like noses, you know. Yeah. We hated the color of our skin. We hated the look of Africa that was in our veins. And in hating our features and our skin and our blood, why, we had to end up hating ourselves . . . Our color became to us a chain. We felt that it was holding us back. Our color became to us like a prison which we felt was

keeping us confined, . . . and it became hateful to us. It made
us feel inferior. It made us feel inadequate. It made us feel
helpless.
—Malcolm X

The Nation of Islam had Fard as its prophet, its original theorist; the
subsequent leader of the sect, Elijah Muhammad, elaborated on Fard's
doctrine (see Chapter 7). But it was not until the political talent of Malcolm X (born Malcolm Little) seized upon the social and political opportunities of the American civil rights movement of the 1950s and the
Black Power movement of the 1960s that the Nation of Islam was integrated into a political movement.

It was not difficult to use this ideology in a campaign of hate against
the white rulers of America. Note the pseudospeciation—the belief that
humans are divided into different species—in the following speech,
which Malcolm delivered in a mosque. In this case pseudospeciation is
combined with a notion of divine legitimation: "These aren't white people . . . You're not using the right language when you say the white man.
You call it the devil. When you call him the devil, you're calling him by
his name, and he's got another name—Satan; another name—serpent;
another name—beast. All these names are in the Bible for the white man.
Another name—Pharaoh; another name—Caesar; another name—France;
French; Frenchman; Englishman; American; all these are just names for
the devil!"[38]

All these groups were to be destroyed. Again, the leader's role was
substantial. In the original Fardian apocalyptic description, the destruction
was by the hand of God, with the virtuous blacks as bystanders. Malcolm
X, in contrast, energized the paranoid dynamic. He advocated organized
struggle and violence. Indeed, he was attracted to Islam in large measure
because it was particularly sympathetic to "fighting (striving) in the way
of God."[39] In this sense he played Peter to Fard's Jesus, Lenin to Fard's
Marx. The environment of America in the 1960s was favorable to such
an adversarial stance. Julius Lester, in a book with the threatening or
mocking title Look Out, Whitey! Black Power's Gon' Get Your Mama!
spoke of the pleasure blacks feel when whites are killed in plane crashes.[40]
His moral dismissal of white society is epitomized in a single comment:

"It is clear that America as it now exists must be destroyed. It is impossible to live within this country and not become a thief or a murderer."[41]

In asserting the divinity, intellectual superiority, moral preeminence, and physical excellence of the black race, Elijah Muhammad had had to deal with the "if-you're-so-smart-why-ain't-you-rich" question. Hitler had faced the same problem in proclaiming the superiority of the Aryans. How was it possible that such superior people were not ruling the world but were themselves being ruled by their "inferiors"?

For Elijah Muhammad as for Hitler, conspiracy provided the explanation. Here again, a paranoid doctrine was added to an ideology to remedy the contradictions. Not only were whites in general working secretly against blacks, but a special role was described for two other groups. "All whites knew they were devils," wrote Malcolm, "especially the Masons." The Masons, he argued, were allied with the devil, the black people with God. The superiority is on God's side with his "360 degrees of knowledge," whereas "the devil has only thirty-three degrees of knowledge—known as Masonry."[42]

Jews, according to this doctrine, were the other conspiratorial group. Malcolm originally resisted including Jews among the black people's enemies because of positive experiences he had had with them. When he was told that *all* whites were devils, "my mind was involuntarily flashing across the entire spectrum of white people I had ever known and for some reason it stopped upon Hymie, the Jew, who had been so good to me."[43] But Malcolm was quickly convinced that in fact the Jew, by treating him fairly in a financial transaction, was taking advantage of him, giving him less than he truly deserved. In later life, Malcolm came to see Jews as the most subtle practitioners of an anti-black conspiracy: "All I held against the Jew was that so many Jews actually were hypocrites in their claim to be friends of the American black man, and it burned me up to be so often called 'anti-Semitic' when I spoke things I knew to be the absolute truth about Jews . . . I gave the Jew credit for being among all other whites the most active and most vocal financier, 'leader' and 'liberal' in the Negro civil rights movement. But I said at the same time I knew that the Jew played these roles for a very careful strategic reason: the more prejudice in America could be focused upon the Negro, then the more the white Gentiles' prejudice would keep diverted off the Jew."[44]

Black groups and individuals critical of Elijah Muhammad and the Nation of Islam were accused of being under Jewish or Zionist control. Black Supreme Court Justice Thurgood Marshall and black American diplomat Ralph Bunche were particular objects of hostility, as was the National Association for the Advancement of Colored People (NAACP). The January 16, 1960, issue of the *Los Angeles Herald-Dispatch,* which had become the official organ of the Nation of Islam, "explained," "In the early 30s, a large percentage of European Jews were engaged in trade, living in the rear of stores, markets and generally making their living from the Negro in the Negro community. Thus they had an excellent opportunity to study the habits and weaknesses of the Negro. The depression of the 30s, through the activities of the Communist Party, allowed the Jews to further intrench themselves into the community, to infect his thinking to the extent that by 1940 the Negro was almost entirely dependent upon the Jews and had accepted the thinking and ideology of the Jewish people. In the late 30s and by the early 50s the Jews had finally gained control of the NAACP."

In 1964, after a pilgrimage to Mecca, Malcolm X renounced the doctrine of black supremacy and separated himself from Elijah Muhammad. Malcolm had derived his power in part from his religious and racist rhetoric, which attracted followers to him, and this recantation led to a split within the movement. Malcolm had been a mentor to Louis Farrakhan, who saw Malcolm's moderation as treason and took his place as head of the Harlem Temple No. 7. In his initial sermon Farrakhan preached, "Only those who wish to be led to hell, or to their doom, will follow Malcolm. Such a man . . . is worthy of death." Malcolm's assassination at the hands of the followers of Elijah Muhammad followed in less than three months.[45]

Although Malcolm X moderated his position and made it more conventional, more religiously orthodox, the doctrine of the Nation of Islam did not change. Malcolm X had the same problem that David Duke and Yasir Arafat would face decades later—how to move away from the extremist followers and doctrines that had brought him political power without alienating those same core supporters. His murder prevents us from knowing whether he would have accomplished this effort.

When Elijah Muhammad died in 1975, he was succeeded by his son

Wallace, who tried to follow the less radical path on which Malcolm X had embarked just before his assassination. Farrakhan rejected this moderate path and in 1978 broke from mainstream Islam and formed his own group, taking the original name, the Nation of Islam, and its tenets.[46] Farrakhan followed Malcolm X in giving a special demonizing role to Jews: "The Jews came at the turn of the century into the black community, . . . and they became strong nursing from the breast of the black community, growing . . . to disrespect the very breast that had nursed them to strength . . . They know someday they will be punished for the bad things they have done to blacks. . . . They didn't apologize for putting my brothers and sisters to live in homes or apartments and charging them the highest rents. [They] don't apologize for setting up liquor stores, when [they] don't drink too much [themselves], feeding my brothers and sisters alcohol. [They] don't apologize for sucking the blood of our poor people that [they] might live well."[47] This externalizing rhetoric of hatred has been a consistent element in Farrakhan's oratory. He regularly claims to be misunderstood—"I am not against the Jews"—arguing that the problem is that "as long as Jewish people control the media, Arabs, blacks, muslims will never have a balanced view. . . . You don't have to be afraid to speak out against Jews if what you are saying is the truth . . . I'm not backing down from Jews, because I know their wickedness." The solution suggested by Farrakhan in a 1985 interview was a race war, which he predicted would occur in 1986. "Some of the white people are going to live, but [God] doesn't want them living with us. Make no mistake, we're going to shake the world." According to Farrakhan, Jews were especially frightened, because they had "an idea of what's rolling around in the back of my brain."[48]

Farrakhan also claimed that the U.S. government is responsible for "pouring drugs into our cities." "Where do drugs come from? Who is the unseen hand? The government of the U.S." This paranoid theme was picked up by black ministers, as exemplified by the Reverend Calvin O. Butts, pastor of New York's Abyssinian Baptist Church: "Drugs hit at such an important time in our community. I don't think that was a co-incidence." Farrakhan also insisted that Africa's AIDS plague is caused by whites trying to steal the region's strategic minerals.[49]

The themes of Jews financially exploiting blacks was a mainstay of Farrakhan's rhetoric and that of the leaders of the organization. Khalid Abdul Muhammad, Farrakhan's deputy, delivered a particularly vicious hate-mongering speech at Kean College, New Jersey, in 1993: "Who are the slumlords in the black community? The so-called Jew. Rundown, dilapidated buildings, huh? Water not working properly. Toilets not working properly . . . Who is sucking our blood in the black community? . . . They're the blood suckers of the black nation and the black community." Later in this address Muhammad calls for the death of all whites in South Africa:

We don't owe the White Man nothin' in South Africa. He's killed millions of our women, our children, our babies, our elders. We don't owe him nothin' in South Africa. If we want to be merciful at all, when we gain enough power from God Almighty to take our freedom and independence from him [the white man], we give him twenty-four hours to get out of town, by sundown. That's all. If he won't get out by sundown, we kill everything white that ain't right in South Africa. We kill the women, we kill the children, we kill the babies. We kill the blind, we kill the crippled, we kill 'em all . . . You say why kill the babies in South Africa? Because they gonna grow up one day to oppress our babies, so we kill the babies. Why kill the women too? They, they . . . because they lay on their back, they are the military or the army's manufacturing center. They lay on their back and reinforcements roll out from between their legs. So we kill the women too. You'll kill the elders too? Kill the old ones too. Goddamit, if they in a wheelchair, push 'em off a cliff in Cape Town, or Johannesburg . . . How the hell you think they got old, they got old oppressing black people. I said kill the blind, kill the crippled, kill the crazy. Goddamit, and when you get through killing 'em all, go to the goddam graveyard and dig up the grave and kill 'em, goddam again. 'Cause they didn't die hard enough. They didn't die hard enough. And if you've killed 'em all and you don't have the strength to dig 'em up, then take your gun and shoot in the goddam grave. Kill 'em again. Kill 'em again, cause they didn't die hard enough.[50]

In response to criticism of this speech, Louis Farrakhan condemned Muhammad's style but confirmed the basic "truth" of his message.

Farrakhan's call for a "March for Atonement" in Washington, D.C., on October 19, 1995, struck a resonant chord in the African-American community. Supporters hoped that the demonstration, dubbed the Million Man March, would ease the climate of racial division. Farrakhan had stated as goals for the demonstration that the participants seek atonement for past wrongs within their communities, seek reconciliation with those they have wronged, and seek the economic, political, and spiritual growth of the black community. But Farrakhan's commentary at the announcement of the demonstration and immediately before the march continued to strike divisive chords and play on the theme of persecution, a theme he echoed at the march itself.

In an interview with Reuters on October 4, 1995, Farrakhan accused Jews and others of exploiting blacks financially and called them bloodsuckers, as had Khalid Muhammad in the Kean College speech. He went on to say, "It was rabbinical scholars that developed the Hamitic myth that we as black folk were the children of Ham, cursed black." After linking Jews to the slave trade, he charged that a failed plot on his life was orchestrated by a Jew who "hated me as a Jew."[51]

The racist paranoid theme that the Nation of Islam propounds resonates with and stimulates a wider group of paranoid beliefs and rhetoric in the black community (see Chapter 2). But Muhammad's poisonous diatribe was not only in continuity with that of Farrakhan; this rhetoric of hatred also bears a remarkable resemblance to the logic and the language of the white members of Christian Identity quoted earlier. Some black groups believe that whites are not human but the creation of the devil. And some white groups believe blacks are not human but the creation of the devil. These groups do, however, agree on one point: the Jews are on the other side and responsible for it all.

## The Communist Witch Hunt

A paranoid message may be adopted by an opportunistic leader who does not believe it. This was the case in the early 1950s with Senator Joseph R. McCarthy, Republican of Wisconsin, the most notorious episode of paranoia and the most infamous "paranoid" leader in United States history. Because it was the receptivity of the audience rather than the psychopathology of the leader that was crucial, we will look at the movement and its audience before we examine the person who fed and rode it.

For many Americans, the term *witch hunt* suggests not Salem, Massachusetts, in the seventeenth century but the entire country in the early 1950s and the phenomenon of McCarthyism. Both McCarthyism and the Salem panic grew from the same paranoid seed, a distorted truth. Arthur Miller wrote *The Crucible,* a play about the Salem witch trials, during the Communist witch hunt of the 1950s. Once, when discussing those years, Miller observed, "McCarthy's power to stir fears of creeping communism was not based entirely on illusion, of course; the paranoid, real or pretended, always secretes his pearl around a grain of fact."[52] Recall that some in Salem practiced what all then believed to be witchcraft and harmed others by doing so. Similarly, in the early 1950s some Americans were indeed willing to subordinate American interests to those of the Soviet Union. The dangers America faced, moreover, were not imaginary. A paranoid leader (Stalin) of a brutally expansionist country had achieved substantial success, possessed nuclear weapons, and was threatening America. And also as in the Salem panic, the damage to innocent (and some not-so-innocent) members of the society was severe but limited in scope and time, and this damage was followed by an almost universal condemnation of the panic.

Like those who were hanged in Salem, McCarthy's victims were chosen within a setting of well-established traditions of belief. Americans have a powerful legacy of being suspicious of government, and so it is not surprising that people were willing to believe the worst about high governmental figures. Another American tradition has been a strong anti-foreign, even xenophobic, sentiment, so it is to be expected that threats from abroad would strike a vulnerable chord.

As in Salem, victims were chosen from those who had angered the accusers or whose humiliation would symbolically or materially enrich the accusers. The extreme anti-Communist movement was very much a populist cause. It was principally the elite who were accused of being allied to Communism, especially leaders and associates of Ivy League universities and officials of the Department of State. Their humiliation

enhanced the status of those who attacked them. In partisan politics, the
replacement of those on the left by those on the right was clearly in the
interest of Republicans like McCarthy. The Democratic Party was able
to maintain its influence (although it lost control of both the presidency
and Congress) only by moving rapidly to the right on issues related to
Communism.

Finally, victims were chosen simply because they had assumed roles,
acquired characteristics, or displayed behaviors that resembled the profile
the accusers described. A suspected Communist showed or had shown
any of the following characteristics: friendliness to Communist or Com-
munist-allied organizations or leaders, association with such people and
organizations, advocacy of doctrines and policies that were especially
identified with Communism (such as Marxism or state ownership of industry), and in a more general, diffuse fashion, connection with those
institutions (liberal newspapers, elite universities) associated with these
doctrines and organizations. Indeed, there was a tendency to castigate
anyone who was less vociferously opposed to Communism than the person doing the accusing.

The McCarthy scare of the early 1950s followed a classic paranoid
pattern of distorting and exaggerating a genuine danger and then finding
and victimizing suitable scapegoats. Like Samuel Parris, the village minister who brought on the Salem panic, Joseph McCarthy was eventually
condemned, in this case by a vote of a special session of the U.S. Senate,
but not before he had wreaked terrible damage.

McCarthy was not without calculation, but his principal characteristics
were impulsiveness and recklessness. As is so often the case with politically successful practitioners of the paranoid style, it is difficult to say
when his accusations sprang from genuinely held beliefs and when they
were calculated efforts at political aggrandizement. McCarthy seems to
have hit upon the Communist issue almost by chance. His accusations in
Wheeling, West Virginia, of widespread Communist influence in government were not based on research or special information but were simply
off the cuff. He was casting about for an issue.

In 1950 McCarthy was only two years away from a reelection campaign. The Republican was unpopular in his own party in the Senate—

he lacked any important committee assignment—and the Wisconsin tax department was investigating him. Once he had hit upon the issue of Communists in government, he rode it blindly, first to frightening power, and eventually into censure, political disgrace, and effective exclusion from American politics.

Although he bore a paranoid message and displayed a paranoid style, McCarthy was not a paranoid. He was driven to seek recognition and was willing to destroy other people's reputations in the process. But after dealing severely and unfairly with people, calling them liars and traitors, he would pathetically attempt to disown responsibility for his behavior. He would then indirectly apologize and try to appease the injured party. When he was rebuffed, he was surprised. This behavior differs from that of the genuine paranoid, who demonizes and depersonalizes his victims. Thus, unlike the classic paranoid, McCarthy lacked any sense of personal enemies.[53] McCarthy also did not have the calculating temperament of the paranoid. He nevertheless opportunistically but clumsily used a paranoid style in promoting his own career. Initially he made reckless accusations, cynically knowing they were untrue. It may be, however, that as these charges were well received and his influence grew, he may have come to believe his own paranoid accusations.

In this case, the ineptness of the leader caused what was probably a premature decline of the movement. McCarthy may have been McCarthyism's greatest handicap. He had substantial though not outstanding political abilities. McCarthy was generally well liked, and among friends and family he was considerate, kind, and relaxed. He had neither the paranoid demagogue's calculating temperament nor the successful political demagogue's sense of choosing the right enemies. The choice of Communism was effective, but the selection of Roy Cohn and G. David Schine as his principal assistants in the Army vs. McCarthy subversion hearings in 1954 missed the demagogic mark. A skillful right-wing demagogue would have attacked the Jews, a traditional target of the American paranoid right, and allied himself to the army, a traditional favorite of the right. McCarthy had it the other way around, in sharp contrast to two thoroughgoing paranoid demagogues, David Duke and Gerald L. K. Smith (see Chapter 9). So, though ruthless in attacking his enemies, he never stooped to assaulting religious or racial minority groups. Yet the paranoid theme was present, for in "the outside world, he saw no friends, only potential adversaries who might oppose his ambitions or frustrate his will."[54]

When McCarthy ultimately was confronted by the system that had acquiesced in his ride to glory, the rapidity of his fall was stunning. After he was censured by the Senate, the press did not report his speeches, and his colleagues in the Senate ignored him whenever possible, even drifting away from him at social occasions. Given his need for recognition and public acclaim, the silence and isolation must have been devastating. But McCarthy did not move in an increasingly paranoid direction; he did not begin to see himself as surrounded by enemies. Rather, he anesthetized himself with alcohol. According to an anecdote related by one of McCarthy's biographers, drinking was not simply a form of escape but a method of suicide: "Back in Washington, Joe ambled into the office of the Secretary of the Senate where two colleagues were having a drink. He filled a drinking glass to the brim with liquor and downed the contents in several uninterrupted gulps. He told his astonished observers that he had been to Bethesda Naval Hospital several times to 'dry out' and that on the last occasion his doctor had said he would die if he had one more drop. He then proceeded to refill the glass and drink it dry."[55]

Joseph McCarthy's reckless political opportunism and manipulation of a paranoid style coincided with a transient receptivity in the American polity to a paranoid message. As the system and the public awakened to the dangerous nature of the messenger, the society rejected him, and McCarthy died largely alone and embittered.

The McCarthy affair demonstrates the crucial nature of the relations among the political context, the political actor, and the message. In this case, the paranoid nature of the message and the erratic nature of the messenger initially went unrecognized. The phenomenon of McCarthyism emphasizes that paranoids do not have exclusive rights to the espousal of paranoid ideas.

# 9

## Paranoia's Organizers and Propagandists

It was a maxim with Foxy: . . . "Always suspect everybody."
—Charles Dickens, *Old Curiosity Shop*

Superabundance of suspicion is a kind of political madness.
—Francis Bacon, *De augmentis scientiarum*

All political theorists are suitors. Each must attract a consort who will create an organization around his worldview. Every Moses must have his Aaron, every Jesus his Peter, every Marx his Lenin. The failure of LaRouchism and the John Birch Society as mass movements can to a substantial extent be attributed to these movements' lack of a brilliant organizer. La-Rouche himself might have been such an organizer, but he lacked the resources to be both theorist and organizer. Welch was more a political hobbyist than a fire-in-the-belly organizer. To some extent, a skillful fomenter—agitator, organizer, promoter—is the most precious asset a movement can have. Many people have paranoid ideologies, but few have the organizational ability to bring that ideology into the mainstream political world.

## Gerald L. K. Smith

Gerald Lyman Kenneth Smith was an American isolationist and anti-Semitic agitator who began his career in the 1920s, rose to regional political influence under the tutelage of Governor Huey Long of Louisiana in the early 1930s, and, after Long's assassination by Baton Rouge physician Dr. Carl A. Weiss, Jr., remained an influential speaker and political figure into the 1960s.[1] In the late 1930s and just after World War II, Smith was widely listened to, and he influenced mainstream politicians and elections. His power was greatest in 1935–36, when his name was known to millions as the advocate of Huey Long's confiscatory Share the Wealth scheme, Francis Townsend's forced spending plans, and Father Charles E. Coughlin's anti-Semitism. He was to the far right of the 1930s and 1940s what David Duke is to the neo-Nazi fringe of today.

Smith drew on well-established American political traditions, especially romantic populism. A simpler, purer America had once existed, Smith said, and was corrupted by big business, big government, and foreign cliques. Smith was hostile to all groups whose origins were not Anglo-Saxon, Scandinavian, or Germanic. The great corrupters and manipulators, according to Smith, were the Jews. It was they who had destroyed the family farm and small business, replacing them with large and impersonal international concerns. Franklin D. Roosevelt, international bankers, Jews, and the Communist Party were joined in a perverse conspiracy to destroy America. Capitalism itself was not wrong; it was its adulteration by "non-American" interests that was at fault.

Although Jews were eventually to become the focus of Smith's paranoid views, his devotion to conspiracy theories preceded his political anti-Semitism. Smith's initial hostility was toward bankers (whom he did not identify with Jews) and their (Gentile) supporters. After Long's assassination on September 8, 1935, Smith suggested that his "mysterious death" was part of the "most subtle plot in American history." He went on to insinuate that the New Orleans district attorney was one of the plotters, as were several federal appointees, and he concluded that President Roosevelt at least acquiesced in the assassination.[2]

Smith was eventually called the "dean of American anti-Semitism." But although anti-Semitism was almost surely present throughout his adult life, he kept it separate from his political rhetoric until at least the early 1940s. In 1934 Smith called the allegation of anti-Semitism the "dirtiest" charge ever leveled against a "friend" of the Jews. He denied ever having any ties with the Ku Klux Klan. He also publicly repudiated the fascist Silver Shirts. In 1936 Richard Gutstadt, midwestern director of the B'nai B'rith's Anti-Defamation League, sent an observer to investigate Smith. The investigator, apparently accepting Smith's own statements, reported that Smith was not an anti-Semite. As late as 1939, Smith criticized Hitler for "hounding" Jews. In 1942, L. M. Burkhead, a Unitarian minister and leader of the anti-Nazi Friends of Democracy, reported that Smith avoided Jew-baiting.[3]

There were, however, early indications of Smith's later overt anti-Semitism. Smith was rumored to have made anti-Semitic remarks in New Orleans in 1936 and advocated a boycott of Jewish merchants in that city. He also associated with notorious anti-Semites, notably Henry Ford, who gave him some modest financial support. Although Smith remained a national influence, his power greatly decreased after his feeble showing as the candidate of the America First Party in the presidential election of 1944.[4] It was only in 1946 that he focused his paranoia on Jews.

After 1946 what had been a "mainstream" paranoia became increasingly idiosyncratic. Smith announced that Roosevelt did not die in 1945 but rather was being kept in a mental institution by Jewish doctors, who planned to return him as "President of the World." He also suggested a hidden meaning in the United Nations flag because it was the same color as "the Jew flag" and subtly resembled the Soviet hammer and sickle in design. These bizarre "special" meanings suggest Smith had progressed from a paranoid personality into a frank paranoid illness. In the 1950s, Smith argued that his hero, Joseph McCarthy, was not only murdered but murdered in an unusual way: "They studied McCarthy's constitution; then they directed their lies, rumors, and innuendos so as to overstimulate certain glands, producing 'glandular murder.' "[5] Clearly Smith's ideology—though never straying far from ideas of conspiracy and always tinged with racism—was neither coherent nor original. Smith was not a theoretician; he was an agitator and organizer possessing conventional political skills, an enormous capacity for hard work, a resilience in the face of defeat, and a nimble wit.

In an age before television and with radio only in its childhood, Smith shone as a public speaker. H. L. Mencken, who had heard orations by William Jennings Bryan, Robert La Follette, Billy Sunday, both Teddy and Franklin D. Roosevelt, and Huey Long, said that Smith was the best public speaker of all. The manner in which Smith's speeches were delivered fit his audience the way the sermons of a charismatic minister fit his. Smith said that the "child-minded" majority could not follow complicated arguments but needed to have the issues dramatized by stories, jokes, and pejorative nicknames. His speeches were long and loud, with heavy doses of patriotism and paranoia, religion, and claims of victimization. The audience was directly or indirectly selected from known Smith supporters (derived from mailing lists), and Smith staff were stationed at the door to exclude anyone who looked like a heckler. Skilled speakers warmed up the crowd in advance, and stirring music was played.

Smith employed innovative forms of audience participation. He led his followers in a kind of reverse cheerleading, or "boo-leading." He would mention Franklin Roosevelt or Bernard Baruch and shout, "Give me a boo!" If the boo were not forceful enough, he would ask for a louder one. And if the audience were not large enough, Smith would send it out to bring others in, and if *they* were not enough, he would do so again. He made many of his speeches in tents erected outdoors for the purpose, and he could hold the audience's attention on the hottest of summer afternoons or when conditions were even more adverse: once, when the tent caught fire as Smith was delivering a speech, the audience kept their seats while his assistants put out the flames.

The capacity to speak vividly, to work hard, and to be resilient could be used in the service of any political cause and in itself did not reflect any defect of personality. Smith's personality, however, also included patterns that were psychologically malign although politically useful. Smith himself had many of the characteristics of those he attacked. As his biographer, Glen Jeansonne, notes: "Smith's own vices were reflected in the evils he saw in Jews. Jews wanted world conquest: Smith wanted power. He denounced Jews for being wealthy, yet he lived in luxury and collected antiques, Bibles, and paintings."[6] Moreover, Smith characterized Jews as parasites, manipulators, clannish, socially assertive, and religiously fanatic—much like Smith was. Indeed, these characteristics (with the exception of religious fanaticism) were those that American populists had long used to describe their wealthy, generally East Coast opponents. This pattern of disowning an intolerable feeling and through projection assigning it to another, who then becomes the object of attack, is at the heart of the paranoid dynamic. In Smith's case, as with Lyndon LaRouche and the militia movement, the traditional (and healthy) American hostility to government offered a fertile ground for the (pathological) belief in governmental conspiracies.

Another projective pattern that is especially complementary to a paranoid style is the belief that, because the paranoid thinks constantly about his enemies, they think constantly about him. In Smith, this belief gave rise to the classic paranoid style of hyperalertness, selective use of evidence, the constant "discovery" of conspiracy, a belief in ultimate victory, and an absolutist view of reality: "He was ceaselessly excited, apprehensive, and keenly alert, finding the most contorted plots in the most innocent conversations. . . . Smith admitted that he might not triumph in his lifetime but he predicted that some day God would intervene to bring victory."[7] There was no room in Smith's mind for doubt or ambiguity. He believed in absolutes, rejecting all evidence contrary to his prejudices or twisting the evidence to make it conform to his beliefs.

When he died in April 1976, Smith was a rich man as a result not of his political activities but of his ownership and financial promotion of the Christ of the Ozarks, a religious theme park in Eureka Springs, Arkansas. Smith was not driven by money, however. He "was neither a cynic nor a hypocrite, but a twisted idealist. He gave away millions of dollars, rejected offers for lucrative positions in industry and public relations, and worked himself to exhaustion every night."[8] A desire for political success would have led him, especially after World War II, to stress anti-Communism and put anti-Semitism on the back burner. But he did not. Smith dramatically revealed the deep roots of his anti-Semitic paranoia to his biographer, who recalled: "Once I was interviewing [Smith] about his childhood when for no apparent purpose he launched into a denunciation of Jews. He went on for twenty minutes and would not let me interrupt him. Finally, he took a deep breath, slumped back into his chair, and said, 'I just had to get that off my chest. I'll answer your questions now.' "[9] Smith was not like his assistant, Frederick Kister, head of Smith's Nationalist Veterans of World War II, who when asked why he engaged in hate work, replied, "I gotta make a living, don't I?"[10]

The question of why Smith had such hatred of non-Anglo-Saxons and bankers is beyond our ability to answer. No evidence suggests that he ever was personally injured by these groups, until late in his career when he had already provoked them by his accusations of disloyalty and conspiracy.

Smith spread the paranoid message and tried to come to power to implement it. He achieved success because he associated this message with a major American political tradition—romantic populism—investing his own great energy, organizational abilities, and speaking ability in the cause. And he employed these ideas during a time of extreme distress—the Great Depression. But as with all paranoid political leaders in well-established democratic societies, Smith's prominence was brief. Although in the late 1930s he had an audience of millions and was in communication with national leaders, when he ran for president he received fewer than two thousand votes. The American political system, then, permits leaders with a paranoid style to flourish indefinitely within a small group, but only briefly within a broader political context.

## David Duke

> The frightening part was that he wasn't a redneck, didn't use
> four letter words, was clean cut.
> —One of David Duke's high school teachers

There was no mistaking the fact that Gerald L. K. Smith proclaimed a paranoid message. He had the paranoid style of "heated exaggeration, suspiciousness, and conspiratorial fantasy" and clearly enunciated a paranoid theme with well-defined enemies, whose elimination would erase the problems his followers felt.[11] The same themes were articulated in the 1990s, but changes in American society, especially in the limits of acceptable political rhetoric and, even more important, in the technology of political communication, brought important alterations in the way the message was presented. David Duke of south Louisiana was the most skillful exploiter of the new "cool" technology of television.[12]

Duke was born in 1950 in Tulsa, Oklahoma, to a white middle-class family. Four years later the family moved to The Hague, Netherlands, where Duke's father, an employee of Shell Oil Company, was assigned. The next year they moved to New Orleans. Duke was often alone. After returning to the United States, Duke's father, David Hedger Duke, was often away from home for business or army reserve duties. Duke's older sister, Dorothy, moved out when she was seventeen and David was twelve. During the 1950s, Duke's mother, Maxine Crick Duke, began to drink excessively, and by the 1960s she was alcoholic and frequently bedridden.[13]

Duke, although not distinguished in school, was a serious reader and learner. In grade school, high school, and college he was unpopular.[14] At fourteen, as part of a high school assignment, Duke interviewed a land developer and White Citizens Council leader, James Lindsay. The adolescent Duke soon became close to Lindsay and began to espouse Nazi causes.

In 1968 Duke enrolled at Louisiana State University in Baton Rouge and, after a quiet freshman year, became a prominent speaker, advocating white supremacy and anti-Semitism. According to an anti-Duke group, the Louisiana Coalition Against Racism and Nazism: "During a local radio program Duke argues that Jews should be exterminated and Blacks sent back to Africa. *Reveille* [the LSU student newspaper] also reports Duke distributing bundles of Nazi newspapers and quotes him as saying: 'I am a National Socialist. You can call me a Nazi if you want.' "[15]

The next year Duke appeared, dressed as a Nazi with brown shirt and swastika armband, to protest a speech by radical attorney William Kunstler at Tulane University. He carried a sign reading "Gas the Chicago Seven" and "Kunstler Is a Communist Jew."

Duke may have been a member of the Ku Klux Klan even in high school. Certainly he was a member in 1973, when he wrote a seventy-page pamphlet, "African Atto," under the pen name Muhammed X. This pamphlet was advertised in black publications and claimed to describe a traditional African method of fighting that could be used "against whitey." Duke later claimed that he wrote and advertised the pamphlet to obtain the names of black militants. Three years later, under the pseudonym Dorothy Vanderbilt, Duke co-wrote *Finderskeepers: Finding and*

*Keeping the Man You Want,* a sex manual directed toward single women that described and advocated various sexual techniques and suggested attending church to meet sexually deprived married men. Duke later claimed that he wrote only the nutritional chapters in the book.[16]

It was Duke's continuing political activities, however, that first won him national exposure. In January 1974, at the age of twenty-four, Duke had achieved sufficient prominence to appear as an interviewee on the Tom Snyder show. Duke made his first foray into electoral politics in the fall of 1975, running as a Democrat for the senatorial seat of the Sixteenth District (near Baton Rouge). Although he lost, he made a respectable showing, receiving a third of the vote. Later that year his mentor, James Lindsay, then the KKK grand wizard, was murdered (his wife was charged but acquitted). Duke, at twenty-five, was soon elected to replace him. He immediately set out to unify and revitalize a divided and outdated Klan, ironically by instituting an affirmative action program of aggressive recruiting of Catholics and women. Another innovation was his dogged courting of the media. In 1979 Duke again ran for state office as a Democrat and received 26 percent of the vote.

Duke's electoral activity and outreach initiatives did not, however, end factionalism within the Klan. Indeed, they probably exacerbated it. Duke left the Klan in 1980, perhaps ousted by an internal coup. He had been accused of selling the Klan mailing list for thirty-five thousand dollars, and fellow Klansmen allegedly caught him selling or possessing pornographic photographs of racially mixed couples. His defense—that he had simply collected the pictures "to show people how bad things had got"—did not persuade the Klansmen. The consequence of these disputes, according to Klan informants, was that Duke was expelled from the Klan for "behavior not befitting a racist." Duke claimed, however, that he left the Klan voluntarily because its reputation made it impossible for its members to participate in mainstream American politics and so acquire power.[17]

In the late 1970s and early 1980s, Duke apparently was earning his living (and maintaining his following in racist circles) from speaking engagements and from his private business, Americana Books, which sold such titles as *Our Nordic Race, Zoological Subspecies of Man,* and *The Six Million Reconsidered.* Always alert to new opportunities, Duke also sold videotapes of *Birth of a Nation, David Duke Speaks at the University of Montana,* and *The Eternal Jew.* This period was the height of Duke's overt racism. In his *National Association for the Advancement of White People News* an article advocated a redivision of the United States into racial or ethnic provinces: Manhattan and Long Island would be assigned to Jews (and named "West Israel"); the New York City area minus West Israel, to Puerto Ricans and those of southern Mediterranean descent ("Minoria"); the western edge of Maine, to those of French-Canadian descent ("Francia"); Dade County, Florida, to Cuban Americans ("New Cuba"); Louisiana, Mississippi, Alabama, the rest of Florida, and part of southern Georgia, to African-Americans ("New Africa"); New Mexico and parts of the surrounding states, to Native Americans ("Navahona"); a strip of land about 150 miles wide running along the Mexican border, with a 20-mile no-man's-land buffer to the north, to Mexican Americans ("Alta California"); and finally Hawaii, to Asian Americans ("East Mongolia"). Duke later distanced himself from this article.[18]

Duke also allied himself with Identity Christianity, which referred to blacks as mud people and to Jews as descendants of Satan. In 1988 he ran for president on the Populist ticket, receiving substantial Nazi support but an insignificant number of votes.

At this time Duke was not a public figure, despite his limited electoral success and public speaking. On the one hand, he recognized that for his racist politics to succeed he would have to welcome groups previously excluded or marginalized, such as women and Catholics, and would have to manipulate rather than fight the media. Indeed, to be a contender for major power, he would have to convince many people that he had left his extremist views behind. On the other hand, his financial situation required that he continue to sell racist books and videos, and he had to maintain his bedrock political support by continuing to associate with well-known racists and racist organizations.

To resolve this contradiction, Duke attempted a remarkable maneuver, one that brought him close to a governorship and a national Senate seat and that made him, for a while, one of the best known and most feared political figures in America. His strategy was to apologize for his racist past while quietly continuing its associations. Publicly he would adopt reasonable, mainstream conservative issues (crime), causes (welfare reform, anti–affirmative action policies), and arguments (welfare leading to dependency) and indeed would associate himself with black as well as white supporters of these causes. To Duke, these were Nazi issues designed to harm black people, but they were presented as if he were a nonracist moderate conservative. In other words, Duke would send different messages to different groups. Racists would be reassured with a wink and a nudge that he was still the old David Duke. Mainstream conservatives, especially those who were frustrated by what they saw as betrayals by those whom they had supported in the past, would view Duke as repentant of his youthful excesses (although these past associations were simultaneously seen as testimony to Duke's sincerity) and as a fresh voice promising a genuine dedication to traditional values. For this strategy to succeed, each group would have to believe the message sent to it and disbelieve or discount the other message. The paranoid groups would have to believe the paranoid message, while the nonparanoid groups would have to either not hear it or discount it.

Style was also to play a large role in his persuasiveness. The days of yelling "nigger" and "kike" and wearing a brown uniform with a swastika on it were past. So, too, was any type of flamboyant speech, clothes, or demeanor. His public speaking would not be any more emotional than other speeches at ordinary political events. More important, the handsome and youthful Duke (who had enhanced his looks by plastic surgery) would shift his energies toward the cool medium of television. With few exceptions, Duke's appearances on radio and television would be models of quiet speech, reasonable argument, and conciliatory and even praising references to such black leaders as Jesse Jackson and Martin Luther King, presented in the context of middle-class sobriety and decency. Duke would abandon the paranoid style. His racist followers, however, would not.

This strategy developed out of his first electoral victory. On January 20, 1989, Duke became one of two candidates for state representative of the Eighty-first District, whose seat is Metairie, Louisiana, a suburb of New Orleans. Because of Louisiana's peculiar electoral system—in the primaries Democrats can vote for Republicans and vice versa, and if no one achieves a majority, the two front-runners, regardless of political affiliation, run against one another in the general election—Duke (now registered as a Republican) faced another Republican, John Treen, in the general election.

Duke's success in the primary and his subsequent hairbreadth victory (a margin of 277 out of nearly 17,000 votes cast) were in many ways a fluke. His victory was dependent on the odd character of the district, divided between Old Metairie silk stockings and New Metairie blue collars; the patrician and off-putting character of Duke's opponent (who was Old Metairie and was obviously reluctant to shake hands with strangers); and the occurrence of a vividly reported anti-white riot in the New Orleans business district just weeks before the primary. Duke, moreover, was a good campaigner—persistent, personable, and, taking a page from his opponents' book, portraying himself as a victim, the subject of unfairness and even conspiracy. He made much of the fact that the *New Orleans Times-Picayune* made its opposition to him obvious in news stories as well as on the editorial page. The national Republican Party declared itself opposed not only to Duke's election but even to his membership in the party. These "outsider" pressures gave Duke the underdog role and irritated many constituents, especially in the blue-collar neighborhoods. As it turned out, this was Duke's only electoral victory. The electorate split, with the (Old Metairie) Republicans and the few liberals voting for Treen and the (New Metairie) Reagan Democrats voting for Duke.

Duke later ran for U.S. senator in 1990 (losing with 44 percent of the vote in a two-way race) and governor of Louisiana in 1991 (losing with 39 percent of the vote in a two-way race). Although he lost the governorship by a substantial margin, the number of votes he gathered was 15 percent more than the number he had won in his senatorial bid, thanks to a much heavier turnout. The very possibility that Duke could win either office, or do as well as he did, caused considerable anxiety and surprise. Duke also sought the Republican presidential nomination in 1991 but won no delegates and only a smattering of votes. Throughout all his races, the heart of Duke's support was white working-class Reagan Democrats, not Republicans. In the 1991 gubernatorial primary, "Duke took 43 percent of the white vote but an estimated 54–57 percent from white Democrats; he received few or no votes from blacks and Republicans.''[19] About 74 percent of the Louisiana electors were registered Democrats, 11 percent independents, and 15 percent Republicans.

After his loss in the gubernatorial race and the debacle of his 1991 try for the Republican presidential nomination, Duke assumed a much lower profile. He had lost his State House seat because he had been prevented from running for two offices at the same time. He tried selling insurance, opened an Irish theme pub, appeared as a radio talk show host, and traveled overseas making speeches. In the September 1996 open primary for U.S. senator, Duke, running on an anti–affirmative action platform, gathered 14 percent of the Republican vote and 6 percent of the total vote.[20] He may now be a has-been, a marginalized crank—but at the writing of this book he is only in his late forties.

Duke's career as an agitator demonstrates several principles about the paranoid theme in politics. First, the theme is not dead. Few of those who voted for him did so because they agreed with his conspiratorial theories of Jewish dominance (although many voted for him because of his hostility to blacks). Nevertheless, it was the paranoid aspect of his political career that gave him his bedrock support and that, had he won, would have supplied him with his closest lieutenants. Second, his paranoid background (and his continued selling of paranoid literature and continued associations with paranoid groups even after he claimed to have reformed) both hurt and helped him. Many voters left Duke when they learned of his double message. But many did not, even though they did not agree with the message. They saw it as harmless and as an indication that "he really means what he says." Third, Duke demonstrated that a paranoid message does not require a paranoid style. On the contrary, a paranoid style—hyperemotionality and the shouting of accusations—is apt to be counterproductive when one is addressing a broad American audience. The paranoid message can be most effective when it is delivered in a calm, reassuring voice. If the devil walked about with a red skin, a pointed tail, and two horns coming out of his head, he would constitute little danger.

One final point concerns both Smith and Duke. They were not opportunists promoting a paranoid message; both believed deeply in the doctrines of hatred they purveyed. Like Smith, Duke would have done much better, after he had won office, to have moderated his message, especially his anti-Semitism. There are only a few thousand Jews in Louisiana. Many are Republicans. The state has had no major tradition of political anti-Semitism, certainly not since World War II. Attacking the Jews as Duke did gained him no voters who were not already attracted to him because of his anti-black message. And the attack on Jews mobilized intense reaction to him nationally by concerned Jewish elites. Why did Duke persist in his anti-Semitism? Because he believed in it even more strongly than he believed in racism.

## Oliver Stone

> The Event was so great; its consequences threatened to be so
> dangerous, that it seemed almost blasphemous to attribute so
> world-shaking a crime to a young, highly unstable, badly
> educated, semi-literate partisan of what he called "Marxism."
> The event deserved a greater cause, to amend Horace.
> —D. W. Brogan, "Death in Dallas"

> When they killed our president.
> —A caller on a talk show on C-SPAN, referring to the
> Kennedy assassination, September 11, 1992

> Always leave them asking for more.
> —Old show business maxim

The entertainment resources of the paranoid message are unrivaled. It offers puzzles, drama, passion, heroes, villains, and struggle. If the story line can be tied to a historical event, especially one that involves romantic characters and unexpected death, then fiction, history, and popular delusion can be joined in the pursuit of profit. The story, moreover, need never end. If evidence appears that refutes the conspiracy, the suppliers of the discrediting material will themselves be accused of being part of the conspiracy. Remember, the paranoid explanatory system is a closed one. Only confirmatory evidence is accepted. Contradictions are dismissed as being naive or, more likely, part of the conspiracy itself.

The death of Marilyn Monroe and the assassination of John F. Kennedy have engendered films, television programs, books, and articles. The Kennedy assassination has even produced study groups and an annual convention in Dallas. One of the most remarkable examples of conspiracy portrayed as entertainment is the film *JFK,* directed by Oliver Stone (Warner Brothers 1992). Our purpose is not to review the controversy concerning the circumstances surrounding President Kennedy's assassination (although we do reject the idea that the assassination was part of a conspiracy). Nor is our purpose to review the film (although we will evaluate the film within an aesthetic and literary tradition). Rather, we intend to show how the paranoid theme added narrative power and commercial value to the film, to illuminate the part that the paranoid message plays in popular entertainment.

Films are not simply entertainment; they are also cultural, intellectual, and political influences.[21] Research demonstrates the influence on beliefs, attitudes, emotions, and behavior of such films as the anti–nuclear war *The Day After,* the anti-Soviet *Amerika, Holocaust,* and the multigenerational saga of a black family, *Roots.*[22] The effect, however, is not so much to change people's minds as to solidify and exaggerate beliefs and attitudes already held. Films do not create cultural trends, but they do accelerate and reinforce them. A survey and analysis of viewer reaction to *JFK* demonstrated that this film and others like it can produce "markedly altered emotional states, belief changes spread across specific political issues, and . . . an impact on politically relevant behavioral changes. [*JFK* viewers] reported emotional changes, [became] significantly more angry and less hopeful . . . Those who had seen the movie were significantly more likely to believe [the various conspiracies depicted in the film]."[23]

*JFK* is not a historical film in the way that William Makepeace Thackeray's *Henry Esmond,* Alexandre Dumas' *Three Musketeers,* and Margaret Mitchell's *Gone with the Wind* are historical novels. Stone does not take fictional characters and put them in a historical context, as the fictional Scarlett O'Hara and Rhett Butler are placed in Civil War Georgia. Stone takes genuine historical characters—New Orleans District Attorney James Garrison and civic activist Clay Shaw, for example—and presents his version of what happened. Films of this sort are called docudramas because they dramatize historical events and historical characters for the screen. A film like *Gone with the Wind* attempts to tell the viewer what sorts of things happened in a past historical period. In contrast, a docudrama like *JFK* attempts to convey a particular version of history; the film does not simply lay out the director's version of history but also seeks to persuade the viewer that the director's version is the truth.

Film as media presents opportunities and limitations that are absent in a written work. These strengths and restrictions were first demonstrated in D. W. Griffith's seminal American film *The Birth of a Nation* (Epic 1915). This film, which set the "grammar and syntax" of cinema as narrative entertainment,[24] carried a powerful racist message. It idealized the Old South, praised slavery, described Klansmen as heroic saviors of the white South from bestial blacks and their Northern white allies, and opposed racial "pollution." Financially it was very successful. Politically it facilitated the revival of the Ku Klux Klan. Its racism was so simplistic and offensive that, even in an era tolerant of racism, it was banned in several cities and became the object of small riots. Griffith saw himself as the victim of the forces (blacks and their Northern sympathizers) that he "exposed" in the film.

From *The Birth of a Nation*'s release in 1915 to the appearance of *JFK* in 1992, American historical films developed a cinematic pattern with the following characteristics:

- The story is presented in a filmic style of seamless visual and aural pattern; the viewer seems to be looking directly at reality.
- The story has a strong moral message.
- The story is simple and definitive. Alternate versions are rarely suggested; if suggested, they are dismissed or mocked.
- The story is about individuals, usually heroic ones, fighting for good in the interest of humanity (that is, the audience).
- The story has a strong emotional tone.[25]

*JFK* adds several other techniques. It seamlessly interweaves newsreel footage from the assassination with fictional material, so that the boundary between historical fact and the director's or writer's fictional elaborations are progressively blurred. It is crammed with information, presented in words and suggested in pictures. It contains not only many short speeches and several long orations but much dialogue. More important, it includes many scenes without dialogue, some seemingly only one or two seconds long, which impart or suggest information. Not one

locus of conspiracy is suggested but eight: the CIA, weapons manu-
facturers, the Dallas police, the armed forces, the White House, the establishment press, renegade anti-Castro Cubans, and the Mafia. The
persuasive value of such an onslaught is to leave the viewer, if not convinced, at least believing that "there has to be something to it." One
viewer said that she and her companion "walked out of the movie feeling
like we had just undergone a powerful 'paranoia induction.' "[26]

These facts, inventions, and insinuations do not necessarily come
from the director's private beliefs. They are driven by the commercial
and narrative needs of the form. Popular art requires continuity and order—elements generally lacking in genuine events. The film depiction of
events must grab the viewer's attention, keep him fixed in his seat, cause
him to identify with the action and principal characters, and induce him
to tell his neighbors to buy a ticket for the next performance. The paranoid
perspective advances these commercial and artistic ambitions:

- It too gives a simplified view of reality. Indeed, the paranoid worldview demands coherence, even when such consistency is lacking.
- It too takes a moral stand: us against them, good against evil, open-
  ness against conspiracy.
- It too presents the "truth" as simple in essence but highly complex
  in details.
- It too describes a struggle, not between abstract forces but between
  individuals and groups.
- It too brings powerful emotions to the narration.

Thus, the paranoid message is uniquely suited to the form of a historical
film drama, or docudrama. This message is seen most powerfully in *JFK*
but also in other paranoid films: *Silkwood, Missing,* and *The Parallax
View*.

The paranoid theme complements another influence: deconstruction,
a prominent feature of late-twentieth-century criticism and art. The most
important part of the deconstructive position for our purposes is its con-
tention that "texts" (novels, films, poems) have no meaning apart from
how they are perceived. If the audience receives the "true" story, then
the "facts" in the text are true. Truth is itself a shifting concept whereby
the political interests of the creator and the audience (generally expressed

in terms of race, gender, and economic position) define what is true. If what is presented persuades people that it is true *and* if this truth is "politically progressive," then the events presented in the text are true.

The political commentator Ronald Steel identifies this dynamic in *JFK:* "Because of the director's ability to cut, splice, fuse, restage, and invent, it is virtually impossible for a viewer of his film to tell if he is seeing a real or a phony event. Stone mixes real black-and-white footage, such as the Zapruder film of Kennedy's murder, with restaged black-and-white episodes that may or may not have happened. The result is a deconstructionist's heaven. Every event becomes a pseudoevent, fictions become fact, imagination becomes reality, and the whole tangible world disappears."[27]

Stone acknowledges that what he shows as happening need not ever have happened. Asked whether he has a responsibility to historical fact, Stone replied that the questioner was getting "into the area of censorship" and that it is "up to the artist himself to determine his own ethics by his own conscience." In any event, Stone argues that he was creating a myth that "represents the inner spiritual meaning of an event."[28]

Stone's reference to myth as central to the film is an appropriate one. Myths are meta-explanations: they explain beyond what we can see or understand. A paranoid message can also have a great role in developing and enhancing a myth.

The life of John F. Kennedy has become an American myth, symbolizing youth, vigor, progress, and glamour. In fact, the historical Kennedy was quite different from the mythic Kennedy, but for the most part the public has set aside the facts in favor of the symbols. There are many reasons for the generation of this myth in the face of the facts.[29] The Kennedy family (and Kennedy himself when he was alive) and their partisans fostered it; they presented Kennedy as associated with other mythic figures (Lincoln, Jefferson, Roosevelt), and they made use of mythic archetypes (New Frontier, Camelot). Most important, however, were the timing and circumstances of Kennedy's death. Had Kennedy lived, he might be remembered as a successful or an unsuccessful president, but not as a legendary hero. His untimely death and the dramatic conditions surrounding it gave rise to his legend: in mythic style, a young king promising a new world was killed in a public place in the presence of his beautiful queen, and his realm changed forever.

What is required in myth-creating circumstances is a destructive force proportional to the event. A nerdish left-wing sympathizer who manages to fire a couple of lucky shots from a cheap mail-order rifle is not a suitable instrument for the destruction of a mythic hero. In real life such things happen. In myth and film, never.

Only two destructive forces are suitable for creating the Kennedy myth. An occurrence that could be interpreted in supernatural terms would be appropriate to ending Kennedy's life and beginning the legend. An earthquake, a meteor, a tornado, the sudden collapse of an ancient bridge, or an unexpected heart attack or stroke during a historic event would all give mythic color to his death. The other possibility is that some great human source of evil was responsible.

Here we return to our initial point, the effectiveness of the paranoid message as a means of completing, or fulfilling, an artistic statement. The paranoid message is a dramatically strong one, like adultery or murder. In the case of Kennedy, it perfects the myth. Because the public has committed itself to believing the rest of the Kennedy myth, there is a natural inclination to believe in a conspiracy. It completes the story and fulfills the audience's desire for understanding. People cling to this belief with remarkable tenacity. For example, Gerald Posner, who wrote the well-reviewed anti-conspiracist *Case Closed*, was the object of threatening telephone calls and picketing by demonstrators carrying signs saying "Case Not Closed." Some conspiracists even advocated a day of national resistance to the book.[30]

Thus, the great strength of the paranoid message in docudrama lies in its capacity to add an element that both explains an event and testifies to its importance. The technique, moreover, adds drama to a film. It also makes for a more profitable film. But such a film is not simply entertainment. As it entertains, it persuades. In fact, if the audience is not persuaded, it will lose interest. The social harm that the film commits goes beyond the distortion of history. It creates a broader intellectual pollution. Each paranoid film gives weight to a popular mentality of paranoid belief. If event after event is "shown to be" the product of a malign conspiracy, then the public will accept that that is how the world works.

When we observe a full-blown instance of political paranoia—in Hitler's Germany or Pol Pot's Cambodia, for example—it appears that masses of people have suddenly been afflicted by a disease. In a sense they have. We have described political paranoia's vectors: individuals and organizations that create an attractive delusion out of distorted facts and contorted logic, individuals who bring that delusion to others, and individuals who make it even more attractive. We have seen that the paranoid theme appears in many places in any society, not only among cranks and psychopaths. It appears in clever books of philosophy and in entertaining and well-made films and novels. It is propounded by all sorts of people, not only by the injured but by those who have injured others with no apparent provocation. Whoever brings it and wherever it is brought, paranoia is the same disease, threatening the same calamities. These calamities are at their greatest when the paranoid is not only the messenger but also its executor or, more appropriately, executioner.

# 10

## Paranoia in Power
### *Pol Pot, Idi Amin, and Joseph Stalin*

I know of no rule which holds so true as that we are always paid for our suspicion by finding what we suspect.
—Henry David Thoreau

Suspicion always haunts the guilty mind.
—William Shakespeare, *Henry VI,* Part 3

When a paranoid leader becomes chief of state, his paranoia infects the nation. The paranoid leader's extraordinary suspicion, hostility, and centrality create a society not simply different in degree but different in kind from any other. Particularly in a totalitarian regime, with all its resources entirely at his disposal, unconstrained by consultation or democratic process, he can shape the society to his psyche's image. The role of any leader is to engender a common ethos in the country he directs. This is no less so with the paranoid leader.

The paranoid leader's catastrophic influence, moreover, operates whether or not the society is itself paranoid. The fact that Stalin rose within and ruled a nation with a strongly paranoid character is well documented.

But an even longer list of leaders came to power in cultures without unusually strong paranoid traits: Francisco Macias Nguema of Equatorial Guinea, Idi Amin of Uganda, Jean-Bédel Bokassa of the Central African Republic, José Rodríguez Gaspar de Francia of Paraguay, and Louis XI of France are only a few.

Paranoids can take power in any society, and their rule ends only with their natural death or with the action of external forces. Paranoids are supremely effective in destroying internal opposition. The inward-turning paranoid leader is among the most common. But all paranoid leaders—whether inward turning or expansionist—must first establish themselves in their own countries. The international community will look the other way as long as the paranoid leader torments only his own people. But paranoia never remains a domestic disorder. Sooner or later, every paranoid leader will go to war with his neighbors.

## Pol Pot of Cambodia

We were so angry when we emerged from the forest that we
didn't want to spare even a baby in its cradle.
—A Khmer Rouge guerrilla

The Khmer Rouge had begun evacuating Phnom Penh, and
among the first people pulled out were the patients at the city's
hospitals. The wounded and disabled walked or crawled; some
were pushed in their beds, a relative holding an intravenous
bag, pretending that might keep a loved one alive. A sobbing
father carried his young daughter in a sling he fashioned from
a bedsheet and tied around his neck. About 20,000 patients
were thrown out that afternoon.
—Becker, *When the War Was Over*

Adolf Hitler, who was responsible for the murders of 10 million people, is history's most notorious paranoid leader. Mass murder was part of his ideology—one that converted his private psychopathology into public policy. Joseph Stalin killed between two and four times that number and leads the list of all-time mass murderers. The boundaries of their countries did not contain the violence of Hitler and Stalin.

But even Hitler's and Stalin's records pale in comparison to that of Cambodia's Pol Pot in terms of the violence and misery that were wreaked upon a single society.[1] In a little less than four years, from the enforced dispersal of Phnom Penh's population on April 17, 1975, to the fall of that same city to the invading Vietnamese on January 7, 1979, 15 percent of Cambodia's population died as a result of his paranoid policies.

Pol Pot's Cambodia illustrates the natural history of political paranoia:

1. A revolution follows a wrenching civil war.
2. A leader and his inner group offer an interpretation of the country's distress requiring the destruction of a demonized group. A millenarian future is promised upon the annihilation of the demons.
3. Policies based on these beliefs are initiated, but they fail to increase happiness or prosperity. Indeed, they greatly increase misery and poverty.
4. The leader rationalizes the failure of these policies in terms of the alleged continuation of demon-group values and conspiracies. The ideologically correct but discredited policies are therefore redoubled, and the hunt for the "conspirators" and "saboteurs" gains strength, destroying many innocent persons.
5. In reaction to these policies, hostility and suspicion, then actual conspiracies and sabotage against the regime, begin to develop.
6. The regime is overthrown.

In the case of Cambodia, hatred of everything non-Khmer (non–ethnic Cambodian) and a pathological idealization of Khmer culture led to irrational and destructive policies. The failure of these policies required an explanation, which the leaders found in a conspiracy by the demonized enemies (especially Westerners and Vietnamese) and a continuation of "impure" non-Khmer influences. This "explanation" was not cynical rationalization offered only for public consumption. Members and leaders of the Khmer Rouge (we use this term as broadly synonymous with the Communist Party of Kampuchea and the government of Democratic Kampuchea), in psychological denial and political desperation, believed it. The consequent purges created a spiral of increasing failure and increasing paranoia.

Why was this? Pre–Pol Pot Cambodia was not a notably paranoid society. Cambodia is a secluded country, at the boundary between two of the world's principal cultural domains. Khmer culture is derived from India, but the culture of neighboring Vietnam is Chinese in origin.

The two cultures and the two peoples are radically different. The Khmer have the reputation of being romantic, artistic, and relaxed, fond of dance and of bright colors. Theravada Buddhism, which teaches the inevitability of suffering, is the defining religious influence. In contrast, the Vietnamese are earnest, practical, goal-oriented, and restrained. Their principal religious influence is Confucianism, which advocates discipline and promises rewards in this world. The two peoples are physically different, the Khmer tending to be more compact and slightly darker. They dress differently: Khmer wear sarongs, Vietnamese, pants. Their cuisines are different, and they eat differently: Khmer with their hands or spoons, the Vietnamese with chopsticks. Their housing styles are different, and, most important, their languages are unrelated.

The two peoples have been in conflict for centuries. Although the record is complex, the general pattern has been for Khmer politics to move from self-rule to civil war to vassalage (Thai, Vietnamese, French) and back to self-rule. From at least the fifteenth century until the French protectorate was established in 1864, Cambodia's national territory shrank greatly. Much of what is South Vietnam today was Cambodia only a few centuries ago. The Khmer are very much aware of that loss. Thus, the Khmer are a people whose politics, internal and external, have been dominated by outsiders. Such a people would likely see outsiders as the source of their problems.

The fall of the capital, Phnom Penh, to the Khmer Rouge occurred in April 1975, two weeks before the fall of Saigon. Substantial foreign involvement in the politics of former French Indochina ceased. The Khmer Rouge was triumphant and unchallenged. The new government proclaimed that all Cambodia's problems could be traced to foreign— that is, non-Khmer—influences. Once these were destroyed, a perfect society would be instituted. All Vietnamese, Chinese, Western, and Thai influences were therefore to be erased. This, of course, proved an impos-

sible task. Although the Khmer clearly retained their cultural distinctive-
ness, they had integrated many external influences over the centuries.
Thus, to the extent that the Khmer Rouge sought a pure Cambodia (to
be renamed Kampuchea, the land of the Khmer), they lived a fantasy.
They could not acknowledge the extent to which Khmer culture had absorbed foreign influences without accusing themselves of contamination.
Perhaps the greatest irony of the Cambodian holocaust is that in purportedly seeking to protect the Khmer from racial pollution, the Khmer
Rouge wreaked by far more pain on their fellow Khmer than had any
foreign influence.[2]

Nevertheless, Pol Pot, the leader of the Khmer Rouge, affirmed that
Cambodia would isolate itself from the rest of the world and that its
population, with few exceptions, would be turned into peasants. Enmity,
hatred, and malevolence toward anything foreign composed the principal
rhetoric of the new policy. But although oratory about independence
abounded, the Khmer Rouge was molding itself upon a foreign model,
Maoist China.[3]

The initial instrument of persecution of those "tainted" with non-
Khmer influences was the Khmer Rouge army. Many of its members were
from nonmodernized rural areas and appeared to be in their early teens.
At first these teenagers with guns impressed the city dwellers with their
earnestness and their alertness. But they also exhibited a certain hostility,
like " 'soldiers on patrol,' and stared at westerners as if they were 'creatures from different planets.' "[4] These soldiers not only appeared illiterate
but even looked on written material as something very strange.

The towns, centers of non-Khmer influence, were the special object
of Khmer Rouge hatred. Within two months, the urban population—about
2.5 million people—had been evacuated to the countryside to be collec-
tivized. Families were broken up, some people were sent to areas where
they were rejected, and others were sent into malarial and unpopulated
regions. City dwellers suffered terribly and died in large numbers, as did
many rural people who were labeled counterrevolutionary. The entire
world of the average inhabitant of cities and towns was eradicated. The
new government abolished private property and the use of money. No
compensation was given for property or for work. Shops, restaurants,

schools, monasteries, and places of religious devotion were closed throughout the country. Travel, reading, writing, and public entertainment were severely restricted. International telephone, telegram, and cable links were cut. International mail was neither sent nor received. No regular airline service existed, and the borders were closed and mined. Medicines and pesticides were not imported (the exclusion of DDT led to a malaria epidemic in 1975–76). Foreigners found in the country were slaughtered; these included not only the traditional enemies, Thais and Vietnamese, but also Indian and Pakistani merchants and students, and American, Australian, British, and New Zealand sailors who had the misfortune or poor judgment to come ashore.

Any indication of a modern or foreign connection could lead to victimization. Eyeglasses, a watch, a ballpoint pen, the use of a foreign expression or word, soft hands, jewelry, or, for women, long hair would identify a person as not truly Khmer. A "newspeak" developed: pronouns suggestive of social hierarchy were stigmatized, peasant dialects were imposed, and, curiously, a superpoliteness was required of all. Khmer Rouge cadres spoke in low, deferential tones. They were extremely clean and neat. Emotions were not to be expressed, and romance, from implied affection to marriage, had to be approved by the authorities. Euphemisms were employed to mask the cruelty: people about to be taken for execution were requested to "help us collect fruit" or to "come with us for further study." Cadres were often promoted just before arrest and execution. This surreal situation was summed up in a popular expression: "Angka [the Khmer Rouge organization] kills but never explains."[5]

As so often with xenophobic movements bent on the destruction of internal groups, references to cleanliness and purification dominated Khmer Rouge rhetoric. Such items as money, telephones, and eyeglasses, which were seen as non-Khmer, were considered "dirty" and were to be exterminated. A Khmer Rouge radio broadcast described Cambodia's history thus: "For thousands of years the colonialists, imperialists and reactionary feudalists have dragged us through the mud. Now with victory . . . we smell good again."[6] Cruelty became embodied in the concept of purity.[7] Blood, symbolizing the Khmer essence, was equated with hatred, as in the opening stanzas of the Khmer Rouge anthem:

Bright red Blood which covers towns and plains
Of Kampuchea, our Motherland,
Sublime Blood of workers and peasants,
Sublime Blood of revolutionary men and women fighters!
The Blood changing into unrelenting hatred.[8]

Even in their methods of torture and murder, the Khmer idealized their past. The gruesome techniques illustrated in the ancient friezes of Angkor Wat were employed by the Khmer Rouge against their "enemies."

In this initial period, in addition to hatred of the non-Khmer and an obsession with cleanliness, the regime had a powerful element of centrality. The Khmer Rouge claimed sole credit for defeating the Americans in Indochina. They believed in the perfection of a Kampuchea isolated from the rest of the world. This exaggerated self-regard was complementary to the new policy of radical self-reliance. In this early period, however, a magnified suspicion and an exaggerated fear of conspiracy were minor themes. The Khmer Rouge was caught up in the exhilaration of its victory and confident of its success.

It was the immediate and catastrophic failure of the inept Maoist-inspired Four Year Plan, drawn up in 1976, that caused the leadership to become increasingly obsessed with conspiracy. The relation between programmatic failure and paranoid belief and behavior was best exemplified in Cambodia's most productive area, Battambang and its environs. The leadership ordered that the crops there be at least doubled. This improvement would be accomplished by the ethnically pure workers inspired by the new Communist government and freed from the "servitude" of receiving material reward for their work. They would also be freed from Western fertilizers and insecticides. Of course, the brutalized, ill-fed, and often inexperienced workers were not up to meeting the previous production levels, much less doubling or tripling them. Productivity plunged. But for the leaders, failure did not lead to doubt of their ideology. Rather, they assigned the blame to ingrained capitalist habits and to traitors in the party.[9]

Treatment of the prisoner-workers degenerated. Sadism mixed with a lunatic revolutionary fervor increased among the political cadres and soldiers, and casual executions multiplied. As all became aware of the failure of the new policies, triumphalist speeches were broadcast more and more often on the radio, and conspiracies and spies were blamed for all shortcomings.

At one point, Pol Pot and his colleagues became convinced that plots were centered in the north, around Siem Reap. They began to accuse their own cadres of disloyalty, and purges of former guerrilla officials began— purges of even greater severity than those practiced against the former regime. "Massive movements of population were re-instituted. . . . Tens of thousands of people [were] jammed upright into trucks and slow-moving freight cars, making their way through an empty landscape toward an uncertain but ominous future."[10] This brutality and the agricultural failures following these purges began to turn even Pol Pot's supporters against him. He soon had reason for suspicion.

Purges and executions accelerated in 1977 and 1978, principally directed against party members. After the Vietnamese had raided Cambodia, those who had failed to stop them were accused of having "Cambodian bodies and Vietnamese minds." Soon troops from the center of the country were fighting the local Khmer Rouge. Approximately a hundred thousand civilians were killed in the Eastern Region alone.[11]

Paranoia now fully gripped Cambodia. The Khmer Rouge leader Ieng Thirith acknowledged, "When the revolution went out of control, the Center began to suspect various zone secretaries and killed them . . . Feeling besieged, the party initiated 'class warfare' in a desperate search for 'enemies' and purged peasants and party members for not coming from an extremely poor . . . class background, or for associating with an ill-defined enemy class bent on sabotaging the revolution. . . . Secrecy, distrust, and isolation became the *modi operandi* of the Khmer Rouge . . . They believed the 'enemy' was everywhere."[12] Pol Pot and his inner circle came to charge the United States, the Soviet Union, and Vietnam with conspiring against them.

As so often with paranoid movements, these fears contained an element of truth, and the measures taken contained an element of rationality. Most important, dispersing the population to small centers facilitated their control by the small Cambodian army. The evacuation of the towns in the first days of the Khmer Rouge regime may have been generated in part by a fear of air strikes. The continued dispersal of the population would also prevent an invading Vietnamese force from swallowing the country. There was, of course, ample historical reason for a fear of Vietnamese invasion. By the end of the Pol Pot regime, all of former French Indochina was a sinkhole of suspicion. Cambodia, Vietnam, and China had all at one time or another betrayed one another, and as so often was the case, paranoia had its rewards. The Chinese, afraid of the Soviet Union, could assert a right to keep Indochina under its control. The Vietnamese similarly claimed a right, based on its fear of China, to dominate Cambodia. Cambodia, remembering its exploitation by the Vietnamese Communist Party and its historic victimization by the Vietnamese, could support the Chinese against the Vietnamese.[13] Vietnam feared that China planned to invade Vietnam through Cambodia, with Cambodian help, and so preempted this move by itself invading Cambodia.

But these reasons, fears, and fantasies were not adequate to account for the destruction of a seventh of Cambodia's population by Cambodia's own leadership. It was the belief in internal conspiracies that drove the Cambodian holocaust. Sometimes suspects were simply taken out and clubbed to death, but in many cases a year passed from the time a person was suspected of being an enemy agent to his arrest. The accused were often called for a "meeting" or for "study" or even for a "celebration." They would be interrogated, perhaps violently, and forced to confess to some crime against the regime. They were then forced to write and revise several times a confession that was little less than an autobiography, which had to implicate friends, associates, and relatives. Those implicated were brought in, and the process continued.[14]

The Khmer Rouge labeled these connections "strings." The strings grew longer and more and more entwined. After opposition to the Khmer Rouge was demonstrated to the interrogators' satisfaction, the prisoners were executed. No effort was made at reeducation, nor was extended imprisonment used as punishment. According to records abandoned by the Khmer Rouge, for example, of the seventeen thousand people brought to the Toul Sleng interrogation center, only seven survived.[15]

By the beginning of 1978, the Khmer Rouge government was obsessed with discovering and fighting enemies. Building the new Cambodia had been abandoned, not only in practice but also largely in the Khmer Rouge's ideology. Pol Pot, in a 1978 conversation with the journalist Jan Myrdal, stated that the Khmer Rouge's main achievement had been the destruction of the ''schemes and activities of interferences, subversions, attempts at coups d'état and aggressions perpetrated by enemies of all kinds.''[16]

On January 7, 1979, Vietnamese forces, accompanied for appearance' sake by some unarmed Cambodian units, occupied Phnom Penh. The Khmer Rouge retreated to bases near the Thai border. There is little reason to think that, without Vietnamese involvement, Pol Pot and the Khmer Rouge would have fallen. Indeed, they continued to operate as recently as late 1996.

Cambodia offers a classic study of the rise and self-destruction of the paranoid dynamic, except for one element. Where is the leader? Who is directing all this? The leader is usually a driving force in the paranoid process, but one seems to be lacking here.

The key to understanding how the Cambodian holocaust was initiated and directed can be found in the ''family'' quality of the Khmer leadership, the personality of Pol Pot, and the Khmer cultural context. In a pattern often encountered in Buddhist countries, the Khmer had no single leader but a collective paranoid leadership composed of the Khmer Rouge inner circle. A member—Pol Pot—played a key role, but his role was far less significant than those of leaders of other paranoid societies, even in comparison to other secretaries of Communist parties. Pol Pot was, however, first among equals and first among those to be feared, so we focus on his life and personality, even while remembering that he was much more constrained than the typical leader of a paranoid regime.

Pol Pot's chief characteristics were persuasiveness in small groups, tenacity, and self-effacement. One of the foremost historians of the regime, Ben Kiernan, even describes him as genteel.[17] It was not until 1976, the year the Khmer Rouge achieved power, that he took Pol Pot (a bland name, like Joe Smith) as his official name. The leader's new public name told the Cambodians little about its holder. Throughout Pol Pot's rule, no cult of personality developed. Indeed, his regime may be called a cult of nonpersonality. No biography was published or broadcast, no collection of works or sayings appeared, no inspirational anecdotes were read on the radio or discussed at party meetings. Until 1978 there were no photographs; no plays or songs were written honoring him. Starting in 1978

there was a hint of some publicity when his title of Brother Number One
was replaced with Uncle Secretary, and a few pictures appeared, but this
all ended a year or so after he "resigned" from the prime ministership.

Pol Pot was born Saloth Sar in May 1928, in the northern province
of Kompong Thom, a Khmer heartland area that was moderate in politics
and historically resistant to foreign influences.[18] His father owned and
worked seven acres of garden land, twenty-two acres of rice land, and
several pairs of buffalo. In the broad Cambodian context Saloth Sar's
father would have been designated a rich peasant, but in this region he
ranked as a middle peasant. The family had distant connections to the
royal family via concubines and court dancers but was otherwise unexceptional. As far as we know, unlike Mao and Stalin, who had strong
conflicts with their fathers, Saloth Sar had good family relations.

Saloth Sar never did any serious work in the fields. At age six he
was sent to Phnom Penh for a year, where he served as a novice at
Botumvody monastery. He also spent some time in a Catholic school. He
was a poor student, however, failing the elementary certification at age
eleven. Eventually he managed to get through a French-style secondary
school. For a while he studied carpentry in a technical school.

The future Pol Pot was drawn into radical nationalist and Communist
politics. The historical record is incomplete, but at the age of twenty-one,
in September 1949, he enrolled (but did not complete a degree) at the
Ecole française de radio-électricité in Paris. He joined the French Communist Party and its Indochinese counterparts. His colleagues described
him as a plodder—kind, pleasant, and unremarkable. A contemporary
said in 1950 that Saloth Sar "would not have killed a chicken."[19] In
December 1952 his government grant was withdrawn, and Saloth Sar had
to leave France. As one of the first French-trained Communists, he put
himself at the disposal of the Vietminh, which he joined at the front. To
his great displeasure he was not given political work but was assigned
menial tasks by his Vietnamese superiors—kitchen work and carrying
excrement. He eventually left the Vietminh and helped found the Cambodian Communist Party in 1960.

From 1960 to about 1967, Pol Pot lay low, probably because the
Cambodian Communists in this period were under the influence of the
Vietnamese. From 1967 until his victory in 1975, Pol Pot fought the

French and especially the pro-American Cambodian governments. We know little of this period. Within the small inner group of the Khmer Rouge, Pol Pot apparently developed a reputation for the Buddhist virtues of self-control, simplicity, and kindheartedness toward close associates. Aside from sharing in the privations, dangers, and uncertainties of the Khmer Rouge's sixteen-year struggle, Pol Pot apparently gained the respect and loyalty of those close to him by his self-effacement. This is not to say that he was not a skillful and brutal infighter. He used lies and deception in internal Khmer Rouge disputes and was willing, outside the inner circle, to use violence. He was, for example, personally responsible for the torture and murder of thousands at the Toul Sleng death center.

Pol Pot's passion for secrecy went beyond himself to his organization and its policies and aims. He and his associates made few speeches or explanations. Long after taking power, Pol Pot declined to acknowledge that Cambodia was ruled by the Communist Party and that he was the former Saloth Sar. Such actions as evacuations and killings were often simply ascribed to Angka or denied.[20] Pol Pot's principal subordinate, the equally self-effacing Nuon Chea, summed up the inner group's policy by saying, "Secret work is fundamental."[21]

Pol Pot continued to follow the same pattern of life while in power as he had as a guerrilla leader. Haunted by the fear of assassination, especially poisoning (he had a long-standing gastric problem, which he ascribed to poisoning), Pol Pot changed his residence frequently and kept his personality hidden. He was also a very hard worker, reading dossiers and otherwise laboring well into the night. Pol Pot's biographer, David Chandler, suggests that one key to the tyrant's personality may be that he was not adequate to the job—he was out of his depth.[22]

Pol Pot's gray persona and the taciturn, clandestine form of tyranny it engendered were well within the Khmer tradition and also served him well.[23] Ho Chi Minh, Pol Pot's principal regional counterpart, cultivated the same image of remoteness. A closer parallel may be Joseph Stalin, who, before he came to power, also had a reputation for blandness (though also for rudeness) and achieved power in part on the basis of that style and reputation.[24] The racist aspect of Pol Pot's policies finds its strongest resonance in Hitler's Germany. In many ways Pol Pot's

Cambodia was a fascist state. It, too, exalted a nationalist racial ideal politically manifested in an autocracy.[25]

The Khmer Rouge holocaust, however, was distinctive not only for the ferocity of its xenophobia but for the leaders' appetite for pushing every idea and every policy as far as they would go, and for their passion to drive their people past their breaking point.[26] And finally, the Cambodian holocaust demonstrates that a paranoid collective leadership can be as destructive as one directed by a single person.

## Idi Amin of Uganda

His Excellency President for Life Field Marshall Al Hadj Dr. Idi Amin Dada, VC, DSO, MC, Lord of All the Beasts of the Earth and Fishes of the Sea, and Conqueror of the British Empire in Africa in General and Uganda in Particular
—Self-assigned full title of Idi Amin

Some journalist asked, "Do you have many visions?" and [Amin] said, "Only when necessary."
—G. I. Smith, *Ghosts of Kampala*

Always found him quite charming, terribly pro-Scottish, loves the bagpipes . . .
—British businessman resident in Kampala

Under Idi Amin, Uganda was a kleptocracy—a government of thieves, ruled by a paranoid tyrant who was dominated by delusions of grandeur and loyal to no ideological principle, no religious ideal, no sense of national purpose. The objective of power was to aid in theft, the government a means to that end.[27] Increasingly, moreover, unchecked grandiosity and brutality were to characterize the regime.

Amin, first, was a person of great impulsivity—a trait that grew more dominant the longer he remained in power. He acted rather than governed. Uganda became a place where the exercise of power was scarcely moderated by law, custom, or tradition. Second, Amin was unprepared by experience or training to be the absolute ruler of a country. Because of this inadequacy and a psychological readiness to blame others for his difficulties, Amin responded with paranoia and compensatory grandiosity.

Amin's rule displayed all the paranoid components—exaggerated fear of conspiracy, exaggerated suspicion, exaggerated fear of loss of autonomy, centrality, hostility, projective thinking, and delusions—but the characteristic coherence of the well-organized paranoid was subordinated to sheer chaos and to his impulsivity, brutality, and criminality. During his rule, from 1971 to 1979, Amin killed approximately 375,000 Ugandans out of a population of 11.5 million. Despite his atrocities, Amin might have ruled indefinitely had he not provoked a Tanzanian invasion. Even then, it took eight months of warfare to overcome him, with little support from inside Uganda.

Amin was born on July 1, 1928, into a fatherless home. Some reports describe his mother as a camp follower. He had at least two years of primary school, but probably not much more. Even as an adult Amin was illiterate or barely literate. In 1946 he enlisted as an assistant cook in the King's African Rifles. This was not unusual, as the British in East Africa recruited especially from minority populations. Amin's ethnic group, the Nubians (a commonly used but anthropologically incorrect term), and his tribe, the Kakwa, were just such marginal groups. His religion, Islam, also was a minority, constituting only 6 percent of Uganda's mostly Christian population.

In the King's African Rifles, Amin's enthusiasm and desire to please gratified his British superiors. Amin, who weighed more than 230 pounds and was six feet three inches tall, appeared to be a friendly, gentle giant; he was cheerful and well liked. He was the heavyweight boxing champion of Uganda for nine years, which delighted his fellow Africans as well as the British officers. Although he lacked formal education and often played the clown, Amin was no fool. He spoke five languages—Kakwa, Luganda (his mother's language), Swahili, English, and Nubian (a popular form of Arabic used by the West Nile colony in Buganda)—and acquired the skills of soldiering. He eventually rose through the enlisted ranks.

The King's African Rifles were not expected to fight on fields of battle. Rather, they were expected to contain intertribal conflict, restrain rural crime (especially smuggling and cattle rustling), and combat anti-British guerrilla activity, including that of the Kenya-based Mau Mau. Much of this conflict was of a type that typically involves intimidation, violent interrogation, and group punishment. The opportunity for abuse is great, and it is the rare military unit that does not become tainted and corrupted by it. Amin himself may have had a cultural predisposition toward this type of violence, for his region of birth had "one of the world's highest homicide rates" and was "renowned for [its] sadistic brutality."[28] Amin acquired an especially strong reputation for brutality, some of it in collusion with his British officers. His own actions, however, went beyond even these broad limits. He was scheduled to be brought up before a military tribunal for a massacre in northwest Kenya just before Uganda became independent in 1962. Deputy Governor Sir Eric Griffith-Jones recommended that Amin be prosecuted, but the governor of Uganda, Sir Walter Coutts, in consultation with the incoming Ugandan president, Milton Obote, decided that because Amin was one of only two Ugandans scheduled to be given a high military post in the new govern-ment, the case would not proceed. Amin was instead promoted from sergeant to major.

In 1965 Obote declared himself dictator and ended constitutional gov-ernment in Uganda. Two years later he appointed Amin commander-in-chief of the Ugandan armed forces. On January 25, 1971, Amin overthrew Obote.

Amin's triumph was well received in many areas. The Americans and Israelis were pleased at the overthrow of the leftist Obote, who was in the process of nationalizing much of the economy. The business com-munity was pleased for the same reason.

As is the case in such changes, groups that were out of power during the Obote period were also pleased at the possibility that they would now benefit from patronage. The Acholi, Lango, and Teso tribes, who were closest to Obote, were unhappy. A general source of popular support for Amin was that he seemed a "real" African, not Westernized like almost all the other leaders. To the average Ugandan, his was a success story with which they could identify.

From the time he entered the King's African Rifles, almost everyone found Amin personally engaging. George Ivan Smith noted that "one of the things we find as a constant is an apparent duality of nature. While he had his harsh paranoid side, he also seemed to have gentleness."[29] Henry Kyemba, a former member of Amin's cabinet, wrote, "Face to face, he is relaxed, simple and charming—he seems incapable of wrongdoing or of sanctioning any crime."[30] Amin appeared warm and considerate of his guests, although one of his habits was to invite his victims to dinner before having them tortured to death. (Stalin, too, was often described as kindly, polite, and seemingly incapable of murder and sometimes invited his prospective victims to dinner.) There was a strong narcissistic strain in Amin's character. But even his arrogance often had a self-mocking, buffoonish quality that suggested an underlying modesty. To some extent Amin probably cultivated this clownishness, to lead his enemies to underestimate him.

At first Amin was moderate in his statements and actions. Immediately after the coup he gave a speech on the radio describing his regime as a "caretaker administration, pending an early return to civilian rule."[31] He promised lower taxes and better relations with neighboring states. He also offered to have the remains of the former Kabaka (paramount chief) of Buganda, who had died in London, returned for a traditional burial. This promise pleased Uganda's largest ethnic group, the Baganda. Amin released many of Obote's political prisoners and also pledged Uganda's continuing membership in the Commonwealth. His appointments were similarly prudent. For the most part Amin's first government was staffed by senior nonpolitical civil servants. A hint of the new style of government was suggested, however, by the fact that they learned of their appointments from the radio news.

Amin was candid in saying he wanted to expand Uganda's frontiers, which greatly disturbed his neighbors. Although Amin was invited to London and even had tea with the queen, his request for sophisticated and advanced weapons from the British was denied. Muammar Qaddafi's Libya and Saudi Arabia soon provided him with substantial amounts of money. Both saw him as a source of Islamic expansion and as a potential ally against Israel.

In 1972 Amin took what was probably his most popular action inside Uganda and indeed in East Africa. He decided to expel (and, if they would not go voluntarily, to eliminate) Uganda's Asian community, almost all of whom had come from what is now India and Pakistan. Numbering about eighty thousand, these Asians dominated Uganda's business, professional, and skilled labor communities. They were, however, unpopular among Africans. The Asians, racially distinct from black Africans, identified themselves and were identified by the Ugandans with the former British rule. Their skills and successes were a silent reproach to the Ugandans, and their wealth made them an attractive target. They were viewed as arrogant exploiters. Genocide was prevented only at the last minute by a massive international rescue. The expulsion permanently separated Amin from Western sympathies. In international affairs he now turned increasingly to the wealthy Arab states and the Communist bloc. Amin's relations with his neighbors began to deteriorate.

Expropriation of the Asians' assets and the flow of Arab aid did not improve life in Uganda. Quite the contrary. From 1973 to 1978 the Soviet Union was Amin's principal military supplier. But just as Amin had dismissed the claims of his former supporters, the business community and the British, so did he behave toward the Soviets. In 1976, when Amin was president of the Organization for African Unity, the Soviets asked him for modest diplomatic support for their efforts in Angola. Amin replied that the Soviet ambassador was "a criminal" who was "trying to dictate" to him. Later, however, he offered the Soviet Union the "biggest military base in the African continent."[32] The Soviets, concerned about Amin's unpredictability and responding to complaints from neighboring African states who feared what Amin would do with Soviet arms, began to distance themselves.

Amin and his rule were impulsive, disorganized, consumed with a diffuse hostility, sadistic, and wildly grandiose. Amin's largely self-awarded official titles—Lord of All the Beasts of the Earth and Fishes of the Sea, and Conqueror of the British Empire in Africa in General and Uganda in Particular, and so on—reflect a deep pathology, betraying not only his massive insecurity underlying such exaggerated grandeur but also his lack of a sense of the impact he had upon his audience. "I myself consider myself the most powerful figure in the world," he said. On several occasions, Amin claimed that God had come to him in a dream and chosen him for this paramount role. God had also told him in a dream to expel Uganda's Asians. To show his importance (and please his supporters), he demanded that "any British citizen who wants to see me must kneel before me."[33] Later in his rule, he had squads of mostly elderly Britishers carry him in a sedan chair for twenty-five miles in public procession (by then he weighed more than three hundred pounds).

In a speech that day he said he would go to London, with or without the British government's permission, and be carried through that city's streets.

Amin wrote and published numerous long and ill-informed advisory cables to world leaders, including one addressed to President Julius Nyerere of Tanzania in 1972: "I want to assure you that I love you very much, and if you had been a woman, I would have considered marrying you, although your head is full of grey hairs, but as you are a man that possibility does not arise."[34] He criticized President Nixon for his conduct during the Vietnam War, and when the Watergate scandal broke, wrote letters of advice to him. This grandiose self-evaluation suggests how threatened and powerless Amin was under his boastful facade and demonstrates how he compensated with grandiosity of ludicrous proportions.

He continued to boast of the honors—such as Britain's Victoria Cross—he received from countries he claimed to despise. Although he praised Hitler and charged Israel with being the enemy of mankind, he nevertheless continued to boast of his Israeli connections and displayed the wings of the Israeli air force on the uniform he wore for his portrait on Ugandan currency.

Although many observers remarked on Amin's cunning and shrewdness, his intelligence was regarded as limited. Amin himself seemed to sense this. Frustrated by his inability to understand policy discussions, he acted without consultation or consideration: "As a military man I know how to act. I am a man of action."[35] He confessed to his British former commanding officer, Iain Grahame, that he could not follow the arguments, explanations, and questions of the British government's ministers and journalists, and asked Grahame to explain them for him.

The one-time sergeant was clearly inadequate for the task of nurturing a national economy, carrying on international relations, and developing social institutions. One of his ministers reported that Amin could not sit in an office very long and could not concentrate on a single topic for half a morning: "It is impossible for him . . . to comprehend" what is going on from the point of view of policy.[36] The Nigerian journalist Peter Enahero, who observed Amin and interviewed those close to him, remarked that Amin "is the kind of man who approaches a thorny problem with an empty mind. It is when he begins to address an audience that solutions suddenly fill his head. Apparently, he then immediately utters these thoughts lest he forget them. And then to prove he does not lack the courage of his convictions he orders his ministers to implement 'the decisions of my government.' ''[37]

Amin always had a paranoid tendency to externalize. Under stress, people with a paranoid disposition become more paranoid. Lacking the education and perhaps the intelligence to cope with the demands of high office, Amin was increasingly faced with his inadequacy. His psychological defense against inadequacy was to blame others and to eliminate the educated class. Amin's diplomatic and domestic failures increased the stress on him, which contributed to his paranoid psychopathology. Criticism could not be tolerated. Failures were the fault of others. Sometimes individuals were blamed for their alleged stupidity or knavery, but the preferred explanation was conspiracy. There were, of course, incompetents, knaves, and conspirators aplenty; several coups were attempted against Amin, and more than one assassination plot was developed. This environment, however, was far more the consequence than the cause of Amin's actions. As with other paranoid leaders, his fear of conspiracy begat repression which begat conspiracy, and conspiracy and fear of conspiracy begat more repression and violence.

Although Amin feared conspiracy, he was a personally brave man. Amin seems to have displayed fear on only one occasion, and it is an instructive one. In November 1966 Amin, then chief of staff, was invited to give a brief speech at Makerere University on the occasion of President Obote's installation as chancellor. Observers reported that Amin "was frightened of his audience; he felt ignorant and foolish." The students jeered at him. Amin was "sweating with fear."[38]

Amin's violence was sweeping, but it was focused particularly on intellectuals and the educated elite. He had initially courted the intellectual elite, but each well-educated, competent individual was a painful reminder to Amin of his own inadequacies. His purge of intellectuals was motivated in part by the wish to eliminate these psychological threats.[39] Moreover, most of the criticism of Amin's leadership came from the educated elite. In effect, he sought to eliminate criticism by literally eliminating the critics. Patrick Marnham, a journalist who spent time in

Amin's Uganda, wrote six years after the tyrant's fall, "Looking back on the Amin days, it was his fear and hatred of educated people that were both the most characteristic and unpredictable aspects of his tyranny."[40]

As Henry Kyemba, Amin's cabinet minister for five years, notes, Amin's weaving of lies and deception engendered a "universal suspicion."[41] The "Killing Muchine,"[42] as the misspelled sign leading to the underground cells of the principal murder building proclaimed, was among the most efficient of the government's activities. Sometimes the victims were picked up more or less at random, killed, then claimed for ransom. Sometimes the victims had been tainted by association with a plot, real or imagined, or were members of some disfavored group, such as the educated or the Christians. Wycliffe Kato, assistant director of civil aviation for the East African Community, served under Amin until his own reputation became tarnished by the Israeli rescue raid on the Entebbe airport on July 4, 1976, which humiliated and enraged Amin. Kato noted how easy it was to end up in the Killing Muchine, "where coming from the wrong tribe, or having a beautiful girlfriend, or driving a shiny car, or being too strict at the office, or asking a messenger boy to make you a cup of tea, was a potential death sentence."[43] Arrest by the State Research Bureau almost always resulted in torture or death.

The fortunate detainees were those who were simply shot. Hammer blows were much more common. Corpses were often found with nails driven through their foreheads. Prisoners would sometimes be permitted to purchase the opportunity to commit suicide, but, so as not to implicate the jailers, they had to break up and eat the razor blades given to them rather than slice their wrists.

A disproportionate number of the more than three hundred thousand murders took place in urban centers, for the money was in the cities, as were most of those inclined to do the killing. At the end of 1978 a press report summarized what had occurred:

*Politicians and civil servants:*
Every member of President Amin's original cabinet who has not fled Uganda is now dead. Many parliamentarians and politicians have also been wiped out. Retired cabinet ministers are not immune . . . Hundreds of civil servants have also been eliminated.

*Religious leaders and followers:*
[The] Archbishop of Uganda . . . was murdered on Amin's orders
in February 1977 . . . other church leaders have subsequently
been picked up and killed.

*Academics, teachers and students:*
Uganda's chief inspector of schools was executed publicly in
September, 1977, at a time when many teachers were being
rounded up.

*Businessmen:*
Almost every Ugandan who represented a foreign company is
now believed to have been killed. Businessmen are particularly
vulnerable because of the near-collapse of Uganda's economy.[44]

At first Amin's lieutenants denied these massacres, blaming white
racism for the reports. As mentioned, Amin was elected president of the
Organization for African Unity as late as 1976, and several black American political figures, such as Stokely Carmichael, and various Western
journalists visited and praised him. But by late 1977 the truth had fully
caught up with Amin. He was condemned on the floor of the United
Nations by chief U.S. delegate Andrew Young, who is black. The Soviet
Union also withdrew support. Only Qaddafi of Libya and Saud of Saudi
Arabia continued their patronage.

There was no organized opposition to Amin within Uganda. And only
after his troops raided neighboring Tanzania did that country invade
Uganda. On June 3, 1979, Kampala was occupied, and Amin fled to Saudi
Arabia. For two years after his removal a reign of terror continued in
Uganda. Paranoia merged with reality, with ''each successive government
[blaming] underground movements from within the country or from bases
in Kenya or the Sudan.''[45]

The coupling of paranoia and grandiosity in Amin's brutal leadership
was responsible for unconstrained bloodshed. Amin was a brutish man
of limited intellectual capacities and background, totally inadequate to the
task of national leadership. In the face of this stress, his characteristic
wariness and readiness to externalize expanded into a full-blown paranoid
state. He defended against his insecurity by developing an exaggerated
sense of his self-importance and by savagely eliminating threats to his

esteem, represented by the educated class. Although political paranoia at times is associated with the most intricate intellectual conceptualizations, Amin's reign showed that it can also flourish under the rule of a cunning buffoon.

## Joseph Stalin

> It's one thing not to trust people. That was his right, even if his extreme mistrust did indicate that he had a serious psychological problem. But it's another thing when a man is compulsively driven to eliminate anyone he doesn't trust.
> —Nikita Khrushchev, *Khrushchev Remembers*

The masked paranoid may reach significant political heights in any society, but his tenure in a healthy democracy will be brief. When, however, the political paranoid reaches the heights of power in a despotic society, his tenure may be long, with devastating consequences. This was the case with Pol Pot in Cambodia and Idi Amin in Uganda, and it was also the case with Joseph Stalin.[46]

Russia has long been a fertile field for conspiracy theories and political violence, but during Stalin's paranoid totalitarian rule, more than 40 million of his enemies, real and imagined, were murdered. With his death, paranoia and totalitarianism eased, but the scars remain.[47]

Stalin found a well-primed canvas on which to paint his paranoid delusions. The czarist state nurtured a society in which beliefs in conspiracy and victimization were pervasive.[48] In fact Russian events often were caused by conspiracies, and this led to the paranoid belief that conspiracy always created policy. A routine assumption in pre-Bolshevik Russia was, for example, either that each ruler's death was caused by murder or that the ruler was not dead at all but continued to live somewhere else. An influential nineteenth-century ideology, Slavophilism, had for its extreme proponents a projective paranoid idea, "the suspicion that the West was plotting against Russia and holding it in contempt, openly or secretly."[49] It may be that historically the paranoid theme resonated far more strongly among the elite than among the masses.[50] Nevertheless, Lenin and Stalin were able to propagate it throughout the Soviet Union.

Well before the Bolshevik Revolution of 1917, dictatorship, centralization, and the manipulation of coercion and propaganda were firmly established in Russia. With the coming of Bolshevism, the full-fledged garrison state was foreshadowed. Under Lenin a single political party, the Communist Party of the Soviet Union, was established and maintained a political monopoly, and a pervasive security apparatus was instituted. Under Stalin a command economy was put in place and subordinated to military demands, and the freedoms of information, of association, and of foreign travel were abolished. Russia was a repressive and suspicious society before Stalin, but his obsession for control brought repression and suspicion to new heights. Maintaining this level of domination required a constant stream of propaganda about the presence of enemies and threats.

Both internal and external threats did exist—the Bolsheviks were unpopular in many areas. It was natural and prudent for the Bolsheviks to publicize and take action against these dangers. The reality of the threat, however, gave rise to an obsession with conspiracy.

Other factors also contributed to the atmosphere of crisis. The secret police had been greatly expanded under Lenin and were increasingly aggressive. Not only did they ferret out genuine conspiracies, but they interpreted as full-fledged conspiracies activities that were only marginally so. Moreover, an explanation had to be found for the increasing number of economic failures under Stalin. A dogma of state ideology was the productive superiority of the Soviet command system over the capitalist system. When socialist projects failed—as was often the case—the system itself could not be blamed, but saboteurs and anti-Soviet conspirators could, and of course the secret police would always "find" them. Finally, a constant flow of cheap and controllable labor was needed for the expanded labor camps, and "conspirators" and "saboteurs" supplied the labor army. This was commonly acknowledged. In the camps, prisoners would describe whether they had a "five," a "ten," or a "fifteen"— numbers that referred to the years of a prisoner's sentence. When one person with a "ten" claimed to have done nothing, not even criticized his drunken foreman, the others laughed and agreed that "for nothing you get a five, for a ten you had to have done something."[51]

This pattern of victimization based on accusations of conspiracy was compounded by three other policies that Stalin introduced, especially after 1928: the concentration of power into even fewer hands than under Lenin, the institution of a system of collective guilt, and an increasing use of terror as a means of resolving economic, social, and cultural problems.

Such was the situation that Stalin had inherited from Lenin and then intensified. Despite the ruthless practices and policies under Lenin's rule, no one has suggested that Lenin was personally paranoid. Lenin and Stalin did have their similarities. Both, for example, were intolerant of opposition. Their differences, however, were crucial. Lenin dealt with his opposition by expulsion or exile, Stalin by extermination.[52] It was Stalin's consuming desire to murder anyone he suspected was or might become an enemy. He brought the paranoid dynamic into what was already a brutal dictatorship.

The difficult circumstances of Stalin's childhood and adolescence foreshadowed his harsh rule. Born Iosif Dzhugashvili in 1879 in Georgia, Stalin was descended from illiterate peasants. He barely survived a severe bout of smallpox at age five, and an accidental injury to his left arm in childhood left him with a permanent impairment. It was, however, the beatings Stalin absorbed from his father, a violent man who drank heavily and who beat his wife as well, that hardened Stalin's nature. A boyhood friend, Joseph Iremashvili, described Stalin's travails and their consequences: "Undeserved and severe beatings made the boy as hard and heartless as the father was. Since all people in authority seemed to him to be like his father, there soon arose in him a vengeful feeling against all people in authority standing above him. From childhood on, the realization of his thoughts of revenge became the aim to which everything else was subordinated."[53]

Unable to identify the intemperate father's viciousness as the problem, the child who is beaten characteristically develops an inner sense of guilt. One way of defending against this is to develop paranoid mechanisms to project the internal "badness" onto outside persecutors. Another way of mastering the intolerable feelings is to identify with the punitive parent, to do to others as had been done to you.[54] It appears that both projection and identification with the aggressor became core features of Stalin's personality and significantly influenced his political leadership.

According to Iremashvili, when Stalin was in the Gori Church School he became fascinated by Georgian literature and tales of Georgian resistance fighters who fought the invading Russians. He especially liked the story of Koba, depicted in *The Patricide*. Based on a historical episode, this tale describes Koba, a Caucasian Robin Hood who, when not helping the poor, avenges himself upon his enemies.[55] Young Dzhugashvili (who was not to assume the pseudonym Stalin until twenty years later) demanded that everyone call him Koba.[56]

At age seventeen, Stalin left Gori to enter the Russian Orthodox theological seminary in Tbilisi, an environment as brutalizing in its own way as the home he had left. The monks spied on their adolescent charges, eavesdropping and searching through their possessions for such banned items as secular books. This environment heightened Stalin's distaste for religion and authority. His daughter Svetlana wrote of the effects of these experiences: "In a young man who had never for a moment believed in the life of the spirit or in God, endless prayers and enforced religious training could only produce contrary results . . . From his experiences at the seminary he came to the conclusion that men were intolerant, coarse, deceiving their flocks in order to hold them in obedience; that they intrigued, [and] lied."[57]

These experiences also sharpened Stalin's skills in dissimulation. He learned to conceal his inner rage, rebellion, and wish for revenge behind a facade of calmness and agreement. Stalin's form of rebellion was to steep himself in banned books, particularly the writings of Marx and Lenin.[58] Just as he hated his father and the monks, he idealized Lenin, calling him a "leader of the highest life, a mountain eagle."[59] Lenin had replaced the "soaring eagle" Koba as Stalin's idealized hero. The eloquence of Lenin's writings on the need to overthrow oppressive authority found fertile ground in young Stalin. Lenin provided an ideological conduit and a political channel for Stalin's vengeful feelings toward authority. According to Robert Tucker, Lenin's beliefs led Stalin to identify his own enemies as history's.[60]

Stalin left the seminary at age twenty and spent the next ten years as a political organizer and agitator.[61] A coworker described the activist Stalin (then still known as Koba), conveying well his paranoid style: "He treated me suspiciously. After lengthy questioning he handed me a stack of illegal literature . . . He saw me to the door with the same guarded, mistrustful expression. Koba would arrive [late] with a book under his shortened left arm and sit somewhere to the side or in a corner. He would listen in silence until everyone had spoken. He always spoke last. Taking his time, he would compare the different views, weigh all the arguments, . . . and make his own motion with great finality, as though concluding the discussion."[62]

Stalin was a leader in the 1901 May Day demonstrations in Tbilisi, in which two thousand workers clashed with the police, and in the labor confrontation in Batum in 1902, in which fifteen striking oil workers were killed by government troops. He was arrested after the Batum confrontation, imprisoned, and sent to exile in Siberia, from which he ultimately escaped to rejoin Lenin in the work of revolution. In an underground press article published in 1905 entitled "The Class of Proletarians and the Party of Proletarians," Stalin emphasized militant aggression and organizational control. The party would now be a "fortress, the doors of which are only open to the worthy."[63] Stalin was often abrasive in his dealings with other revolutionary leaders; he was quick to take slight, resentful of their superior education and intellectual attainments.

A lasting humiliation to Stalin was his failure to play a leading role in the culminating events of 1917. Indeed, Trotsky played a much more consequential role in the seizure of power, second only to Lenin in his importance. When Lenin returned from exile, Stalin's presence was not noted in the records of the meeting in Petrograd. In his official biography, Stalin recast his role, claiming that he rather than Trotsky orchestrated the events, falsely identifying himself as Lenin's equal.

Stalin's rivalry with Trotsky was bitter, for Trotsky occupied the position Stalin coveted. After Lenin's death, Stalin systematically moved to consolidate his control and to rewrite Trotsky's role in the history of the revolution. He characterized Trotsky's "permanent revolution" as the very opposite of Lenin's theory of "proletarian revolution." After Trotsky's forced resignation in 1925, Stalin, characteristically concealing his aggressive, paranoid, controlling nature behind a temperate facade, counseled moderation in responding to those Bolsheviks who disagreed with the preferred party line. The man who was to cut off 40 million heads stated that "cutting off heads is fraught with major dangers for the party."[64] Stalin was not able to heed his own sage warning concerning the dire consequences of "cutting off heads," and, as he noted, once the process was initiated, there was no stopping it.

The following description of Stalin's terror is quoted at length to show that what occurred under his rule was not simply political conflict in a revolutionary period in a brutal society. It was a madness that devoured the society:

> It is simply impossible to evoke in words the full measure of the individual and collective human suffering that Stalin inflicted. In the name of socialism, several million peasant families were deported under the most primitive of conditions, with the survivors resettled in distant Siberia. Stalin was also responsible for the mass starvation of several million Ukrainian peasants during the Great Famine of the early 1930s—a famine deliberately exploited to accelerate the process of collectivization, but to a significant degree also generated by the same brutal collectivization itself. During the purges, the party itself was decimated, with most of its top leaders executed and with their families cruelly persecuted. Arrests and executions cut across the entire Soviet society and ran into the millions. According to Soviet data, in the military sector alone no less than 37,000 army officers and 3,000 navy officers were shot in the years 1937 and 1938, more than actually perished during the first two years of the Nazi-Soviet war.
>
> The GULAG [a system of forced labor camps] kept swelling under Stalin. Individual and group arrests were a massive and continuous occurrence. Even entire ethnic groups were targeted for genocidal extinction. Just before the outbreak of the war in 1939, the entire Polish population living on the Soviet side of the then Soviet-Polish border, numbering several hundred thousand, suddenly disappeared, with only the women and children resettled in Kazakhstan. The men simply perished. In the last stages of [World War II], the Tatars of Crimea and the Chechen-Ingush of northern Caucasus, numbering also in the hundreds of thousands, were uprooted and deported to Siberia. After the war, and despite the revelations of the Nazi Holocaust of the Jews,

the Jewish community in Moscow and Leningrad was suddenly targeted, and its leadership was decimated. In 1949, mass deportations to Siberia were inflicted on hundreds of thousands of Balts. According to scrupulously kept Soviet accounting, . . . the victims included 108,362 from Lithuania alone. On the eve of Stalin's death, preparations were in progress for new show trials of the "Jewish doctors' plot," with the victims accused of having conspired to kill the top Kremlin leadership. . . .

Though the total number of Stalin's victims will never be known, it is absolutely safe to estimate the number at no less than twenty million and perhaps as high as forty million. . . . All in all, Stalin was probably the biggest mass murderer in human history, statistically overshadowing even Hitler.[65]

Stalin killed those who were close to him as well as those he designated as enemies or potential enemies. In the late 1930s alone, Stalin killed the chief of the general staff, the chief political commissar of the army, the supreme commanders of all important military districts, 99 percent of all Soviet ambassadors, 98 of 139 members of the Central Committee of the Seventeenth Party Congress, and, eventually, the two chiefs of his secret service, who had been responsible for killing all those just listed.[66]

Stalin enjoyed inflicting pain upon his foes and would sometimes specify the type of torture to be used on prisoners. A particular source of pleasure to him was maintaining life-and-death control through random terror. An example of what Erich Fromm has characterized as Stalin's "non-sexual sadism" concerns Sergei Ivanovich Kavtaradze, who had once hidden Stalin from detectives. Stalin rehabilitated the Trotsky-tainted Kavtaradze, who returned the favor by writing an adulatory newspaper article. This was not enough for Stalin, however, and he had Kavtaradze and his wife arrested, tortured, and sentenced to be shot. Kavtaradze, after being kept in his cell for months, was suddenly taken to the office of the chief of the secret police, Lavrenti Beria, where he was reunited with his wife, who seemed to have aged by years. Although the couple was permitted to resume their life, Stalin continued his cat-and-mouse game, having Kavtaradze to dinner and even unexpectedly dropping in for an occasional social call with Beria. At dinner Stalin would play the host, serving his former savior, joking and reminiscing. Yet Stalin's menace would suddenly appear. At one dinner Stalin said to the fearful Kavtaradze, "And still you wanted to kill me."[67]

Stalin would reassure anxious officials that they were in his favor, only to arrest them days later. As Fromm recounts, one evening the wife of a deputy commissar who was hospitalized received an unexpected phone call from Stalin: " 'I hear you are going about on foot,' Stalin said. 'That's no good. People might think what they shouldn't. I'll send you a car if yours is being repaired.' And the next morning a car from the Kremlin garage arrived . . . But two days later her husband was arrested right from the hospital."[68]

During the purges Stalin frequently watched the trials from behind a curtain, revealing his presence only by the occasional flare of the matches as he lit and relit his pipe. To oppose Stalin was to ensure lifelong enmity. He never forgot a slight and would often avenge it many years later. Discussing his idea of a perfect day with some comrades, Stalin indicated, "Mine is to plan an artistic revenge upon an enemy, carry it out to perfection, and then go home and go peacefully to bed."[69]

Stalin's pleasure in revenge was not simply an indulgence. It sprang from the relief of eliminating an enemy. Believing he was surrounded by enemies, Stalin was paranoid to the core. One of his principal lieutenants, Nikita Khrushchev, commented, "Sometimes [Stalin] would glare at you and say 'Why don't you look me in the eye today? Why are you averting your eyes from mine?' or some other such stupidity . . . Stalin had instilled in the consciousness of us all the suspicion that we were surrounded by enemies, that we should try to find an unexposed traitor or saboteur in everyone. Whenever we had a dinner with him, Stalin wouldn't touch a single dish or hors d'oeuvre or bottle until someone else had tested it. This shows he had gone off the deep end." Khrushchev also recalled that, after distributing to his inner circle information about what he called the "doctors' plot," a murderous conspiracy headed by a cabal of Jewish doctors, Stalin said, "You are blind like young kittens . . . What will happen without me? The country will perish because you do not know how to recognize enemies."[70]

The ruthless rooting out of enemies is the sine qua non of the paranoid despot. In order to survive, a despot must trust no one. But the very action of accusing imagined enemies creates enemies. The severity of Stalin's paranoia left no one free of suspicion, no matter how dedicated and loyal his previous service. According to Stalin's daughter, if Stalin suspected anyone of disloyalty he would try to destroy him, regardless of their previous relationship.[71]

Moreover, Stalin did not have to suspect someone of disloyalty to have him murdered. His fear of betrayal was projective, prospective, and prophylactic. Stalin had many high military officers killed before World War II because he reasoned that it would be in their interest to betray the Soviet Union and cooperate with the far better equipped Germans. He decided to have them killed before the idea occurred to them. Furthermore, the terror of 1934–1939 had no political necessity.[72] The Communists and Stalin were secure by that time. The terror was simply a reflection of Stalin's personal pathology.

How could Stalin, who displayed his paranoia so obviously to intimates, avoid acquiring the reputation of a paranoid? Above all, the events in question took place in an intensely partisan context, and the world had an imperfect idea of what was going on. Another reason concerned Stalin's personality and the paranoid dynamic.

Stalin's favorite image in describing his enemies was that of "masks."[73] Stalin was projecting on others what he himself was doing. Paranoids live in a world in which everyone is in disguise. It is not surprising that they also veil their nature behind a false personality. Stalin did this throughout his life, and it served him well. Unlike Hitler and such lesser leaders as Gerald L. K. Smith and Joseph McCarthy, Stalin presented himself to all but his closest intimates as the most moderate of men. He manifested nothing of the paranoid style.

Stalin's own mask was remarkably effective. At Lenin's death the Bolsheviks, still operating within the collegial context that Lenin had fostered, sought a leader who would be "practical and sober minded," someone bland and unexceptional.[74] Many feared that another Napoléon Bonaparte would arise, and they focused their fear on Trotsky, not Stalin. Ironically, Stalin was selected in part because he was seen as an unthreatening, gray bureaucrat.

Not all the Bolsheviks, however, were convinced of Stalin's meekness. Lenin himself, in a final testament, warned against Stalin. Nikolai Bukharin, an intellectual who had spent most of his life outside Russia and who became one of the founders of the Soviet Union, sensed Stalin's inexorable consolidation of power and one-man rule. Desperate, he warned Lev Kamenev, one-time politburo chairman, that Stalin was a "Ghengis Khan [whose] line is ruinous for the whole revolution . . . He has made concessions only so that he can cut our throats later." In his notes of a meeting with Lenin, Kamenev observed, "Stalin knows only one method: . . . to plant a knife in the back."[75]

But for the most part Stalin's disguise was effective. In face-to-face encounters with nonintimates, Stalin wore a mask of reasonableness and moderation, even kindliness. To the observing world, he was genial "Uncle Joe."

But what of those who were politically sophisticated and hostile to him and to Communism? American ambassador and historian George F. Kennan, who was deeply antagonistic to Communism and aware of Stalin's crimes, notes in his memoirs, "In manner—with us, at least—he was simple, quiet, unassuming. There was no striving for effect. His words were few. They generally sounded reasonable and sensible; indeed, they often were. An unforewarned visitor would never have guessed what depths of calculation, ambition, love of power, jealousy, cruelty, and sly vindictiveness lurked behind this unpretentious facade."[76] Another shrewd anti-Communist American ambassador, Averell Harriman, noted, "It is hard for me to reconcile the courtesy and consideration that he showed me personally with the ghastly cruelty of his wholesale liquidations."[77]

Stalin was as effective in disguising his destructive paranoia with scholars as he was with politicians and diplomats. Isaac Deutscher, one of his early biographers and sometime Trotskyite critic, called Stalin a person of "almost impersonal personality."[78] E. H. Carr described him as a creature of circumstance, a person who rode the whirlwind, whose personality did not matter.[79] Evidently, even these critical scholars not only were ignorant of facts that would later emerge but also were affected by Marxist doctrine, which denies the decisive influence of personality on history.

Even when, during World War II, Stalin sought to develop a charismatic appeal, his demeanor was more avuncular than dramatic.[80] Stalin's image was that of a calm and kindly figure, a distant czarlike god. As a Marxist leading a Marxist revolution, Stalin should have found conspiratorial explanations—among the most personal of behaviors—unattractive. The fact that they so obsessed him points to the crucial role that his personal psychology played in creating the terror.

The case of Stalin again illustrates that a paranoid leader need not display a paranoid style. Indeed, the concealed paranoid can be far more destructive than the open one. To survive in the conspiracy-ridden Kremlin, one would benefit from an awareness of plots. But what is the boundary between prudent suspicion and paranoia? In such a society, can there be a boundary?

If, early in his career, there was a fit between Stalin's paranoid personality and the requirements of leadership, with the passage of years his paranoia deepened. By the time of the so-called doctors' plot just before his death in 1953, when he was convinced that a group of Jewish doctors was part of a larger conspiracy to murder him, he was in a clinical paranoid state, consumed by paranoid fears, obsessed with conspiracies, trusting no one, fearing everyone. Stalin's case demonstrates how context affects the diagnosis. The Stalin of the 1930s would have been considered paranoid in a Western democracy, but not in the Kremlin. But by the early 1950s, even in the treacherous Soviet Union he had created, Stalin's paranoia far exceeded the norm. Lavrenti Beria, his last chief of political police, adroitly manipulated Stalin's paranoia to rid himself of rivals, feeding Stalin's fears and suggesting "enemies" to be destroyed.

The stroke that claimed Stalin's life prevented another purge of innocent victims. They would have joined the millions of casualties of Stalin's insatiable, paranoid search for security from the enemies that surrounded him—the enemies within.

# 11

## Adolf Hitler
### *Destructive Charisma*

It is only a step from the primitive medicine-man to
the paranoiac, and from both of them to the despot of
history.
—Elias Canetti, *Crowds and Power*

The Nazi propaganda machine was powerfully effective
in drawing the German population into support of Hitler's destructive cause. A poster, for example, featured
Hitler in a white doctor's coat, a stethoscope in his
pocket, with a legend describing him as physician to the
diseased German nation.[1] The theme of the German nation as a "national organism" that was disintegrating is
stressed throughout Hitler's writings and speeches, as is
the image of the Jew as the contaminant in the German
body politic, responsible for the "ferment of decomposition."[2] This imagery reflects Hitler's personal psychology externalized through paranoid dynamics to the
national scene.[3] Although the material on Hitler's early
years is sketchy, it does provide clues to the origins of
Hitler's paranoid psychodynamics.

### Hitler's Background and Early Years

Accurate scholarship can
Unearth the whole offence . . .

276

> That has driven a culture mad, . . .
> What huge imago made
> A psychopathic god: . . .
> Those to whom evil is done
> Do evil in return.
> —W. H. Auden, "September 1, 1939"

Hitler's uncertainty over his genealogy on his father's side was to plague him throughout his life and was probably the basis for his preoccupation with racial purity.[4] The Schickelgrubers, Hitler's paternal grandmother's family, were Austrian farmers whose history contained a significant amount of family intermarriage and psychological instability. Hitler's grandmother, Maria Ann Schickelgruber, left the farming community to enter domestic service. In 1837, at the age of forty-one, she gave birth to Alois Schickelgruber; the child's father was unrecorded in the baptismal registry. Five years later she married a millworker, Johann Georg Hiedler (also spelled Hitler), who refused to care for her son. Hiedler's older brother, a farmer, took young Alois in and raised him until, at age thirteen, he became an apprentice to a bootmaker.

Alois was both bright and ambitious, and at age eighteen he managed to secure a position in the Austrian civil service, a notable achievement. When he was thirty-nine, Alois, by now an established civil servant, persuaded his foster father to alter the baptismal records in order to correct the blemish in his past, and Georg Hitler was recorded as his father.

We dwell on the confusing family background because Hitler dwelled on it. In 1930, an alarmed Hitler called in his attorney, Hans Frank. A relative of Hitler's was threatening blackmail, indicating that he had documentary evidence that Hitler's paternal grandfather was Jewish. Frank investigated and reported that he had found corroborating evidence that Hitler's mother had worked in the home of a Jewish family named Frankenberger and that Frankenberger had paid financial support to Maria Ann for Alois for fourteen years; an obvious conclusion was that Frankenberger had fathered Alois. According to Frank, Hitler denied the implication, indicating that his grandmother had said she accepted the money because her family was poor.

A compelling indication of Hitler's suspicion that his grandmother had been impregnated by a Jew and that he carried Jewish blood can be found in the Nuremberg Racial Laws of 1935, which Hitler called *Blutschutzgesetz* (''law for the protection of the blood'').[5] Paragraph 3, which was written by Hitler, declared, ''Jews cannot employ household servants of German or related blood who are under 45 years of age.'' Forty-five, of course, was the presumptive age of cessation of fertility. Had this law been in place when his forty-one-year-old grandmother was working as a domestic, she could not have become pregnant by her Jewish employer, as Hitler feared she had.

Hitler's preoccupation with his physical appearance and with the physiognomy of Jews also indicates that he was concerned that he was ''tainted by Jewish blood.'' He often observed Jewish noses and spoke with disgust of the ''characteristic odor'' that emanated from them. Hitler himself had a large nose, which he took pains to camouflage with his moustache. The idealized concept of the pure Aryan that Hitler promoted was very different from his own appearance, which has been described as resembling that of an ''apprentice waiter in a second-class Viennese cafe.''[6]

It does not matter whether Hitler actually had a Jewish grandfather. What matters is that he feared, perhaps believed, that he was part Jewish. The intensity of his compulsion to rid the German body politic of the ''Jewish pestilence'' suggests he was playing out his own pathological dynamics on the national scene. Having identified himself with the nation, he was projecting the devalued aspects of his self upon the Jews. This is the paranoid dynamic writ large.

Hitler's father, described as an authoritarian and self-centered man with little concern for his wives or children, was twenty-two years older than his second cousin Klara, his third wife. Klara, already Alois's mistress, was pregnant with Adolf when Alois's second wife died.[7] Adolf was born on April 20, 1889.

Although Hitler, in *Mein Kampf,* attempts to convey that his family had economic difficulties, this was apparently not the case, although they moved frequently in connection with his father's career as an Austrian civil servant. If the economic circumstances were not harsh, however, the disciplinary ones were. Adolf's older brother, Alois, Jr., described their father's discipline in the severest of terms: ''Alois Sr. frequently beat

[Alois, Jr.,] with a hippopotamus whip. He demanded the utmost obedience . . . Every transgression was another excuse for a whipping . . . [He was a man of] a very violent temper [who] often beat the dog until the dog would . . . wet the floor. He often beat the children, and on one occasion . . . his wife, Klara.'' According to another report, the father once beat Alois, Jr., until he was unconscious and on another occasion beat Adolf and left him for dead. His children reportedly were required to call him Herr Vater. He would call Adolf by whistling for him, as he did for the dog.[8]

Reports from teachers and his half-brothers indicate that Adolf was a bright but willful boy of unstable temperament who easily lost his temper. He did poorly in school, except in drawing. In *Mein Kampf*, Hitler attributes his poor school performance to rebellion against his authoritarian father's demands that he prepare for the civil service. He depicted an ongoing power struggle with his father: ''No matter how firm and determined my father might be, . . . his son was just as stubborn and obstinate . . . My father did not give up his 'never' and I strengthened my 'nevertheless.' ''[9] This emphasis on the power of will colored all Hitler's political writing, and the refusal to yield to superior force would characterize all his relationships and his leadership of the fatherland. (Hitler later became enamored of the works of Arthur Schopenhauer, especially *The World as Will and Idea*. He gave Schopenhauer's collected works to Benito Mussolini because he was so impressed by Mussolini's ability to reverse, by an act of will—his march on Rome—his nation's decline.)

In his adolescence Hitler began to form the attitudes that were to shape his political ideology. Between the ages of sixteen and eighteen, he developed a grandiose view of himself as an artistic genius. This self-concept was shaped by Richard Wagner. Hitler was fascinated by Wagner's heroic operas and the theme of Aryan superiority he championed. His youthful companion, August Kubizek, recalls Hitler's being so transported by Wagner's *Rienzi* that he vowed to one day rescue Germany as Rienzi had rescued Rome.

Hitler's rejection at the art academy was a major blow. Several psychoanalytically oriented biographers have written of Hitler's ''identity crisis,'' which Erik Erikson believed occurred between 1907, when Hitler was rejected at the art academy, and 1908, when his mother died. When the adolescent crisis is not mastered and healthy identity is not consolidated, lifelong psychological problems ensue. In Hitler's case, Erikson believed, this lack of resolution of the identity crisis resulted in Hitler's remaining "the unbroken adolescent who had chosen a career apart from civilian happiness, mercantile tranquillity and spiritual peace."[10]

The death of Hitler's mother and a second rejection at the academy of art ushered in an extended period of wandering. During this time, according to *Mein Kampf,* his zealous anti-Semitism consolidated. Hitler's principal psychobiographer, Robert Waite, hypothesizes that his mother's death while under the care of a Jewish doctor led Hitler to seek vengeance.[11] He also "found" the reason for his having been turned down at the academy of art: four of the seven members of the jury were Jews. Hitler was so incensed that he wrote a letter to the director of the academy, ending with the threat "For this the Jews will pay!"[12] He immersed himself in the study of Marxism and its relationship with Jewry.

Confronted by failure, with no clear course before him, Hitler employed the classic paranoid dynamic of denying his own inadequacy, in this case blaming the Jews for his failures. He read widely but was particularly fascinated by articles on or by anti-Semitic politicians. After he had spent his small inheritance, he lived in extremely poor circumstances, moving from flophouse to flophouse. "For two years," he wrote, "I had no other mistress than sorrow and need, no other companion than eternally unsatisfied hunger."[13] After two years of homelessness (1908–1910), he moved into a men's hostel supported by a charitable foundation, where he stayed for the next three years.

During these difficult five years, the "Vienna period," he had no focus other than hatred. Reflecting on this period of his life in *Mein Kampf,* he saw his experiences as the foundation of his determination and resolve; this was when "the Goddess of Suffering" and "Dame Care" taught him hardness.[14] The outbreak of World War I ended this aimless time and gave purpose to Hitler's life.[15] He immediately volunteered and became a good soldier—he was awarded the Iron Cross, first class—but was not promoted beyond corporal because his superiors felt he lacked leadership qualities. His fellow soldiers were horrified by the brutality of war, but Hitler exulted in it, his superpatriotism alienating many of his military comrades.

In October 1918, Hitler was caught in a British gas attack, which temporarily blinded him. He was in the hospital when he learned that the war was over. Hitler had been psychologically lost before the war and had found himself in fighting for German supremacy and identifying with German nationalism. The end of the war was thus devastating to him. It signified not only a humiliating defeat but also a loss of his newfound role as heroic soldier.

But in this loss came the consolidation of Hitler's dreams of avenging the defeat and playing a heroic role in Germany's history. He was obsessed with the "November criminals" who had betrayed Germany. In the hospital, voices came to him, telling him to "rescue his Motherland from the Jews who had violated her."[16] His destiny became clear to him: "With the Jews there can be no bargaining. There can only be the hard either/or. I had resolved to become a politician."[17] Hitler identified the Jews as responsible for Germany's humiliation, and "hard" vengeance against the Jews was central to Hitler's role as Germany's savior.

Hitler plunged into political activity, working with rightist movements to overthrow the Weimar Republic. He soon made a mark with his oratorical gifts and drew thousands to his nationalist speeches. An early admirer, Hermann Rauschning, wrote, "Hatred is like wine to him. It intoxicated him. One must have heard his tirades of denunciation to realize how he can revel in hate."[18]

## Paranoid Director of Hatred

Hitler had already recognized the organizing importance of words. He had developed a reputation as an authority on the "Jewish question" and was making two or three speeches a day in which he railed bitterly against the Jews, identifying them as the cause of Germany's moral decay. In response to a request from a senior military officer, in September 1919 he wrote a guide for the rightist military, "The Dangers of Jewry," in which he emphasized the goal of "the removal of the Jews altogether [by] the ruthless intervention" of national leaders.[19] Jews, according to Hitler, constitute a race, not a religious community—a race that pretends to be part of the nation in which it lives but that, through guile, manipulation, and the use of wealth, destroys the moral and then the material quality of the host nation. Jews, who are completely materialistic, seek only power and money. With Jews there can be no compromise, only complete removal. It was in this context that Hitler sounded his dominant theme of racial purity, the belief that the "source of a people's whole power [lies in] its racial value."[20]

Anti-Semitism followed from, even was required by, this doctrine of racial purity. In Hitler's view, racial purity was threatened by three poisons, each of which the Jews represented: internationalism, or an undue interest in things foreign and an insufficient valuing of the nation, which in turn leads to miscegenation; egalitarianism, democracy, and majority rule, which devalue individual creativity and individual contributions to the nation's good; and pacifism, which subverts a nation's willingness to fight for self-preservation.[21] The Jews promoted all these poisons by seeking the "enslavement of productively active people, . . . by the promiscuous bastardization of other people, . . . [and] through the extirpation of the völkisch intelligentsia and its replacement by members of its own people."[22]

One need not be paranoid to manipulate the paranoid dynamic so as to inflame mass hatred. But when the leader has a personal psychological stake in the hatred he trumpets, his sincerity is indubitable, and his conviction and persuasive strength powerful. It is clear that Hitler had a strong personal psychological stake in identifying Jews as the cause of Germany's decline from its pre–World War I status. But it is equally clear that he fully understood how his focused message of malice had a forceful organizing effect on the wounded German society. He knew that mass movements spread with greatest ferocity when they have a palpable enemy, a devil to fear, hate, and attack. The more visible the devil, the more powerful a rallying point for the unifying force of hatred. Asked whether he thought the Jew must be destroyed, he replied, "No . . . We should then have to invent him. It is essential to have a tangible enemy, not merely an abstract one."[23]

The paranoid dynamic colored and dominated Hitler's leadership. Consider, for example, the oath of loyalty he drew up for the officers of the *sturm-abteilung* (SA, or Brown Shirts). Given his fear of submission, it is revealing that his first demand was that of total obedience.[24] The SA swore loyalty to Hitler, not to the constitution or the German people. This reflected the magnitude of Hitler's inner doubts. Moreover, Hitler knew all too well that many saw him as a "queer duck."[25] After the Night of the Long Knives (June 30, 1934), when Hitler and his co-conspirators killed his political enemies within the Nazi movement, many of whom had assisted him in his rise to power, Hitler exulted, "They underestimated me . . . because I haven't had an education, because I haven't the manners that their sparrow brains think right! . . . But I don't need them to assure me of my historical greatness. . . . They thought I was their tool. And behind my back they laughed at me."[26]

By 1938, when he confronted Austrian chancellor Kurt von Schuschnigg and demanded Austria's capitulation, his compensatory grandiosity had reached supreme heights. Hitler said, "Providence had selected me" to carry out a historical mission, and "I have travelled the hardest road that any German ever had to tread and I have achieved more in German history than it was given to any other German to bring out."[27] Two weeks after the Night of the Long Knives, Hitler gave a speech defending his actions and describing the conspirators—international disintegrators, disaffected domestic leaders, pre–World War I revolutionaries, and nihilists—that he had thwarted.[28] This speech seems to be a description of Hitler and his followers, projected upon his enemies.

The orchestrated campaign of hatred that Hitler directed through his formidable propaganda apparatus was a critical element in the engine of death and destruction he mobilized. Its demonic force was fueled by the enmity that burned within Hitler and was projected upon the Jews. His power as chief communicator of this doctrine was a direct reflection of his fervid belief in his message, a dark loathing that required the Jewish enemy. His internal terrifier was externalized and became the object of destruction.

## The Psycho-Logic of Hitler's Hatred

Hitler's rhetoric reflects the deepest recesses of the unconscious, and the themes were ones of primal force.[29] These themes included the following:

- *The country as a living organism.*

  What remains is the substance, a substance of flesh and blood, our nation.[30]

  Could anyone believe that Germany alone was not subject to exactly the same laws as all other human organisms?[31]

  And if the nation is an organism, a "body corporate pulsing through and through with a vital inner life,"[32] it follows that loss of territory is like an amputation.

  The Polish corridor is like a strip of flesh cut from our body, . . . a national wound that bleeds continuously and will continue to bleed until the land is returned to us.[33]

  France was tearing piece after piece out of the flesh of our national body.[34]

- *Ensuring the integrity of the nation.* It therefore follows that the purpose of politics is to ensure the integrity and the purity of the nation.

  The body formed by the people must . . . secure in the future the maintenance of this body which is the people.[35]

  The purpose of every idea and of every institution within a people can . . . be only to maintain the substance of the people . . . in bodily and mental health, in good order and in purity.[36]

- *The disintegration of the nation.*

  This [is a] period of [the] incipient and slowly spreading decomposition of our nation.[37]

  The political disintegration of the body of a people must . . . mean the end of every authority.[38]

- *The Jew as the cause of the nation's disintegration.*

  The Jew . . . is the demon of the disintegration of peoples, the symbol of the unceasing destruction of their lives.[39]

  The Jew is a ferment of decomposition in peoples.[40]

- *The need to prevent disintegration.*

  We will not capitulate before these ferments of disintegration.[41]

  We want to burn out the symptoms of decomposition.[42]

- *The Jew as the cause of the nation's disease.*

  The international carrier . . . of the bacillus [Jews] must be fought.[43]

  Against the infection of materialism, against the Jewish pestilence, we must hold aloft the flaming ideal.[44]

- *The Jew as parasite.*

  [The Jew's] spreading is a typical phenomenon for all parasites; he always seeks a new feeding ground for his race.[45]

  [The Jew] was . . . only and always a parasite in the body of other people's pores.[46]

- *The Jew as poison, defiling racial purity.*

  [The Jew] poisons the blood of others.[47]

  All great cultures of the past perished . . . from blood poisoning.[48]

The specter of the defiling of the race leads to a special paranoid fear, for the poisoning is not only through the spreading of culture but, even more important, through sexual contamination of the Aryan race.

  With satanic joy in his face, the black-haired Jewish youth lurks in wait for the unsuspecting girl whom he defiles with his blood, thus stealing her from her people. With every means he tries to destroy the racial foundations of the people he has set out to subjugate.[49]

The emphasis on purity requires elimination of the Jew.

  We will not pause . . . until the last trace of this poison is removed from the body of our people.[50]

• *The crisis is upon the German people.*

> [We] find ourselves in the midst of a struggle, . . . concerned
> . . . with the questions of the maintenance or the annihilation
> of the whole inherited human order of society and its civi-
> lizations. The organization of human society is threatened.[51]

In this language, Hitler depicts a war between the forces of
order and the forces of disintegration, between good and evil,
and Hitler claimed the vision to lead his people in this struggle
for their survival.

The skillful leader adroitly manipulates symbols. For the German
people, the image of the marching army aroused strong feelings of national pride. It was because the army had such symbolic significance for
the German people that the humiliation of the army concretized in the
harsh terms of the Treaty of Versailles was so painful—which Hitler
understood very well. He employed the slogan of the *Diktat* of Versailles
with great effectiveness, inviting the German people to follow his banner,
to join him in strength, regaining pride by reversing the humiliation of
the *Diktat,* the humiliation of forced submission.[52]

In the next selections, Hitler first argues that the German will is weak
and that the German nation must struggle against submission. Then, echoing Schopenhauer, he emphasizes the need for will, and he offers himself
as an object for the weakened nation to identify and fuse with. At the
same time, Hitler makes clear his identification of himself with the nation.

• *The need for national will and the fusion of Hitler with the nation.*

> We Germans have been . . . lacking in any will power and
> determination.[53]

> The strength of our people . . . lies in our inner unity of
> will.[54]

> You must fuse your will with mine.[55]

• *War as the struggle for the nation's existence.*

> We fight not for theories and dogmas. We fight for the ex-
> istence of the German people.[56]

The world is now struggling to dissolve the German nation.[57]

No power in the world will be able again to force us to our knees.[58]

- *Hitler as Christ the Redeemer.* Hitler identified himself as the rescuer of the German people and identified the Jews as crucifying the German body politic. He also used language of resurrection.

We want to prevent our Germany from suffering, as Another did, the death upon the Cross.[59]

Through us and in us the nation has risen again.[60]

All these themes—the German nation as an organism; the threat of dissolution and disintegration; the Jew as the agent of disintegration, the contaminant, the bacillus, the poison; the need to purify the Aryan nation; the need not to submit in the battle for the soul of the Aryan nation, and so on—can be found in Hitler's personal testament, *Mein Kampf* (*My Struggle*), and are echoed throughout his writings and his oratory. Hitler well understood the organizing effect of an enemy. But these ideas, a clear display of the paranoid dynamic, reflected the deepest recesses of Hitler's psychology. His impressive rhetorical gifts were made the more effective by the conviction with which he endowed his rhetoric of hatred.

## The Popular Readiness to Respond to Anti-Semitism

The belief in conspiracy and its related doctrine of anti-Semitism were central to Nazism, but how large did they figure in Hitler's appeal? This may seem like an odd question, because these doctrines were so prominent in the Hitler period. But we know that fascism elsewhere—not only in Italy but also in Argentina and Spain—has been politically successful without the Hitlerian obsession with conspiracy and anti-Semitism.

Nineteenth-century anti-Semitism found its origin in the idea of Jew as outsider, but a new type of anti-Semitism developed from about 1914—one in which Jews were resented because they were connected in the public mind with bourgeois liberal society.[61] This hostility to bourgeois society was associated in Germany with idealization of a tribal past, the so-called völkisch era of Saxons, Goths, and Franks. Nazism was not the originator of these ideas but was their amplifier and beneficiary.

Six powerful sources of anti-Semitism were particularly strong in Weimar Germany: many Jewish members of the Reichstag refused to vote for war credits during World War I; it was commonly believed that Jews were reluctant to enlist in the army during the war; Jews were prominent in the government that surrendered to the Allies; it was believed that a disproportionate number of left-wingers were Jews; many thought that Jews had profited from the war; and Germany experienced an influx of poor and culturally unassimilated East European Jews about this time.[62]

Whatever the nature of anti-Semitism in 1933, it was not proportional to the persecution that was to come. "Most [Germans] continued to harbour unflattering stereotypes of Jews and to regard them as unassimilated outsiders. . . . Indifference was in far greater supply than antagonism. Acts of violence against Jews comparable to the pogroms in Russia and the riots that accompanied the Dreyfus Affair in France were unheard of in Germany."[63]

William Sheridan Allen, in *The Nazi Seizure of Power: The Experience of a Single German Town, 1922–1945,* has offered a thorough description of how Jews were viewed and treated in ordinary circumstances. The Hanoverian town of Northeim, with a population of 10,000, had a small and stable Jewish population of 120 with a history going back at least two centuries. The Jewish population constituted the same percentage of Northeim as it did the national urban average. This Jewish population consisted of several families occupying different social classes.

Anti-Semitism was manifested in jokes and in expressions of mild distaste. Jews, however, were active in shooting societies, choral groups, and patriotic organizations; indeed, they were frequently officers in these groups. In 1933, Nazi activists began a public campaign of anti-Semitism—boycotts of Jewish businesses, anti-Semitic slogans painted on walls, and so on. At first the campaign had little effect, and a Nazi report as late as 1935 complained that Jewish shops were still being patronized. In this community at least, anti-Semitism was not part of Nazism's appeal: "Northeimers were drawn to anti-Semitism because they were drawn to Nazism, not the other way around."[64] The persecution had its effect, however, and Northeimer's Jews began to withdraw from public life, eventually leaving the town for the larger cities where they thought they would be safer. The attitude of their one-time Gentile friends was seldom hostile, but neither was it supportive. The Gentiles were not willing to take risks.

Norman Cohn, in his classic history of the *Protocols of the Elders of Zion* forgeries, notes that the "one thing on which all witnesses seem to agree is that the Germany in which Hitler came to power was not in fact a country gripped in a frenzy of antisemitism, hypnotized by the myth of the world-conspiracy and thirsting for the blood of the Jews . . . Nor can it be taken for granted that even the whole of the Nazi party itself, with its relatively small membership of about one million, was fanatically antisemitic."[65]

Nearly half the early members of the National Socialist German Workers' Party reported being uninterested in the Jewish question.[66] Hitler's principal appeal to the German people was his stress on national renewal and anti-Marxism, not his anti-Semitism. Many Germans, however, found it cognitively consistent to be anti-Jewish: Jews were thought of in the public mind as "not really German" and as Marxists. From the standpoint of political tactics, individual political enemies—socialists, more extreme Marxists, and certain financial leaders—could be attacked for being Jewish as well as for whatever other "bad" characteristic the Nazis found. The major effect of Nazi propaganda was to encourage indifference toward anti-Semitic policies.[67] Only about 11 percent of Nazi party members were extreme anti-Semites. Of the general population, about 40 percent were what has been called the don't-bother-me vote.[68] They were interested only in their personal lives.

Thus it was not a matter of Hitler cynically exploiting anti-Semitism because the society was ripe to respond to this theme. The rabid anti-Semitism that pervaded Hitler's rhetoric sprang from deep irrational sources within himself. Hitler persisted in pursuing his Jewish demons when it was against his political-military interests to do so. There is no question that the Holocaust—with its diversion of vitally needed men and matériel from the war against the Allies to the murdering of Jews, and with the refusal to coerce Jewish scientists and technicians in support of the German war effort—cost him dearly. Hitler's adherence to anti-Semitism went far beyond its immediate instrumental utility, although the intensity of those beliefs had earlier contributed to his charismatic appeal.

What explains his appeal, the power and effectiveness of his leadership? Why did so many in the nation follow him on his destructive path? To some extent, Hitler's popularity was rational and instrumental. He was an effective counter to German Bolshevism, his economic policies were a great improvement over those of the Weimar Republic, and his pan-Germanism struck a responsive chord in Germany and in the German diaspora. But there was more to Hitler's attractiveness than cold logic and popular self-interest.

The reassuring "salvationist" message Hitler offered was based on a paranoid fantasy of conspiracy: the Germans were not responsible for their plight but were the victims of Jewish intrigue. They had been tricked into the loss of World War I by a Jewish-led conspiracy. With this paranoid explanation, Hitler held out an enabling promise: "If you will follow me, you will realize your true greatness and achieve happiness." Without this encouraging paranoid explanation, Hitler would not have won over his audience. He merged this hopeful message, moreover, with both conventional and extraordinary political abilities—resilience, a good memory, an ability to evaluate what people wanted or feared, a facility in intimidation, charm in personal encounters, and a talent for public speaking and self-advertisement. But the power of his leadership derived from the image he projected, with consummate skill, of himself as rescuer. With high drama, he promised to save the German nation from its distress.

Glory, Eric Hoffer notes, is largely a theatrical concept.[69] The leader, in striving to realize his dreams of glory, always has in mind an audience to his heroic performance. Hitler was masterful in his manipulation of audiences. It was in the frequent public rallies that Hitler's complex charismatic appeal was most evident. In today's age of television it may be difficult to realize the emotional effect of the living presence not only of the leader but also of the members of the audience.

Rallies were scheduled for early evening, when the audience would be psychologically susceptible, tired from work and a little hungry. Patriotic and emotional songs were sung as twilight descended. When it was nearly time for Hitler to arrive, the coming of his plane would be announced, and the crowd would look up in the heavens, searching for him and cheering when they saw the plane. Singing would begin again. After a while it would be announced that the Führer was on the autobahn and approaching. Again cheers and revival of spirit. At last his arrival outside the stadium would be announced, and silence would fall, with all waiting. Just as the crowd was getting restless, the gates would open, the lights would come up on the central field, and Hitler would sweep in, standing in his Mercedes-Benz, with motorcycle escort. He would mount the rostrum and then stand alone in the huge stadium, with the only spotlight in use riveted on him.

It was at this point, when the audience expected a histrionic and florid speech, that Hitler was most effective. He appeared small, even defenseless. He would begin to speak in a low voice, barely audible. He would seem to be musing to himself as if the crowd were not there. He told his audience, now leaning forward as one, of experiences he had had—of the afternoon when he had seen a cold and nearly frozen motorcyclist with wife and small child crammed in a sidecar because they could not afford an automobile; of the fall day when his sergeant began to cry when he learned that Germany had surrendered, had lost the war, while its armies were still standing in the field. These anecdotes tied Hitler to his audience; they sensed that he was one of them, that he understood and felt as they did. Slowly and much later the speech would reach the maniacal crescendo that is so often shown in films, but it was during the quiet soliloquy that he bonded the audience to him and called for help, even for sympathy. It was in the frenzied zenith of the speech that the paranoid message was delivered—the "why" of Germany's condition, the identification of the enemy, and the call for their destruction.

Among Hitler's techniques was the suggestion that he was the underdog.[70] This clever tactic was made all the more effective by virtue of its perhaps being unconscious. It was also complementary to Hitler's paranoid appeal. The paranoid is always the underdog, always the victim.

Hitler was accurate when, in the early 1930s on an auto tour through the German countryside, he turned to his companion and said, "Heretofore only one German has been hailed like this: Luther. When he rode through the country, people gathered from far and wide to cheer him. As they do for me today!"[71] There was a potent connection between Hitler and the German people, a connection he fostered. It was a bond of charismatic force.

## Hitler's Charismatic Appeal

The concept of charisma can be traced to biblical times. In the Bible, charisma was always a gift from God and from God alone.[72] Charisma could be a private truth revealed to only one person so that he could better understand God's will, or it could be a truth enabling the hearer to lead others in a holy mission.

Moses, who in the Old Testament led the Hebrews out of Egypt and gave them the Ten Commandments, and John the Baptist, who in the New Testament predicted the coming of the Messiah, are examples of charismatic leaders. In each case the revealed truth promised relief from suffering. Because charisma was a gift bestowed by God, its recipients were blessed. This concept conformed with the pre-modern world in which religion was the fount of art, literature, and philosophy, the source of all goodness.

Early scholars of charisma attributed the phenomenon to unusual characteristics of the leader. Max Weber, the nineteenth-century German social theorist, defined the modern use of the term. Observing that in a secular age the extraordinary no longer had to be traced to God, he wrote that charismatic authority exists when people willingly submit to a person whom they believe has extraordinary qualities.[73] The charismatic's followers view him as superhuman, blindly believe whatever he says, unconditionally follow his orders, and give him unqualified emotional support.[74]

The bond between the charismatic leader and his followers can have deep and diverse sources. Most charismatic leaders use only one of these sources. Hitler simultaneously drew on four of the most forceful:

- that of a parent or lover who gives love and reassurance to his children or loved one and receives love and reassurance from them—the charisma of nurturance and dependency;
- that of a demonic figure who does what the followers wish they could do but are inhibited from doing—the charisma of the outrageous;
- that of a teacher who guides his pupils to achieve what they desire—the charisma of the ideal self;
- that of a leader who assumes the responsibility for determining for

his followers what is good and what is evil—the charisma of moral certainty.[75]

Crucial to Hitler's political success was his ability to appeal to people in ways that they did not expect, to strike unanticipated emotional chords. Being able to appeal on multiple levels simultaneously magnified the power of Hitler's charisma.

## The Paranoid as Charismatic Lover and Loved One

Hitler was able to gain not only the respect of many of those who saw him in public and in private, but also a type of love or a desire to nurture him. And he was not only the nurturing parent and the defenseless child to his followers; he was also the lover. This status was certainly not won through a prepossessing physical appearance. If anything, Hitler looked mousy. It was his message, his position, and the political theater that surrounded him that gave him his erotized appeal.[76] Hitler said that the good speaker should always treat an audience as if it were a woman. Sometimes this woman was a mother to whom he appealed for protection and love, but sometimes she was a lover to be seduced. Hitler produced, directed, and starred in a theater of seduction. At first the powerful man showed himself in a public arena as being worthwhile, then the same man quietly subordinated himself in private humility, seeking and then receiving the woman's surrender. His rallies were bonding events, part political ceremony, part theater, part symbolic consummation.

Hitler combined these diverse appeals, which were in some ways contradictory, and addressed them to both men and women. The image of Hitler as vulnerable object is difficult to imagine today, but it was present. Diana Mitford Mosley, wife of the British fascist leader Sir Oswald Mosley and member of the politically prominent Mitford family, had fallen under Hitler's charismatic spell. She was not, however, a mindless follower. In her memoirs, published from the perspective of a different era, she notes: "The truth is that in private life he [Hitler] was exceptionally charming, clever, and original, and that he inspired affection. He also inspired fear, perhaps, but he was essentially one of those rare beings who make people want to please them, want to work for them, eager to sacrifice. He identified himself with Germany and this identification was accepted by his countrymen. In his make-up there was both pride and a modesty, even vulnerability, which aroused chivalrous feelings, a very powerful motive force. His public appearances, his speeches, had this dual effect which must have come from something in his personality; they excited to action while at the same time arousing a deep desire to protect and cherish. He probably appealed in equal measure to women and to exactly the sort of men he needed.''[77] Hitler was even more effective in evoking these emotions publicly than privately. To a remarkable degree he combined the images of the mysterious erotized leader, the powerful father figure, the caring mother, and the vulnerable child.

### The Paranoid as Charismatic Embodiment of the Outrageous

To the extent that the Nazi movement exhibited a charisma of the outrageous, it was manifested principally in the use of pagan symbolism. This un-Christian activity was particularly strong among some members of the elite. Within the Nazi elite there existed an active, though semi-secret, cosmology based in part on the Cather (''pure'') heresy of the Middle Ages. The Cathers had strong non-Christian roots and were accused of blood sacrifices.[78]

The charisma of the outrageous also came from the direct appeal that something known to be evil has for many. Much of the attraction of Hitler today is of this nature, based on the atrocities committed by the Nazis. Was some part of Hitler's appeal in his rise to power based on a foreshadowing of what he would do? Were the policies of aggression and genocide evident in his program? Did the theater of the torchlit rallies, the use of massed images of eagles, the militarization of the society call upon some collective destructive unconscious? We believe it did.

Some sensed Hitler's evil designs and were attracted, and some sensed them and were repelled. Many did not detect them at all. Those who are not attracted to the paranoid charismatic do not take him or his doctrines seriously. Charismatic paranoids like Hitler have a bizarre quality to nonbelievers, both in their style and in their paranoid beliefs. Nonbelievers found it incredible that anyone would follow such an absurd man as Hitler, and if the masses were to follow him, surely the leaders must know better—his message was just a sham, an act to fool the foolish that would be dropped once he came to power.

The leaders of the Social Democratic Party of Germany (Hitler's principal democratic opposition, and a party in which 10 percent of the leaders were Jews) believed that the Nazi leadership and their associates were cynical in advocating anti-Semitism—that they did not believe in it. The Nazis, the SDP leaders believed, "were too intelligent to believe in such racist nonsense. Only a minority thought it likely that Jews would be subject to severe persecution in the event of a Nazi take-over, and none sensed that the Nazis might eventually resort to genocide."[79]

## The Paranoid as Teacher

One of the most important functions of the leader is to create meaning for his followers, who are lost and overwhelmed. This diagnostic sense-making provides clarity in the midst of confusion, a prescription for action in the midst of paralysis. When the leader suggests a clear path out of the chaos, it is of great relief to the followers. But the path may be one of healing and peace or one of hatred and aggression.

The bearer of the paranoid message is first of all a teacher. He comes with information that he believes to be of vital importance to his audience; he "teaches" them that their problems are due to the hostility and conspiracy of others. He then instructs them to destroy those others.

Both the charismatic and the paranoid claim to know something very important that others do not—something that enables them to understand the world immeasurably better. Hitler's "truth" was the genetic superiority of the Aryan people and the evil and conspiratorial role of Jews in frustrating the exercise of that superiority. Although he referred to various works of history and biology, his real claim was not that he had derived this "truth" from scholarly study but that he was personally infallible.[80] His valet commented that Hitler was always irritated if anyone suggested that he could not foresee the future. Hitler firmly believed that Providence had chosen him, and he propounded this belief with unshakable confidence.[81]

Hitler also had a genius for simplification.[82] Conspiracy has a great appeal as an explanation because it is a mental form of one-stop shopping. Once one accepts the paranoid explanation, so many other things seem to fall into place. In this perverted sense, paranoia follows the scientific principle of parsimony: "Three hundred men who know one another dominate the world."[83] The paranoid explanation also resonates with the human ability to find conspiracy where it exists and to suspect it where it may not. Thus, it not only explains, it confirms what many had always suspected.

The essential quality of the paranoid theme in Hitler's ideology can be seen by comparing Nazism to its predecessor, Mussolini's fascism. Mussolini's fascism was harmful, but not nearly to the degree of Hitler's Nazism. In part the difference can be traced to the rigor of Nazism's Germanic context.[84] But far more important was the paranoid dimension of Nazism. Mussolini did not identify conspiracy as the motive force in history, nor did he trace Italy's problems to a racial cabal.

## The Paranoid as Charismatic Moral Leader

Every charismatic is imbued with a touch of the sacred; his followers believe that he possesses a special ability to determine what is right and wrong. It is not that Hitler and his followers lacked a sense of right and wrong. Quite the contrary. They had a keen sense, but a perverted one. They believed that the millenarian perfection they sought excused any action in gaining it.

The extraordinary quality of the leader endowed with charismatic powers by his followers is at its greatest when it is manifested, as it was with Moses, in a salvationist truth revealed to a distressed community.[85] Hitler's salvationist message, his "remarkable truth," was that human perfection could be achieved through racial purity.

Hitler's paranoid description of the world as a battleground between absolute good and absolute evil, with the destruction of evil leading to earthly perfection, came to define his followers' moral universe. Their enemies were so evil and the end to be reached so good that any action against the evil ones would be not only legitimate but morally required. Sadism and callousness were common among the perpetrators of the Holocaust, and other Germans were profoundly repulsed by what they were doing, yet the followers persevered because they believed their actions were necessary for the greater good as defined by Hitler.

Arthur Koestler describes the same situation in Stalin's Soviet Union in his novel *Darkness at Noon*, in which the leading character, Rubaschov, is persuaded that Stalin's mass murders are historically progressive, a form of "social vivisection." "History will absolve me" is a phrase associated with Hitler, but it is the moral basis for the immorality of all such regimes. The charismatic leader draws the boundaries of morality, and his followers yield their moral compass to him. What he defines as moral is moral; those whom he defines as evil are evil. It becomes a moral imperative to eliminate those who are responsible for the decay in society.

Hitler had always seen himself as a leader with a moral mission. Early in his career, he saw himself as a harbinger of someone else's moral leadership; he was playing John the Baptist to some as yet unarrived Christ.[86] His confidant, Albert Speer, wrote that Hitler viewed himself, and wanted others to see him, as the founder of a religion more than as a political leader. Hitler's use of the term *Thousand-Year Reich* was deliberately chosen for its overtones of millenarian greatness.[87] In an unconscious irony, Hitler even compared himself to Jesus when criticizing Jews.[88]

Hitler was aware of this morally legitimating aspect of his charismatic appeal, and at times he mused on his moral legacy. Perhaps the most remarkable mis-evaluation of the twentieth century was made late on the night of September 28–29, 1941: "Thank God," Hitler remarked, "I have always avoided persecuting my enemies."[89] It was his charisma of the sacred that endowed him with the ability to convince others, and himself, that they could do no wrong in the pursuit of a higher moral cause: restoring Germany to its former greatness. Yielding their own individual sense of morality and responsibility, provided with a legitimating channel for their own projected hate and aggression, Nazi officials, civil and military, committed the unspeakable atrocities of the Holocaust. Without Hitler's religious charisma, the self-restraints that act, though imperfectly, in wartime would have been more in evidence. The paranoid dynamic, however, leaves no room for gray areas; no room for rivals, only for enemies; no room for compromise, only for destruction.

Because the leader takes on complete moral responsibility for his people, he is difficult to remove. For how can one remove the person one acknowledges as the source of all morality? More important, the leader becomes the conduit for his followers' hatred and aggression. As the mass movement of hatred swells, the liberated followers exult as they destroy and are freed from the restraint of conscience, for the leader has declared their acts to be a moral good. Without elevating ideology to the level of a sacred cause, it is difficult to persuade followers to yield their lives. But to die for a holy cause is ennobling, and Hitler's explicit identification of himself as a religious leader with a sacred cause was critical to the power of his leadership.

None of these forms of charisma derives from the leader alone. Rather, these powerful bonds reflect a psychological fit between leader and follower.

## Hypnotic Leader and Wounded Nation

Much has been written about the power of Hitler's charismatic leadership, but to understand this destructive movement we must look beyond the individual and examine the lock-and-key fit between Hitler and his followers. However impressive Hitler's rhetorical gifts or political skills, however sincere his convictions, however driven his projected hatred, how can we explain his capacity to mobilize the nation, to place the German body politic under his charismatic spell? Hitler composed the score and conducted the orchestra of death before a rapt audience. The nation enabled his rise to power, was co-creator of the Third Reich, and participated in this destructive charismatic movement.

Charisma is not a special quality that a person has but, rather, a powerful relationship between leader and follower that tends to occur at moments of historical crisis. We should not speak of charismatic leaders but rather of charismatic leader-follower relationships.[90] The leader and the led each finds a psychological need fulfilled in the other. At the core, the charismatic relationship is one between a wounded individual, a mirror-hungry personality who under his grandiose facade thirsts for recognition and adulation, and ideal-hungry followers, who seek an all-wise, all-powerful leader who has the answers and can lead them out of the desert of their distress. But at times of social crisis, otherwise psychologically independent individuals, temporarily overwhelmed by societal disintegration, seek a strong leader to rescue them. They swell the numbers of the followership, transforming a small organization into a mass movement.

When a nation is wounded, it seeks—indeed, may create—a charismatic leader to rescue it from its distress. These moments of crisis offer a choice. A reparative charismatic, like Gandhi or Martin Luther King, can help to heal the nation's wounds, peacefully resolving the divisions within his country. But societies in great distress are especially vulnerable to the paranoid appeal of the destructive charismatic. At these times, the people, unable to cope, look to a strong leader and are ready to believe that there is an external cause for their difficulties. The politically gifted paranoid leader, like Hitler or Khomeini, can provide a sense-making conspiratorial explanation to his followers, one that provides solace but can fuel genocidal violence.

In the wake of World War I, Germany was suffering from major social and economic dislocations as the consequence of the harsh conditions of the Treaty of Versailles. The economy was in shambles, characterized by hyperinflation and fathers unable to provide for their families. The climate was one of despair.

Germany had not only suffered more than most countries in the Great Depression but had also experienced great distress during the 1920s, when most other countries had prospered. German youth, having been seriously deprived as a consequence of World War I, were especially vulnerable to Hitler's promises of restored greatness. Many of the German youth raised during World War I were raised without fathers, who were either away at the front or killed in battle. Such an experience can produce an idealization of the absent father, a searching for a strong, powerful, nurturing figure. Moreover, widespread unemployment led to fewer opportunities for apprenticeships and entry-level jobs.[91] Thus Germany's youth was needy both psychologically and economically.

Hitler and his inner circle intuitively understood this and appealed directly to youth through such slogans as "National Socialism is the organized will of youth." The approach worked. Those aged eighteen to thirty constituted 31 percent of the German population of 1933, but they represented 42 percent of the National Socialist German Workers' Party. By contrast, the Social Democratic Party reported that less than 8 percent of their membership was under twenty-five and less than half was under forty.[92]

It can be argued that the nation would have responded to any leader who healed the nation's wounds, who brought it together. The tragedy was that the most politically effective person available was Adolf Hitler, who found the German polity ripe for his paranoid psychology. If the German people did not require a paranoid leader with hatred of the Jews as a central value, Hitler did require the canvas of the wounded German people upon which to paint his vision of hatred. Jews were not the inevitable victims. It required a politically skillful charismatic leader with a paranoid ideology and a personal hatred of Jews to make them such. That is to say, it required Hitler.

Some individuals undergoing major stress deal with painful reality by relying on the primitive defenses of denial, distortion, and projection, and so they retain some temporary serenity by escaping from reality—the paranoid "solution." Still others fall into paralytic depression. The psychologically mature individual accepts the pain and adapts to reality. An effective therapist helps his patients to recognize and deal with painful reality, to take responsibility for shortcomings, and to master loss, making fleeing from reality unnecessary.

Hitler was a malign therapist to his German patients. The German people were in genuine distress. They had been humiliated in war, had suffered terrible economic reversals, and faced a disintegrating society. The Democratic Socialists were ineffectual, and the Bolsheviks offered a future even more hellish than what the Germans had already experienced. Hitler's paranoid ideology found a people all too willing to accept it. It "explained" their plight by blaming others and offered them a "treatment" that required the destruction of those others.

Paranoid teacher, sense-making leader, malign therapist, physician to the ailing German body politic—in these roles Hitler identified a pathway to redemption for the wounded German people. They eagerly embraced his paranoid message, and together they created one of the most evil chapters in the history of mankind.

# 12

## Concluding Note

Although clinical paranoia is associated with severe mental illness, the readiness to blame others for our misfortune is deeply rooted in human nature. Political paranoia is widespread in every society, especially in those undergoing rapid change.

How preferable it is to exult righteously in a full-throated roar of hatred of the enemies conspiring to destroy us rather than to acknowledge the humiliation of helplessness. The political paranoid's identification of the enemies responsible for our collective misery provides a deceptively comforting explanation for our problems. Worse, the paranoid call sanctions a ''solution'': the destruction of an ''enemy.'' This message has recurrently bred mass murder—political in the Soviet Union and Uganda, genocidal in Germany and Cambodia.

The would-be leader propagating a paranoid theme in a time of tranquillity will appeal only to a small audience. Even in a time of stress such an appeal will fail if the leader lacks conventional political skills. But when the politically skillful leader or propagandist with a persuasive paranoid message calls to an overwhelmed society, the conditions are ripe for a violent and widespread response. As we have demonstrated in these pages, behind every destructive mass movement of this, history's blood-iest century, are the dark forces of political paranoia.

Hitler's charismatic force, for example, and the dogmatic certainty and simplicity of his paranoid diagnosis of Germany's plight, met the needs of a wounded nation desperately seeking a leader who was strong and powerful and knew the answers to their many problems. The lock-and-key fit between Hitler and his followers opened a gate into the horrors of World War II and the Holocaust. This was political paranoia of Wag-nerian proportions, engulfing the globe in carnage. The same chorus is singing today, with different members and at different places but voicing the same dissonant chant—racial mob violence and hate crimes in the United States, religious persecution in Bangladesh, genocidal slaughter in Rwanda and Burundi, and "ethnic cleansing" in Bosnia.

One might think that the resolution of any major international conflict would be a blessing. But we need our enemies. They provide a comforting explanation of what is wrong with ourselves. Their loss removes the ex-ternal focus for our difficulties. This loss of enemies has contributed to the post–Cold War explosion of ethnic and nationalist tension, of increas-ing prejudice and hatred, of internal disorder and terrorism. Long-muted hatreds have surfaced, stimulated by paranoid leaders and paranoid doc-trines, malign therapists offering deceptively sense-making prescriptions of hate to wounded populations.

There are still-locked rooms with their stores of atrocities. We are not speaking of the chambers of horror already open and richly displayed in the morning newspaper or on the evening news. We are cautioning about societies that are prosperous but undergoing stress, with substantial and growing inequalities of social condition: societies like Russia in 1917 or Mexico or Indonesia today. We are pointing to racially, ethnically, and religiously diverse societies like India, where beneath the deceptively qui-escent surface are dangerous, potentially destabilizing tensions. It was not so long ago that Sarajevo was a thriving, multiethnic metropolis with an appearance of peaceful harmony. These diverse multiethnic societies are especially at risk, for in the face of social and economic distress, or the dissolution of legitimate government authority, hate-mongering leaders trumpeting a divisive paranoid message can exploit the underlying ten-sions with violent and tragic consequences. Nor is the United States immune to such dangers. As witnessed by the increase of hate crimes and the bombing of the federal building in Oklahoma City, it can happen here, and already has.

This book offers no prescription against paranoia, for something so deeply rooted in the human condition cannot be eliminated. We can, however, be alert to the danger political paranoia poses. To be indifferent to early expressions of the paranoid mobilization of hatred is to be complicit with evil. Unnoted, the paranoid propensity can fester, and exploited, it can erupt into the psychopolitics of hatred.

# Notes

### Introduction

1. A. Shapiro 1992, p. 63.
2. Volkogonov 1994, pp. 425–427.
3. This book is the product of over a decade of professional collaboration on the topic of politics and paranoia. Earlier publications include Post and Robins 1993 and Robins and Post 1987, which grew out of our numerous professional papers and presentations. Each of us has also published independently in this area. See, for example, Post, "Notes," 1984; Post, "Hostilité," 1986; Post 1990; Robins, "Psychopathology," 1977; Robins, "Pathological Deviants," 1977; Robins 1986.
4. This description is drawn from *DSM IV: The Diagnostic and Statistical Manual of Mental Disorders of the American Psychiatric Association* (Washington, D.C.: American Psychiatric Association, 1994), pp. 637–638.
5. Bleuler 1950.
6. Although it is true that both men and women suffer from paranoia, in this book the masculine pronoun is used to refer to individual paranoids, reflecting both our desire for brevity and also the fact that every political paranoid discussed in this work is male.
7. Freedman, Kaplan, and Saddock 1972, p. 250.
8. Akhtar 1990, p. 18.
9. Bruck 1996, p. 96.

### 1
### The Mind of the Paranoid

1. Houseman 1990, p. 176.
2. Kovar 1966.
3. D. Shapiro 1967.
4. In his initial considerations of paranoia, Sigmund Freud conceptualized it as an intellectual disorder, grouping it with obsessional disorders, an intellectual psychosis. Seeing paranoia as a pathological defense, Freud indicated, "People become paranoiac over things that they cannot put up with, provided

that they possess the peculiar psychical disposition for it." Freud [1892–1899] 1966, pp. 206–207.

5. Arieti 1959, p. 478.
6. Von Domarus 1944.
7. Cameron, "Paranoid Conditions," 1959, p. 518.
8. Knight 1940, pp. 149–159.
9. Akhtar 1990; M. J. Hamilton 1974; D. Shapiro 1967.
10. D. Shapiro 1967, pp. 73–88.
11. Fromm 1975.
12. Renshon 1974.
13. Meissner 1978, p. 4.
14. D. Shapiro 1967, pp. 69–71.
15. Bonime 1979.
16. Rosen and Kiene 1947.
17. Akhtar 1990.
18. Kovar 1966, p. 297.
19. Blum 1981, pp. 789–813; Kernberg 1975; D. Shapiro 1967.
20. H. S. Sullivan 1956.
21. Meissner 1979.
22. Murray 1964.
23. Meissner 1979, pp. 532–533.
24. Waite 1971.
25. Meissner 1978, pp. 50–53; Rothstein 1964, 1965, 1971.
26. Salzman 1960.
27. Tausk [1919] 1948.
28. Citizens for LaRouche 1980.
29. Tucker 1965.
30. Ambrose 1987, p. 32.
31. Ambrose 1987, p. 618; Greenstein 1977, p. 80.
32. Lemert 1972.
33. Aitkin 1993, p. 115.
34. Aitkin 1993, pp. 129, 130.
35. Ambrose 1987, pp. 218, 297.
36. Greenstein 1977, p. 83.
37. White 1962, p. 338.
38. Walter Reich 1980.
39. Stalstrom 1980, pp. 149–150.
40. Dickinson 1976, p. 209.
41. D. Martin 1980.
42. D. Martin 1980; Mangold 1991.

2

**Paranoid Culture and Conspiracy Thinking**

1. Hofstadter 1967, p. 9.
2. Hofstadter 1967, p. 8.

3. Hofstadter 1967, p. 8.

4. Hofstadter 1967, p. 7.

5. We observe in Chapter 8 that one need not be paranoid to exploit a paranoid message. McCarthy's demons were ones of reckless opportunism rather than paranoia. But he found the political moment ripe for a paranoid message and rode the Communist witch hunt with unconstrained demagoguery.

6. Glass 1985.

7. Vovelle 1982.

8. Chartier 1982.

9. Chartier 1982.

10. Darnton 1985.

11. L. B. Smith 1986.

12. Understanding conspiracy was, not surprisingly, the foremost route to Tudor political power: Thomas More and William Tyndale gained their reputation for political sagacity by being analysts of conspiracy.

13. L. B. Smith 1986, p. 139.

14. Although paranoia permeated the entire society, its ruler, Elizabeth, was not paranoid. Given the circumstances, she was as trusting as she could be and had Essex executed only when he committed treason one time too many.

15. Cohn [1957] 1961.

16. Cohn [1957] 1961, p. 75.

17. Cohn 1975.

18. C. Hansen 1971, pp. 59–60.

19. See Thomas 1971 for a comprehensive study of the relation between magic and religion in this period.

20. C. Hansen 1971, p. 119.

21. Rosenthal 1993, p. 50.

22. Weisman 1984, pp. 17, 135. Strictly speaking, the doctrines surrounding witchcraft included no reason why witches were more likely to be women than men. In practice, however, women were seen as being morally weaker than men, more driven by sexual appetite, and thus more likely to give way to the devil's temptations. During the panic the primary suspect was typically a woman, with a man as accomplice. Demos 1982, pp. 60, 62.

23. Levin 1952, p. 12.

24. Rosenthal 1993, p. 7. The judges differed on whether "spectral evidence" (reports of seeing spirits, especially when others present could not see them) should be admitted. On reconvening, the judges agreed to consider reports that a figure looking like the accused had tormented the afflicted, but they would not consider such evidence conclusive without corroboration. The devil, they believed, could take the shape of an innocent person. Reluctance to accept firsthand accounts of spectral evidence was well established. Although there was near-universal belief in witchcraft, the public as well as courts were suspicious of specific allegations.

25. Godbeer 1992, p. 204.

26. Godbeer 1992, p. 203.

27. Godbeer 1992, p. 203.

28. Demos 1982, p. 71.

29. Godbeer 1992, p. 205.
30. Weisman 1984, p. 136.
31. Cohn 1981.
32. Demos 1982, pp. 78–79.
33. Demos 1982.
34. Demos 1982, p. 86.
35. Quoted in Godbeer 1992, p. 173.
36. Demos 1982, pp. 79–84.
37. *Records* 1864, pp. 172–180.
38. Demos 1982, pp. 84–86.
39. Boyer and Nissenbaum 1974.
40. Boyer and Nissenbaum 1974, pp. 80–109.
41. Quoted in Godbeer 1992, p. 198.
42. Demos 1982, p. 72.
43. Demos 1982, p. 73.
44. Demos 1982, pp. 78–79.
45. Benedict 1934.
46. Benedict 1934, p. 172.
47. Benedict 1934, pp. 172, 151.
48. LeVine 1973, p. vii ff.
49. Cole et al. 1971, p. 213.
50. Linton 1956.
51. Savage, Leighton, and Leighton 1965.
52. Draguns 1980; Lonner 1979.
53. Another example of such pervasive distrust may be found in the Andean region of Colombia, which has suffered decades of conflict between Protestants and Catholics. This conflict, called La Violencia, has become intertwined with many social and political issues. It has resulted in two societies, Catholic and Protestant, each paranoid not only toward the other but internally as well. Houses are built in such a way that visitors must reveal themselves well in advance, agricultural systems are so arranged that cultivation and harvest may be carried out in semi-secrecy, and social relations, even within families, are tainted by mistrust. Schor 1974.
54. Cited in Pipes 1989, p. 18. Pipes's *Hidden Hand: Middle East Fears of Conspiracy* (1996) was published too late to receive here the recognition it deserves. Containing a wealth of examples, it is the best analysis of this phenomenon in the Middle East.
55. Laffin 1975, pp. 169–170.
56. Laffin 1975, p. 166.
57. Quoted in Pipes 1991, p. 27.
58. Pipes 1991, p. 29.
59. Quoted in Zonis and Joseph 1994, p. 445.
60. Popham 1994.
61. Cited in Pipes 1989, p. 24.
62. Cited in Zonis and Joseph 1994, p. 446.
63. Pipes 1983, p. 184.

64. This section draws significantly upon Bar Tal and Antebi 1989.
65. Bar Tal 1986.
66. Bar Tal and Antebi 1988.
67. Quoted in Bar Tal and Antebi 1988, p. 3.
68. Gothelf 1970, cited in Bar Tal and Antebi 1988, pp. 14–15.
69. *Newsweek,* March 13, 1973, cited in Bar Tal and Antebi 1988, p. 15.
70. *Newsweek,* January 25, 1989, cited in Bar Tal and Antebi 1988, p. 16.
71. Pastor 1988, p. 91.
72. Pastor 1988, p. 91.
73. Castañeda 1988, pp. 63–69.
74. Castañeda 1988, pp. 67, 68.
75. Pye 1985, p. 46.
76. Pye 1985, p. 242.
77. Pye 1985, p. 293.
78. Pye 1985, p. 259.
79. Levinson 1992; McMillen 1994; "No Man" 1994; Turner 1994. It has been suggested that these beliefs are to be taken not literally but as a metaphor for the suffering that blacks have experienced (Lance Hill, interview, April 2, 1996).
80. Lefkowitz 1993. We acknowledge that every people, every race, every religion will tend to emphasize its contributions. The point here is the charge of a conscious conspiracy; that charge puts the belief over the paranoid line.
81. Levinson 1992, p. A19.
82. Quoted in Levinson 1992, p. A19.
83. Quoted in Levinson 1992, p. A19.
84. See also see Bates 1990; Cooper 1990.
85. Thomas and Quinn 1991, p. 1499, as quoted in Goertzel 1995; Levinson 1992, p. A19.
86. Goertzel 1995, p. 734.
87. Quoted in Athill 1987, p. ix.
88. McMillen 1994.
89. DeParle 1993, sec. 4, p. 1.
90. C. Sullivan 1993, p. A4.
91. T. Friedman 1989, p. 30.
92. T. Friedman 1989, pp. 42, 43.
93. Holsti 1967.
94. Holsti 1967.

3
**The Roots of Paranoia**

1. Gould 1990, p. 34.
2. Alexander 1987, pp. 63–65, 70.
3. Alexander 1979, pp. 58–65; Barash 1982, chap. 9; Bonner 1980, pp. 96–102; G. Johnson 1995, p. 252.
4. G. Johnson 1995, pp. 252–254.
5. Alexander 1987, pp. 63–65.

6. W. D. Hamilton 1964.
7. R. R. Dawkins 1976; Krebs and Dawkins 1984; M. J. Smith 1972, 1974, 1976, 1979, 1983, 1986.
8. Trivers 1985, p. 85.
9. Krebs and Davies 1984; see esp. Krebs and Dawkins 1984.
10. Gazzaniga 1992, p. 90.
11. Krebs and Dawkins 1984, pp. 380–381.
12. Krebs and Dawkins 1984.
13. Humphrey 1976.
14. Krebs and Dawkins 1984, p. 389.
15. Alexander 1987, esp. pp. 73–74.
16. These observations on the evolutionary theory of social cooperation are drawn from a personal communication from Roger Masters, October 5, 1995.
17. Trivers 1985, p. 57.
18. Byrne and Whitten 1988; Cheney and Seyfarth 1981, 1990; DeWaal 1982; Packer 1977; Thornhill 1979.
19. Trivers 1985, p. 395.
20. Cited in Gazzaniga 1992, p. 119.
21. MacLean 1990.
22. Van Buren, Li, and Ojemann 1966.
23. MacLean 1990, p. 139.
24. P. Kramer 1993, pp. 301–303.
25. P. Kramer 1993, pp. 144–249.
26. This section draws heavily on Meissner 1978.
27. Spitz 1965.
28. Wilhelm Reich 1949.
29. Vaillant 1993, p. 36. Drawing on the work of Elvin Semrad, Vaillant has played a major role in clarifying the hierarchical organization of ego defenses. The most primitive defenses, characteristic of certain ages and of individuals vulnerable to psychosis—and of regressive psychotic states—are denial, distortion, and delusional projection. At a higher level of functioning are the immature defenses: projection, fantasy, hypochondriasis, passive aggression, acting out, and dissociation. Projection, the sine qua non of paranoia, is a key defense mechanism at both the most primitive psychotic level and the immature level. The intermediate or neurotic defenses comprise displacement, isolation/intellectualization, repression, and reaction formation. The mature defenses include altruism, sublimation, suppression, anticipation, and humor.
30. Freud [1892–1899] 1966, p. 207.
31. Klein uses the term *objects* to refer not only to persons and physical objects but also to such abstract concepts as capitalism and racial homogeneity. According to Klein, we all have these "objects" in our minds (the idea of capitalism, the idea of the president), and to the extent that our behavior is determined by psychological forces, it is determined by the nature and relations of these mental objects. Kleinian theory, for this reason, is called object relations theory.
32. Klein [1932] 1960, 1952, 1957, 1964.
33. Clinical studies of young children confirm this primitive splitting of the me and

the not-me, and the identification of the not-me with the enemy. Hundreds of four- to six-year-old American and West German children were asked to draw pictures of enemies (Hesse and Poklemba 1988; also see Keen 1986). Enemies were depicted as different in appearance from the children. For example, they lacked a body part or had too many body parts, such as additional arms. The enemies were also seen as strong and angry. In follow-up interviews the children were asked to describe the enemies further. According to the children, enemies are born bad; they cannot become good. The children themselves, they said, could never be enemies.

34. Money-Kyrle 1951, pp. 52–53, 159.
35. Klein 1955, p. 311.
36. Bacal and Newman 1990, pp. 64–66.
37. A. Freud, [1936] 1966, p. 122.
38. Rochlin 1973, p. 176.
39. Meissner 1978, p. 12.
40. Meissner 1986, p. 253.
41. "The use of 'projection,' together with a 'denial' of destructiveness, are among the most developed of early childhood defenses. They are the unconscious means, beginning in childhood and carried forward into adult life, by which we may disengage ourselves from being concerned over wishes and impulses which are a source of conflict. To attribute disquieting aims to others and thus unwittingly deny one's egocentric wishes and . . . aggressive inclinations . . . affords a measure of relief. Under these conditions, a child's fear of what might happen to him, a blameless victim of circumstances, are apt to become prominent." Rochlin 1973, p. 165.
42. Alford 1989, p. 43.
43. Post and Semrad 1965.
44. Winnicott 1965.
45. Maltsberger and Buie 1980.
46. James [1902] 1960, pp. 162, 176.
47. Meissner 1986, pp. 321–322.
48. Post and Semrad 1965.
49. Grotstein 1987.
50. Grotstein 1987.
51. Ostow 1994.
52. Freud [1911] 1958.
53. Freud [1911] 1958, p. 11.
54. Alford 1994.
55. Bion 1961; Colman and Bexton 1975; Colman and Geller 1985; Rutan and Stone 1993. Wilfred Bion's work moves systematically from the clinical to the organizational setting. See Bion 1955 and Rioch 1971. Elliot Jaques has devoted his career to the psychological analysis of organizations. A major paper that reflects the Kleinian influence is "Social Systems as a Defense Against Persecutory and Depressive Anxiety" (Jaques 1957).
56. Bion 1961; Rioch 1971; Rioch [1971] 1975.
57. Bion (1961) made important contributions to the understanding of the powerful

effects of group psychology that have become the foundation of group relations theory and practice, as developed at the Tavistock Institute of Human Relations in London. His insights are more illuminating than his language, which is often dense and abstruse. The reader interested in pursuing how Bion's insights have been applied to the study of organizational pathology will find useful the papers collected in *Group Relations Reader 1* (Colman and Bexton 1975) and *Group Relations Reader 2* (Colman and Geller 1985). In Bion's terminology, when the group is pursuing its avowed task (such as conceptualizing a new curriculum or developing a business plan), it is functioning as a work group. When it seems to be operating under basic psychological assumptions, it is a basic assumption group. The descriptions of the three basic assumption groups identified by Bion are drawn from Rutan and Stone 1993.

58. Bion 1955, p. 448.
59. Hopper 1995.
60. Bion 1961, pp. 67, 123, 188.
61. Schiffer 1973.
62. Jaques 1965, p. 479.
63. Jaques 1965, p. 479. Analysis of the Glacier Corporation, a British manufacturer, provided persuasive evidence that identical mechanisms operated between labor and management—splitting, idealization, and projection of aggressive impulses against the other. Insofar as other members of the labor or management group shared the same feelings, drew upon the same reservoir, the shared distorted perceptions could not be subjected to critical scrutiny and so became "reality." What is compelling about this and similar analyses is the readiness of the organizational components to fall into extreme suspiciousness and aggressivity of near-psychotic proportions. See Jaques 1951, 1965.
64. Post 1987.
65. Hoffer [1951] 1966, p. 149.

4
**The Need for Enemies**

1. A pioneer in applying psychoanalytic analysis to the collective psychology of war is Fornari (1975). A major contributor to political psychology is the psychoanalyst Vamik Volkan. In his study *The Need to Have Enemies and Allies* (1988), Volkan traces the roots of international conflict to the crib, persuasively demonstrating that fear and hatred of the stranger are deeply rooted in the human psyche. The political anthropologist Howard Stein greatly influenced the social construction of nationalism and the "us-them" dichotomization with *Developmental Time, Cultural Space* (1987). The works of Fornari, Volkan, and Stein have strongly contributed to the conceptualization in this chapter.
2. Volkan 1988, p. 32.
3. Volkan 1988, pp. 32–33.
4. Volkan 1985, p. 236.
5. Stein 1987, p. 109.
6. Stein 1987, pp. 188–189.

7. Stein 1987, p. 193.
8. Stein 1987, p. 179.
9. Jaques 1957, p. 483.
10. Elias Canetti analogizes the crowd to forces of nature in *Crowds and Power* (1962, pp. 75–90).
11. Canetti 1962, pp. 75–80.
12. Frosch 1967.
13. See Canetti 1962, pp. 22–24, on the persecutory feelings of the social movement.
14. Quoted in Berindranath 1966.
15. Fromm 1941.
16. Hoffer [1951] 1966, p. 31.
17. Galanter 1980; Galanter, Rabkin, Rabkin, and Deutsch 1979.
18. Zonis 1984.
19. Alford 1989, p. 44.
20. Nechayev, *Catechism of the Revolutionist* (1869), quoted in Laqueur and Alexander 1987, pp. 68–72.
21. Rauschning, *Hitler Speaks* (New York, 1939), pp. 234–235, cited in Hoffer [1951] 1966, pp. 92–93.
22. The utility of the Jew in unifying hatred, and the expression of lament by the Japanese visitor, are cited in Hoffer [1951] 1966, p. 91.
23. Fornari 1975.
24. Hoffer [1951] 1966, pp. 59–60.
25. Hoffer [1951] 1966, p. 65. It must also be noted that the British were not willing to employ the brutal, much less the genocidal, means employed by the Nazis.
26. Pascal 1965, p. 277; Konrad Heiden, *Der Fuehrer* (Boston, 1944), cited in Hoffer [1951] 1966, p. 81.
27. Heifitz 1994.
28. Post, "Hostilité," 1986.
29. Post 1990.
30. Ferracuti 1982.
31. Sturm 1972, p. 57.
32. Spietel 1980, p. 35.
33. Baeyer-Kaette 1983.
34. Post 1990, p. 34.
35. Erikson 1968; Stein 1987, p. 181.
36. Eros 1991.
37. Eros 1991.
38. Poem, by anonymous author, recited on "All Things Considered," National Public Radio, November 1991.
39. Batkata 1989.
40. Harden 1990.
41. Brumberg 1991, p. 72.
42. Demoskop Research Agency 1991.
43. S. Nowotny, interview with JMP, November 1991, Warsaw. Other surveys found that the percentage of Poles who believed that Jews had too much influence in

Polish politics was as high as 60 percent (Ray Taras, personal communication, January 1996).

44. *Gazeta Wyborcza,* June 24, 1990, cited in Brumberg 1991.
45. Brinkley 1991, p. A5.
46. Foreign Broadcast Information Service–Eastern Europe Report, March 18, 1991.
47. Shafir 1991, pp. 24–25.
48. Shafir 1991, pp. 25–26.
49. Shafir 1991, pp. 25–26.
50. Champion 1991, p. A14.
51. Kamm 1991, p. 8.
52. Foreign Broadcast Information Service–Eastern Europe Report, March 18, 1991.
53. Hunčík 1992.
54. Schifter 1990.
55. Even though Jews rarely rose to senior levels, in fact Jews were represented in disproportionate numbers in the Communist Party. Both in the Soviet Union and the socialist nations of Eastern Europe, the prospect of eradicating expressions of nationalism meant the prospect of eradicating expressions of anti-Semitism. Of course, Jews also had impeccable anti-Nazi credentials. Thus it was that many Jews joined the Communist Party in the hope of finding asylum from persecution. Even today's minorities (including Jews) tend to vote for the former Communist parties because they pledge to protect minority rights.
56. Personal communication to JMP, November 1996.
57. Personal communication with a senior minister in the government of Czechoslovakia, November 1991.
58. One calculation has it that the anti-Semitic fringe received less than .5 percent of the vote in the 1993 Polish parliamentary elections. It may be that anti-Semitism is sufficiently defuse to make it impractical as a principle for any one political party to focus on.

5
**From the Individual to the Collective Apocalypse**

1. Ostow 1994, p. 226.
2. Ostow 1994, p. 227.
3. "Psychiatrist Rejects" 1979.
4. Zee 1980, p. 347.
5. Reiterman and Jacob 1982, p. 17.
6. Olsson 1994.
7. Maguire and Dunn 1978, p. 79.
8. Reiterman and Jacob 1982, pp. 40–41.
9. Zee 1980, p. 360; Klineman, Butler, and Conn 1980.
10. Wright 1993, p. 70.
11. Wright 1993, p. 70.
12. Wright 1993, p. 71.
13. Some alternative religious movements have relatively easy access and egress, and hence are considered "open." In others, powerful psychological pressures are

exerted to block exit from the group, making it difficult if not impossible to leave, and hence are considered "closed." Group dynamics are extremely powerful in the closed groups.

14. Goldberg 1996, cited in Olsson 1994, p. 94.
15. Reston 1981, p. 244.
16. Hall 1982.
17. Wright 1993, p. 75.
18. Larson 1993, p. 16.
19. Ulman and Abse 1983.
20. Lasaga 1980.
21. This profile draws primarily on investigative journalistic reports: Applebome 1993; Kantrowitz et al. 1993; Lacayo 1993; McGee and Claiborne 1993; Pressley 1993; Puente 1993; Verhovek 1993.
22. Verhovek 1993; Puente 1993.
23. McGee and Claiborne 1993.
24. McGee and Claiborne 1993, p. A19.
25. Kantrowitz et al. 1993, pp. 56–58.
26. Applebome 1993.
27. McGee and Claiborne 1993, p. A19.
28. Kantrowitz et al. 1993.
29. Jordan and Pressley 1993.
30. Kantrowitz et al. 1993.
31. Asahara 1988, pp. 86–87.
32. Asahara 1988, pp. 87, 90.
33. Strasser and Post 1995, p. 40.
34. Asahara 1988, p. 91.
35. Spaeth 1995, p. 57.
36. Strasser and Post 1995, p. 36.
37. Spaeth 1995, p. 57.
38. Asahara 1988, p. 93.
39. C. Smith 1995, p. 15.
40. The Chemical Arms Unit was headed by Masami Tsuchiya, who was reportedly working on a doctorate in organic chemistry at Tokyo University. In 1991 Tsuchiya wrote, "Asahara will be imprisoned in the 1990s, but his trial will prove the existence of supernatural power and all 100 million Japanese will become followers of Aum." Rafferty 1995, p. 19.
41. Campbell 1996.
42. Kiyoyasu 1995, p. 377.
43. Strasser and Post 1995, p. 41.
44. C. Smith 1995, p. 15.
45. The biographic material concerning Asahara draws on profiles by Sayle (1996), Reid ("Doomsday Guru," 1995), and Kristof ("Tokyo," 1995).
46. Reid, "Doomsday Guru," 1995.
47. K. Sullivan 1995.
48. WuDunn, "Japan Sect," 1995.
49. Reid, "Children," 1995.

50. WuDunn 1996 and "Ex-Cult Members," 1995.
51. "Japanese Find Dead Child" 1995.
52. Sayle 1996, pp. 64, 65.
53. Sayle 1996, p. 66.
54. Kristof, "Tokyo," 1995.
55. Kristof, "Japanese Indict," 1995.

6
## Killing in the Name of God

1. Hazani, in press.
2. Hazani, in press.
3. Quoted in Hazani, in press.
4. Juergensmeyer 1988, p. 179.
5. Hoffer [1951] 1966.
6. Pascal 1965, p. 277.
7. Bahrani 1994.
8. Lax 1994, p. 248.
9. Lax 1994, p. 253.
10. Haberman 1995.
11. Juergensmeyer 1988, pp. 178–179.
12. This section is particularly informed by the writings of John Esposito and Nicole O'Neill's unpublished manuscript, "Allahu Akbar: Islam and Political Violence."
13. Although *jihad,* in common parlance, is often taken to mean "holy war," the word comes from *jahada,* which means "to struggle in God's course," an obligation of all Muslims. Its most common meaning is "to propagandize and to proselytize." Sometimes this struggle is peaceful, sometimes violent (F. Robert Hunter, personal communication, October 1995). Also see J. A. Williams 1971, chap. 5. R. Martin (1987) asserts that *jihad* originally referred to struggle in the service of God in a variety of contexts, and the word's connotation of violent struggle is a late development. The extremity of violence in pursuit of the struggle is justified only by circumstances that override other usual constraints. Radical clerics, by diagnosing the circumstances as exceptional, provide a religious rationale for religiously sanctified violent struggle. It is at these "exceptional" times that the paranoid propensity is mobilized in Islamic civilizations. Hence the violent examples of jihad cited in this work on political paranoia, although we recognize that the religiously prescribed struggle or jihad is generally peaceful.
14. Esposito 1988, p. 24.
15. See Canetti 1962 for a discussion of Islam as a religion of war.
16. Qu'ran 56:12–37. All Qu'ranic quotations from *Islam* 1992.
17. Esposito 1988, pp. 169–170. But see Roy 1994, who distinguishes between the Islamist regimes (such as Iran), which seek to modernize and spread Islam through governments that are at once participatory and authoritarian, and traditional fundamentalist regimes (such as Saudi Arabia), which believe that pious government arises as a reflection of a godly society. Roy predicts the ultimate failure of the Islamist regimes, which are becoming what he calls neofundamen-

talist, an "Islam of resentment," that is already sinking into the cynicism and moral evasion characteristic of the last stages of all puritanical movements.

18. Taheri 1987, p. 34.
19. Cited in Taheri 1987, p. 17.
20. Taheri 1987, p. 32.
21. "Though God's promise of good is for all / He has granted His favour of the highest reward / to those who struggle / in preference to those who sit at home" (Qu'ran 4:95). Also see 47:4.
22. Zonis and Brumberg 1987.
23. Khomeini, June 20, 1983.
24. "Khomeini" 1987, p. 8.
25. Martin Kramer 1990.
26. Interview with Sadiq al-Musawi, al-Nahar al-arabi wal-duwali, July 28, 1986, cited in Martin Kramer 1990, p. 151.
27. Interview with Fadlallah, *Politique internationale* (Paris) 29 (Autumn 1985), p. 268, cited in Martin Kramer 1990, p. 145.
28. Jansen 1986.
29. Bernstein 1995.
30. The following analysis is drawn principally from Abu-Amir 1993 and Jubran and Drake 1993.
31. Quoted in Maqsdi 1993.
32. Quoted in Maqsdi 1993.
33. Quotations from the charter are taken from Taheri 1987.
34. After considerable negotiations, the PLO managed to effect an accommodation with Hamas, with the result that in the January 1996 election the PLO apparently temporarily brought Hamas under substantial control.
35. This section draws largely on Keppel 1994, pp. 154–170, and Sprinzak [1987] 1988.
36. Quoted in Aran 1988, pp. 263–264.
37. See the statement of one of the radicals, Yehuda Etzion, as quoted in Sprinzak [1987] 1988, p. 206.
38. Etzion 1984, p. 26, cited in Sprinzak [1987] 1988, p. 207.
39. Gideon Aran, cited in Keppel 1994, p. 168.
40. R. Friedman 1994, p. 54.
41. Osmer [1988] 1994, pp. C1, C4, from an interview with Baruch Goldstein in the spring of 1988, conducted by Ellen Osmer, editor-at-large for *Multinational Monitor*. The interview was conducted in the settlement of Kiryat Arba, on the outskirts of Hebron.
42. Berachot 58.
43. Kahane 1971, p. 150.
44. Sanhedrin 73.
45. M. Maimonides, *Hilchot Melachim* 5:1.
46. M. Maimonides, *Hilchot Rotzeyasch* 1:6.
47. Schmemann, November 8, 1995, p. 1.
48. Kifner, November 8, 1995, pp. A1, A12.
49. Schmemann, "Police," 1995, p. A1.

50. Greenberg 1995, p. A3.
51. Schmemann, November 11, 1995.
52. D. Williams 1995, p. A35.
53. Paris 1995, p. 127. Some of the conversos had genuinely become Christian, although many continued to practice Judaism in secret.
54. Lewis 1952, pp. 50–51.
55. Keppel 1994, pp. 117–118.
56. Among the best sources on the anti-abortion movement are the following works by Kaplan: 1993; "Right-Wing Violence," 1995; "Absolute Rescue," 1995; "Politics of Rage," 1996; *Religion in America,* 1996.
57. Melton 1989, p. 53. Also see Chu and Clary 1994, pp. A1, A19.
58. C. Allen 1994, p. 12.
59. Blanchard and Prewitt 1993, p. 51.
60. Blanchard and Prewitt 1993, pp. 39, 46, 60.
61. Hed, Bowermaster, and Headden 1994, p. 55.
62. C. Allen 1994, p. 14.
63. Niebuhr, "Church's Dismay," 1995, p. A12.
64. Niebuhr, "Church's Dismay," 1995, p. A12. Also see C. Allen 1994, pp. 16, 17, 76, for other examples.
65. Waelder 1960.
66. This section draws on Brass 1974; Daljeet Singh 1984; Fox 1985; McLeod 1989; and Tully and Jacob 1985.
67. Brass 1974, p. 286.
68. The Sikh radicals elevated a "temporal struggle to the level of the cosmic, [bypassing] the usual moral restrictions on killing ... By clothing their actions in the moral garb of religion, they have given their actions legitimacy. Because their actions are morally sanctioned by religion, they are fundamentally political actions: they break the state's monopoly on morally sanctioned killing." Juergensmeyer 1988, pp. 182–183.
69. Excerpts from speeches of Bhindranwale, cited in Juergensmeyer 1988, pp. 175–176.
70. Juergensmeyer 1988, pp. 185–190.
71. Ostow 1994, pp. 228–229.
72. On the equilibrium of the group, see Lax 1994, p. 253.

7

## Paranoia's Theorists

1. This section draws largely on Barkun 1994.
2. Cited in Barkun 1994, p. 131.
3. Barkun 1994, p. ix.
4. Barkun 1994, pp. 154–155.
5. Langer 1990. While many Anglo-Israelites embraced the pre-Adamite theory, most of the important pre-Adamite writers were not themselves Anglo-Israelites. Michael Barkun, personal communication, 1995.
6. Hiss 1978, cited in Barkun 1994.

7. Barkun 1994, p. 23.
8. Sawyer 1921, cited in Barkun 1994, p. 25.
9. Barkun 1994, pp. 150–151.
10. Barkun 1994, pp. 136–137.
11. This section draws heavily on Goldman 1974; Lincoln 1961; Malcolm X 1964; and Perry 1991. Perry's work is both valuable and problematic. His was the first biography to check facts in Malcolm X's autobiography. His psychological orientation is also helpful. We do not, however, accept the book uncritically. See Decaro (1996), who focuses on Malcolm X's religious life, for an invaluable perspective.
12. Perry 1991, p. 143.
13. Goldman 1974, p. 36.
14. Lincoln 1961, p. 73.
15. Lincoln 1961, p. 77.
16. Broyles 1964, p. 27.
17. Lyons 1937.
18. Welch 1952, p. 61.
19. Welch 1964, p. xxxv; Welch 1961, pp. 30–31.
20. Welch 1961.
21. Broyles 1964, p. 7.
22. R. Rose 1991.
23. Welch 1961, p. 181.
24. R. Rose 1991.
25. R. Rose 1991.
26. Grupp 1972.
27. Grupp 1972.
28. Baeyer-Kaette, Classens, Feiger, and Neihardt 1982.
29. This section owes a substantial debt to Johnson 1983 and King 1989.
30. Johnson 1983, p. 200.
31. Johnson 1989, p. 7.
32. Paranoid movements and paranoid ideologies do not disappear easily. We doubt but do not dismiss the possibility of a LaRouche revival. His organization continues to advertise on national television, carries on substantial direct mailing, publishes a newspaper, and has local meetings. Furthermore, LaRouche himself contested 1996 Democratic primaries.

### 8
### Paranoia's Agitators and Activists

1. This chapter benefits from a number of excellent publications on right-wing extremism: Aho 1990, 1995; Barkun 1994; Lake 1985; Merkl and Weinberg 1993; Sargent 1995; Sederberg 1994; and Wood 1996. Also see the following works by Kaplan: 1993; "Right-Wing Violence," 1995; "Absolute Rescue," 1995; "Politics of Rage," 1996; *Religion in America,* 1996.
2. R. Wood, interview with JMP, Fargo, N.Dak., August 16, 1995; Wood 1996, p. 219.

3. Wood 1996, p. 218, drawing on Finch 1983; W. E. Barker, unpublished manuscript "The Aryan Nations: A Linkage Profile," 1986; and Zeskind 1986. Also see L. Weinberg, "The Radical Right and Varieties of Right-Wing Politics in the United States," a manuscript cited in Wood 1996, p. 219.
4. Barkun 1990; Ostling 1986.
5. Barkun 1994, p. 190.
6. Barkun 1994, pp. 229–230.
7. Barkun 1994, p. 228.
8. Lake 1985, p. 100.
9. Lake 1985, p. 102.
10. Major sources for this discussion of the Posse Comitatus are Audsley 1985; Wood 1996; and Yaeger 1994.
11. Yaeger 1994, p. 17.
12. As with other extremist groups of the radical right, there are many overlapping memberships. Posse members are affiliated with such radical groups as the Covenant, Sword and the Arm of the Lord, the Ku Klux Klan, the National Party for Emancipation of the White Seed (NEWS), Aryan Nation, the Order, and the American Nazi Party. Posse chapters frequently used such titles as Patriots, Constitutionalists, Educated Citizens of Iowa, America First, and Protection Society of [county name] County, in order to confuse and evade law-enforcement authorities. Some other names associated with the Posse are Christian Liberty Academy, New York Patriots, National Patriots Association, Christian Conservative Churches, and the Arizona Patriots. See Yaeger 1994, p. 17.
13. Yaeger 1994, p. 17. As is so often the case with organizations that deny the legitimacy of the government they are opposing, the Posse invented a legalistic rhetoric in describing how it will execute its opponents: "In some instances of record, the law provides for the following prosecution of officials of government who commit criminal acts or who violate their oaths of office. He shall be removed by the Posse to the most populated intersection of streets in the Township and at high noon hung by the neck, the body remaining until sundown, as an example to those who would subvert the law." Yaeger 1994, p. 18.
14. Lake 1985, p. 22. Also see Barkun 1994, p. 110, for another illustration.
15. Pierce 1980.
16. Lake 1985, p. 97. Although almost all the members of the militias are white and although many of the texts they mention have a strong anti-Semitic and racist character, not all militias or militia members are racists.
17. Pierce 1980, p. 210.
18. "Pro-Life Hate" 1994. Note that Bishop's distinction between preventing white abortions and encouraging black ones is not characteristic of the anti-abortion movement, which opposes all abortions.
19. An excellent discussion entitled "Right-Wing Extremism and the Problem of Rural Unrest," by Robert Wood (1996), and an extensive interview with Professor Wood (Fargo, N.Dak., August 16, 1995) were especially helpful in informing this section, as were several of the books and articles on extremism cited earlier. In addition, this section draws on investigative reporting in the wake of the 1995

Oklahoma City explosion, primarily from the *New York Times* and the *Washington Post.*

20. Kovaleski 1995, p. A13.
21. Trochman, quoted in Goshko and Swardson 1995, p. A22.
22. Schneider 1994, p. A1.
23. Egan, "Federal Uniforms," 1995, p. A1.
24. Robertson 1991, p. 6.
25. Robertson 1991, pp. 9–14, 82, 83.
26. The conspiracy theorist Phillips O'Halloran, a physician, has published an article that provides a detailed description of the "syringe implantable biochip," which he characterizes as a "fearsome potential threat in the surveillance arsenal." The chip emits low-frequency FM waves that would provide "information on the exact location of the 'chipee': his latitude, longitude, and elevation to within a few feet anywhere on the planet." O'Halloran (1994), cited in McHugh 1995.
27. Goshko and Swardson 1995, p. A23.
28. Quoted in Lake 1985, p. 98.
29. Barkun 1995.
30. Schmidt and Kenworthy 1995, p. A5.
31. Fisher and McCombs 1995, p. D6.
32. "Two Militia Figures" 1995, p. A13.
33. Doskoch 1995.
34. Janofsky 1995; Mintz 1995.
35. Kovar 1966, p. 289.
36. Fenichel 1945.
37. The following discussion about the role of the Rambo films (*First Blood,* Carolco 1982; *Rambo: First Blood, Part Two,* Anabassis Investments NVC/Buzz Feitshans 1985; *Rambo III,* Columbia TriStar/Carolco [Buzz Feitshans] 1988) and the importance of archaic myth and man as warrior and protector owes a substantial debt to Gibson 1994.
38. Goldman 1974, p. 67. See DeCaro 1996 for a full description of the central role of religion in Malcolm X's life and thought. DeCaro suggests that the Nation of Islam be understood as a cult (p. 6) and that the Sunni Islam later adopted by Malcolm X be known as "orthodox Islam." We describe both as religions.
39. DeCaro 1996, p. 249.
40. Lester 1968, p. 195.
41. Lester 1968, p. 194.
42. Malcolm X 1964, pp. 252, 253.
43. Malcolm X 1964, p. 253.
44. Malcolm X 1964, pp. 490, 491.
45. George and Wilcox 1996, pp. 319-320.
46. For a comprehensive study of Farrakhan and his relation to the Nation of Islam, see Magida 1996.
47. Kramer 1985, pp. 16–17.
48. Kramer 1985.
49. Cooper 1990, pp. 30–31.

50. Muhammad 1993.
51. Fletcher and Harris 1995.
52. Miller 1996, p. 158.
53. Landis 1987.
54. Oshinsky 1983, p. 14.
55. Reeves 1982, p. 671.

9

**Paranoia's Organizers and Propagandists**

1. This section owes a substantial debt to Jeansonne 1986, 1991; and Ribuffo 1983.
2. Ribuffo 1983, p. 140.
3. Ribuffo 1983, pp. 157, 167.
4. Ribuffo 1983, p. 175.
5. Jeansonne 1986, p. 120.
6. Jeansonne 1986, p. 104.
7. Jeansonne 1986, pp. 104, 110.
8. Jeansonne 1986, p. 114.
9. Jeansonne 1991, p. 248.
10. Jeansonne 1986, p. 95.
11. Hofstadter 1967, p. 3.
12. This section draws on the essays in D. Rose 1992, and on the direct observation and research of one of the authors of this book (RSR).
13. Bridges 1994, pp. 5, 6.
14. Bridges 1994, p. 7.
15. Louisiana Coalition 1991, p. 1.
16. Louisiana Coalition 1991, p. 3.
17. Louisiana Coalition 1991, p. 3; Berry 1989, p. 12.
18. Louisiana Coalition 1991, the section titled "One Nation under Duke: A Plan to Scapegoat America."
19. D. Rose and Esolen 1992 in D. Rose 1992, p. 221.
20. "Poll," 1996.
21. This section draws substantially on Butler, Koopman, and Zimbardo 1995. See also Zelizer 1992 on the role of the news media in creating and exploiting narratives about the Kennedy assassination.
22. On *The Day After,* see Schofield and Pavelchak 1985; on *Amerika,* see Lenart and McGraw 1989, p. 22; on *Holocaust,* see de Block and van Lil 1981; and on *Roots,* see Surlin 1978.
23. Butler, Koopman, and Zimbardo 1995, p. 249.
24. Boorstin 1992, p. 743.
25. Rosenstone 1992.
26. L. Butler, personal communication, September 11, 1995.
27. Steel 1992, p. 30.
28. Quoted in Morrow and Smilgis 1991, p. 74.
29. Felkins and Goldman 1993.
30. NBC news interview, 8:15 A.M. central time, November 21, 1993.

## 10
### Paranoia in Power

1. This section draws principally on Becker 1986; Burgler 1990; Chandler 1983, 1991, 1992; Etcheson 1984; Kiernan 1985, 1996; and Shawcross 1984.
2. This is the concluding point of Kiernan's *Pol Pot Regime* (1996).
3. David Chandler, personal correspondence, June 15, 1995.
4. Chandler 1991, p. 250.
5. Chandler 1991, p. 259.
6. Burgler 1990, p. 58.
7. Becker 1986, pp. 168, 169.
8. Quoted in Becker 1986, p. 219.
9. Chandler 1991, p. 252.
10. Chandler 1991, pp. 260, 261, 270.
11. Chandler 1991, p. 271.
12. Becker 1986, pp. 221, 222.
13. Becker 1986, p. 355.
14. Burgler 1990, pp. 150, 114.
15. Ablin and Hood 1987, p. 412.
16. Quoted in Chandler 1991, p. 271.
17. Kiernan 1996, p. 448.
18. This description of Saloth Sar's life is largely derived from Chandler 1992.
19. Kiernan 1985, p. 119.
20. Becker 1986, p. 207.
21. Chandler 1992, p. 158.
22. Chandler 1992, p. 139.
23. Chandler 1992, p. 157.
24. Stalin, like Pol Pot, for the most part avoided a charismatic appeal—although he certainly fostered a cult of personality. Stalin's purges and economic policies in the Soviet Union bear striking similarity to Pol Pot's. Unlike Pol Pot, however, Stalin sought to abolish the somewhat collective decision making that existed under Lenin, and he succeeded in this goal.
25. Becker 1986, p. 136.
26. Becker 1986, p. 201.
27. G. I. Smith 1980, which draws on Colin Legum's archives, is one of the few extended post-Amin scholarly evaluations of his rule. Many other sources are firsthand accounts written close to the time by journalists, political figures, and victims. They have the advantages and disadvantages of those perspectives. Aside from G. I. Smith 1980, our principal sources for this section are Avirgan and Honey 1982; Grahame 1980; Kato 1987; Kyemba 1977; Listowel 1973; Mamdani 1983; Marnham 1985; D. Martin 1974; Mazrui 1977; Melady and Melady 1977; Mutibawa 1992; and Mallory Weber 1973.
28. D. Martin 1974, p. 14.
29. G. I. Smith 1980, p. 103.
30. Kyemba 1977, p. 7.
31. Listowel 1973, p. 77.

32. Mamdani 1983, pp. 73, 74.
33. Melady and Melady 1977, pp. 17, 18, 19.
34. D. Martin 1974, p. 11.
35. Melady and Melady 1977, p. 167.
36. G. I. Smith 1980, p. 101.
37. Listowel 1973, pp. 183, 184.
38. Marnham 1985, pp. 80, 82.
39. Melady and Melady 1977, p. 167.
40. Marnham 1985, p. 80.
41. Kyemba 1977, p. 107.
42. A Ugandan 1977, p. 33.
43. Kato 1987, p. 79.
44. Jacobson 1978, p. 10.
45. Avirgan and Honey 1982, p. 298.
46. Valuable sources for this portrait of Stalin include Bullock 1992; Conquest 1968; and Tucker 1973, 1990.
47. This section draws substantially upon Groth and Britton 1993; and Tucker 1965, 1973, 1977, 1990.
48. From "the beginning [of the nineteenth century] Russia displayed a nation-wide passion for secret societies and circles." Ulam 1977, p. 74.
49. Laqueur 1993, p. 8.
50. Herman Freudenberger, personal communication, October 1995.
51. Paraphrased from Conquest 1979, p. 228.
52. Groth and Britton 1993, p. 635.
53. Iremashvili 1932, quoted in Tucker 1973, p. 73.
54. Anna Freud (1966) first called attention to this ego defense mechanism, which she called "identification with the aggressor."
55. Bullock 1992, p. 7.
56. Cited in Tucker 1973, p. 80.
57. Alliluyeva 1969, pp. 313–314.
58. Deutscher 1966, p. 19, cited in Bullock 1992, p. 31.
59. Address to the Kremlin military school after the death of Lenin in 1924. Deutscher 1966, p. 98. This was not merely the idealization often found in a eulogy, for, as Bullock (1992, p. 36) notes, similar sentiments were expressed in a letter of 1904.
60. Tucker 1973, p. 120.
61. Bullock 1992, p. 27.
62. Translated from Arsenidze, *Novyi Zhurnal,* cited in Bullock 1992, p. 27.
63. Stalin 1952–1955, vol. 1, pp. 62–73.
64. Stalin 1952–1955, vol. 6, p. 246.
65. Brzezinski 1990, pp. 23, 27.
66. Snow 1966, pp. 266, 267.
67. Fromm 1973, pp. 287–288.
68. Fromm 1973, p. 285.
69. As quoted in Tucker 1973, p. 211.
70. Khrushchev 1970, pp. 254, 299, 601.

71. Tucker 1973, p. 449.
72. Conquest 1968; Tucker 1965.
73. Tucker 1973, p. 453.
74. Tucker 1973, p. 463.
75. Bullock 1992, p. 210.
76. Kennan 1967, p. 279.
77. Harriman and Abel 1975, p. 535.
78. Deutscher 1967, p. 273.
79. Carr 1968, pp. 177–190.
80. Tucker 1979.

## 11
### Adolf Hitler

1. A photo of the poster was provided by Richard Koenigsberg, whose textual analysis of Hitler's language in *Hitler's Ideology* (1975) provides persuasive confirmatory evidence of Hitler's personal psychological investment in his anti-Semitic rhetoric and tends to support the psychoanalytic hypotheses suggested by Waite (1971, 1976).
2. Hitler 1962, p. 464.
3. Particularly valuable sources are Bromberg and Small 1983; Bullock 1992; Fest 1975; Hoffer [1951] 1966; Koenigsberg 1975; Payne 1973; and Waite 1976.
4. The material on Hitler's father's background is drawn largely from Waite 1976, pp. 124–128, and that on Hitler's boyhood is drawn from Bullock 1992, pp. 7–9, and Waite 1976, pp. 131–141.
5. This line of reasoning and the supporting evidence is laid out in Waite 1976, pp. 126–130.
6. Waite 1976, pp. 5–6.
7. Bullock 1992, p. 7.
8. Bromberg and Small 1983, pp. 32–33.
9. Hitler 1962, pp. 7, 10–14.
10. Erikson 1963, p. 337.
11. This hypothesis is developed at greater length in Binion 1973 and Stierlin 1976. John Kafka (1978; personal communication, 1990) offers evidence that the hypothesis is overdrawn.
12. Cited in Waite 1976, p. 190.
13. Quoted in Payne 1973, p. 61.
14. Payne 1973, p. 21.
15. Hitler 1962, pp. 145, 146.
16. Waite 1971, p. 204.
17. Hitler 1962, p. 225.
18. Rauschning 1939, p. 257.
19. Bromberg and Small 1983, p. 85. The text of the guide can be found in Payne 1973, pp. 129–131.
20. Hitler 1961, pp. 22, 24.
21. Bullock 1992, p. 144.

22. Hitler 1961, pp. 212–213.
23. Rauschning 1939, p. 234, cited in Hoffer [1951] 1966, p. 91.
24. Payne 1973, p. 277.
25. Fest 1975, p. 252.
26. Rauschning 1939, pp. 172–173, cited in Payne 1973, p. 280.
27. Payne 1973, p. 304.
28. Hitler 1941, p. 257.
29. Richard Koenigsberg has subjected Hitler's speeches to a psychoanalytically in-
    formed content analysis. The themes and illustrations in this section are drawn
    from Koenigsberg's 1975 analysis in *Hitler's Ideology: A Study in Psychoanalytic
    Sociology*.
30. Baynes 1942, p. 433.
31. Hitler 1962, p. 155.
32. Baynes 1942, p. 1253.
33. Baynes 1942, p. 995.
34. Hitler 1962, p. 133.
35. Baynes 1942, p. 780.
36. Baynes 1942, p. 441.
37. Hitler 1962, p. 279.
38. Baynes 1942, p. 453.
39. Baynes 1942, p. 68.
40. Baynes 1942, p. 17.
41. Baynes 1942, p. 259.
42. Baynes 1942, p. 240.
43. Baynes 1942, p. 693.
44. Baynes 1942, p. 108.
45. Hitler 1962, p. 305.
46. Hitler 1962, p. 304.
47. Hitler 1962, p. 316.
48. Hitler 1962, p. 289.
49. Hitler 1962, p. 325. The sexual defiling of German womanhood by the Jew is a
    recurrent theme. Recall Hitler's fear that his father was fathered by a Jew. Other
    reasons for sexual concerns have been theorized. According to the Soviet autopsy,
    Hitler had an undescended testicle. A number of anecdotes indicate that he had
    significant sexual difficulties and possibly perversions. In the psychoanalytically
    oriented biographies by Waite (1976) and Langer (1972), the psychodynamic
    significance of the sexual defect is given particular emphasis. Self-doubts about
    sexual ability may have contributed to Hitler's profound sense of failure and
    inadequacy.
50. Baynes 1942, pp. 240, 117.
51. Baynes 1942, p. 683.
52. Canetti 1962, pp. 181–183.
53. Hitler 1962, p. 431.
54. Baynes 1942, p. 231.
55. Baynes 1942, p. 265.
56. Baynes 1942, p. 1136.

57. Hitler 1941, p. 775.
58. Hitler 1941, p. 758.
59. Baynes 1942, p. 60.
60. Baynes 1942, p. 584.
61. Pulzer 1964. This section draws on Carmichael 1993 and Wistrich 1991, as well as on the sources cited.
62. Gordon 1984, pp. 51–53.
63. Niewyk 1980, p. 9. In his controversial *Hitler's Willing Executioners,* Daniel Goldhagen argues that anti-Semitism itself was insufficient to explain the Holocaust, that it was the fit between Hitler's malignant leadership and a deeply entrenched anti-Semitism that permitted Hitler's views to find a receptive audience. Goldhagen argues that the climate of anti-Semitism in Germany was particularly virulent, what he calls "eliminationist anti-Semitism." This doctrine, widespread in German society during and before the Nazi period, maintained that "Jews were different from Germans, that these putative differences resided in their biology, conceptualized as race, and were therefore immutable; that the Jews were evil and powerful, had done great harm to Germany and would continue to do so. The conclusion drawn by Germans who shared this view was that Jews and Jewish power had to be eliminated somehow to be secure and prosper. The German perpetrators of the Holocaust were motivated to kill Jews principally by their belief that the extermination was necessary and just" (Goldhagen 1996b, p. 37).

   In Goldhagen's view, it was a unique combination of these circumstances that explained the Holocaust: "First, the most committed and virulent anti-Semites in history [came] to power and decided to turn murderous fantasy into the core of state policy. Secondly, they did so in a society in which their essential views of Jews were widely shared. Third, it was only Germany that was in the geo-military situation to carry out a genocide of this sort" (Goldhagen 1996b, p. 43).
64. W. S. Allen 1984, p. 84.
65. Cohn 1981, p. 198.
66. Gordon 1984, pp. 51–53.
67. Dietrich 1988, p. 402; also see Gordon 1984, pp. 51–55.
68. Both statistics from Balfour 1988, p. 57.
69. Hoffer 1951 [1966], p. 68.
70. Bullock 1952, p. 344.
71. Speer 1970, p. 65.
72. Vince et al. 1984, pp. 461, 477.
73. Max Weber 1946, pp. 295, 296.
74. Wilner 1984.
75. Adapted from Camic 1980.
76. Waite 1976, p. 54.
77. Mosley 1977, p. 150.
78. Angebert 1974.
79. Niewyk 1971, pp. 217, 218.
80. Langer 1972, p. 32.

81. Fest 1975, p. 179; Waite 1976, p. 28.
82. Langer 1972, p. 61.
83. Hitler 1941, p. 535.
84. Fest 1975, p. 376.
85. Tucker 1968.
86. Fest 1975, p. 157.
87. Speer 1976, p. 262; also see Rhodes 1980.
88. Langer 1972, p. 35.
89. Waite 1976, p. 40.
90. Post, ''Dreams,'' 1984.
91. Loewenberg 1969, p. 264.
92. Loewenberg 1969, p. 251.

# References

Ablin, D. A., and M. Hood (Eds.). *The Cambodian agony.* London: Sharpe, 1987.

Abu-Amir, Z. HAMAS: A historical and political background. *Journal of Palestine Studies* 22 (Summer 1993): 5–19.

Aho, J. A. *The politics of righteousness: Idaho Christian patriotism.* Seattle: University of Washington Press, 1990.

———. *This thing of darkness: A sociology of the enemy.* Seattle: University of Washington Press, 1995.

Aitkin, J. *Nixon.* London: Weidenfeld and Nicholson, 1993.

Akhtar, S. Paranoid personality disorder. *American Journal of Psychotherapy* 44 (1990): 5–25.

Alexander, R. D. The evolution of social behavior. *Annual Review of Ecology and Systematics* 5 (1974): 325–383.

———. *Darwinism and human affairs.* Seattle: University of Washington Press, 1979.

———. *The biology of moral systems.* Hawthorne, N.Y.: Aldine de Gruyter, 1987.

Alford, C. F. *Narcissism: Socrates, the Frankfurt School, and psychoanalytic theory.* New Haven: Yale University Press, 1988.

———. *Melanie Klein and critical social theory.* New Haven: Yale University Press, 1989.

———. *Group psychology and political theory.* New Haven: Yale University Press, 1994.

Allen, C., Jr. Pro-life hate: Violence in the name of God. *Reform Judaism* 10–17 (Summer 1994): 76.

Allen, W. S. *The Nazi seizure of power: The experience of a single German town, 1922–1945.* Rev. ed. New York: Watts, 1984.

Alliluyeva, S. *Only one year.* New York: Norton, 1969.

Ambrose, S. E. *Nixon: The education of a president.* New York: Simon and Schuster, 1987.

Angebert, J.-M. *The occult and the Third Reich.* L. Sumberg (Trans.). New York: Macmillan, 1974.

329

Applebome, P. Bloody Sunday's roots in deep religious soil. *New York Times,* March 2, 1993, p. A16.

———. A bombing foretold in extreme-right "Bible." *New York Times,* April 26, 1995, p. A22.

———. Anger of the '60's takes root in the violent right. *New York Times,* May 7, 1995, pp. A1, A36.

Aran, A. A mystico-messianic interpretation of modern Israeli history: The Six-Day War as a key event in the development of original religious culture of Gush Emunim. *Studies in Contemporary Jewry* 4 (1988): 263–275.

Arieti, S. Schizophrenia: The manifest symptomatology, the psychodynamic, and formal mechanisms. In S. Arieti (Ed.), *American handbook of psychiatry,* vol. 1. New York: Basic Books, 1959, pp. 456–484.

Asahara, S. *Supreme initiation: An empirical spiritual science for the supreme truth.* N.p., 1988.

———. *Beyond life and death.* Shizuoka, Japan: Aum Publishing, 1993.

Assassination in Israel. *New York Times,* November, 5, 1995, p. A1.

Athill, D. Introduction. In Jean Rhys, *Collected short stories.* New York: Norton, 1987.

Audsley, D. Posse Comitatus: An extremist tax protest group. *TVI Journal* 2 (Summer 1985): 13–16.

Avirgan, T., and M. Honey. *War in Uganda.* London: Zed Press, 1982.

Bacal, H. A., and K. N. Newman. *Theories of object relations.* New York: Columbia University Press, 1990.

Baeyer-Kaette, W. von. A left-wing terrorist indoctrination group. Paper presented at the sixth annual meeting of the International Society of Political Psychology, Oxford, England, July 1983.

Baeyer-Kaette, W. von, D. Classens, H. Feiger, and F. Neihardt. *Analyzen zum Terrorismus 3: Gruppenprozesse.* Darmstadt: n.p., 1982.

Bahrani, Y. The Rushdie specter: For Muslim intellectuals, the danger deepens. *Washington Post,* August 14, 1994, p. 1.

Balfour, M. *Withstanding Hitler in Germany, 1933–1945.* London: Routledge and Kegan Paul, 1988.

Barash, D. P. *Sociobiology and behavior.* 2nd ed. New York: Elsevier, 1982.

Barkun, M. Racist apocalypse: Millennialism on the far right. *American Studies* 31 (Fall 1990): 121–140.

———. *Religion and the racist right.* Chapel Hill: University of North Carolina Press, 1994.

———. Political paranoia on the paranoid right. Paper presented at the annual meeting of the International Society of Political Psychology, Washington, D.C., July 6, 1995.

Bar Tal, D. The Masada syndrome: A case of central belief. In N. A. Milgrim

(Ed.), *Stress and coping in time of war.* New York: Bruner/Mazel, 1986, pp. 32–51.

Bar Tal, D., and D. Antebi. Beliefs about negative intentions of the world: A study of Israeli siege mentality. Paper presented at the annual meeting of the International Society of Political Psychology, New Jersey, July 1988.

———. Siege mentality in Israel. Paper presented at the annual meeting of the International Society of Political Psychology, Tel Aviv, July 1989.

Bates, K. D. Is it genocide? *Essence,* September 1990, pp. 76–117.

Batkata, M. Largest rally in Prague since '69 ends violently. *Washington Post,* November 18, 1989, pp. A1, A21.

Baynes, N. H. *The speeches of Adolf Hitler, 1922–1939.* 2 vols. Oxford: Oxford University Press, 1942.

Becker, E. *When the war was over.* New York: Simon and Schuster, 1986.

Benedict, R. *Patterns of culture.* Boston: Houghton-Mifflin, 1934.

Berindranath, D. *Nasser: The man and the miracle.* New York: Afro-Asian Publications, 1966.

Bernstein, R. Biggest U.S. terrorist trial begins as arguments clash. *New York Times,* January 13, 1995, p. A1.

Berry, J. Duke caucus. *Gambit,* September 11, 1989, pp. 11–12.

Binion, R. Hitler's concept of Lebensraum. *History of Childhood Quarterly* 1 (1973): 187–215.

Bion, W. Group dynamics: A re-view. In M. Klein, P. Heiman, and R. E. Money-Kyrle (Eds.), *New directions in psycho-analysis.* London: Tavistock, 1955, pp. 440–477.

———. *Experiences in groups and other papers.* London: Tavistock, 1961.

———. *Learning from experience.* New York: Basic Books, 1962.

Blanchard, D. A., and T. J. Prewitt. *Religious violence and abortion: The Gideon Project.* Gainesville: University of Florida, 1993.

Bleuler, E. Dementia praecox; or, The group of schizophrenias. J. Zinkin (Trans.). New York: International Universities Press, 1950.

Blum, H. Object inconstancy and paranoid conspiracy. *Journal of the American Psychoanalytic Association* 29 (1981): 789–813.

Bonime, W. Paranoid psychodynamics. *Contemporary Psychoanalysis* 15, no. 3 (1979): 514–527.

Bonner, J. T. *The evolution of culture in animals.* Princeton: Princeton University Press, 1980.

Boorstin, D. *The creators.* New York: Random House, 1992.

Boyer, P., and S. Nissenbaum. *Salem possessed: The social origins of witchcraft.* Cambridge: Harvard University Press, 1974.

Brass, P. *Language, religion, and politics in north India.* Cambridge: Cambridge University Press, 1974.

Breitman, G. (Ed.). *Malcolm X speaks.* New York: Merit, 1965.

————. *The last year of Malcolm X.* New York: Schocken, 1967.

Bridges, T. *The rise of David Duke.* Jackson: University Press of Mississippi, 1994.

Brinkley, J. Walesa, in Israel, regrets Poland's anti-Semitism. *New York Times,* May 21, 1991, p. A5.

Brogan, D. W. Death in Dallas. *Encounter,* December 1964, pp. 20–26.

Bromberg, N., and V. Small. *Hitler's psychopathology.* New York: International Universities Press, 1983.

Broyles, A. *The John Birch Society: Anatomy of a protest.* Boston: Beacon Press, 1964.

Bruck, C. The wounds of war. *New Yorker,* October 19, 1996, pp. 64–91.

Brumberg, A. Polish intellectuals and anti-Semitism. *Dissent* (Winter 1991): 72–77.

Brzezinski, Z. *The grand failure.* New York: Collier, 1989.

Bullock, A. *Hitler.* London: Odhams Press, 1952.

————. *Hitler and Stalin: Parallel lives.* New York: Knopf, 1992.

Burgler, R. A. *The eyes of the pineapple: Revolutionary intellectuals and terror in democratic Kampuchea.* Saarbrucken, Germany: Beitenbach, 1990.

Butler, L., C. Koopman, and P. Zimbardo. The psychological impact of viewing the film *JFK. Political Psychology* 16 (1995): 237–258.

Byrne, R. W., and A. Whitten. *Machiavellian intelligence: Social expertise and the evolution of intellect in monkeys, apes, and humans.* New York: Oxford University Press, 1988.

Cameron, N. The paranoid pseudo-community. *American Journal of Sociology* 49 (1943): 32–38.

————. Paranoid conditions and paranoia. In S. Arieti (Ed.), *American handbook of psychiatry,* vol. 1. New York: Basic Books, 1959, pp. 508–539.

————. The paranoid pseudo-community revisited. *American Journal of Sociology* 65 (1959): 52–58.

Camic, C. Charisma: Its varieties, preconditions, and consequences. *Sociological Inquiry* 50 (1980): 5–24.

Campbell, J. K. Terrorism and weapons of mass destruction. Master's thesis, Navy Post-Graduate School, Monterey, 1996.

Canetti, E. *Crowds and power.* New York: Continuum, 1962.

Carmichael, J. *Satanizing of the Jews: Origin and development of mystical anti-Semitism.* New York: Fromm International Publishing, 1993.

Carr, E. H. *Socialism in one country, 1924–1926,* vol. 1. New York: Macmillan, 1968.

Castañeda, J. A. From Mexico looking out. In R. A. Pastor and J. A. Castañeda, *Limits to friendship.* New York: Knopf, 1988, pp. 55–77.

Champion, M. Jews meeting in Romania cite new antisemitism. *Washington Post,* July 5, 1991, p. A14.

Chandler, D. P. *A history of Cambodia.* Boulder: Westview Press, 1983.

———. *The tragedy of Cambodian history.* New Haven: Yale University Press, 1991.

———. *Brother number one.* Boulder: Westview Press, 1992.

Chartier, R. Intellectual history or sociocultural history? The French trajectories. In D. LaCapra and L. S. Kaplan (Eds.), *Modern European intellectual history: Reappraisals and new perspectives.* J. P. Kaplan (Trans.). Ithaca: Cornell University Press, 1982, pp. 13–45.

Cheney, D. L., and R. M. Seyfarth. Selective forces affecting the predator alarm calls of vervet monkeys. *Behavior* 76 (1981): 25–61.

———. *How monkeys see the world.* Chicago: University of Chicago Press, 1990.

Citizens for LaRouche. The psychiatric shock troops. In *Stamp out the aquarian conspiracy* (n.p.: 1980), pp. 15–24.

Cohn, N. *The pursuit of the millennium.* 1957. Reprint, New York: Harper Torchbooks, 1961.

———. *Europe's inner demons. An enquiry inspired by the great witch hunt.* New York: Basic Books, 1975.

———. *Warrant for genocide.* 3rd ed. Chico, Calif.: Scholars Press, 1981.

Cole, M., et al. *The cultural context of learning and thinking.* New York: Basic Books, 1971.

Colman, A., and W. H. Bexton (Eds.). *Group relations reader 1.* Washington, D.C.: A. K. Rice Institute, 1975.

Colman, A., and M. Geller (Eds.). *Group relations reader 2.* Washington, D.C.: A. K. Rice Institute, 1985.

Conquest, R. *The great terror.* New York: Macmillan, 1968.

———. *Kolyma.* Oxford: Oxford University Press, 1979.

Cooper, M. The return of the paranoid style in American politics. *U.S. News and World Report,* March 12, 1990, pp. 30–31.

Daljeet Singh. *The Sikh ideology.* New Delhi: Guru Nanak Foundation, 1984.

Darnton, R. *Great cat massacre.* New York: Vintage, 1985.

Dawkins, R. *The selfish gene.* Oxford: Oxford University Press, 1976.

de Bock, H., and J. van Lil. "Holocaust" in the Netherlands. In G. C. Wilhoit and H. de Bock (Eds.), *Mass communication review yearbook,* vol. 2. Newbury Park, Calif.: Sage, 1981, pp. 639–646.

DeCaro, L. A. *On the side of my people.* New York: New York University Press, 1996.

Delgado-García, J. M., et al. Behavioral inhibition induced by pallidal stimulation in monkeys. *Experimental Neurology* 49 (1975): 580–591.

Demos, J. P. *Entertaining Satan.* New York: Oxford University Press, 1982.

Demoskop Research Agency. *Democracy, economic reform, and Western assistance in Poland.* Warsaw: Demoskop Research Agency, 1991.

DeParle, J. Those people. *New York Times,* December 26, 1993, p. D1.

Deutscher, I. *Stalin: A political biography*. 2nd ed. New York: Oxford University Press, 1967.

DeWaal, F. B. M. *Chimpanzee politics*. New York: Harper and Row, 1982.

Dewhurst, K., and J. Todd. The psychosis of association: Folie deux. *Journal of Nervous and Mental Diseases* 124 (1956): 451–459.

Dickinson, Emily. *The Complete Poems of Emily Dickinson*. Thomas H. Johnson (Ed.). Boston: Little, Brown, 1976.

Dietrich, D. D. National renewal, anti-Semitism, and political continuity: A psychological assessment. *Political Psychology* 9 (1988): 385–411.

Doskoch, P. Mind of the militia. *Psychology Today* 12 (July–August 1995): 12–14.

Draguns, J. G. Psychological disorders of clinical severity. In H. C. Triands and J. C. Draguns (Eds.), *Handbook of cross-cultural psychology: Psychopathology,* vol. 6. Boston: Allyn and Bacon, 1980, pp. 99–174.

Egan, T. Federal uniforms become cause of wave of threats and violence. *New York Times,* April 25, 1995, pp. A1, A20.

——. Trying to explain contacts with paramilitary groups. *New York Times,* May 2, 1995, p. A19.

Epstein, E. Extremist groups' bizarre fears of U.N. conspiracy. *San Francisco Chronicle,* May 4, 1995, pp. A1, A13.

Erikson, E. *Childhood and society*. 2nd rev. ed. New York: Norton, 1963.

——. Ontogeny of ritualization. In R. M. Loewenstein et al. (Eds.), *Psychoanalysis: A general psychology*. New York: International Universities Press, 1966.

——. *Identity, youth, and crisis*. New York: Norton, 1968.

Eros, F. The construction of Jewish identity in Hungary in the 1980s. Paper presented at a seminar entitled "Identity renewal: Studies in Eastern European Jewish life histories," Tel Aviv, October 6–10, 1991.

Esposito, J. *Islam: The straight path*. Oxford: Oxford University Press, 1988.

——. Political Islam: Beyond the green menace. *Current History* (January 1994): 19–24.

Etcheson, C. *The rise and demise of democratic Kampuchea*. Boulder: Westview Press, 1984.

Etzion, Y. From the laws of existence to the laws of destiny (in Hebrew). *Nequda* 75 (1984).

——. *Temple mount* (in Hebrew). Jerusalem: E. Caspi, 1985.

Fadlallah, S. H. H. Interview. *Middle East Insight* 7, no. 2 (June–July 1985): 10–19.

Felkins, P. K., and I. Goldman. Political myth as subjective narrative. *Political Psychology* 14 (1993): 447–467.

Fenichel, O. *The psychoanalytic theory of neurosis*. New York: Norton, 1945.

Ferenczi, S. The problem of acceptance of unpleasant ideas. In *Further contri-*

*butions to the theory and technique of psychoanalysis.* London: Hogarth Press, 1926.

Ferracuti, F. A sociopsychiatric interpretation of terrorism. *Annals of the American Academy of Sciences* 463 (September 1982): 136–137.

———. Ideology and repentance: Terrorism in Italy. In W. Reich (Ed.), *Origins of terrorism.* Cambridge: Cambridge University Press, 1990, pp. 59–64.

Fest, J. C. *Hitler.* R. Winston and C. Winston (Trans.). New York: Vintage, 1975.

Finch, P. *God, guts, and guns.* New York: Seaview/Putnam, 1983.

Fisher, M., and S. Coll. Hate groups: An international cooperative. *Washington Post,* May 11, 1995, pp. A31, A35.

Fisher, M., and P. McCombs. The book of hate. *Washington Post,* April 25, 1995, pp. D1, D6.

Fletcher, M., and H. Harris. Rift between Farrakhan, Jewish leader reemerges. *Washington Post,* October 14, 1995, pp. A1, A12.

Fornari, F. *The psychoanalysis of war.* A. Pfeifer (Trans.). Bloomington: Indiana University Press, 1975.

Fox, R. G. *Lions of the Punjab.* Berkeley: University of California Press, 1985.

Fraser, A. *Cromwell.* London: Weidenfeld and Nicolson, 1973.

Frazier, G. J. *The golden bough.* London: St. Martin's, 1927.

Freedman, A., H. Kaplan, and B. Saddock. *Modern synopsis of psychiatry.* Baltimore: William and Wilkins, 1972.

Freud, A. *The ego and the mechanisms of defense.* 1936. Rev. ed., London: Hogarth Press and Institute of Psychoanalysis, 1966.

Freud, S. *Moses and monotheism.* K. Jones (Trans.). London: Hogarth Press, 1951.

———. Psycho-analytic notes on an autobiographical account of a case of paranoia (1911). In *Standard edition of the complete psychological works of Sigmund Freud,* vol. 12. James Strachey (Trans.). London: Hogarth Press, 1958, pp. 9–82.

———. Constructions in psychoanalysis (1937). In *Standard edition of the complete psychological works of Sigmund Freud,* vol. 22. James Strachey (Trans.). London: Hogarth Press, 1964, pp. 225–269.

———. *The ego and the mechanisms of defense.* Rev. ed. New York: International Universities Press, 1966.

———. Extracts from the Fliess papers, 1892–1899. In *Standard edition of the complete psychological works of Sigmund Freud,* vol. 1. James Strachey (Trans.). London: Hogarth Press, 1966, pp. 173–281.

Friedman, R. An unholy rage. *New Yorker,* March 7, 1994, pp. 54–56.

Friedman, T. *From Beirut to Jerusalem.* New York: Doubleday, 1989.

Fromm, E. *Escape from freedom.* New York: Farrar and Rinehart, 1941.

———. *The anatomy of human destructiveness.* New York: Holt Rinehart, 1973.

———. Paranoia and policy. *New York Times,* December 11, 1975, p. 45.

Frosch, J. Delusional fixity, sense of conviction, and the psychotic conflict. *International Journal of Psychoanalysis* 48 (1967): 475–495.

Galanter, M. Psychological induction into the large group: Findings from a modern religious sect. *American Journal of Psychiatry* 137 (1980): 1574–1579.

———. *Cults.* New York: Oxford University Press, 1989.

Galanter, M., R. Rabkin, J. Rabkin, and A. Deutsch. The "Moonies": A psychological study of conversion and membership in a contemporary religious sect. *American Journal of Psychiatry* 136 (1979): 165–170.

Gaylin, W. *The rage within.* New York: Simon and Schuster, 1984.

Gazzaniga, M. S. *Nature's mind.* New York: Basic Books, 1992.

Gibson, J. S. *Warrior dreams.* New York: Hill and Wang, 1994.

Glass, J. M. *Delusion: Internal dimensions of political life.* Chicago: University of Chicago Press, 1985.

Godbeer, R. *The devil's dominion: Magic and religion in early New England.* Cambridge: Cambridge University Press, 1992.

Goertzel, T. Belief in conspiracy theories. *Political Psychology* 15 (1995): 731–742.

Goldberg, C. *Speaking with the devil.* New York: Viking, 1996.

Goldhagen, D. *Hitler's willing executioners: Ordinary Germans and the Holocaust.* New York: Knopf, 1996.

———. Motives, causes, and alibis. *New Republic,* December 23, 1996, pp. 37–45.

Goldman, P. *The death and life of Malcolm X.* London: Gollancz, 1974.

Gordon, S. *Hitler and the Jewish question.* Princeton: Princeton University Press, 1984.

Goshko, J., and A. Swardson. Militias, an angry mix hostile to government. *Washington Post,* April 21, 1995, pp. A1, A23, A24.

Gothelf, Y. Old and new antisemitism. *Davar,* March 13, 1970.

Gould, S. J. Cardboard Darwinism. In *An urchin in the storm.* London: Penguin, 1990, pp. 26–50.

Grahame, I. *Amin and Uganda.* London: Granada, 1980.

Greenberg, J. Israeli police question two rabbis in Rabin assassination. *New York Times,* November 27, 1995, p. 3.

Greenstein, F. A president is forced to resign: White House organization and Nixon's personality. In A. P. Sindler (Ed.), *America in the seventies.* Boston: Little, Brown, 1977, pp. 50–102.

Groth, A. J., and S. Britton. Gorbachev and Lenin: Psychological walls of the Soviet garrison state. *Political Psychology* 14 (1993): 627–650.

Grotstein, J. Meaning, meaninglessness, and the black hole: Self and interactional regulation as a new paradigm for psychoanalysis and neuroscience. Manuscript, 1987, p. 5. Cited in J. Lachkar, *The narcissistic/borderline couple.* New York: Brunner Mazel, 1992, pp. 28–29.

Grupp, F. W. Personal satisfaction derived from membership in the John Birch Society. In S. Kirkpatrick and L. Pettit (Eds.), *The social psychology of political life*. Belmont, Calif.: Duxbury Press, 1972, pp. 368–371.

Haberman, C. Israelis mourn, but Rabin says talks continue. *New York Times,* January 24, 1995, p. A1.

Hall, J. R. The apocalypse at Jonestown. In K. Levi (Ed.), *Violence and religious commitment*. University Park: Pennsylvania State University Press, 1982, pp. 35–54.

Hamilton, M. J. *Fish's clinical psychopathology*. Bristol: John Wright and Sons, 1974.

Hamilton, R. F. *Who voted for Hitler*. Princeton: Princeton University Press, 1982.

Hamilton, W. D. The genetical evolution of social behavior I and II. *Journal of Theoretical Biology* 7 (1964): 1–52.

Hansen, C. *Witchcraft at Salem*. London: Arrow, 1971.

Harden, B. Anti-Jewish bias rising in Poland: Catholic leaders aim to dispel myths, head off violence. *Washington Post,* July 16, 1990, pp. A1, A19.

Harrall, J. R. *The golden triangle*. Flora, Ill.: Christian Conservative Church, 1982.

Harriman, W. A., and E. Abel. *Special envoy to Churchill and Stalin, 1941–1946*. New York: Random House, 1975.

Hazani, M. Dualism, violence, and hostility: The spiritual belligerent. In G. Cromer and G. Shavit (Eds.), *Studies in violence*. Ramat Gan, Israel: Bar-Ilan University Press, in press.

Hed, S., D. Bowermaster, and S. Headden. Abortion: Who's behind the violence? *U.S. News and World Report,* November 14, 1994, pp. 50–67.

Heifitz, R. *Leadership without easy answers*. Cambridge: Harvard University Press, 1994.

Hesse, P., and D. Poklemba. The development of enemy images: Universal and culture-specific themes. *Center Review* (Center for Psychological Studies in the Nuclear Age, Harvard Medical School) (Spring 1988): 6, 7.

Hiss, W. C. Shiloh: Frank W. Sandford and the kingdom, 1893–1948. Ph.D. dissertation, Tufts University, 1978.

Hitler, A. *My new order*. R. de Sales (Ed.). New York: Reynal and Hitchcock, 1941.

———. *Hitler's secret book*. S. Attanasio (Trans.). New York: Grove Press, 1961.

———. *Mein Kampf*. J. Chamberlain et al. (Ed. sponsors). New York: Sentry Edition, 1962.

Hoffer, E. *The true believer*. 1951. Reprint, New York: Harper and Row, 1966.

———. *The passionate state of mind*. New York: Perennial Library, 1954.

Hoffman, D. The battle to understand Israel's siege mentality. *Washington Post,* February 15–21, 1993 (weekly edition), p. 16.

Hofstadter, R. The paranoid style in American politics. In *The paranoid style in American politics and other essays.* New York: Vintage, 1967, pp. 3–40.

Holsti, O. R. Cognitive dynamics of the enemy. In D. J. Finley et al., *Enemies in politics.* Chicago: Rand McNally, 1967, pp. 25–96.

Hopper, E. The incohesion basic assumption. Paper presented at a panel on the narcissistic group leader, at the annual scientific meeting of the American Group Psychotherapy Association, Atlanta, Georgia, February 1995.

Houseman, C. The paranoid person: A biopsychosocial perspective. *Archives of Psychiatric Nursing* 4, no. 3 (June 1990): 176–181.

Hughes, A. *Psychology and the political experience.* London and New York: Cambridge University Press, 1975.

Huizinga, J. *The waning of the middle ages.* F. Hopman (Trans.). 1924. Reprint, London: Penguin, 1976.

Humphrey, N. D. The social function of intellect. In P. P. G. Gateson and R. A. Hinde (Eds.), *Growing points in ethology.* Cambridge: Cambridge University Press, 1976, pp. 303–317.

Hunčík, P. The deformation of personality in Eastern Europe as a consequence of four decades of communist rule. Paper presented at the annual meeting of American Psychiatric Association International Scholar's series, Washington, D.C., 1992.

Iremashvili, J. *Stalin und die Tragodie Georgiens.* Berlin: Volksblatt-Druckerei, 1932.

*Ishtar Gate, The.* Mainz: Verlag Phillip von Zabern, n.d. (c. 1994).

*Islam: The Qu'ran.* A. Ali (Trans.). In J. Pelikan (Ed.), *Sacred Writings,* vol. 3. Princeton: Princeton University Press, 1992.

Jacobson, P. How Amin chooses his victims. *London Times,* October 22, 1978, p. 10.

James, W. *The varieties of religious experience.* 1902. Reprint, London: Fontana Library, 1960.

Janofsky, M. Senators question five paramilitary leaders. *New York Times,* June 11, 1995, p. A23.

Jansen, J. *The neglected duty: The creed of Sadat's assassins and Islamic resurgence in the Middle East.* New York: Macmillan, 1986.

Japanese find dead child linked to cult. *New York Times,* September 11, 1995.

Jaques, E. *The changing culture of a factory.* London: Tavistock, 1951.

———. Social systems as defense against persecutory and depressive anxiety. In M. Klein, P. Heimann, and R. Money-Kyrle (Eds.), *New directions in psychoanalysis.* New York: Basic Books, 1957, pp. 478–498.

———. Social analysis and the Glacier Project. In W. Brown and E. Jaques

(Eds.), *Glacier Project Papers*. London: Heinemann Educational Books, 1965.

Jeansonne, G. *Gerald L. K. Smith*. New Haven: Yale University Press, 1986.

———. Personality, biography, and psychobiography. *Biography* 14, no. 3 (Summer 1991): 241–255.

Johnson, G. *Architects of fear*. Los Angeles: Jeremy Thatcher, 1983.

———. Review of *Lyndon LaRouche and the new American fascism*, by D. King. *New York Times Book Review* (June 1989): 7, 8.

———. The evolutionary origins of government and politics. In A. Somit and J. Losco (Eds.), *Human nature and politics*. Greenwich, Conn.: JAI Press, 1995, pp. 243–305.

Jordan, M., and S. A. Pressley. Gruesome contest to raise dead led to Koresh's takeover of cult. *Washington Post*, March 7, 1993, p. A3.

Jubran, M., and L. Drake. The Islamic fundamentalist movement in the West Bank and Gaza Strip. *Middle East Policy* 2, no. 1 (1993): 1–115.

Juergensmeyer, M. The logic of religious violence. In D. Rapoport (Ed.), *Inside terrorist organizations*. New York: Columbia University Press, 1988, pp. 172–193.

Kafka, J. Review of *Adolf Hitler*, by H. Stierlin. *Psychiatry* 41 (May 1978): 221–225.

Kahane, M. *Never again!* Los Angeles: Nash Publications, 1971.

Kamm, H. Anti-Semitic taunt at Wiesel talk in Romania. *New York Times*, July 3, 1991, p. A8.

Kantrowitz, B., et al. The messiah of Waco. *Newsweek*, March 15, 1993, pp. 56–58.

Kaplan, J. America's last prophetic witness. *Terrorism and Political Violence* 5 (Autumn 1993): 60–75.

———. Right-wing violence in North America. *Terrorism and Political Violence* 7 (Spring 1995): 46–95.

———. Absolute rescue: Absolutism, defensive action, and the resort to force. *Terrorism and Political Violence* 7 (Autumn 1995): 128–163.

———. Politics of rage. *Christian Century*, June 19–26, 1996, pp. 657–662.

———. *Religion in America: Millenarian movements from the far right to the children of Noah*. Syracuse: Syracuse University Press, 1996.

Kato, W. An escape from Kampala. *Granta*, no. 22 (1987): 77–121.

Keen, S. *Faces of the enemy*. New York: Harper and Row, 1986.

Kennan, G. F. *Memoirs, 1925–1950*. Boston: Little, Brown, 1967.

Kenworthy, T., and G. Lardner, Jr. The militias: Guns and bitter. *Washington Post*, May 4, 1995, pp. A23, A26.

Keppel, G. *The revenge of God*. State College: Pennsylvania State University Press, 1994.

Kernberg, O. F. *Borderline conditions and pathological narcissism.* Northvale, N.J.: Aronson, 1975.

Khomeini, R. Foreign Broadcast Information Service. SAS–83. June 7, 1983. Broadcast June 5, 1983.

———. Foreign Broadcast Information Service. SAS–83–119. June 20, 1983. Broadcast June 18, 1983.

———. Foreign Broadcast Information Service. SAS–83–160. August 17, 1983. Broadcast August 16, 1983.

———. Foreign Broadcast Information Service. SAS–82–237. December 8, 1983. Broadcast December 7, 1983.

"Khomeini, the ultimate theocrat." *London Independent,* August 8, 1987, p. 8.

Khrushchev, N. *Khrushchev remembers.* S. Talbott (Trans. and Ed.). Boston: Little, Brown, 1970.

Kiernan, B. *How Pol Pot came to power: A history of Communism in Kampuchea, 1930–1975.* London: Verso Press, 1985.

———. *The Pol Pot regime: Race, power, and genocide in Cambodia under the Khmer Rouge, 1975–1979.* New Haven: Yale University Press, 1996.

Kifner, J. Assassination in Israel: The inquiry; Israelis investigate far right; may crack down on speech. *New York Times,* November 8, 1995, p. A1.

King, D. *Lyndon LaRouche and the new American fascism.* New York: Doubleday, 1989.

Kiyoyasu, K. Aum Shinriko: Society begets an aberration. *Japan Quarterly* 42, no. 2 (October 1995): 376–383.

Klein, M. *The psychoanalysis of children.* 1932. Reprint, New York: Grove Press, 1960.

———. A contribution to the psychogenesis of manic-depressive states. In *Contributions to psychoanalysis.* London: Hogarth Press, 1948, pp. 40–70.

———. Notes on some schizoid mechanisms. In M. Klein et al. (Eds.), *Developments in psychoanalysis.* London: Hogarth Press, 1952.

———. On identification. In M. Klein, P. Heimann, and R. Money-Kyrle (Eds.), *New directions in psychoanalysis.* New York: Basic Books, 1957, pp. 309–345.

———. *Contributions to psychoanalysis, 1920–1945.* New York: McGraw-Hill, 1964.

Klineman, G., S. Butler, D. Conn, with research by A. O. Miller. *The cult that died: The tragedy of Jim Jones and the People's Temple.* New York: Putnam, 1980.

Knight, R. P. The relationship of latent homosexuality to the mechanism of paranoid delusions. *Bulletin of the Menninger Clinic* 4 (1940): 149–159.

Koenigsberg, R. *Hitler's ideology: A study in psychoanalytic sociology.* New York: Library of Social Science, 1975.

Koestler, A. *Darkness at noon.* D. Hardy (Trans.). London: Cape, 1940.

Kovaleski, S. "One world" conspiracies prompt Montana militias' call to arms. *Washington Post,* April 29, 1995, pp. A1, A13.

Kovar, L. A reconsideration of paranoia. *Psychiatry* 29 (1966): 289–305.

Kramer, Martin. The moral logic of hizballah. In W. Reich (Ed.), *Origins of terrorism.* Cambridge: Cambridge University Press, 1990, pp. 131–157.

Kramer, Michael. The charmer. *New York Magazine,* October 7, 1985, pp. 16–17.

Kramer, P. *Listening to prozac.* New York: Viking, 1993.

Krauss, C. A rash of conspiracy theories. *Washington Post,* July 5, 1991, p. C18.

Krebs, J. R., and N. B. Davies (Eds.). *Behavioral ecology: An integrated approach.* Oxford: Blackwell Scientific, 1984.

Krebs, J. R., and R. Dawkins. Animal signals: Mind reading and manipulation. In J. R. Krebs and N. B. Davies (Eds.), *Behavioral ecology: An integrated approach.* Oxford: Blackwell Scientific, 1984.

Kristof, N. (with S. WuDunn). A guru's journey—a special report: The seer among the blind; Japanese sect leader's rise. *New York Times,* March 26, 1995, p. A1.

———. How Tokyo escaped even deadlier subway attack. *New York Times,* May 18, 1995, p. A14.

———. Japanese indict leader of cult in gas murders. *New York Times,* June 7, 1995, p. A6.

Kyemba, H. *A state of blood: The inside story of Idi Amin.* New York: Ace, 1977.

Lacayo, R. In the grip of a psychopath. *Time,* May 3, 1993, pp. 34–35.

Lachkar, J. *The narcissistic/borderline couple.* New York: Brunner Mazel, 1992.

Laffin, J. *The Arab mind considered.* New York: Taplinger, 1975.

Lake, P. An exegesis of the radical right. *California Magazine* 10, no. 4 (April 1985): 95–102.

Landis, M. *Joseph McCarthy: The politics of chaos.* Selingrove, Pa.: Susquehanna University Press, 1987.

Langer, E. The American neo-Nazi movement today. *The Nation,* July 16–23, 1990, pp. 82–107.

Langer, W. C. *The mind of Adolf Hitler.* New York: Basic Books, 1972.

Laqueur, W. *Black hundred: The rise of the extreme right in Russia.* New York: HarperCollins, 1993.

Laqueur, W., and Y. Alexander (Eds.). *The terrorist reader.* New American Library, 1987.

LaRouche, L. *The aquarian conspiracy.* Washington, D.C.: Schiller Institute, 1980.

Larson, R. K. In reading "Orphans of Jonestown." Letter to the editor, *New Yorker,* December 27, 1993, pp. 14, 16.

Lasaga, J. Death in Jonestown: Techniques of political control by a paranoid leader. *Suicide and Life-Threatening Behavior* 10 (Winter 1980): 210–213.

Lax, R. Thou shalt not kill: Some aspects of superego pathology. In A. K. Richards and A. Richards (Eds.), *The spectrum of psychoanalysis: Essays in honor of Martin S. Bergman*. Madison, Conn.: International Universities Press, 1994, pp. 248–255.

Lay, S. (Ed.). *The invisible empire in the West*. Urbana: University of Illinois Press, 1992.

Lee, H. Y. *The politics of the Chinese cultural revolution*. Berkeley: University of California Press, 1978.

Lefebvre, G. *The great fear of 1789*. J. White (Trans.). New York: Pantheon, 1970.

Lefkowitz, M. Afrocentrists wage war on ancient Greeks. *Wall Street Journal*, April 7, 1993, p. A3.

Lemert, E. Paranoia and the dynamics of exclusion. In *Human deviance, social problems, and social control*. 2nd ed. Englewood Cliffs, N.J.: Prentice-Hall, 1972, pp. 246–264.

Lenart, S., and K. M. H. McGraw. America watches "Amerika." *Journal of Politics* 51, no. 3 (1989): 697–712.

Lester, J. *Look out, whitey! Blackpower's gon' get your mama*. New York: Dial Press, 1968.

Levin, D. Introduction. In D. Levin (Ed.), *What happened in Salem?* Boston: Twayne, 1952, pp. 7–17.

LeVine, R. A. *Culture, behavior, and personality*. Chicago: Aldine de Gruyter, 1973.

Levinson, A. White paranoia grips black sector. *New Orleans Times-Picayune*, February 16, 1992, p. A18 ff.

Lewis, C. S. *Mere Christianity*. Rev. ed. New York: Macmillan, 1952.

Lifton, R. J. *The Nazi doctors*. London: Macmillan, 1986.

Lincoln, C. E. *The Black Muslims in America*. Boston: Beacon, 1961.

Linton, R. *Culture and mental disorders*. G. Devereux (Ed.). Springfield, Ill.: Thomas, 1956.

Listowel, J. *Amin*. Dublin: IUP Books, 1973.

Loewenberg, P. The psychohistorical origins of the Nazi youth cohort. In *Decoding the past*. Berkeley and Los Angeles: University of California Press, 1969, pp. 240–283.

Lonner, W. L. Issues in cross-cultural psychology. In A. J. Masella, R. G. Tharp, and T. J. Ciborowski (Eds.), *Perspectives on cross-cultural psychology*. New York: Academic Press, 1979, pp. 17–45.

Louisiana Coalition Against Racism and Nazism. *Resource packet*. New Orleans: Louisiana Coalition Against Racism and Nazism, 1991.

Lyons, E. *Assignment in utopia*. New York: Harcourt Brace, 1937.

MacDonald, A. *The Turner diaries*. Hillsboro, W.Va.: National Vanguard Books, 1980.

McGee, J., and W. Claiborne. The transformation of the Waco "Messiah." *Washington Post,* May 9, 1993, pp. A1, A18, A19.

McHugh, D. Conspiracy theories grow. *Detroit News and Free Press,* April 29, 1995, pp. A1, A6.

MacLean, P. *The triune brain evolution*. London: Plenum Press, 1990.

McLeod, W. H. *The Sikhs*. New York: Columbia University Press, 1989.

McMillen, L. The power of rumor. *Chronicle of Higher Education,* March 23, 1994, pp. A6, A15.

Magida, A. J. *Prophet of rage: A life of Louis Farrakhan and the Nation of Islam*. New York: Basic Books, 1996.

Maguire, J., and M. Dunn. *Hold hands and die: The incredible true story of the People's Temple*. New York: Dale Books, 1978.

Malcolm X. *Autobiography*. New York: Grove, 1964.

Malcolm X and J. Farmer. Separation or integration: A debate. In F. L. Broderick and A. Meier (Eds.), *Negro protest thought in the twentieth century*. New York: Bobbs-Merrill, 1966, pp. 357–383.

Maltsberger, T., and D. Buie. The devices of suicide: Revenge, riddance, and rebirth. *International Review of Psychoanalysis* 7 (1980): 61–72.

Mamdani, M. *Imperialism and fascism in Uganda*. London: Heinemann, 1983.

Mangold, T. *Cold warrior: James Jesus Angleton, the CIA's master spy hunter*. New York: Simon and Schuster, 1991.

Maqsdi, M. (Trans.). Charter of the Islamic resistance movement (HAMAS) of Palestine. *Journal of Palestine Studies* 22, no. 4 (Summer 1993): 122–134.

Marnham, P. In search of Amin. *Granta* 17 (1985): 69–82.

Martin, D. *General Amin*. London: Faber and Faber, 1974.

Martin, D. *Wilderness of mirrors*. New York: Harper and Row, 1980.

Martin, R. Religous violence in Islam: Toward an understanding of the discourse on Jihad in modern Egypt. In P. Wilkinson and A. M. Stewart (Eds.), *Contemporary research on terrorism*. Aberdeen: Aberdeen University Press, 1987, pp. 54–71.

Mazrui, A. Boxer Muhammad Ali and soldier Idi Amin as international political symbols. *Comparative Studies in Society and History* 19 (April 1977): 189–215.

Meissner, W. W. *The paranoid process*. New York: Aronson, 1978.

———. Narcissism and paranoia: A comment on paranoid psychodynamics. *Contemporary Psychoanalysis* 15, no. 3 (1979): 527–538.

———. *Psychotherapy and the paranoid process*. Northvale, N.J.: Aronson, 1986.

Melady, T. and M. Melady. *Idi Amin Dada*. Kansas City: Sheed Andrews and McMeel, 1977.

Melton, J. G. (Ed.). *The churches speak on abortion*. Detroit: Gale Research, 1989.

Merkl, P., and L. Weinberg (Eds.). *Encounters with the contemporary radical right*. Colorado Springs: Westview Press, 1993.

Miller, A. Why I wrote *The Crucible*. *New Yorker,* October 21 and 28, 1996, pp. 158–164.

Mintz, J. Militias meet the Senate with conspiracies to share. *Washington Post,* June 16, 1995, pp. A1, A10.

Money-Kyrle, R. E. *Psychoanalysis and politics*. Westport, Conn.: Greenwood Press, 1951.

Morrow, L., and M. Smilgis. Plunging into the labyrinth. *Time,* December 23, 1991, pp. 74–76.

Mosley, D. M. *A life of contrasts*. New York: New York Times Books, 1977.

Mosse, G. L. *Germans and Jews*. New York: Howard Fertag, 1970.

Muhammad, K. The secret relationship between Blacks and Jews. Speech delivered at Kean College, New Jersey, November 29, 1993. Transcript of recorded speech provided by the Anti-Defamation League of B'nai B'rith.

Murray, J. Narcissism and the ego-ideal. *Journal of the American Psychoanalytic Association* 12 (1964): 477–511.

Mutibawa, P. *Uganda since independence*. London: Hurst, 1992.

Niebuhr, G. A vision of an apocalypse: The religion of the far right. *New York Times,* May 22, 1995, p. A8.

————. To Church's dismay, priest talks of "justifiable homicide" of abortion doctors. *New York Times,* August 24, 1995, p. A12.

Niewyk, D. L. *Socialist, anti-Semite, and Jew*. Baton Rouge: Louisiana State University Press, 1971.

————. *The Jews in Weimar Germany*. Baton Rouge: Louisiana State University Press, 1980.

No man in the moon. *London Independent,* July 22, 1994, p. 14.

Olsson, P. In search of their fathers-themselves: Jim Jones and David Koresh. *Mind and Human Interaction* 5 (August 1994): 85–96.

Oshinsky, D. M. *A conspiracy so immense*. New York: Free Press, 1983.

Osmer, E. Did he kill the peace? Baruch Goldstein in his own words. *Multinational Monitor,* 1988. Reprint, *Washington Post,* March 6, 1994, pp. C1, C4.

Ostling, R. A sinister search for identity. *Time,* October 20, 1986, p. 74.

Ostow, M. Apocalyptic and fundamentalist thinking in mental illness and social disorder. In A. K. Richards and A. Richards (Eds.), *The spectrum of psychoanalysis: Essays in honor of Martin S. Bergman*. Madison, Conn.: International Universities Press, 1994, pp. 221–232.

Packer, C. Reciprocal altruism in olive baboons. *Nature* 265 (1977): 441–443.

Paris, E. *The end of days: A story of tolerance, tyranny, and the expulsion of Jews from Spain.* Amherst, N.Y.: Prometheus Books, 1995.

Pascal, B. *Pensées.* W. J. Trotter (Trans.). H. S. Thayer and E. B. Thayer (Eds.). New York: Washington Square Press, 1965.

Pastor, R. A. From the United States looking in. In R. A. Pastor and J. A. Castañeda, *Limits to friendship.* New York: Knopf, 1988, pp. 78–92.

Payne, R. *The life and death of Adolf Hitler.* New York: Praeger, Popular Books, 1973.

Perry, B. *Malcolm.* Barrytown, N.Y.: State Hall, 1991.

Pierce, W. [Andrew MacDonald, pseud.]. *The Turner diaries.* 2nd ed. Washington, D.C.: National Alliance, 1980.

Pipes, D. *In the path of God.* New York: Basic Books, 1983.

———. Whodunit? *Atlantic* 263 (May 1989): 18–24.

———. Israel, America, and Arab delusions. *Commentary* 91 (March 1991): 26–31.

———. Dealing with Middle East conspiracy theories. *Orbis* 36 (Winter 1992): 41–56.

———. *The hidden hand: Middle East fears of conspiracy.* New York: St. Martin's, 1996.

"Poll." *New Orleans Times-Picayune,* September 22, 1996, pp. A1, A16.

Popham, P. Talk of the devil. *London Independent,* July 23, 1994, p. 12.

Posner, G. L. *Case closed.* New York: Random House, 1993.

Post, J. M. On aging leaders: Possible effects of the aging process on the conduct of leadership. *Journal of Geriatric Psychiatry* 6 (1973): 109–116.

———. The seasons of a leader's life. *Political Psychology* 2 (1980): 36–49.

———. Dreams of glory and the life cycle. *Journal of Political and Military Sociology* 12 (1984): 49–60.

———. Notes on a psychodynamic theory of terrorism. *Terrorism* 7, no. 3 (1984): 241–256.

———. Hostilité, fraternité, conformité: The group dynamics of terrorist behavior. *International Journal of Group Psychotherapy* 36, no. 2 (1986): 211–224.

———. Narcissism and the charismatic leader-follower relationship. *Political Psychology* 7 (1986): 675–688.

———. The basic assumptions of political terrorists. In J. Z. Kranz (Ed.), Irrationality in social and organizational life. *Proceedings of the Eighth A. K. Rice Institute Scientific Meeting.* Washington, D.C.: A. K. Rice Institute, 1987.

———. Terrorist psycho-logic: Terrorist behavior as a product of psychological forces. In W. Reich (Ed.), *Origins of terrorism.* Cambridge: Cambridge University Press, 1990.

Post, J. M., and R. S. Robins. *When illness strikes the leader: The dilemma of the captive king.* New Haven: Yale University Press, 1993.

Post, J. M., and E. Semrad. The psychosis-prone personality. *Mental Hospitals* 16, no. 2 (February 1965): 81–84.

Pressley, S. A. For Rachel Koresh and kin, a deadly deception. *Washington Post,* April 28, 1993, pp. A1, A4.

Pro-life hate violence in the name of God. *Reform Judaism* (Summer 1994).

Psychiatrist rejects public view that cult survivors are "crazy." *New York Times,* October 11, 1979, p. A10.

Puente, M. Koresh ruled with scripture. *USA Today,* April 20, 1993, p. 2A.

Pulzer, P. G. J. *The rise of political anti-Semitism in Germany and Austria.* New York: Wiley, 1964.

Pye, L. (with M. Pye). *Asian power and politics.* Cambridge: Harvard University Press, 1985.

Rafferty, K. Shokotactics. *Manchester Guardian,* May 16, 1995, p. T2.

Rapoport, D. (Ed.). *Inside terrorist organizations.* New York: Columbia University Press, 1988.

———. Sacred terror. In W. Reich (Ed.), *Origins of terrorism.* Cambridge: Cambridge University Press, 1990, pp. 103–130.

*Records of Salem witchcraft.* 2 vols. Roxbury, Mass.: W. Elliot Woodward, 1864.

Reeves, T. S. *The life and times of Joe McCarthy.* New York: Stein and Day, 1982.

Reich, Walter. The case of General Grigorenko: A psychiatric re-examination of a dissident. *Psychiatry* 43 (1980): 303–323.

Reich, Wilhelm. *Character-analysis.* New York: Orgone Press, 1949.

Reid, T. R. The doomsday guru: Japanese sect leader rose to venerated master after failure as acupuncturist, tonic vendor. *Washington Post,* March 24, 1995, p. A25.

———. Children of Japan cult describe spartan life. *Washington Post,* April 19, 1995, p. A26.

Reiterman, T., and J. Jacob. *Raven: The untold story of the reverend Jim Jones and his people.* New York: E. P. Dutton, 1982.

Renshon, S. A. *Psychological needs and political behavior.* New York: Free Press, 1974.

Reston, J. *Our father who art in hell.* New York: Times Books, 1981.

Rhodes, J. M. *The Hitler movement: A modern millenarian revolution.* Stanford: Hoover Institution Press, 1980.

Ribuffo, L. P. *The old Christian right.* Philadelphia: Temple University Press, 1983.

Ringwald, J. W. An investigation of group reaction to central figures. In G. Gibbard et al., *Analysis of groups.* San Francisco: Jossey-Bass, 1974, pp. 220–246.

Rioch, M. J. All we like sheep (Isaiah 53:6): Followers and leaders. In A. D. Coleman and W. Harold Bexton (Eds.), *Group relations reader 1*. Washington, D.C.: A. K. Rice Institute, 1975, pp. 159–177. First published in *Psychiatry* (1971): 258–273.

―――. The work of Wilfred Bion on groups. *Psychiatry* (1971): 33, 56–66.

Robertson, P. *The new world order*. Dallas: Word Publishing, 1991.

Robins, R. S. *Political institutionalization and the integration of elites*. Beverly Hills: Sage, 1976.

―――. Introduction to R. S. Robins (Ed.), *Psychopathology and political leadership*. New Orleans: Tulane Studies in Political Science, 1977, pp. 1–33.

―――. Recruitment of pathological deviants into political leadership. In R. S. Robins (Ed.), *Psychopathology and political leadership*. New Orleans: Tulane Studies in Political Science, 1977, pp. 53–78.

―――. Disease, political events, and populations. In H. Rothschild (Ed.), *Biocultural aspects of disease*. New York: Academic Press, 1981, pp. 153–175.

―――. Paranoid ideation and charismatic leadership. *Psychohistory Review* 5 (1986): 15–55.

Robins, R. S., and J. Handler. The paranoid theme in the career of José Gaspar de Francia of Paraguay. *Biography* 16 (1993): 346–368.

Robins, R. S., and J. M. Post. The paranoid political actor. *Biography* 10 (1987): 1–19.

Robins, R. S., and H. Rothschild. Hidden health disabilities and the presidency: Medical management and political considerations. *Perspectives in Biology and Medicine* (1981): 240–266.

―――. Ethical dilemmas of the president's physician. *Politics and the Life Sciences* 7 (August 1988): 3–11.

Rochlin, G. *Man's aggression: The defense of the self*. Boston: Gambit, 1973.

Rose, D. (Ed.). *The emergence of David Duke and the politics of race*. Chapel Hill: University of North Carolina Press, 1992.

Rose, D., and E. Esolen. Duke for governor. In D. Rose (Ed.), *The emergence of David Duke and the politics of race*. Chapel Hill: University of North Carolina Press, 1992, pp. 197–241.

Rose, R. Will Communists take over in 2002? Ask a John Bircher. *Wall Street Journal*, October 2, 1991, p. A1.

Rosen, H., and H. E. Kiene. The paranoiac officer and the officer paranee. *American Journal of Psychiatry* 103 (March 1947): 614–621.

Rosenstone, R. A. *JFK*: Historical fact/historical film. *American Historical Review* 97 (1992): 506–511.

Rosenthal, B. *Salem story*. Cambridge: Cambridge University Press, 1993.

Rothstein, D. Presidential assassination syndrome. *Archives of General Psychiatry* 11 (1964): 245–254.

————. Presidential assassination syndrome, 2: Applications to Lee Harvey Oswald. *Archives of General Psychiatry* 15 (1965): 260–266.

————. The assassin and the assassinated as non-patient subjects of psychiatric investigation. In J. Fawcett (Ed.), *Dynamics of violence.* Chicago: American Medical Association, 1971.

Roy, O. *The failure of political Islam.* C. Volk (Trans.). Cambridge: Harvard University Press, 1994.

Rutan, S., and W. Stone. *Psychodynamic group psychotherapy.* 2nd ed. New York: Guilford Press, 1993.

Salzman, L. Paranoid state: Theory and therapy. *Archives of General Psychiatry* 2 (1960): 679–693.

Salzman, L. Review of *The paranoid,* by D. W. Swanson, J. P. Bohnert, and J. A. Smith. *Psychiatry* 34 (1971): 442–445.

Sargent, L. T. (Ed.). *Extremism in America: A reader.* New York: New York University Press, 1995.

Savage, C., A. H. Leighton, and D. C. Leighton. The problem of cross-cultural identification of psychiatric disorders. In J. M. Murphy and A. H. Leighton (Eds.), *Approaches to cross-cultural psychiatry.* Ithaca: Cornell University Press, 1965, pp. 21–63.

Sawyer, R. H. The truth about the invisible empire knights of the Ku Klux Klan: A lecture delivered at the municipal auditorium in Portland, Oregon, on December 22, 1921, to six thousand people. In Shawn Lay (Ed.), *The invisible empire in the West: Toward a new appraisal of the Ku Klux Klan of the 1920s.* Urbana: University of Illinois Press, 1992, pp. 11–12.

Sayle, M. Nerve gas and the four noble truths. *New Yorker,* April 1, 1996, pp. 56–71.

Schiffer, I. *Charisma.* Toronto: University of Toronto Press, 1973.

Schifter, R. The legacy of Communism. Paper presented at the thirteenth annual meeting of the International Society of Political Psychology, Washington, D.C., July 1990.

Schmemann, S. Assassination in Israel: The politics; now the finger pointing begins. *New York Times,* November 10, 1995, p. A8.

————. Police say Rabin killer led sect that laid plans to attack Arabs. *New York Times,* November 11, 1995, p. A1.

Schmidt, S., and T. Kenworthy. Michigan fringe group's leader has national reputation. *Washington Post,* April 25, 1995, p. A5.

Schneider, K. Fearing a conspiracy, some heed a call to arms. *New York Times,* November 14, 1994, pp. A1, A14.

————. Manual for terrorists extols "greatest cold-bloodedness." *New York Times,* April 29, 1995, p. A10.

Schofield, J., and M. Pavelchak. *The day after:* The impact of a media event. *American Psychologist* 40 (1985): 542–548.

Schor, T. S. The structure and stuff of rural violence in a north Andean valley. In M. Richardson (Ed.), *The human mirror*. Baton Rouge: Louisiana State University Press, 1974, pp. 269–299.

Sederberg, P. C. *Fires within: Political violence and revolutionary change*. New York: HarperCollins, 1994.

Shafir, M. Anti-Semitism without Jews in Romania. *Report on Eastern Europe* 2, no. 24 (June 14, 1991): 22–28.

Shapiro, A. Notes on illness and death in American presidents. *Advances* 8, no. 3 (Summer 1992): 62–69.

Shapiro, D. *Neurotic styles*. New York: Basic Books, 1967.

Shawcross, W. *The quality of mercy: Cambodia, holocaust, and modern conscience*. New York: Simon and Schuster, 1984.

Smith, C. Soul Searching. *Far Eastern Economic Review* 158, no. 21 (May 25, 1995): 14–16.

Smith, G. I. *Ghosts of Kampala*. London: Weidenfeld and Nicolson, 1980.

Smith, L. B. *Treason in Tudor England: Politics and paranoia*. Princeton: Princeton University Press, 1986.

Smith, M. J. *On evolution*. Edinburgh: Edinburgh University Press, 1972.

———. The theory of games and the evolution of animal conflict. *Journal of Theoretical Biology* 47 (1974): 209–221.

———. Evolution and the theory of games. *American Scientist* 64 (1976): 41–45.

———. Game theory and the evolution of behavior. *Proceedings of the Royal Society, London* 205 (1979): 474–488.

———. *Evolution and the theory of games*. Cambridge: Cambridge University Press, 1983.

———. Ownership and honesty in competitive interactions. *Behavioral Brain Science* (1986): 742–744.

Snow, C. P. *Varieties of men*. New York: Scribners, 1966.

Spaeth, A. Engineer of doom. *Time*, June 12, 1995, p. 57.

Speer, A. *Inside the Third Reich*. R. Winston and C. Winston (Trans.). New York: Macmillan, 1970.

———. *Spandau: The secret diaries*. R. Winston and C. Winston (Trans.). New York: Macmillan, 1976.

Spietel, V. We wanted everything and nothing. *Der Spiegel* 33 (July 20, 1980): 35.

Spitz, R. *The first year of life: A psychoanalytic study of normal and deviant object relations*. In collaboration with W. G. Coblines. New York: International Universities Press, 1965.

Sprinzak, E. From Messianic pioneering to vigilante terrorism: The case of the Gush Emunim underground. *Journal of Strategic Studies* (October 4, 1987):

194–216. Also published in D. Rapoport (Ed.), *Inside terrorist organizations.* New York: Columbia University Press, 1988, pp. 195–216.

Stalin, J. *Collected works,* vols. 1–13. Moscow: n.p., 1952–1955.

Stalstrom, O. W. Querulous paranoia: Diagnosis and dissent. *Australian and New Zealand Journal of Psychiatry* 14 (1980): 145–150.

Starkey, M. L. *The devil in Massachusetts.* New York: Knopf, 1949.

Steel, R. Mr. Smith goes to the twilight zone. *New Republic,* February 3, 1992, pp. 30–32.

Stein, H. *Developmental time, cultural space.* Norman: University of Oklahoma Press, 1987.

Stevens et al. Stimulation of caudate nucleus: Behavioral effects of chemical and electrical stimulation. *Archives of Neurology* 4 (1961): 47–54.

Stierlin, H. *Adolf Hitler: A family perspective.* New York: Psychohistory Press, 1976.

Strasser, S., and T. Post. A cloud of terror—and suspicion. *Newsweek,* April 3, 1995, pp. 36–41.

Sturm, B. In the trenches for the wrong cause. *Der Spiegel* 7 (1972): 57.

Sullivan, C. The facts of King's death still hidden, observers say. *New Orleans Times-Picayune,* April 4, 1993, p. A4.

Sullivan, H. S. *Clinical studies in psychiatry.* New York: Norton, 1956.

Sullivan, K. Tokyo judge sets in motion seizure of Aum cult assets. *Washington Post,* October 31, 1995, p. 8.

Surlin, S. H. "Roots" research: A summary of findings. *Journal of Broadcasting* 22 (1978): 309–320.

Swanson, D. W., J. P. Bohnert, and J. A. Smith. *The paranoid.* Boston: Little, Brown, 1970.

Swardson, A. Guns have kept us free. *Washington Post,* April 23, 1995, p. A22.

Taheri, A. *Holy terror.* Bethesda: Adler and Adler, 1987.

Tausk, V. On the origins of the "influencing machine" in schiozophrenia. In *Psychoanalytic reader,* ed. R. Fliess, vol. 1. 1919. Reprint, New York: International Universities Press, 1948, pp. 52–85.

Thomas, K. *Religion and the decline of magic.* New York: Scribners, 1971.

Thomas, S. B., and S. C. Quinn. The Tuskeegee syphilis study, 1932–1972. *American Journal of Public Health* 60 (1991): 1498–1505.

Thornhill, R. Adaptive female mimicking behavior in a scorpion fly. *Science* 205 (1979): 412–415.

Trivers, R. *Social evolution.* Menlo Park, Calif.: Benjamin Cummings, 1985.

Tucker, R. C. The dictator and totalitarianism. *World Politics* 17 (1965): 555–583.

———. The theory of charismatic leadership. *Daedalus* 97 (1968): 731–756.

———. *Stalin as revolutionary, 1879–1929.* New York: Norton, 1973.

———. (Ed.). *Stalinism.* New York: Norton, 1977.

————. The rise of Stalin's personality cult. *American Historical Review* 84 (1979): 347–366.

————. *Politics as leadership.* Columbia: University of Missouri Press, 1981.

————. Does big brother really exist? *Psychoanalytic Inquiry* 2 (1982): 118–132.

————. *Stalin in power, 1929–1941.* New York: Norton, 1990.

Tully, M., and S. Jacob. *Amritsar: Mrs. Gandhi's last battle.* London: Pan Books, 1985.

Turner, P. A. *I heard it through the grape-vine: Rumor in African-American culture.* Berkeley: University of California Press, 1994.

Turquet, P. M. Leadership: The individual and the group. In G. Gibbard, J. J. Hartman, and R. D. Mann (Eds.), *Analysis of groups.* San Francisco: Jossey-Bass, 1974, pp. 349–371.

Two militia figures lose platforms. *Washington Post,* April 1995, p. A13.

Ugandan, A. In Uganda, dead, dead, dead, dead. *New York Times,* September 12, 1977, p. 33.

Ulam, A. B. *In the name of the people: Prophets and conspirators in pre-revolutionary Russia.* New York: Viking, 1977.

Ulman, R. B., and D. W. Abse. The group psychology of mass madness: Jonestown. *Political Psychology* 4 (1983): 637–662.

Vaillant, G. *The wisdom of the ego.* Cambridge: Harvard University Press, 1993.

Van Buren, J. M., C. L. Li, and G. A. Ojemann. The fronto-striatal arrest response in man. *Electroencephalography Clinical Neurophysiology* 21 (1966): 114–130.

Verhovek, S. "Messiah" fond of rock, women, and Bible. *New York Times,* March 3, 1993, pp. A1, B10.

Vine, W. E., et al. *An expository dictionary of biblical words.* Nashville: Nelson, 1984.

Volkan, V. Narcissistic personality organization and reparative leadership. *International Journal of Group Psychotherapy* 30 (1980): 121–152.

————. The need to have enemies and allies: A developmental approach. *Political Psychology* 6 (1985): 219–248.

————. *The need to have enemies and allies.* Northvale, N.J.: Jason Aronson, 1988.

Volkogonov, D. *Lenin.* New York: Free Press, 1994.

Von Domarus, E. The specific laws of logic in schizophrenia. In J. S. Kasinin (Ed.), *Language and thought in schizophrenia.* Berkeley: University of California Press, 1944, pp. 104–113.

Vovelle, M. Ideologies and mentalities. J. Dunne (Trans.). In R. Samuel and G. S. Jones (Eds.), *Culture, ideology, and politics.* London: Routledge and Kegan Paul, 1982, pp. 2–11.

Waelder, R. Characteristics of totalitarianism. In W. Muensterberger and S. Axelrad (Eds.), *The psychoanalytic study of society*. New York: International Universities Press, 1960, pp. 11–25.

Waite, R. G. L. Adolf Hitler's anti-Semitism. In B. B. Wolman (Ed.), *The psychoanalytic interpretation of history*. New York: Harper Torchbooks, 1971, pp. 192–230.

———. *The psychopathic god*. New York: Basic Books, 1976.

Weber, Mallory. An attempt on the mind of Idi Amin. *The Listener* 90 (September 6, 1973): 297–299.

Weber, Max. *From Max Weber*. M. M. Gerth and C. W. Mills (Trans. and Eds.). New York: Oxford University Press, 1946.

Weisman, R. *Witchcraft, magic, and religion in seventeenth-century Massachusetts*. Amherst: University of Massachusetts Press, 1984.

Welch, R. *May God forgive us*. Chicago: Henry Regnery, 1952.

———. *The blue book of the John Birch society*. Belmont, Mass.: Belmont Publishing, 1961.

———. *The politician*. Belmont, Mass.: Belmont Publishing, 1964.

White, T. *The making of the president, 1960*. London: Jonathan Cape, 1962.

Williams, D. Rabbi's reaction to killing: We have to make a tear in our shirt. *Washington Post,* November 10, 1995, p. A35.

Williams, J. A. (Ed.). *Themes of Islamic civilization*. Berkeley: University of California Press, 1971.

Wilner, A. R. *The spellbinders*. New Haven: Yale University Press, 1984.

Wilson, J. *Lectures on our Israelite origin*. 5th ed. London: James Nisbet, 1876.

Winnicott, D. *The motivational process and the facilitating environment*. New York: International Universities Press, 1965.

Wistrich, R. S. *Anti-semitism: The longest hatred*. New York: Pantheon, 1991.

Wood, R. Right-wing extremism and the problem of rural unrest. In T. D. McDonald, R. A. Wood, and M. A. Flug (Eds.), *Rural criminal justice*. N.p.: Sheffield Publishing, 1996, pp. 217–234.

Wright, L. Orphans of Jonestown. *New Yorker,* November 22, 1993, pp. 66–89.

WuDunn, S. Secretive Japan sect evokes both loyalty and hostility. *New York Times,* March 24, 1995, p. A1.

———. For ex-cult members in Japan, a hard, slow recovery. *New York Times,* June 5, 1995, p. 3.

Yaeger, C. Armageddon tomorrow: The Posse Comitatus prepares for the future. *TVI Report* 11, no. 2 (1994): 16–20.

Zee, H. J. The Guyana incident: Some psychoanalytic considerations. *Bulletin of the Menninger Clinic* 44 (1980): 345–363.

Zelizer, B. *Covering the body*. Chicago: University of Chicago Press, 1992.

Zeskind, L. *The "Christian Identity" movement: A theoretical justification for racist and anti-Semitic violence*. Atlanta: National Council for the Churches of Christ in the U.S.A., 1986.

Zonis, M. Self-objects, self-representation, and sense-making crises: Political instability in the 1980s. *Political Psychology* 5, no. 2 (1984): 267–285.

Zonis, M., and D. Brumberg. Khomeini, the Islamic republic of Iran, and the Arab world. Cambridge: Harvard Middle East Papers, 1987.

Zonis, M., and C. Joseph. Conspiracy thinking in the Middle East. *Political Psychology* 15, no. 3 (1994): 443–459.

# Index